THE PROCESS OF LEGAL RESEARCH

How to use your Connected Casebook

Step 1: Go to **www.CasebookConnect.com** and redeem your access code to get started.

Access Code:

Step 2: Go to your **BOOKSHELF** and select your Connected Casebook to start reading, highlighting, and taking notes in the margins of your e-book.

Step 3: Select the **STUDY** tab in your toolbar to access a variety of practice materials designed to help you master the course material. These materials may include explanations, videos, multiple-choice questions, flashcards, short answer, essays, and issue spotting.

Step 4: Select the **OUTLINE** tab in your toolbar to access chapter outlines that automatically incorporate your highlights and annotations from the e-book. Use the My Notes area for copying, pasting, and editing your book notes or creating new notes.

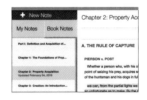

Step 5: If your professor has enrolled your class, you can select the **CLASS INSIGHTS** tab and compare your own study center results against the average of your classmates.

Is this a used casebook? Access code already scratched off?

You can purchase the Digital Version and still access all of the powerful tools listed above. Please visit CasebookConnect.com and select Catalog to learn more.

ASPEN COURSEBOOK SERIES

THE PROCESS OF LEGAL RESEARCH

Practices and Resources

Ninth Edition

Deborah A. Schmedemann
Professor of Law Emerita
William Mitchell College of Law
(now Mitchell Hamline School of Law)

Ann L. Bateson
Library Director, Associate Dean, and Professor of Law
University of St. Thomas School of Law

Mehmet Konar-Steenberg
Professor of Law and Briggs & Morgan/Xcel Energy Chair in Energy and
Environmental Law
Mitchell Hamline School of Law

CONTRIBUTING AUTHORS:

Simon Canick
Professor of Law and Associate Dean of Information Resources
Mitchell Hamline School of Law

Anthony S. Winer
Professor of Law
Mitchell Hamline School of Law

Sarah Deer
Professor of Law
Mitchell Hamline School of Law

Published by Wolters Kluwer in New York.

Wolters Kluwer Legal & Regulatory US serves customers worldwide with CCH, Aspen Publishers, and Kluwer Law International products. (www.WKLegaledu.com)

To contact Customer Service, e-mail customer.service@wolterskluwer.com, call 1-800-234-1660, fax 1-800-901-9075, or mail correspondence to:

Wolters Kluwer
Attn: Order Department
PO Box 990
Frederick, MD 21705

Printed in the United States of America.

1 2 3 4 5 6 7 8 9 0

ISBN 978-1-4548-6333-5

Names: Schmedemann, Deborah A., 1956- author. | Bateson, Ann L., author. | Konar-Steenberg, Mehmet, author.
Title: The process of legal research : practices and resources / Deborah A. Schmedemann, Professor of Law Emerita, William Mitchell College of Law (now Mitchell Hamline School of Law), Ann L. Bateson, Library Director, Associate Dean, and Professor of Law, University of St. Thomas School of Law, Mehmet Konar-Steenberg, Professor of Law and Briggs & Morgan/Xcel Energy Chair in Energy and Environmental Law, Mitchell Hamline School of Law.
Description: Ninth edition. | New York : Wolters Kluwer, [2016] | Series: Aspen coursebook series | Includes index.
Identifiers: LCCN 2016007495 | ISBN 9781454863335
Subjects: LCSH: Legal research — United States.
Classification: LCC KF240 .S36 2016 | DDC 340.072/073 — dc23 LC record available at http://lccn.loc.gov/2016007495

About Wolters Kluwer Legal & Regulatory US

Wolters Kluwer Legal & Regulatory US delivers expert content and solutions in the areas of law, corporate compliance, health compliance, reimbursement, and legal education. Its practical solutions help customers successfully navigate the demands of a changing environment to drive their daily activities, enhance decision quality, and inspire confident outcomes.

Serving customers worldwide, its legal and regulatory portfolio includes products under the Aspen Publishers, CCH Incorporated, Kluwer Law International, ftwilliam.com, and MediRegs names. They are regarded as exceptional and trusted resources for general legal and practice-specific knowledge, compliance and risk management, dynamic workflow solutions, and expert commentary.

*This book is dedicated to those who have
taught us the importance of learning and the joy of discovering,
in particular Aynur Konar and Luke Bowmann Arents.*

Summary of Contents

Contents	*xi*
Boxes	*xv*
Preface	*xix*
Acknowledgments	*xxi*

UNIT I
THE BASICS   1

CHAPTER 1   The Landscapes of Legal Research   3
CHAPTER 2   The Ten Practices of Skilled Legal Researchers   25

UNIT II
SECONDARY SOURCES   57

CHAPTER 3   Secondary Sources   59

UNIT III
PRIMARY AUTHORITY FROM THE U.S.   101

CHAPTER 4   Case Law   103
CHAPTER 5   Enacted Law   165
CHAPTER 6   Rules of Procedure and Professional Responsibility   239
CHAPTER 7   Administrative Agency Materials   271

UNIT IV
BEYOND U.S. LAW   305

CHAPTER 8   Tribal Law and International Law   307

Index   *323*

CONTENTS

Boxes	*xv*
Preface	*xix*
Acknowledgments	*xxi*

UNIT I
THE BASICS   1

CHAPTER 1
THE LANDSCAPES OF LEGAL RESEARCH   3

The Lawyer-Client Relationship	4
The U.S. Government: Primary Authority	5
Secondary Sources and Finding Tools	12
Legal Publishing: Resources	17
Build Your Understanding	20

CHAPTER 2
THE TEN PRACTICES OF SKILLED LEGAL RESEARCHERS   25

1. Master Your Client's Situation	26
2. Develop Your Research Terms	28
3. Create a Research Plan	31
4. Choose Resources with Care	32
Content	32
Credibility	33
Ease of Use	33
Cost-Effectiveness	33
5. Piggyback on Others' Work	34
6. Work Several Access Angles	35
Writer-Driven Access Methods	35
Researcher-Driven Searching	40
7. Take a Look Back	42
8. Get Up to Date	45
9. Manage Your Information File	49
10. Stop When You're Done	52
Build Your Understanding	53

UNIT II
SECONDARY SOURCES   57

CHAPTER 3
SECONDARY SOURCES   59

Treatises   61
The Reading and Mining of a Secondary Source   68
Encyclopedias   69
Legal Periodical Articles   72
Restatements of the Law   77
Jury Instruction Guides   83
American Law Reports Annotations   85
Practice Guides   89
Build Your Understanding   96

UNIT III
PRIMARY AUTHORITY FROM THE U.S.   101

CHAPTER 4
CASE LAW   103

The U.S. Case Law System   103
    Round 1: State Courts   103
    Round 2: Federal Courts   111
    Round 3: Selecting Cases   122
The Reading and Mining of a Case   123
Recommended Approaches to Researching Case Law   124
    The Backdrop: Case Reporters   124
    Overview   126
    Court Websites   129
    High-End Commercial Resources   129
    Economy-Class Commercial Resources   148
    Google Scholar   154
Build Your Understanding   159

CHAPTER 5
ENACTED LAW   165

The U.S. Statutory System   166
    Round 1: The Legislative Process and Statute Design   166
    Round 2: The Legislature and the Courts   170
    Round 3: Federal and State Statutes   177
The Reading and Briefing of a Statute   177

Recommended Approaches to Researching Statutes   178
   Overview   178
   Print Codes   179
   Legislative Websites   186
   High-End Commercial Resources   191
   Economy-Class Commercial Resources   202
Constitutions   204
Charters and Ordinances   205
Legislative Materials   207
   Situations for Researching in Legislative Materials   207
   The Legislative Process and Documents   207
   Researching Legislative History   210
   Researching Pending Legislation   231
Build Your Understanding   233

CHAPTER 6
RULES OF PROCEDURE AND PROFESSIONAL RESPONSIBILITY 239

Rules of Procedure   240
   Understanding the Rules and Related Sources   240
   Researching Rules of Procedure   244
Rules of Professional Responsibility   258
   Understanding the Rules and Related Sources   258
   Researching Rules of Professional Responsibility   264
Build Your Understanding   266

CHAPTER 7
ADMINISTRATIVE AGENCY MATERIALS   271

Regulations   272
   Understanding Regulations   272
   Researching Regulations   276
Decisions and Orders   289
   Understanding Decisions and Orders   289
   Researching Decisions and Orders   294
Interpretive Rules and Other Guidance Materials   297
Build Your Understanding   302

UNIT IV
BEYOND U.S. LAW   305

CHAPTER 8
TRIBAL LAW AND INTERNATIONAL LAW   307

American Indian Tribal Law   *307*
Federal Indian Law   308

Tribal Law   309
Public International Law   *310*
Foreign Law   310
Public International Law   311
    Treaties and Conventions   312
    Customary International Law   315
    Decisions by Courts and Arbitration Panels   317
    UN Materials   318
    Commentary and General Principles   320
Private International Law   321

Index   *323*

BOXES

CHAPTER 1
THE LANDSCAPES OF LEGAL RESEARCH

1.1	Our Clients' Situations	5
1.2	Primary Authorities and Quasi-Authorities	6
1.3	Statute (Employment Discrimination)	8
1.4	State Case (Employment Defamation)	10
1.5	Legal Periodical Article (Social Media Policy)	14
1.6	Case Citator Report (Employment Defamation)	16
1.7	Secondary Sources and Finding Tools	17

CHAPTER 2
THE TEN PRACTICES OF SKILLED LEGAL RESEARCHERS

2.1	Leading Dictionaries and Thesauri	29
2.2	Legal Dictionary Definition (Covenant Not-to-Compete)	30
2.3	Tables of Contents (Employment Discrimination Statute)	37
2.4	Index (Employment Discrimination Statute)	40
2.5	Key-Word Search and Results (Employment Discrimination Statute)	42
2.6	Federal District Court Case (Constitutional Rights of Public School Student)	43
2.7	Federal Court of Appeals Decision (Constitutional Rights of Public School Student)	46

CHAPTER 3
SECONDARY SOURCES

3.1	Six Major Secondary Sources	60
3.2	Treatise Text (Employment Defamation)	63
3.3	Treatise Table of Contents (Employment Defamation)	65
3.4	Treatise Index (Employment Defamation)	66
3.5	Treatise Notes (Employment Defamation)	68
3.6	Encyclopedia (Driving While Using Cell Phone)	71
3.7	Student Note (Constitutional Rights of Public School Student)	74
3.8	Article (Constitutional Rights of Public School Student)	76
3.9	Restatement of the Law Subjects	78

3.10 Restatement Rule and Supporting Materials
      (Covenant Not-to-Compete)   80
3.11 Citator Report for Restatement (Covenant Not-to-Compete)   82
3.12 Jury Instruction Guide (Employment Defamation)   84
3.13 American Law Reports (Employment Defamation)   87
3.14 Looseleaf Checklist (Social Media Policy)   90
3.15 Looseleaf Sample Document (Social Media Policy)   91
3.16 Newsletter Article (Social Media Policy)   94

CHAPTER 4
CASE LAW

4.1   State Case from Westlaw (Employment Defamation)   105
4.2   Federal Court of Appeals Case from Lexis (Constitutional
      Rights of Public School Student)   112
4.3   Federal Appellate Courts Map   120
4.4   Case Brief and Research Notes (Employment Defamation)   125
4.5   West Reporters   127
4.6   Approaches to Case Law Research   128
4.7   Westlaw Terms-and-Connectors Search
      (Employment Defamation)   130
4.8   Westlaw Key-Number Search (Employment Defamation)   132
4.9   Keycite Report (Employment Defamation)   135
4.10 Lexis Search (Constitutional Rights of Public School Student)   141
4.11 Shepard's Report (Constitutional Rights of Public
      School Student)   143
4.12 Case from Fastcase (Covenant Not-to-Compete)   150
4.13 Authority Check Report (Covenant Not-to-Compete)   152
4.14 Case from Google Scholar (Covenant Not-to-Compete)   156
4.15 How Cited Display (Covenant Not-to-Compete)   158

CHAPTER 5
ENACTED LAW

5.1   Statute Main Section (Driving While Using Cell Phone)   168
5.2   Statute Definition Section (Driving While Using Cell Phone)   170
5.3   Statutory Interpretation Case (Driving While Using
      Cell Phone)   173
5.4   Statutory Brief and Research Notes (Driving While Using
      Cell Phone)   178
5.5   Approaches to Statutes Research   180
5.6   Print Code Popular Name Table (Employment Discrimination)   182
5.7   Print Code Statute Text (Employment Discrimination)   183
5.8   Print Code Annotation (Employment Discrimination)   184
5.9   Legislative Website Popular Name Tool (Family Leave Rights)   188

5.10 Legislative Website Statute Section (Family Leave Rights) 189
5.11 Westlaw Notes of Decisions (Driving While Using Cell Phone) 192
5.12 Westlaw Context & Analysis (Driving While Using Cell Phone) 193
5.13 Statutory Keycite Report (Driving While Using Cell Phone) 194
5.14 Lexis Statute with Annotations (Family Leave Rights) 196
5.15 Statutory Shepard's Report (Family Leave Rights) 200
5.16 Fastcase Statute with Case Excerpt (Family Leave Rights) 203
5.17 City Ordinance (Driving Regulation) 206
5.18 Legislative Documents 209
5.19 Bill (Family Leave Rights) 211
5.20 Proposed Amendment (Family Leave Rights) 213
5.21 Hearing Testimony (Family Leave Rights) 214
5.22 Committee Report (Family Leave Rights) 215
5.23 Floor Debate (Family Leave Rights) 217
5.24 Presidential Signing Statement (Family Leave Rights) 218
5.25 Approaches to Legislative Materials Research 219
5.26 Annotated Code History Information (Family Leave Rights) 222
5.27 Congress.gov Information (Family Leave Rights) 225
5.28 Proquest Congressional Legislative History Report
     (Family Leave Rights) 227
5.29 Congress.gov Bill Tracking Report (Family Leave Rights) 232

CHAPTER 6
RULES OF PROCEDURE AND PROFESSIONAL RESPONSIBILITY

6.1 Federal Rule of Civil Procedure (Preliminary Injunction) 241
6.2 Approaches to Rules of Procedure Research 245
6.3 Treatise Discussion (Preliminary Injunction) 247
6.4 Annotated Rules (Preliminary Injunction) 251
6.5 Local Rules (Electronic Filing) 256
6.6 Sample Form (Preliminary Injunction) 257
6.7 Rule of Professional Responsibility (Client Confidentiality) 259
6.8 Ethics Opinion (Client Confidentiality) 263

CHAPTER 7
ADMINISTRATIVE AGENCY MATERIALS

7.1 Regulation (Employee Data) 273
7.2 Approaches to Regulations Research 277
7.3 Annotated Code (Employee Data) 279
7.4 Agency Website Posting (Employee Data) 280
7.5 Regulation in e-CFR (Employee Data) 281
7.6 *Federal Register* Daily Edition (Employee Data) 283
7.7 Keycite Report for Regulation (Employee Data) 285
7.8 Explanation of Regulation (Employee Data) 287

7.9   Board Decision and Order (Social Media Policy)   290
7.10 Agency Website Digests of Decisions (Social Media Policy)   296
7.11 Guidance Document (Social Media Policy)   298

CHAPTER 8
TRIBAL LAW AND INTERNATIONAL LAW

8.1   Major Treaty Resources   313
8.2   Components of Customary International Law   316

PREFACE

You are about to learn a skill that requires curiosity and diligence, precision and creativity. To most novices, legal research is daunting—yet we believe you will find it rewarding. Although legal research can seem ponderous at times, it is also the basis for legal work that helps individuals and organizations maintain their well-being, achieve their goals, and resolve their conflicts. Indeed, the research that we do as lawyers makes our pursuit of justice possible.

We are honored that you are learning this important skill through our book. This book is the ninth edition of *The Process of Legal Research*; the first edition was published in 1986. Over the years, we, along with the co-authors of previous editions and those who have taught research with us, have picked up certain ideas about learning legal research. Here are our observations, along with suggestions for how to use this book to maximize your learning.

Discussion of sources and resources. As you will see, *sources* are the texts created by lawmakers and those who write about the law; *resources* are publications that contain sources. Our complex government produces an abundance of sources, and you must have a solid grasp of what they are and how they interact. In recent decades, with the development of online publishing, we now have an even more dizzying array of legal research resources. This book explains what you need to know about both legal sources and resources.

To help you solidify this knowledge, we have italicized key concepts throughout the text, provided visual presentations, and included some detailed information in matrix charts. In addition, near the end of most chapters you will find a "Build Your Understanding" component. Under the title "Test Your Knowledge" is a set of questions designed to reinforce the key concepts. Indeed, you may want to read those questions before you read the chapter, to prime your reading. The answers to those questions appear at the very end of each chapter.

Ten practices of skilled legal researchers. The point of the title of this book, *The Process of Legal Research*, is that legal research is an activity—indeed a rather challenging one, as you will soon see. Furthermore, it should be purposeful, not random, as set out in Chapter 2's discussion of the ten practices of skilled legal researchers. Thus, most chapters not only discuss sources and resources, but also generally how to research in them, drawing on these ten practices.

To help you fully understand these practices, we have provided demonstrations throughout the book. In Chapter 1, we set out some client situations, covering a range of (we hope) interesting topics. Along the way, we recount how we researched these situations. Carefully read our narratives; study the documents that we have included here; and think about how what we did fits into the ten practices. Indeed, ponder what you might have done differently and what you would do next.

In addition, in the "Build Your Understanding" component under the title "Put It into Practice," we have provided a scenario for you to research, along with specific tasks tracking our research steps. We encourage you to engage in this extended research project so that you can replicate what we have demonstrated and see how the sources covered in the separate chapters combine into a complete research file for a client's situation. Note that the answers do not appear in the book for two reasons: there are no fixed answers for most questions, and answers change over time. Nonetheless, "Put It into Practice" is designed so that you can achieve good results with solid effort and be able to recognize those results yourself.

Your responsibility for your own learning. As you learn to research, you prepare to learn throughout your career; as lawyers, we have to discover over and over what the law is for our next client's situation. So too legal research itself is an activity that will change during your career. Although the types of sources and ten practices discussed in this book will hold steady, the resources that you are likely to use will change in small and big ways. Thus, as you learn legal research, it is important to be a self-teacher and to reflect on this enterprise from time to time.

To help you with this, we have not provided a high level of detail as to any specific resource; we do not tell you where on a screen to click to accomplish a particular task, for example. By and large, many resources have understandable interfaces, tutorials, or training staff to help you with this.

We have provided at the end of each chapter a question to prompt you to think more broadly about legal research, in the "Build Your Under-standing" component under the title "Make Connections." As you might guess, there are no fixed answers to these questions, so none are provided.

A final word. Among us, we have over 100 years of experience in researching in the law. We continue to find it fascinating, and we hope you do too.

Deborah A. Schmedemann
Ann L. Bateson
Mehmet Konar-Steenberg

February 2016

ACKNOWLEDGMENTS

This is the ninth edition of a book that debuted in 1986. Although much of it is new — legal research being a *very* fast-changing field — we owe a great deal to those who started and sustained this endeavor over the years. The list is long, but we must single out Christina Kunz, who generated the idea for the book and "drove the bus" as William Mitchell's Legal Writing Program coordinator for decades, and Matthew Downs, a strong contributor during his tenure as William Mitchell's library director.

This book is nourished on an ongoing basis by those in our respective professional communities. Thus we thank the many students who have been our research learners; the colleagues with whom we have taught research, including the library staffs and adjunct faculty; the faculties and administrations of our respective law schools; and the wider legal writing and law library communities. For this edition, we thank Lynette Fraction at Mitchell Hamline School of Law for her able and cheerful administrative assistance.

We write a manuscript; a publishing team produces a book. Thus we thank the following people for their highly skilled and ever patient work on various aspects of the creation of this book: Kathy Langone (developmental editor), Sarah Hains (production editor), Susan McClung (copyeditor), Marla Cook (proofreader); S4Carlisle Publishing Services (composition team); and Keithley and Associates, Inc. (designers).

Many pages in this book are documents drawn from legal resources. While some are from government resources, others are drawn from commercial publications. We acknowledge, with deep thanks, the permissions to reprint materials, as listed below.

Finally, as always, this book is nourished, as we are nourished, by our respective personal support crews. They know who they are; thanks yet again!

Box 1.6. List of 20 Citing References for Luttrell v. United Telephone System, Inc. Copyright © 2016 Thomson Reuters. Reprinted by permission.

Box 2.2. Covenant, Black's Law Dictionary (10th ed. 2014). Copyright © 2016 Thomson Reuters. Reprinted by permission.

Box 2.4. 2014 Minnesota Statutes Index (Topics), Index (Employment Discrimination Statute). Copyright © 2016 Thomson Reuters. Reprinted by permission.

Box 3.2. Dobbs' Law of Torts, § 519, Elements of Defamation, Treatise Text (Employment Defamation). Copyright © 2016 Thomson Reuters. Reprinted by permission.

Box 3.3. Chapter 44, Defamation, Treatise Table of Contents (Employment Defamation). Copyright © 2016 Thomson Reuters. Reprinted by permission.

Box 3.4. Defamation, DOBBLOT Index, Treatise Index (Employment Defamation). Copyright © 2016 Thomson Reuters. Reprinted by permission.

Box 3.6. § 315, Wireless Telephones, 8 Cal. Jur. 3d Automobiles, Encyclopedia (Driving While Using Cell Phone). Copyright © 2016 Thomson Reuters. Reprinted by permission.

Box 3.10. Restatement (Second) of Contracts, § 188; § 188 Comments a, b, g; § 188 Illustrations 2, 3, 4, 5, 6, 7. Copyright © 1981 The American Law Institute. Reprinted by permission.

Box 3.11. Shepard's: Contracts 2d § 188 cmt. g, Citator for Restatement (Covenant Not-to-Compete). Copyright © 2016 LexisNexis. Reprinted by permission.

Box 3.12. 127.51 Defamation, Pattern Inst. Kan. Civil 127.51, Jury Instruction Guide (Employment Defamation). Copyright © 2016 Thomson Reuters. Reprinted by permission.

Box 3.13. 47 A.L.R. 4th 674, American Law Reports (Employment Defamation). Copyright © 2016 LexisNexis. Reprinted by permission.

Box 3.14. § 47,268 Checklist: What Topics Should Be Covered in a Social Media Policy? WL 5470799, Looseleaf Checklist (Social Media Policy). Copyright © 2016 Thomson Reuters. Reprinted by permission.

Box 3.15. § 2429 Sample Social Media Communication Policy, WL 1830890, Looseleaf Checklist (Social Media Policy). Copyright © 2016 Thomson Reuters. Reprinted by permission.

Box 3.16. Balancing Protection of Information With Employee Rights in Confidentiality Policies, 2015 WL 1883380, Newsletter Article (Social Media Policy). Copyright © 2016 Thomson Reuters. Reprinted by permission.

Box 4.1. Luttrell v. United Telphone System, 683 P.2d 1292, 47 A.L.R. 4th 669, State Case from WestLaw (Employment Defamation). Copyright © 2016 Thomson Reuters. Reprinted by permission.

Box 4.2. B.H. v. Easton Area School District, Federal Court of Appeals Case from Lexis (Constitutional Rights of Public School Student). Copyright © 2016 LexisNexis. Reprinted by permission.

Box 4.7. WestLaw Terms and Connectors Search (Employment Defamation). Copyright © 2016 Thomson Reuters. Reprinted by permission.

Box 4.8. WestLaw Key-Number Search (Employment Defamation). Copyright © 2016 Thomson Reuters. Reprinted by permission.

Box 4.9. List of 20 Citing References for Luttrell v. United Telephone System, Inc., Keycite Report (Employment Defamation). Copyright © 2016 Thomson Reuters. Reprinted by permission.

Box 4.10. Lexis Search (Constitutional Rights of Public School Student). Copyright © 2016 LexisNexis. Reprinted by permission.

Box 4.11. Shepard's Report (Constitutional Rights of Public School Student). Copyright © 2016 LexisNexis. Reprinted by permission.

Box 4.12. Walker Employment Service v. Parkhurst (Covenant Not-to-Compete). Copyright © 2016 Fastcase. Reprinted by permission.

Box 4.13. Authority Check Report. Authority Check Report (Covenant Not-to-Compete). Copyright © 2016 Fastcase. Reprinted by permission.

Box 5.1. West's Ann. Cal. Vehicle Code § 23123 [Statute Main Section (Driving While Using Cell Phone). Copyright © 2016 Thomson Reuters. Reprinted by permission.

Box 5.2. Vehicle Code VEH, Statute Definition Section (Driving While Using Cell Phone). Copyright © 2016 Thomson Reuters. Reprinted by permission.

Box 5.3, People v. Spriggs, 224 Cal. App. 4th 150 (2014), Statutory Interpretation Case (Driving While Using Cell Phone). Copyright © 2016 Thomson Reuters. Reprinted by permission.

Box 5.6, Popular Name Table, Print Code Popular Name Table (Employment Discrimination). Copyright © 2016 Thomson Reuters. Reprinted by permission.

Box 5.7. § 363A.04 Human Rights, Print Code Statute Text (Employment Discrimination). Copyright © 2016 Thomson Reuters. Reprinted by permission.

Box 5.8. § 363A.08 Human Rights, Print Code Annotation (Employment Discrimination). Copyright © 2016 Thomson Reuters. Reprinted by permission.

Box 5.11. List of 8 Notes of Decisions for 23123, WestLaw Notes of Decisions (Driving While Using Cell Phone). Copyright © 2016 Thomson Reuters. Reprinted by permission.

Box 5.12. List of 17 Context & Analysis for § 23123, WestLaw Context & Analysis (Driving While Using Cell Phone). Copyright © 2016 Thomson Reuters. Reprinted by permission.

Box 5.13. List of 2 Validity for § 23123.5, Statutory KeyCite Report (Driving While Using Cell Phone). Copyright © 2016 Thomson Reuters. Reprinted by permission.

Box 5.14. 29 USCS § 2611, Lexis Statute With Annotations (Family Leave Rights). Copyright © 2016 LexisNexis. Reprinted by permission.

Box 5.15. Shepard's Report Content: Comprehensive Report for 29 U.S.C. § 2611, Statutory Shepard's Report (Family Leave Rights). Copyright © 2016 LexisNexis. Reprinted by permission.

Box 5.16. Fastcase Document — Statute with Case Excerpt (Family Leave Rights). Copyright © 2016 Fastcase. Reprinted by permission.

Box 5.20. Proposed Amendment (Family Leave Rights). Copyright © 2016 Thomson Reuters. Reprinted by permission.

Box 5.23. Floor Debate (Family Leave Rights). Copyright © 2016 Thomson Reuters. Reprinted by permission.

Box 5.26. 29 § 2611, Annotated Code History Information (Family Leave Rights). Copyright © 2016 Thomson Reuters. Reprinted by permission.

Box 6.1. Rule 65. Injunctions and Restraining Orders, Federal Rule of Civil Procedure (Preliminary Injunctions). Copyright © 2016 Thomson Reuters. Reprinted by permission.

Box 6.3. Federal Practice & Procedure § 2951 Temporary Restraining Orders, Treatise Discussion (Preliminary Injunction). Copyright © 2016 Thomson Reuters. Reprinted by permission.

THE PROCESS OF
LEGAL RESEARCH

THE BASICS

Chances are that, no matter what your background, legal research will be more challenging than the research that you have conducted thus far, at least some of the time. There are various reasons for this:

- First, legal research involves many essential sources because it is aimed at locating the law, and various entities act together to make law in the U.S. legal system.
- Second, not surprisingly, the law is available in many resources, and with plenty comes the dilemma of choice. Some resources are published by the government, others by commercial companies or nonprofit organizations. Some are basic; some are expansive and elaborate; some are in between.
- Third, legal research is exacting: you must find the specific law that controls your client's particular situation, in that location, at that time — not something more or less pertinent.
- Fourth, your clients will rightly expect you to conduct your research in an efficient, cost-effective manner. You will need to be a smart consumer of these resources.
- Fifth, for at least a while, much of the terminology will be unfamiliar to you, and some seemingly familiar words will have unexpected meanings.

Chapter 1 examines the first and second points by providing an overview of the legal research landscapes that you must understand in order to undertake legal research. Chapter 2 explores the third and fourth points by setting out ten practices of skilled legal researchers, practices that will serve you well no matter how simple or substantial a particular project is. As for the fifth point, we hope that this book, along with the rest of your law school classes, helps to ease you into the language of the law.

<table>
<tr><td>

THE LANDSCAPES OF
LEGAL RESEARCH

</td><td>

CHAPTER

1

</td></tr>
</table>

Before you undertake legal research, you need to be grounded in the territory, so to speak, in which legal research happens. One way to think of this territory is as a set of landscapes:

- One landscape is the structure of the U.S. government. At each of three levels (federal, state, and local), the three branches of government — the legislature, the judiciary, and the executive — create the law, or *primary authority.*
- A second landscape is the phenomenon of legal commentary. Given the volume and complexity of law created in the United States, many individuals and organizations generate extensive analyses of it every day; they create *secondary sources* and also *finding tools.*
- A third landscape — really a different slant on the other two — is the world of legal publishing, which is a highly competitive industry composed of a wide range of government, commercial, and nonprofit organizations producing *resources,* which are publications of various kinds containing primary authority, secondary sources, and finding tools.

This chapter presents an overview of these three landscapes, providing key terminology and concepts used in all the other chapters of this book.

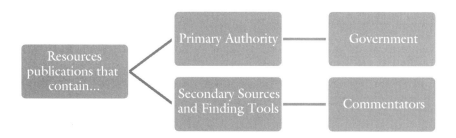

Yet the most important landscape in the territory of legal research is the lawyer-client relationship, which gives rise to legal research and is governed by rules of professional ethics and standards of performance. So this chapter begins there.

THE LAWYER-CLIENT RELATIONSHIP

Lawyers[1] research the law not out of idle curiosity, but because clients need them to do so. Thus the goal of legal research is to find the law that provides the rules for — or, as lawyers say, *controls* — a client's situation. Only when the lawyer finds the controlling law can the lawyer appropriately counsel the client, select a course of action (in consultation with the client), and implement that course of action.

The situations that bring clients to lawyers in the United States run a wide gamut indeed, given the pervasiveness of law in our economy and culture. To help you appreciate this point, and also to provide concrete examples, we will refer throughout this book to various fictional client matters that a typical small or midsized law firm might handle. Many involve topics falling within courses taught in the first year of law school; the more advanced topics arise in employment law, a fairly accessible area. Note that our situations are set in various states; in real life, a firm typically would handle client situations mostly in one state. The client situations are summarized in Box 1.1 and are developed further in the following chapters of this book.

In some of these situations, the lawyer would advise the client before the client acts so that the actions accord with the law. In others, the client has already acted, a dispute is in progress, and the lawyer's role is to represent the client in resolving that dispute, which is likely to involve negotiation, but may entail litigation before some tribunal.[2] Regardless of the situation, the lawyer must get the law right — that is, find and understand the controlling law.

Getting the law wrong means that the advice will be skewed, so that the action taken will be off-target or the positions asserted in litigation erroneous. Furthermore, serious consequences may follow for the lawyer. One may be a violation of the first rule of professional responsibility for lawyers, which could lead to professional sanctions: "A lawyer shall provide competent representation to a client [which includes] the legal knowledge . . . reasonably necessary for the representation."[3] Incompetent research may also have financial consequences for a lawyer, through a legal malpractice award paid to the client or sanctions paid to the opposing party.[4]

---

1. In some situations, paralegals conduct legal research under the supervision of lawyers. For the most part, this book can be read to include paralegals within the term "lawyers."

2. As a very rough estimate, nine out of ten legal disputes are resolved by negotiation. For a wide-ranging discussion of U.S. dispute resolution, see Marc Galanter, *The Vanishing Trial: An Examination of Trials and Related Matters in Federal and State Courts*, 1 J. Empirical Legal Stud. 459 (2004).

3. This language comes from Rule 1.1 of the ABA Model Rules of Professional Conduct. For an example of a court's discussion of a lawyer's failure to comport with Rules 1.1 and 1.3, which requires acting with "reasonable diligence," see *Massey v. Prince George's Cty.*, 918 F. Supp. 905 (D. Md. 1996).

4. For an example of a malpractice award of $100,000, see *Smith v. Lewis*, 530 P.2d 589 (Cal. 1975), *disapproved of on other grounds, In re Marriage of Brown*, 544 P.2d 561 (Cal. 1976). For a discussion of sanctions cases, see Marguerite L. Butler, *Rule 11 Sanctions and a Lawyer's Failure to Conduct Competent Legal Research*, 29 Cap. U. L. Rev. 681 (2002).

| Box 1.1 | **OUR CLIENTS' SITUATIONS** |

All-Day Wellness: A Minnesota company that provides health-care consulting services to employers—a very competitive business—would like to keep its employees from working for its competitors when they leave its employ. (This matter involves a contract, as well as issues of professional responsibility.)

Bower's Bounty: A grocery store in Kansas has received a complaint from a recently fired employee charging it with defamation. (This matter involves torts.)

Cassie Collins: A client in California was ticketed for driving while using her cell phone after she was involved in a car accident while pulling out of a parking lot into traffic. (This matter involves criminal law.)

Daniel de la Cruz: A public school student in Pennsylvania was suspended for shaving a message in his hair in support of his sister, who has breast cancer. (This matter involves constitutional law and rules of civil procedure.)

Exact Electronics, Inc.: This rapidly growing company manufactures parts for consumer electronics in plants in small towns around the country. Its new human resources manager has raised several questions involving employment law:

May the company decline to hire an applicant for a position on the grounds that he would be working closely with, although not supervised by, his spouse? This issue has arisen in Minnesota.

Is the company obligated to find a position at one of its plants for an employee who is seeking to return from a family leave following an adoption of a child? This issue has arisen in Oklahoma.

The company is developing a policy governing employee use of its communications systems, as well as their own social media accounts and technology, such as Facebook and Twitter. Are there any legal parameters to follow?

Finally, it merits note that, as you research on behalf of a client, you have other responsibilities as well. In the words of the preamble to the American Bar Association (ABA) Model Rules of Professional Conduct for Lawyers, on which many state codes of professional responsibility are based: "A lawyer, as a member of the legal profession, is a representative of clients, an officer of the legal system and a public citizen having special responsibility for the quality of justice." Ours is indeed a high calling.

THE U.S. GOVERNMENT: PRIMARY AUTHORITY

Getting the law right is not that easy because there are so many forms of U.S. law. One useful way to think of U.S. law is as a three-by-three matrix.

First, the United States has three levels of government: federal, state, and local (with the latter consisting of units such as counties and cities). Not surprisingly, the United States generally follows a geographically based system of governmental power: the federal government governs matters affecting the nation as a whole, such as interstate commerce, national security, and implementation of the U.S. Constitution; the states govern matters within their borders, such as many crimes, contracts, and passing of property; and local governments handle matters such as zoning and delivery of public services. Thus, a client's situation could be controlled by federal, state, or local law; indeed in some situations, more than one of these could control. As you begin a research project, a key task is to determine the location of your client's situation — and thus the potential *jurisdictions* whose law could control. In this context, *jurisdiction* refers to a geographic area over which a particular lawmaking body's laws are controlling.

Second, at each of the three levels of government, there are three branches — the legislature, the judiciary, and the executive — each of which is comprised of various bodies. For example, at the federal level, the legislative branch is comprised of Congress (the Senate and the House of Representatives); the main elements of the judiciary are the U.S. Supreme Court, the federal courts of appeals, and the federal district courts; and the executive branch is comprised of the President, fifteen cabinet-level departments, and several hundred administrative agencies.

These many bodies have the capacity to make law, that is, *primary authority*.[5] Each branch of government creates its own types of primary authority, as shown in the middle column of Box 1.2. Each primary authority follows a format that reflects its mode of creation.

Box 1.2	**PRIMARY AUTHORITIES AND QUASI-AUTHORITIES**	
Branch of Government	**Primary Authority**	**Quasi-Authority**
Legislature	Constitutions Statutes	Legislative history documents
Judiciary	Cases Rules of procedure	Advisory comments to rules of procedure
Executive	Legislative agency rules Decisions and orders	Interpretive agency rules Explanations of rules Guidance memos

---

5. Some writers use the term *authority* to refer to a very wide range of sources and, accordingly, use *primary* to distinguish the texts discussed in this part from texts that are not the law. We use *authority* only for texts that are the law. We retain *primary* to drive that point home, as well as to distinguish the law itself from quasi-authorities.

As an example, consider the issue posed by Exact Electronics concerning the hiring of a spouse of a current employee. Box 1.3 contains portions of a statute enacted by the Minnesota Legislature that controls this situation. Note that this text is fairly straightforward in (1) defining what *marital status* means (see subdivision 24) and (2) specifying that it is an unfair employment practice — that is, illegal — for an employer to discriminate in hiring based on marital status (among other things) (see subdivision 2). In other provisions of the statute, the consequences of engaging in an unfair employment practice are stated, including paying damages to the applicant.[6] This statute is a *legal rule*: it identifies behavior that a client engages in and states its legal consequences.

As another example, consider the issue posed by the Bower's Bounty situation, in which the client has been sued for defamation by a fired employee. Box 1.4 contains a case from a Kansas state court controlling this situation. This case differs considerably from the statute in Box 1.3. It states a legal rule in the penultimate paragraph, but it also does much more. It sets out the facts of the dispute that the court was asked to decide, presents the views of the parties[7] and the ruling of the lower court, discusses various earlier cases on the legal issues, and explains why the court selected its chosen rule.

The branches of government interact in a system of checks and balances. In brief, the legislature enacts statutes, which courts then interpret and apply to specific situations. However, courts also have the power to invalidate statutes that do not conform to the requirements of the applicable constitution.[8] Where the legislature has not acted, the courts may create *common law* by deciding cases, but that law may be displaced by statutes enacted by the legislature.

Furthermore, administrative agencies come into being by statute. Depending on their statutory powers, they act both in ways that resemble legislatures (i.e., creating rules) and ways that resemble courts (i.e., issuing decisions and orders). In both capacities, their actions are reviewed by the courts for conformity to statutory and constitutional requirements.

An additional body of law controls the operation of legal procedures. Thus, when your client's matter involves litigation in court, you will often research in two related areas. First, you will research the controlling *substantive law*, which determines the legality of the client's conduct and its consequences. Second, you will research the *procedural law*, such as rules of civil or criminal procedure, which control such matters as how a case is brought and defended. Rules of procedure generally are created by courts.

Each branch of government also creates texts that are not law in and of themselves but are nonetheless important because they either are generated during the process of creating primary authority or reveal the thinking of

---

6. *See* Minn. Stat. §§ 363A.29, 363A.33 (2014).

7. The parties in a simple case are the plaintiff (here, the employee) who is suing the defendant (here, the employer).

8. Federal statutes must comport with the U.S. Constitution, the supreme law of the land; state statutes must comport with the U.S. Constitution and their respective state constitutions.

Box 1.3   **STATUTE (Employment Discrimination)**

2014 Minnesota Statutes

363A.03 UNFAIR DISCRIMINATORY PRACTICES RELATING TO EMPLOYMENT OR UNFAIR EMPLOYMENT PRACTICE.

Subdivision 1. **Labor organization.** Except when based on a bona fide occupational qualification, it is an unfair employment practice for a labor organization, because of race, color, creed, religion, national origin, sex, marital status, status with regard to public assistance, familial status, disability, sexual orientation, or age:

(1) to deny full and equal membership rights to a person seeking membership or to a member;

(2) to expel a member from membership;

(3) to discriminate against a person seeking membership or a member with respect to hiring, apprenticeship, tenure, compensation, terms, upgrading, conditions, facilities, or privileges of employment; or

(4) to fail to classify properly, or refer for employment or otherwise to discriminate against a person or member.

Subd. 2. **Employer.** Except when based on a bona fide occupational qualification, it is an unfair employment practice for an employer, because of race, color, creed, religion, national origin, sex, marital status, status with regard to public assistance, familial status, membership or activity in a local commission, disability, sexual orientation, or age to:

(1) refuse to hire or to maintain a system of employment which unreasonably excludes a person seeking employment; or

(2) discharge an employee; or

(3) discriminate against a person with respect to hiring, tenure, compensation, terms, upgrading, conditions, facilities, or privileges of employment.

Subd. 3. **Employment agency.** Except when based on a bona fide occupational qualification, it is an unfair employment practice for an employment agency, because of race, color, creed, religion, national origin, sex, marital status, status with regard to public assistance, familial status, disability, sexual orientation, or age to:

(1) refuse or fail to accept, register, classify properly, or refer for employment or otherwise to discriminate against a person; or

(2) comply with a request from an employer for referral of applicants for employment if the request indicates directly or indirectly that the employer fails to comply with the provisions of this chapter.

Subd. 4. **Employer, employment agency, or labor organization.** (a) Except when based on a bona fide occupational qualification, it is an unfair employment practice for an employer, employment agency, or labor organization, before a person is employed by an employer or admitted to membership in a labor organization, to:

(1) require or request the person to furnish information that pertains to race, color, creed, religion, national origin, sex, marital status, status with regard to public assistance, familial status, disability, sexual orientation, or age; or, subject to section 363A.20, to require or request a person to undergo physical examination; unless for the sole and exclusive purpose of national security, information pertaining to national origin is required by the United States, this state or a political subdivision or agency of the United States or this state, or for the sole and exclusive purpose of compliance with the Public Contracts

Box 1.3 *(continued)*

[Section 363.08 definitions]

Subd. 15. **Employee .** " Employee " means an individual who is employed by an employer and who resides or works in this state. Employee includes a commission salesperson, as defined in section 181.145, who resides or works in this state.

Subd. 16. **Employer.** "Employer" means a person who has one or more employees.

Subd. 17. **Employment agency.** "Employment agency" means a person or persons who, or an agency which regularly undertakes, with or without compensation, to procure employees or opportunities for employment.

Subd. 18. **Familial status.** "Familial status" means the condition of one or more minors being domiciled with (1) their parent or parents or the minor's legal guardian or (2) the designee of the parent or parents or guardian with the written permission of the parent or parents or guardian. The protections afforded against discrimination on the basis of family status apply to any person who is pregnant or is in the process of securing legal custody of an individual who has not attained the age of majority.

Subd. 19. **Fixed route system.** "Fixed route system" means a system of providing public transportation on which a vehicle is operated along a prescribed route according to a fixed schedule.

Subd. 20. **Historic or antiquated rail passenger car.** "Historic or antiquated rail passenger car" means a rail passenger car:

(1) that is at least 30 years old at the time of its use for transporting individuals;

(2) the manufacturer of which is no longer in the business of manufacturing rail passenger cars; or

(3) that has consequential association with events or persons significant to the past or embodies, or is being restored to embody, the distinctive characteristics of a type of rail passenger car used in the past or to represent a time period that has passed.

Subd. 21. **Human rights investigative data.** "Human rights investigative data" means written documents issued or gathered by the department for the purpose of investigating and prosecuting alleged or suspected discrimination .

Subd. 22. **Labor organization.** "Labor organization" means any organization that exists wholly or partly for one or more of the following purposes:

(1) collective bargaining;

(2) dealing with employers concerning grievances, terms or conditions of employment; or

(3) mutual aid or protection of employees.

Subd. 23. **Local commission.** "Local commission" means an agency of a city, county, or group of counties created pursuant to law, resolution of a county board, city charter, or municipal ordinance for the purpose of dealing with discrimination on the basis of race, color, creed, religion, national origin, sex, age, disability, marital status, status with regard to public assistance, sexual orientation, or familial status.

Subd. 24. **Marital status.** "Marital status" means whether a person is single, married , remarried, divorced, separated, or a surviving spouse and, in employment cases, includes protection against discrimination on the basis of the identity, situation, actions, or beliefs of a spouse or former spouse.

Subd. 25. **National origin.** "National origin" means the place of birth of an individual or of any of the individual's lineal ancestors.

Subd. 26. **Open case file.** "Open case file" means a file containing human rights investigative data in which no order or other decision resolving the alleged or suspected discrimination has been made or issued by the commissioner, a hearing officer, or a

STATE CASE (Employment Defamation)

9 Kan. App. 2d 620 (1984)
683 P.2d 1292

MARVIN G. LUTTRELL, Appellant,

v.

**UNITED TELEPHONE SYSTEM, INC., Appellee. Affirmed 236 Kan. 710, 695
P.2d 1279 (1985).**

No. 56,031

Court of Appeals of Kansas.

Opinion filed July 19, 1984.

Richard M. Smith, of Smith & Winter-Smith, of Mound City, for appellant.

Paul Hasty, Jr., of Wallace, Saunders, Austin, Brown & Enochs, Chartered, of Overland Park, for
appellee.

Before FOTH, C.J., PARKS and SWINEHART, JJ.

PARKS, J.:

Plaintiff Marvin G. **Luttrell** appeals the dismissal of his defamation action against the defendant,
United Telephone System, Inc.

Plaintiff alleges in his petition that several managerial employees of defendant maliciously
communicated defamatory remarks about him between themselves while acting within the scope of
their employment. Particularly, he alleges that on or about April 6 or 7 of 1982, Mr. R.H. Baranek, an
employee of defendant, stated to Mr. R.L. Flint, plaintiff's supervisor, that plaintiff was illegally taping
telephone conversations on April 1 and that Baranek had requested him to stop but plaintiff persisted
in this illegal activity the rest of the afternoon despite the direct order given him to stop by his
supervisor. He further alleged that the communication of the same defamatory information was made
by Mr. Flint to Mr. T.V. Tregenza and by Mr. Tregenza to Mr. W. Soble, all while acting within the
scope of their employment. Defendant filed a motion to dismiss pursuant to K.S.A. 60-212(*b*)(6) on
the grounds that intracorporate communications did not constitute "publication." The trial court
sustained the motion to dismiss for failure to state a claim upon which relief may be granted.

621   The tort of defamation includes both libel and slander. The elements of the wrong include false and
defamatory words (*Hein v. Lacy,* 228 Kan. 249, 259, 616 P.2d 277 [1980]) communicated *621 to a
third person (*Schulze v. Coykendall,* 218 Kan. 653, 657, 545 P.2d 392 [1976]) which result in harm to
the reputation of the person defamed. *Gobin v. Globe Publishing Co.,* 232 Kan. 1, 6, 649 P.2d 1239
(1982) (*Gobin III*). A corporation may be liable for the defamatory utterances of its agent which are
made while acting within the scope of his authority. *Bourn v. State Bank,* 116 Kan. 231, 235, 226 Pac.
769 (1924).

Box 1.4   *(continued)*

In this case, the defendant argued and the district court agreed that there can be no communication to a third person, or "publication," when the defamatory words are exchanged by agents of a single corporate defendant. This issue of first impression is more precisely whether interoffice communications between supervisory employees of a corporation, acting within the scope and course of their employment, regarding the work of another employee of the corporation, constitute publication to a third person sufficient for a defamation action.

There is a considerable division of authority concerning this issue. For example, courts recently considering the laws of Nevada, Missouri, Arkansas, Georgia and Louisiana have all accepted the assertion that intracorporate defamation is simply the corporation talking to itself and not publication. See, *e.g., Jones v. Golden Spike Corp.,* 97 Nev. 24, 623 P.2d 970 (1981); *Ellis v. Jewish Hospital of St. Louis,* 581 S.W.2d 850 (Mo. App. 1979); *Halsell v. Kimberly-Clark Corp.,* 683 F.2d 285 (8th Cir.1982); *Monahan v. Sims,* 163 Ga. App. 354, 294 S.E.2d 548 (1982); *Commercial Union Ins. Co. v. Melikyan,* 424 So.2d 1114 (La. App. 1982). The contrary conclusion has been reached in courts applying the laws of Kentucky, Massachusetts, New York and California. See, *e.g., Brewer v. American Nat. Ins. Co.,* 636 F.2d 150 (6th Cir.1980); *Arsenault v. Allegheny Airlines, Inc.,* 485 F. Supp. 1373 (D. Mass.), *aff'd* 636 F.2d 1199 (1st Cir.1980); *Pirre v. Printing Developments, Inc.,* 468 F. Supp. 1028 (S.D.N.Y.), *aff'd* 614 F.2d 1290 (2d Cir.1979); *Kelly v. General Telephone Co.,* 136 Cal. App.3d 278, 186 Cal. Rptr. 184 (1982). The latter opinions have held that while communications between supervisory employees of a corporation concerning a third employee may be qualifiedly privileged, they are still publication. Prosser also favors the view that such communications are
622   publication and dismisses those cases holding otherwise as confusing *622 publication with privilege. Prosser, Law of Torts § 113, p. 767 n. 70 (4th ed. 1971).

Undeniably, the district court's holding in this case is not without support or technical appeal; however, we believe it ignores the nature of the civil injury sought to be protected in a defamation action. Damage to one's reputation is the essence and gravamen of an action for defamation. It is reputation which is defamed, reputation which is injured, reputation which is protected by the laws of libel and slander. *Gobin III,* 232 Kan. at 6. Certainly, damage to one's reputation within a corporate community may be just as devastating as that effected by defamation spread to the outside. Thus, the injury caused by intra-corporate defamation should not be disregarded simply because the corporation can be sued as an individual entity.

Defendant argues that corporate employers must be free to evaluate and comment on their employees' work performance and that this freedom will be unduly restrained if they are liable for intracorporate defamation. However, the law in this state has already extended protection to comments made within a work situation by means of a qualified privilege. A communication is qualifiedly privileged if it is made in good faith on any subject matter in which the person communicating has an interest, or in reference to which he has a duty, if it is made to a person having a corresponding interest or duty. The essential elements of a qualifiedly privileged communication are good faith, an interest to be upheld, a statement limited in its scope to the upholding of such interest and publication in a proper manner only to proper parties. *Dobbyn v. Nelson,* 2 Kan. App.2d 358, 360, 579 P.2d 721, *aff'd* 225 Kan. 56 (1978). Thus, in *Dobbyn* the Court held that a letter written by an employee of the Kansas State University library concerning the conduct of another employee and

| Box 1.4 | *(continued)* |

transmitted to the second employee's superior was qualifiedly privileged. *Dobbyn*, 2 Kan. App.2d at 361. As a result, the plaintiff was required to prove that the defendants acted with knowledge of falsity or reckless disregard for the truth before the privilege could be overcome. See also *Scarpelli v. Jones*, 229 Kan. 210, 216, 626 P.2d 785 (1981).

By virtue of the qualified privilege, the employer who is evaluating or investigating an employee in good faith and within the bounds of the employment relationship is protected from the threat of 623 defamation suits by the enhanced burden of proof *623 which the plaintiff would have to bear. We see no reason for greater freedom from liability for defamation to be accorded the corporate employer than that already available to all employers through the qualified privilege.

We conclude that remarks communicated by one corporate employee to another concerning the job performance of a third employee are publication for the purposes of a defamation action against the employer. Since the dismissal motion was granted in this case prior to the commencement of any discovery, we make no findings concerning the possible application of qualified privilege to the communications alleged.

The dismissal for failure to state a claim upon which relief may be granted is reversed and the case is remanded for further proceedings.

lawmakers as they exercise their governmental functions. These *quasi-authorities*, listed in the right-hand column of Box 1.2, are discussed in later chapters.

In summary, a client's situation could be controlled by one or more of a wide variety of primary authorities and guided by various quasi-authorities. And these authorities could come from the federal, state, or local level, or from multiple levels.

SECONDARY SOURCES AND FINDING TOOLS

To help you discern where in the landscape of primary authority to research, as well as to ground your research in other ways, you generally will research in materials written by commentators. These materials are not law because they are not written by lawmakers in a lawmaking process.[9] Rather, they are written

---

9. Sometimes lawmakers do write secondary sources, e.g., a judge may write an article in a law journal. This article is not primary authority but a secondary source.

by individuals (typically professors, practicing lawyers, and judges) and organizations (such as segments of the bar[10] and public interest organizations) to comment on the law; thus, they are *secondary sources*.

Secondary sources describe the law in various ways, but they all more or less state what the law is, and many seek to present the law on a specific topic in a clear framework, knitting together the various primary authorities (some in considerable detail, and with abundant references to primary authorities). Some also critique the law and propose reforms. Others provide background on the law, such as its evolution or empirical studies, or provide practical guidance for lawyers in carrying out specific tasks for clients. Secondary sources come in various formats, and some are kept current, with updates as frequent as daily in the most notable situations, quarterly or annually in the more typical situation.

As an example, consider the request by Exact Electronics for a social media policy for its employees. Box 1.5 contains the first two pages of an article in a legal periodical addressing this issue. Note how this text compares to the statute in Box 1.3 and the case in Box 1.4. It does state legal concepts and the facts of the case that it is discussing. But it also ranges more widely in describing the situations that employers face and closes (at thirty-eight pages) with practical advice for employers.

As you research in primary authority and secondary sources, you also will use research materials that in and of themselves say fairly little; these materials are *finding tools*. Some of these resemble tools that you may have used before in other fields, such as tables of contents and indexes. Others are more specific to law, including case citators and statutory annotations. Some help you to locate a pertinent authority early in your research. Others help you to continue your research by building upon a pertinent authority that you already have found; in legal research, one find often leads to another.

For example, the case in Box 1.4, *Luttrell v. United Telephone System, Inc.*, is a useful case for the Bower's Bounty situation involving an employee claiming defamation against our client. A *case citator* is a finding tool that lists later sources that have referred to, or cited, the case that you are currently reading. Box 1.6 contains excerpts from the citator report for *Luttrell*.

In summary, secondary sources themselves provide useful content; finding tools point you to sources with useful content, as summarized in Box 1.7.

---

10. *Bar* is a term referring to all attorneys and derives from the railing in a courtroom that separates the general public from the lawyers, judges, parties, and court officials.

Box 1.5   **LEGAL PERIODICAL ARTICLE (Social Media Policy)**

The First Facebook Firing Case Under Section 7 of the National Labor Relations Act: Exploring the Limits of Labor Law Protection for Concerted Communication on Social Media

Christine Neylon O'Brien[1]

ABSTRACT

The emergence of social media, from Facebook to Myspace and Linkedin to Twitter—much like the earlier evolution of email, IM, and web 2.0—have changed the way people communicate, expanding the virtual horizons for social networking and business promotion on these popular communications platforms. Smartphones and other portable internet data generators such as iPads, and even internet hotspots incorporated into motor vehicles, have encouraged the blurring of work and personal time such that people are tethered to their devices, checking their work and personal messages wherever they are and whatever else they are doing.

In the first case of its kind, the National Labor Relations Board (Labor Board or NLRB) issued a complaint against an employer, American Medical Response of Connecticut (AMR), for the suspension and firing of an employee who posted negative comments about her supervisor on her Facebook page. The federal agency alleged that the employer retaliated against the terminated employee for her postings and for requesting the presence of her union representative at an investigatory interview that led to discipline. Most importantly, the Labor Board maintained that the employer's rules on blogging and internet posting, which included social media use, standards of conduct relating to discussing co-workers and superiors, and solicitation and distribution, were overbroad, interfering with employees' right to engage in concerted activities for mutual aid and protection under section 7 of the National Labor Relations Act (NLRA). The NLRB, as the federal agency that enforces the statutory rights of all employees covered by the NLRA—not just those who belong to unions—signaled that it is ready to prosecute companies

---

1. Professor and Chair of Business Law, Carroll School of Management, Boston College. B.A., Boston College, J.D., Boston College Law School. The author wishes to express her sincere appreciation for the research assistance and ideas of Margo E. K. Reder, Research Associate & Adjunct Lecturer, Boston College, and Jaspreet Dosanjh, M.B.A./J.D. candidate, Boston College. She also wishes to thank Professors David P. Twomey and Stephanie Greene, Boston College, and Jonathan J. Darrow, S.J.D. candidate, Harvard Law School, for their review of the manuscript and helpful comments.

Box 1.5   *(continued)*

30   *SUFFOLK UNIVERSITY LAW REVIEW*   [Vol. XLV:29

with policies that unduly interfere with employee communication about work matters such as wages, hours, and working conditions, even on social media. The AMR case puts employers on notice that rules affecting employee communication, including the use of email and social media during nonwork time, should be reviewed to ensure that the rules do not violate the NLRA. This article outlines tips for employers and employees to stay within the boundaries of labor law.

I. INTRODUCTION

In the first labor law case of its kind in the United States, Region 34 of the NLRB issued a complaint against AMR. The complaint alleged AMR's firing of Emergency Medical Technician (EMT) Dawnmarie Souza for posting derogatory comments about her supervisor on the social media website Facebook violated sections 7, 8(a)(1), and 8(a)(3) of the NLRA.[2] The Board

---

2. Region 34 of the NLRB issued its complaint against AMR on October 27, 2010 in *American Medical Response of Connecticut, Inc.*, No. 34-CA-12576 (NLRB Region 34) [hereinafter AMR Case]. *See* Complaint & Notice Hearing, Am. Med. Response of Conn., Inc., No. 34-CA-12576 (NLRB Region 34 Oct. 27, 2010) [hereinafter AMR Complaint], *available at* http://www.scribd.com/doc/41010696/American-Medical-Response-of-CT-NLRB-Nov-2010. The Board issued a complaint after investigation of charges filed by the International Brotherhood of Teamsters, Local 443, that AMR of Connecticut had been engaging in unfair labor practices in violation of sections 7 and 8 of the National Labor Relations Act. 29 U.S.C. §§ 151, 157, 158(a)(1), 158(a)(3) (2006). Section 7 provides:

> Employees shall have the right to self-organization, to form, join, or assist labor organizations, to bargain collectively through representatives of their own choosing, and to engage in other concerted activities for the purpose of collective bargaining or other mutual aid or protection, and shall also have the right to refrain from any or all of such activities except to the extent that such right may be affected by an agreement requiring membership in a labor organization as a condition of employment as authorized in Section 8(a)(3).

29 U.S.C. § 157. Section 8(a)(1) provides: "It shall be an unfair labor practice for an employer . . . to interfere with, restrain, or coerce employees in the exercise of the rights guaranteed in Section 7." 29 U.S.C. § 158(a)(1). Section 8(a)(3) provides in relevant part: "It shall be an unfair labor practice for an employer . . . by discrimination in regard to hire or tenure of employment or any term or condition of employment to encourage or discourage membership in any labor organization . . . ." 29 U.S.C. § 158(a)(3). The Board's Office of Public Affairs issued a news release on the AMR case on November 2. *See* News Release, NLRB, Office of the Gen. Counsel, Complaint Alleges Connecticut Company Illegally Fired Employee over Facebook Comments, Release No. R-2794 (Nov. 2, 2010), *available at* http://mynlrb.nlrb.gov/link/document.aspx/09031d45803c4e5e.

Recent reports of similar Facebook firing cases in Canada and France reflect that the employee terminations were upheld by labor tribunal or board. *See* Jeremy Hainsworth, *Canadian Labor Board Upholds Firings of Workers for Negative Facebook Postings*, Daily Lab. Rep. (BNA) No. 213, at A3 (Nov. 11, 2010) (citing Lougheed Imps. Ltd. (W. Coast Mazda) v. United Food & Commercial Workers Int'l Union, Local 1518, 2010 CanLII 62482 (B.C. Labour Relations Bd.)), *available at* http://canlii.ca/s/15r09 (upholding employer's right to fire employees because of derogatory postings about company and supervisors on Facebook); Rick Mitchell, *French Labor Tribunal Upholds Firings over Facebook Comments*, Daily Lab. Rep. (BNA) No. 225, at A4 (Nov. 23, 2010) (citing Southiphong v. Societe Alten SIR, No. RG-F 09/316 (Conseil de Prud'hommes de Boulogne-Billancourt Nov. 19, 2010) and Barbera v. Societe Alten SIR, No. RG-F 09/343 (Conseil de Prud'hommes de Boulogne-Billancourt Nov. 19, 2010)) (referencing "first in France" case where firing of

Box 1.6   CASE CITATOR REPORT (Employment Defamation)

List of 20 Citing References for Luttrell v. United Telephone System, Inc.

Citing References (20)

Treatment	Title	Date	Type	Depth	Headnote(s)
Examined by	**1.** Naab v. Inland Container Corp. 1994 WL 70268, *1+ , D.Kan. Ronald Naab worked for Inland Container until he was terminated on the basis of an appraisal completed by his supervisor, Joseph Miller. Naab has sued Inland and Miller alleging...	Feb. 28, 1994	Case	▪▪▪▪	6 7 8 P.2d
Discussed by	**2.** Hall v. Kansas Farm Bureau 50 P.3d 495, 504+ , Kan. BUSINESS ORGANIZATIONS - Association. President of cooperative marketing association could not be removed by vote of board of directors.	July 12, 2002	Case	▪▪▪	2 5 6 P.2d
Discussed by	**3.** Dominguez v. Davidson 974 P.2d 112, 117+ , Kan. TORTS - Defamation. Qualified privilege protected supervisor's statement that employee filed false injury claim.	Mar. 05, 1999	Case	▪▪▪	2 5 P.2d
Discussed by	**4.** Lindemuth v. Goodyear Tire and Rubber Co. 864 P.2d 744, 750+ , Kan.App. Former employee brought suit against former employer, alleging intentional infliction of emotional distress, defamation, outrage and tortious interference with contract. The...	Dec. 10, 1993	Case	▪▪▪	5 6 7 P.2d
Discussed by	**5.** Gearhart v. Sears, Roebuck & Co., Inc. 27 F.Supp.2d 1263, 1277+ , D.Kan. Former employee brought action against former employer and supervisor, alleging that they discriminated against her on basis of age, disability, and gender, harassed her on basis...	Oct. 19, 1998	Case	▪▪▪▪	5 P.2d
Discussed by	**6.** Etzel v. Musicland Group, Inc. 1993 WL 23741, *7+ , D.Kan. Richard Todd Etzel filed this action against his former employer, The Musicland Group, Inc. (Musicland), for outrageous conduct during the events surrounding his termination and...	Jan. 08, 1993	Case	▪▪▪	2 7 8 P.2d

1

Box 1.7	**SECONDARY SOURCES AND FINDING TOOLS**

Type	Purposes
Secondary Sources	Describe law and cite authorities Critique law and propose reforms Provide background Provide practical guidance
Finding Tools	Locate pertinent authorities (e.g., table of contents, index) Build on pertinent authorities (e.g., case citator, statutory annotation)

LEGAL PUBLISHING: RESOURCES

To build on the landscape metaphor a bit, consider the government and the writers of commentary as "farmers" that produce various "crops" (i.e., primary authorities, secondary sources, and finding tools). These crops need a way to get to market—to the lawyers who will use them on behalf of their clients. This is the role of legal publishing.

Think for a moment of the many locations at which an apple can be sold: at the orchard, at a farmer's market, or at a grocery store offering a very wide range of products. Furthermore, an apple may be sold alone, in a bag of apples, or in a bag with other fruits. Indeed, it may be offered in a wide range of processed versions, including sliced apples, canned apple pie filling, and applesauce.

As with an apple, a creator of a legal text can market the product itself or have others, who are specialists in production and distribution, do so. A legal text can be marketed by itself or combined with others. It can be marketed in its pure form, exactly as it was created, or it can be enhanced before being presented to the legal marketplace.

Each publication in which a legal text appears is known as a *resource*. Consider the statute in Box 1.3. You could find it in the following resources (among others): the website of the Minnesota Legislature; a set of books titled *Minnesota Statutes*, published by the state of Minnesota; a set of books titled *Minnesota Statutes Annotated,* published by a commercial company; and commercial online resources such as Bloomberg Law, Casemaker, Fastcase, LexisNexis (commonly known as "Lexis"), and Westlaw. Some of these resources are in print, and others are online. Some provide the statute and little else; others provide significant editorial enhancements. Some provide basic methods of finding pertinent material; others provide more sophisticated methods.

As the list above suggests, the marketing of legal materials diverges from the crop analogy in one key respect. A legal text consists of words that can be packaged and sold over and over and over; once created, it can be marketed by any number of publishers to many buyers. Over time, given the volume of legal research materials created in the United States and the necessity that lawyers research well, legal publishing has become a major industry. It has been revolutionized, as you would expect, by developments in information technology. An April 2015 article in the *ABA Journal* identified digitized research as number five on a list of 100 innovations in law in the past century: "More than 40 years ago, Mead Data Central introduced Lexis, offering digitized legal research through electronic copies of Ohio and New York legal codes and cases. That action pushed legal research from the world of leather-bound books to clumsy computer terminals, then to CD-ROMS, and now to the Internet. The next wave in legal research may already be here: Google Scholar went beta in 2004, making hundreds of millions of cases, research articles, and filings easily searchable and free."[11]

Each segment of the legal publishing industry has its relative advantages and disadvantages. One obvious trade-off is that, in general, the more that a resource offers in terms of range of materials, editorial enhancements, and searching capabilities, the more expensive it is likely to be. The main categories of participants are government, commercial, and nonprofit publishers; alternative models have become increasingly viable recently.

- Government publishing operations generally produce the official versions of primary authority. Although print versions can take a long time to be published, many government websites are good resources because the information comes directly from the originator of the information, use of the resource is free, and the information is often posted quickly.
- Commercial companies play a significant role in U.S. legal publishing, particularly in producing enhanced versions of primary authorities, secondary sources, and sophisticated finding tools. Some of these are expansive, elaborate, and expensive.[12] Others are less comprehensive and less costly.
- Nonprofit organizations from various sectors—such as law schools, the bar, and public interest groups—publish various types of secondary sources. Furthermore, some of these organizations also provide access to selected primary authorities.
- In recent years, alternative models have come to challenge these traditional categories. Non-legal publishers have entered the market; foremost among these is Google, which provides free access to a considerable amount of legal content. Also noteworthy is the development of free commercial providers of selected legal content, such as Findlaw, Justia, and Law.com.

---

11. Jason Krause, *Innovations in the Law*, A.B.A. J. (Apr. 2015) at 34, 37.

12. Some of the major companies do provide limited-scope databases for free.

Throughout this book, we will feature the resources that we consider the most credible for each research task we cover — at this time. You may expect this roster of resources to change from time to time during your career.

As this chapter ends, take note of a critical distinction: when you research, your main focus should be on the materials that you need to read, i.e., which primary authority or secondary source, not which resource you like or want to use. Just as you are not likely to shop efficiently when you go to a grocery store if you just buy whatever happens to be on sale that day, you are not likely to research efficiently by choosing a resource and going with whatever sources you find within it. Rather, you should identify the materials that you need to read, assess the options that you have for researching those materials, and choose your best option.

This point is supported by recent studies of the research patterns of lawyers, which found that lawyers use a mix of resources. In one study, the lawyers spent an average of 7.7 hours per week on paid-for online research, 4.5 hours on free or low-cost online research, and 2.1 hours on books/printed research.[13] In another, over forty percent of the lawyers used print resources frequently or very frequently, over sixty percent used free Internet resources frequently or very frequently, and sixty-seven percent used fee-based databases frequently or very frequently.[14]

In addition, studies support the idea that research will play a key role in your career, especially early on. New lawyers spend about thirty percent of their time researching.[15] So it is not surprising that in a 2015 study of 300 hiring partners and supervising lawyers, eighty-six percent rated the research skills of new associates as highly important.[16] Indeed, the need to conduct legal research does not abate: A 2013 study of over 600 attorneys from a wide range of practice settings and ages found that nearly half spent up to fifteen percent of their workweek doing research.[17]

---

13. Stephen A. Lastres, *Rebooting Legal Research in a Digital Age* 3 (2013).

14. Am. Law Libraries Special Interest Section Task Force on Identifying Skills & Knowledge for Legal Practice, Am. Ass'n of Law Libraries, *A Study of Attorneys' Legal Research Practices and Opinions of New Associates' Research Skills* 30, 32, 33 (2013).

15. Am. Bar Ass'n, *Legal Technology Survey Report* viii (Joshua Poje, ed. 2014); Stephen A. Lastres, *Rebooting Legal Research in a Digital Age* 1 (2013).

16. *White Paper: Hiring Partners Reveal New Attorney Readiness for Real-World Practice* 3 (LexisNexis 2015) (also estimating that new associates spent forty to sixty percent of their time researching).

17. Am. Law Libraries Special Interest Section Task Force on Identifying Skills & Knowledge for Legal Practice, Am. Ass'n of Law Libraries, *A Study of Attorneys' Legal Research Practices and Opinions of New Associates' Research Skills* 8 (2013).

BUILD YOUR UNDERSTANDING

Test Your Knowledge

This chapter has introduced a number of key terms and concepts. To solidify your understanding of them, answer the following questions:

1. Define each of the following categories of research materials, making it clear how each differs from the others:
   - Primary authority
   - Quasi-authority
   - Secondary source
   - Finding tool

2. How does the concept of *resource* differ from all four of the items listed in question 1?

3. For each of the following types of authority, identify (a) which branch of government creates it and (b) whether it is a primary authority or quasi-authority:
   - Advisory comments to rules of procedure
   - Cases
   - Constitutions
   - Decisions and orders
   - Legislative history documents
   - Legislative agency rules
   - Policy statements
   - Rules of procedure
   - Statutes

4. State the basic design of a legal rule.

5. What is the common law?

6. To explain our system of checks and balances, describe the ways in which:
   - A court follows the legislature's lead.
   - A court may override the legislature.
   - A legislature may override a court.
   - A legislature interacts with an administrative agency.
   - A court interacts with an administrative agency.

7. Explain the difference between substantive law and procedural law. Is it possible that you would research both for the same client situation? Explain your answer.

Put It into Practice

To help you apply the concepts and skills discussed in the book, we have created the following client situation for you to consider:

———————————

Emmet Wilson is thirty-three years old, a cook in a local restaurant, and a veteran who saw active combat. Several months ago, he developed symptoms of post-traumatic stress disorder (PTSD), diagnosed by his Army physicians as stemming from his wartime experience. He finds it difficult to sleep, is edgy when awake, has disturbing flashbacks, and can be confrontational. He is in counseling and on medication. Another helpful strategy is a therapy dog, which provides a calming influence, especially when he is at home alone. Mr. Wilson's employer is fine with having the dog around.

However, Mr. Wilson's landlord has raised concerns because the building is a no-pets building. Indeed, the lease (which is for a year) so specifies, and the landlord says that other tenants have raised the issue. So she has given Mr. Wilson notice that if does not give up the dog, he will be evicted in a month. Mr. Wilson likes the apartment, believes that he would be hard-pressed to find another suitable apartment at the same price, and does not believe that he should have to move for this reason.

You are the law clerk in a small firm that is representing Mr. Wilson. Mr. Wilson does not have the money to pay for his representation, but the firm has decided to represent him for free as part of its commitment to provide pro bono services to those who cannot pay.[18]

Unless otherwise instructed, you will research this situation in West Virginia.

———————————

1. Can you think of reasons why the federal government, the state of West Virginia, and the city of Charleston might each undertake to create law for this situation?

2. There is not a lot of money involved in this situation. Assume that Mr. Wilson does not seem to be the type of person who would sue if things did not go well. Why, then, does it matter that you do a competent job of researching this topic? That is, why would you not simply write the land- lord a letter stating that Mr. Wilson has a lawyer and that she should think again before evicting him? Such a letter could bring a quick end to the dispute.

3. It is unlikely that the landlord in this situation consulted a lawyer before acting. Why not, do you suppose?

Make Connections

What is the authority structure of the field that you have researched most often? Compare it to that of the law as described in this chapter.

———————————

18. *Pro bono* is short-hand for *pro bono publico* (for the good of the public). According to ABA Model Rule 6.1, a lawyer should provide fifty hours of pro bono service annually, of which a substantial amount should be free legal services to clients who cannot afford to pay for it.

Answers to Test Your Knowledge Questions

1. The categories can be defined as:
   - A primary authority is a law made by a government entity operating in a lawmaking capacity.
   - A quasi-authority is a text created by a lawmaking authority as it makes law, but it is not law; it provides insight into what the law means.
   - A secondary source is created by someone other than a lawmaker (or by a lawmaker operating in a non-lawmaking capacity) to comment on the law; it provides references to the law and may provide useful information, such as historical background, empirical studies, and arguments for law reform, in addition to explaining the law.
   - A finding tool does not state legal propositions and is not citable; rather it assists you in finding sources that are.

2. A resource is a publication in which the items listed in question 1 are found.

3. The following types of authority can be identified as:
   - Advisory comments to rules of procedure — judiciary, quasi-authority
   - Cases — judiciary, primary authority
   - Constitutions — legislature, primary authority
   - Decisions and orders — executive (administrative agency), primary authority
   - Legislative history documents — legislature, quasi-authority
   - Legislative agency rules — executive (administrative agency), primary authority
   - Policy statements — executive, quasi-authority
   - Rules of procedure — judiciary, primary authority
   - Statutes — legislature, primary authority

4. The basic design of a legal rule is that it identifies behavior that a client engages in and states its legal consequences.

5. The common law is a body of cases that establishes a controlling rule of law in the absence of law created by the legislature.

6. Under our system of checks and balances:
   - A court follows the legislature's lead — by interpreting the language enacted by the legislature.
   - A court may override the legislature — by overturning an unconstitutional statute.
   - A legislature may override a court — by enacting a statute to modify the common law.
   - A legislature interacts with an administrative agency — by creating the agency and specifying its powers.

- A court interacts with an administrative agency—by evaluating its conduct according to legislative and constitutional requirements.

7. Substantive law specifies the legal consequences of client conduct. Procedural law governs how court proceedings are conducted. Both would be researched when a client situation involves litigation.

THE TEN PRACTICES OF SKILLED LEGAL RESEARCHERS

The process of legal research is in many ways a set of interlocking practices. We use the word "practice" here in all of its meanings: an action that is repeated, that aims toward proficiency, and that is employed within a profession. Whatever the project, skilled legal researchers engage in ten practices, which are covered in concentrated form in this chapter and further developed in the following chapters.

1. Master your client's situation.
2. Develop your research terms.
3. Create a research plan.
4. Choose resources with care.
5. Piggyback on others' work.
6. Work several access angles.
7. Take a look back.
8. Get up to date.
9. Manage your information file.
10. Stop when you're done.

Note that our diagram for the set of ten practices is a circle. By this, we intend to convey the idea that research is not an entirely linear process. Rather, it is often recursive. You will execute some of these practices multiple times, with various secondary sources and primary authorities. Furthermore, a research project may entail more than one topic, requiring more than one complete round of research. And it is not uncommon to start off in one direction, find it unproductive, and decide to go in a different direction. (The practices covered here are intended to make this experience as rare as possible, of course.)

Before we start discussing the ten practices, a word about terminology: In Chapter 1, a line is drawn between *primary authority*, which refers to the law, and *secondary sources*, which consist of commentary on the law. For conciseness, this and other chapters use the word *source* to refer to both primary authority and secondary sources. By distinction, a *resource* is a publication (whether a print book, government website, commercial database, or other publication) in which you find the source.

1. Master Your Client's Situation

You will conduct legal research to solve a real problem for a client, not as an exercise in idle curiosity. Thus, the first practice is to master your client's situation.

Investigating the facts of a client's situation is a complicated process well beyond the scope of this book. Suffice it to say that the process starts with interviewing the client; it often expands to include reviewing documents, interviewing other people, visiting pertinent locations, consulting experts, and perhaps conducting non-legal research. The latter may involve examining public records about the companies or organizations involved in a client's situation; it may also include non-legal research on a client's situation. For example, if you were working for All-Day Wellness as it seeks to constrain its departing employees from competing with it, you would research labor conditions within its industry.

The next step is to synthesize and summarize what you have learned for the purposes of your legal research. Synthesizing entails combining information from various sources on a single topic. For example, your client may tell you about a topic that is also covered in various documents; you would synthesize these bits of information. Summarizing entails identifying the main points from the reams of information that you obtain and deleting the unnecessary ones. Of course, before you conduct your legal research, you may not know what will prove to be legally important, so the best approach is to err on the side of including most points.

Many of the main points to identify in your summary are the facts of your client's current situation — what lawyers like to call the "real-world" facts (as distinct from what happens within the legal system). These facts can be captured through the classic questions journalists ask: who, what, when, where, why, and how. Similar questions should be asked about the ultimate desired outcome of the representation.

Sometimes you will research the law pertaining to a dispute, and the events will already have occurred. These questions are easy to answer in such situations, unless you have conflicting views from different sources about what happened. Then you will need to encompass a range of possible facts in your summary. Sometimes you will research the law to prepare for a client's future transaction, such as a contract or will, and you will frame the questions about events that are anticipated to occur.

Equally important to identify in your summary is your client's legal and practical context. Before you start your research, you should know your client's legal context: Is the client involved in litigation? If so, are the proceedings criminal or civil?[1] At what stage is the litigation? Is the client involved in some other form of legal proceeding aimed at dispute resolution?[2] If the situation does not involve a dispute, what is the nature of the actual or potential transaction? As a further refinement, attend to the client's goals as to the outcome. For example, does the client seek to take an aggressive or conciliatory stance in litigation? Does the client seek a contract that benefits itself primarily or benefits both sides equally?

Furthermore, before you start your research, you should be clear about your client's expectations for your research, which set the practical parameters of your assignment. In what form is your research to be presented? How much time may you reasonably spend on the project? Are there any limitations on the resources you may use? Legal research is expensive because it takes your time and may involve fee-for-use resources. To provide your research services in a truly professional manner, you must respect your client's cost parameters.

Real-World Facts	• Who are the important actors? • What happened between them or may happen? • When did or will the events occur? • Where did or will the events occur? • Why did or will the events occur? • How did or will the events occur?
Research Task	• What is my client's legal context? • What are my client's goals? • What form is my work to take? • What is the time frame for my research? • Are there limits on resources I may use?

---

1. In broad strokes, criminal prosecution involves the state bringing charges that may lead to fines and imprisonment. The classic civil case involves private parties suing each other.

2. This could be a proceeding before an administrative agency or in a private dispute resolution forum, such as mediation or arbitration.

2. DEVELOP YOUR RESEARCH TERMS

In a way, research is an elaborate word-find task, in which your goal is to find the few small portions of a huge trove of legal sources — each of which contains thousands of words — that pertain to your client's situation. Your research terms are the key to success. All of the ways that you access legal resources require you to use words; if you do not have the right words, you will not find what you need.

As discussed in Chapter 1, legal research sources consist of legal rules, the materials that lawmakers generate as they create legal rules (such as the facts of the dispute that judges include when writing a case), discussion of rules (as in an article), or some mix of these. Thus, in developing your research terms, your aim is to anticipate the words that the writers of sources pertinent to your client's situation may have used.

As you work on developing your research terms, keep two goals in mind. First, you want to achieve high *recall* — that is, to find a high percentage of the texts that pertain to your client's situation. Second, you also want to achieve high *precision* — that is, to avoid retrieving a large number of non-pertinent texts — because doing so will bog down your research. Too many required research terms lead to recall problems, whereas too broad terms lead to precision problems.

Some of your research terms will be fact-based. So begin by thinking about every facet of the real-world facts of your client's situation; work through the who, what, when, where, why, and how questions. Describe each one at a middle level of generality. For example, if your client's situation involves Cassie Collins, a driver involved in a car accident, the appropriate way to frame the *who* dimension of the situation is neither *Cassie Collins* (too specific), nor *person* (too general), but *driver* (which reflects the role that she played in the event). Then think about alternative terms for your initial terms; alternatives include synonyms, broader and narrower terms, words commonly used together, and even antonyms. For example, for the various questions posed by Exact Electronics, which arise out of the workplace, one good term would be *employee*; others might be *worker*, *laborer*, *employer*, *manager*, and *employment*.

Your other research terms will be legal words. So think next about whether you already know any legal concepts that are or may be pertinent. Concepts such as *liability*, *plaintiff*, and *damages* may be too broad to be of much use because they are so commonly used. For example, for the de la Cruz situation involving the boy suspended from public school for a statement that he shaved into his hair, a potentially pertinent area of law would be constitutional law, a major legal topic would be freedom of speech, and a subtopic would be the speech rights of a public school student.

To expand your initial framing of your legal research terms, incorporate your client's legal context. If your client is involved in litigation, a procedural term reflecting the phase of the litigation is likely to be very useful. Again, for example, if you were seeking to keep Daniel de la Cruz in school, you would be researching a preliminary injunction.[3] On the other hand, if your client is

---

3. A preliminary injunction is a court order that some action be taken while the litigation is pending.

planning a transaction, the legal term for that transaction is likely to be very useful. For example, in advising All-Day Wellness, which is trying to keep its employees from working for its competition when they leave their jobs, the probable solution would be a type of contract called a "covenant not-to-compete," which would be a good research term.

Of course, the paradox of research is that you do not yet know what you are seeking to know, so developing research terms can be a bit of a shot in the dark. Some legal words are uniquely legal words, whereas others (such as the contracts term "consideration") are used outside the law but have different meanings in legal and non-legal usage. You can reduce the risk of missing a useful word or — even worse — using a word improperly by spending some time with a legal thesaurus or dictionary. A thesaurus provides alternatives to the listed words; a legal dictionary provides the legal meanings of the listed words and may provide alternatives. See Box 2.1 for references to leading legal dictionaries and thesauri, along with their online availability.

Box 2.1   LEADING DICTIONARIES AND THESAURI

Black's Law Dictionary (10th ed. 2014)	Available on Westlaw
Ballentine's Law Dictionary (3d ed. 2010)	Available on Lexis
The Law Dictionary (7th ed. 1997)	Available on Lexis
Steven H. Gifis, *Barron's Law Dictionary* (6th ed. 2010)	Available on Bloomberg Law
Merriam-Webster's Dictionary of Law (rev. & updated 2011)	1996 edition available at http://dictionary .findlaw.com/
Daniel Oran, *Oran's Dictionary of the Law* (4th ed. 2008)	Third edition available online via EBSCOhost
Wex	Available at https://www .law.cornell.edu.wex
Bryan A. Garner, *Garner's Dictionary of Legal Usage* (3d ed. 2011)	
William C. Burton, *Burton's Legal Thesaurus* (5th ed. 2013)	

Legal dictionaries provide an impressive amount of information. As you can see in Box 2.2, for example, the entry from *Black's Law Dictionary* (generally regarded as the premier legal dictionary) for *covenant not to compete*

| Box 2.2 | **LEGAL DICTIONARY DEFINITION (Covenant Not-to-Compete)** |

COVENANT, Black's Law Dictionary (10th ed. 2014)

Black's Law Dictionary (10th ed. 2014), covenant

COVENANT

Bryan A. Garner, Editor in Chief

Preface | Guide | Legal Abbreviations

covenant (kəv-ə-nənt) *n.* (14c)   **1.** A formal agreement or promise, usu. in a contract or deed, to do or not do a particular act; a compact or stipulation.
- **absolute covenant** (17c) A covenant that is not qualified or limited by any condition. Cf. *conditional covenant.*
- **active covenant** (1933) A covenant that obligates the promisor to do something. See *affirmative covenant.* Cf. *passive covenant.*
- **affirmative covenant** (18c) A covenant that obligates a party to do some act; esp., an agreement that real property will be used in a certain way. • An affirmative covenant is more than a restriction on the use of property. For the real-property sense, see *affirmative covenant* [under] COVENANT (4). Cf. *negative covenant.*
- **assertory covenant** (ə-sər-tə-ree) One that affirmatively states certain facts; an affirming promise under seal.
- **auxiliary covenant** (awg-zil-yə-ree) (18c) A covenant that does not relate directly to the primary subject of the agreement, but to something connected to it. Cf. *principal covenant.*
- **collateral covenant** (kə-lat-ə-rəl) (17c) A covenant entered into in connection with the grant of something but not immediately related to the thing granted; esp., a covenant in a deed or other sealed instrument extraneous to the property being conveyed. Cf. *inherent covenant.*
- **concurrent covenant** (1819) A covenant that requires performance by one party at the same time as another's performance.
- **conditional covenant** (17c) A covenant that is qualified by a condition. Cf. *absolute covenant.*
- **conservation covenant** See *conservation easement* under EASEMENT.
- **continuing covenant** (18c) A covenant that requires the successive performance of acts, such as an agreement to pay rent in installments.
- **covenant in deed** See *express covenant.*
- **covenant in law** See *implied covenant.*
- **covenant in restraint of trade** (1827) See *covenant not to compete.*
- **covenant not to compete** (1978) A promise, usu. in a sale-of-business, partnership, or employment contract, not to engage in the same type of business for a stated time in the same market as the buyer, partner, or employer. • Noncompetition covenants are valid to protect business goodwill in the sale of a company. In employment contexts, requiring the employee, after leaving the employment, not to do a particular type of work, they are disfavored as restraints of trade. Courts generally enforce them for the duration of the relationship, but provisions that extend beyond that relationship must be reasonable in scope, time, and territory. — Also termed *noncompetition agreement; noncompete covenant; noncompetition covenant; restrictive covenant; covenant in restraint of trade; promise not to compete; contract not to compete.*
- **covenant not to execute** (18c) A covenant in which a party who has won a judgment agrees not to enforce it. • This covenant is most common in insurance law.
- **covenant not to sue** (18c) A covenant in which a party having a right of action agrees not to assert that right in litigation. — Abbr. CNS. — Also termed *contract not to sue.*

> "A covenant not to sue is a promise by the creditor not to sue either permanently or for a limited period. If the promise is one never to sue it operates as a discharge just as does a release. The theory is that should the creditor sue despite his promise not to, the debtor has a counterclaim for damages for breach of the creditor's covenant not to sue which is equal to and cancels the original claim… If the covenant is not to sue for a limited time, the modern view is that the covenant may be raised as an affirmative

provides not only a definition and alternative terms, but a legal rule as well. It can be tempting, but unwise, to use a dictionary as your authority. Rather, you should use a dictionary to help you understand legal terminology during your research, then work your way into primary authorities such as cases and statutes to find the controlling legal rules.[4]

Furthermore, if you are researching in an unfamiliar field using terms you do not understand, consider using a source from that field to help you understand the terminology before you dive too deeply into your research.

3. CREATE A RESEARCH PLAN

Developing a strong set of research terms does not by itself prepare you to delve into legal resources. You must also plan the probable course of your research.

The course of your research is set, in part, by its parameters of time and jurisdiction. First, what is the date of your client's situation? If the situation involves a dispute that took place two years ago, your task is to find the controlling law as of that date. If the situation involves a potential transaction, your task is to discover the law in effect now and to anticipate any probable changes.

Second, which jurisdictions encompass the events? As discussed in Chapter 1, an event taking place in Chicago (for example) could be controlled by the law of the city of Chicago, Cook County, the state of Illinois, the United States, or any combination — including the laws made by their respective legislative bodies, courts, and administrative agencies.

The course of your research project is also set, in part, by the legal context of the project. If, for example, you were researching covenants not-to-compete for an employer contemplating using one, you would focus on the legal rules and sample language. On the other hand, if you were representing an employee sued for violating a covenant not-to-compete with her former employer, you would be researching procedural issues and litigation strategies.

Furthermore, the course of your research project is set, in part, by the options and constraints of your setting. To continue with the same example, if you work at a large law firm hired by a large employer, you may have access to high-end, commercial resources. However, if you work for a small firm representing individual employees, you may well be expected to work with low-cost or free resources. In both examples, cost efficiency would matter, of course, but it may be more crucial in the latter situation.

Finally, the course of your research is set, in part, by what you already know or can quickly learn. At some point, you will be an expert in an area

---

4. It may be that you will find a dictionary useful later when an authority (such as a statute) or an important document (such as a contract) uses a term without defining it.

of law and may need to do little to no research to know the law controlling a new project. On the other end of the spectrum, you may find yourself at times researching truly unfamiliar topics. As you begin, always take stock of what you may already know (e.g., that the topic could be controlled by a federal statute). Furthermore, especially when a topic is unfamiliar, ask trusted advisors, such as a reference librarian or a colleague with experience in the area of law, for good starting points, such as a useful secondary source.

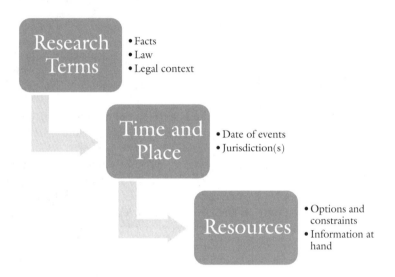

4. CHOOSE RESOURCES WITH CARE

Most research projects entail multiple sources, and hence the possibility, if not the necessity, of using various resources. Do not make one choice for an entire project and stick with it out of convenience or inertia. Rather choose the resource that best suits your needs for each step, based on the factors discussed generally here and developed throughout the rest of this book.

The first point should be obvious: you can choose only from what is available to you. This book covers a wide range of resources, and you likely will not have access to all of them. Law offices and libraries choose to buy some and not others; some resources may be available for certain clients or projects but not others. As you choose among the resources available to you, consider the following four factors.

Content

The content factor has several dimensions: jurisdiction, time range, and breadth and depth of materials.

JURISDICTION. Does the resource cover the jurisdictions you need? For example, if your topic is a matter of well-settled state law, you do not need a resource that encompasses federal law or the law of other states.

TIME RANGE. This factor has two reference points. How far back in time does the resource go, and how up to date is the resource? The necessary historical reach of a resource will depend on the dates of your client's situation and the creation of the controlling authority (a complex topic covered in subsequent chapters). The currency of a resource varies by type of resource as well as the preferences of the authors and publishers; you will want to pick a resource that is reasonably up to date and then use updating strategies as needed.

BREADTH AND DEPTH OF MATERIALS. How much material and what types of materials does the resource provide? For example, if you are selecting a secondary source for the covenant not-to-compete topic, you might prefer one that would have sample contract language if you were researching the project for All-Day Wellness. As another example, if you are researching a student's right to free speech for the de la Cruz situation, a topic on which cases abound, you would choose a resource that provides not only the cases but also summaries of the cases, to help you sort through them.

Credibility

The credibility factor varies depending on the source involved. For a primary authority, does the resource have a track record for reliability and accuracy? This is certainly true of official government publications and those of the major commercial publishers; other resources vary in their credibility, so that you need to evaluate them carefully before using them or supplement them with additional resources. For secondary sources, is the source known for thoughtful analysis, frequently updated, and often cited? Consulting with advisors in the area of your research topic or with librarians will help you discern the credibility of newer resources and those in unfamiliar areas.

Ease of Use

First, are you able to find pertinent information within the resource fairly readily? And then, are you able to maneuver within the resource and extract information fairly readily? For example, can you highlight text, and can you copy documents into a folder? The more user-friendly a resource the better, because then it will take you less time to use it.

Cost-Effectiveness

One element in the cost-effectiveness equation is the value of your time to access and use the resource. A second element is the cost of the resource itself, which may be a fee based on your use of it, a prorated cost of owning the resource, or paying a flat subscription rate for a resource. Of course, free resources, such as government websites, do not entail this cost. If resource A is as useful in terms of content, credibility, and ease of use as resource B and costs less than resource B, it is more cost-effective to research using resource A, and you should do so.

Law school is the time for you to learn about a wide range of resources, to develop your proficiency using many of them, and to develop the habit of performing cost-effective research.

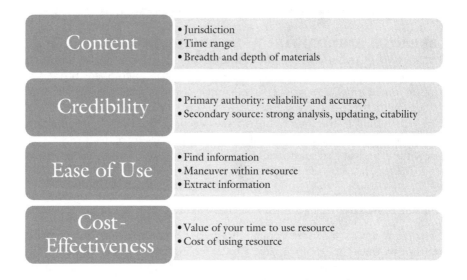

Content	• Jurisdiction • Time range • Breadth and depth of materials
Credibility	• Primary authority: reliability and accuracy • Secondary source: strong analysis, updating, citability
Ease of Use	• Find information • Maneuver within resource • Extract information
Cost-Effectiveness	• Value of your time to use resource • Cost of using resource

5. PIGGYBACK ON OTHERS' WORK

The law on a topic generally is not a single text, but rather an amalgam of texts created by various lawmakers over time. If you are lucky, someone may have pieced together the law before you, and you should take advantage of your predecessors' efforts.

Sometimes the most obvious step is easily overlooked: find out whether your own law office has any existing research on the topic. Many law offices do the same type of work repeatedly, and it makes little sense to start from scratch if the office has useful work that you can update and tailor to your client's situation.

Another way to piggyback on others' work is to start your research in secondary sources, as discussed in detail in Chapter 3 of this book. While it might seem that you are simply delaying getting to the primary authorities that you must rely on, this time is well spent for several reasons. First, secondary sources generally are more readable than primary authorities. Second, you will obtain an overview of the law when you read secondary sources. Third, you will find references to primary authorities, so your search for primary authorities will get off to a good start. Fourth, you may find some materials that assist you in creating the work needed to solve your client's problem, such as a sample litigation document or contract.

You can also piggyback on the work of others when you use the editorial enhancements provided along with primary authority in some resources. While it is not necessary to use every enhancement of every resource available to you — indeed, it could be dizzying and inefficient to do so — piggybacking on others' work is a good means of streamlining and checking your work.

6. WORK SEVERAL ACCESS ANGLES

In an era where non-legal research is primarily done online, when you envision "looking something up," you probably think of typing some words into a computer, which then runs a search and produces pertinent information. Most of the time, you will indeed do something like this when you conduct legal research — but not always. Rather, you will use your research terms in various ways in legal research resources. The main access methods are using tables of contents and indexes on the one hand and key-word searching on the other.

Writer-Driven Access Methods

First, consider the two time-honored tools that can help you gain access to pertinent information within a resource in any field: a table of contents and index. This is also true in legal research.

Many legal sources contain a vast amount of information on an interlocking series of topics. The authors or editors — we will use "writers" here to refer to both — seek to present the information according to some logical organization. That overall organization reflects the nature of the source, and within each major division are subdivisions. To help you locate the pertinent information, writers create tables of contents and indexes; thus, these two access methods are *writer-driven access methods*.

Many legal sources have multiple tables of contents; typically, a summary table of contents shows the largest level of organization and one or more detailed tables of contents show the subdivisions. Consulting these tables of contents when you first turn to a resource is a fine way of piggybacking on writers' work. Not only will you discern where to locate useful information for your topic within the source, you will also discern the writers' framework for the subject into which your topic falls.

An *index* is an alphabetical list of major and minor topics covered in a source; each entry provides a direction to the location where the topic is discussed. Legal indexes are very intricate, with not only subtopics and sub-sub-topics but also cross-references that direct you to other topics. An index may use a wider range of terminology than is used in the table of contents, so it may unlock a resource that is not easily understood by its table of contents. Thus, using the index, in addition to the tables of contents, may help you find pertinent information in a nonobvious location within a resource.

Tables of contents and indexes developed with print books but are equally useful with online resources. Using them online permits you both to tap into the insights of the experts who created the resource and to navigate easily to the pertinent portions of the resource.

As an example, consider this issue posed by Exact Electronics: may it legally decline to hire a spouse of a current employee at one of its Minnesota plants? At the Minnesota Legislature's website, we found a list of statutory chapters—this is a high-level table of contents. See Box 2.3. Realizing that "human rights" is one common term for statutes banning discrimination, we found the pertinent statute this way. At the beginning of that statute, we found a detailed table of contents in the form of a list of the sections. Again, see Box 2.3.

Exploring the Minnesota Legislature website's index, we also found the statute in various ways.[5] The listings under *discrimination* and *labor and employment* had no specific references to married employees or marital status discrimination in employment, but both pointed to the pertinent statute under other subtopics. The topic *marital status* had a subtopic, *discrimination,* and a sub-subtopic, *labor and employment,* pointing to the pertinent statute (see Box 2.4).

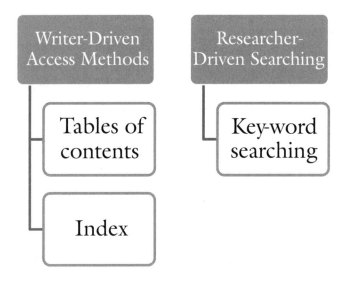

---

5. When we looked under *spouse,* we were directed to a different section of the same statute (exempting from coverage one spouse's employment of another), but not the legal rule controlling the client's situation.

| Box 2.3 | TABLES OF CONTENTS (Employment Discrimination Statute) |

2014 Minnesota Statutes

Statutes are laws that apply to all citizens and cover a variety of topics, including the following: the legislature, the executive branch, state departments, the judiciary and courts, tax policy, public safety and police authority, towns, cities, counties, commerce and trade, private property and private rights, civil injuries and remedies, and crimes against people and property and the penalties associated with them. Read more... Statutes for prior years are also available.

Search by Keyword

Document	Title
Contents	Table of Contents
Index 1	Index
Index 2	Index, Part 2
Preface	Preface
Table I	Local Special Acts
Table II	New Statutes

Table of Chapters

Chapters	Title
1 - 2A	JURISDICTION, CIVIL DIVISIONS
3 - 3E	LEGISLATURE
4 - 9	CONSTITUTIONAL OFFICES AND DUTIES
10 - 12B	GOVERNMENT MISCELLANY
13 - 13C	DATA PRACTICES
13D	MEETINGS OF PUBLIC BODIES
14 - 15A	STATE AGENCIES
15B	CAPITOL AREA
15C - 16	FRAUDULENT STATE CLAIMS
16A - 16E	ADMINISTRATION AND FINANCE
17 - 43	AGRICULTURE
43A	STATE EMPLOYMENT
44	CITY MERIT SYSTEMS
44A - 45	COMMERCE
46 - 59	BANKING
59A - 79A	INSURANCE
80 - 80A	SECURITIES
80B - 81A	COMMERCIAL REGULATIONS
82 - 83	REAL ESTATE SALES REGULATIONS
83A - 84	NATURAL RESOURCES
84A - 84D	CONSERVATION
85 - 87A	RECREATION
88 - 91	FORESTRY
92 - 94	LANDS AND MINERALS
97 - 102	GAME AND FISH
103A - 114B	WATER
114C - 116I	ENVIRONMENTAL PROTECTION

Box 2.3   *(continued)*

Chapters	Title
116J - 116O	ECONOMIC DEVELOPMENT AND PLANNING
116P - 116Q	ENVIRONMENTAL PROTECTION FUNDS
116R - 116W	BUSINESS DEVELOPMENT
117 - 119	EMINENT DOMAIN; LOCAL DEPOSITORIES AND INVESTMENTS
119A - 119B	CHILDREN AND FAMILIES
120 - 129C	EDUCATION CODE: PREKINDERGARTEN - GRADE 12
129D - 133	ARTS
134 - 135	LIBRARIES
135A - 137	POSTSECONDARY EDUCATION
138 - 140	STATE HISTORY
141 - 142	PROPRIETARY SCHOOLS
144 - 159	HEALTH
160 - 174A	TRANSPORTATION
175 - 186	LABOR, INDUSTRY
190 - 195	MILITARY AFFAIRS
196 - 198	VETERANS
200 - 212	ELECTIONS
214 - 215	EXAMINING AND LICENSING BOARDS
216 - 217	UTILITIES
218 - 222	CARRIERS
223 - 236A	FARM PRODUCTS, COMMERCIAL PRACTICES
237 - 238	TELECOMMUNICATIONS
239	WEIGHTS AND MEASURES
240 - 240A	SPORTS
241 - 244	CORRECTIONS
245 - 267	PUBLIC WELFARE AND RELATED ACTIVITIES
268 - 269	EMPLOYMENT AND ECONOMIC DEVELOPMENT
270 - 271	TAXATION, SUPERVISION, DATA PRACTICES
272 - 289	PROPERTY TAXES
289A - 295	VARIOUS STATE TAXES AND PROGRAMS
296 - 299	EXCISE AND SALES TAXES
299A - 299N	PUBLIC SAFETY
300 - 323A	BUSINESS, SOCIAL, AND CHARITABLE ORGANIZATIONS
324 - 341	TRADE REGULATIONS, CONSUMER PROTECTION
343 - 348	ANIMALS AND PROPERTY
349 - 350	GAMING
351	VACANCY IN PUBLIC OFFICE
352 - 356B	RETIREMENT
357 - 359	COURT AND FILING FEES; ATTESTATIONS
360 - 362	AERONAUTICS
362A	RURAL DEVELOPMENT
363 - 363A	HUMAN RIGHTS
364	CRIMINALS; REHABILITATION
365 - 368	TOWNS
370 - 403	COUNTIES, COUNTY OFFICERS, REGIONAL AUTHORITIES

Box 2.3 *(continued)*

2014 Minnesota Statutes

CHAPTER 363A. HUMAN RIGHTS

Section	Headnote
363A.001	*MS 2006 [Renumbered 15.001]*

GENERAL PROVISIONS

363A.01	CITATION.
363A.02	PUBLIC POLICY.
363A.03	DEFINITIONS.
363A.04	CONSTRUCTION AND EXCLUSIVITY.
363A.05	DEPARTMENT OF HUMAN RIGHTS.
363A.06	POWERS AND DUTIES OF COMMISSIONER.
363A.07	LOCAL COMMISSIONS.

UNFAIR DISCRIMINATORY PRACTICES

363A.08	UNFAIR DISCRIMINATORY PRACTICES RELATING TO EMPLOYMENT OR UNFAIR EMPLOYMENT PRACTICE.
363A.09	UNFAIR DISCRIMINATORY PRACTICES RELATING TO REAL PROPERTY.
363A.10	REAL PROPERTY; DISABILITY DISCRIMINATION.
363A.11	PUBLIC ACCOMMODATIONS.
363A.12	PUBLIC SERVICES.
363A.13	EDUCATIONAL INSTITUTION.
363A.14	AIDING AND ABETTING AND OBSTRUCTION.
363A.15	REPRISALS.
363A.16	CREDIT DISCRIMINATION.
363A.17	BUSINESS DISCRIMINATION.
363A.18	*[Reserved]*
363A.19	DISCRIMINATION AGAINST BLIND, DEAF, OR OTHER PERSONS WITH PHYSICAL OR SENSORY DISABILITIES PROHIBITED.

EXEMPTIONS TO UNFAIR DISCRIMINATORY PRACTICES

363A.20	EXEMPTION BASED ON EMPLOYMENT.
363A.21	EXEMPTION BASED ON REAL PROPERTY.
363A.22	EXEMPTION BASED ON FAMILIAL STATUS IN HOUSING.
363A.23	EXEMPTION BASED ON EDUCATION.
363A.24	EXEMPTION BASED ON PUBLIC ACCOMMODATIONS.
363A.25	EXEMPTION BASED ON DISABILITY.
363A.26	EXEMPTION BASED ON RELIGIOUS ASSOCIATION.

LEGAL PROCEEDINGS AND ACTIONS

363A.27	CONSTRUCTION OF LAW.
363A.28	GRIEVANCES.
363A.29	HEARINGS.
363A.30	DISTRICT COURT, REVIEW ORDERS OF PANEL OR EXAMINER; ENFORCEMENT; MISDEMEANOR.
363A.31	LIMITATIONS ON WAIVER.

Box 2.4	INDEX (Employment Discrimination Statute)

2014 Minnesota Statutes Index (topics)   Select Index

A B C D E F G H I J K L M N O P Q R S T U V W X Y Z **Search**

MARITAL STATUS

Affidavits, instruments affecting title to real property, evidence, Minn. Statutes 2014 507.29

Definitions, Human Rights Act, Minn. Statutes 2014 363A.03

Determination, joint bankruptcy, exempt property, Minn. Statutes 2014 550.371

Discrimination

Credit, Minn. Statutes 2014 363A.16

Dwellings, *see* Discrimination under DWELLINGS

Education, Minn. Statutes 2014 363A.13

Exemptions, Minn. Statutes 2014 363A.21

Labor and employment, Minn. Statutes 2014 363A.08

Labor organizations, Minn. Statutes 2014 363A.15

Public accommodations, Minn. Statutes 2014 363A.11

Real property, Minn. Statutes 2014 363A.09

School districts, flexible learning year program, Minn. Statutes 2014 124D.123

Health and accident insurance, marital status-based underwriting and premium rates, Minn. Statutes 2014 62A.306, 2014 62A.65

Joint bankruptcy, exempt property, Minn. Statutes 2014 550.371

Null and void status, Minn. Statutes 2014 518.01

Small employer health benefit plans, marital status-based premiums, Minn. Statutes 2014 62L.08

Researcher-Driven Searching

Online research affords another method of finding information: typing in words that the resource's program matches to the text of the documents in the database through some sort of algorithm to yield documents meeting the requirements of the search. This access method differs from the traditional methods of using a table of contents or index in that it is *researcher-driven*: you choose the words to match to the text rather than work with the words that writers have selected.

If a source's table of contents and index are available online, you will have the option of using either writer-driven or researcher-driven access methods. The better choice generally is: use both. You will learn something about the vocabulary and structure of the law by tapping into tables of contents and indexes. And you can tailor your research to your client's situation by writing your own key-word searches.[6]

---

6. Indeed an online resource may permit you to both browse an index and table of contents and conduct a key-word search in them.

The types of searches that you may run vary widely from online resource to online resource, from basic to highly sophisticated. Many resources permit you to build searches based on a terms-and-connectors system, in which you essentially translate your answers to the following questions into the resource's search protocol:

1. What words (or word stems) do I want to look for?
2. How do I want those words to appear relative to each other? For example, do they form phrases; are they alternatives to each other; should they appear within a certain sequence?
3. Do I want to narrow my search to only a portion of the resource? For example, do I want to confine my search to a certain time frame? Do I want to search only some documents within the resource, or only some segments of some documents?

Some systems bolster your search capability (e.g., by providing alternatives to your search terms). Indeed, the more elaborate resources permit natural-language searching, in which the resource's program takes your loosely framed search and runs a nontransparent search based on a sophisticated algorithm. You should always learn about the search protocols and options of each resource before you use it, so that you fully understand your search results.

To return to the same example, the Minnesota Legislature's website permitted key-word searching with the following options: using * to truncate a word, selecting several words as all necessary, selecting several words as alternatives, searching for an exact phrase, combining a phrase and a word, searching for a specific statute by number, and searching within a specific component of the website (a specific chapter of the statutes or the index). We chose to search for all of the following words in the current statutes: *married discrim* employee*. See Box 2.5.

Select words or word stems.	• Selected *married, employee* • Truncated *discrim**
Connect the words to each other.	• Selected all words as necessary
Select the components of the resource in which to run the search.	• Ran search in entire 2014 Minnesota Statutes

| Box 2.5 | **KEY-WORD SEARCH AND RESULTS (Employment Discrimination Statute)** |

Minnesota Statute Search   Advanced Search   New Search   Order by Relevance   Help

3 Minnesota Statutes Found Containing **"married discrim* employee"**

Type	Year	Document	Chapter
Statutes	2014	Section 62A.041 Maternity Benefits. found 7 Occurrences	Chapter 62A Accident And Health Insurance
Statutes	2014	Section 363A.03 Definitions. found 17 Occurrences	Chapter 363A Human Rights
Statutes	2014	Section 518B.01 Domestic Abuse Act. found 15 Occurrences	Chapter 518B Domestic Abuse

Note that the key-word search yielded a different section of the statute than using the table of contents and index did. The table of contents and index led to the prohibition on discrimination (section 363A.08), whereas the key-word search led to the definition of discrimination on the basis of marital status (section 363A.03). These two sections appear in Chapter 1 at pages 8-9.

This outcome is neither surprising nor troubling. Different access methods operate differently, so they may well direct you to slightly different places; that is why you should use more than one. Furthermore, you should always read around the first portion of a source that you find, in search of additional pertinent portions.

7. TAKE A LOOK BACK

Again, the law on a topic generally is not a single text, but rather an amalgam of texts created by various lawmakers over time. Thus, when you find one strongly pertinent authority, you should see it as not only important in itself but also as a source of references to other potentially useful authorities. As you decide which of them to pursue, consider the topics discussed in Chapter 1, such as the nature of authority and jurisdiction.

As an example, if you were researching the topic of the public school student who was suspended for shaving a message into his hair, you might at some point find and read the decision in *H. v. Easton Area School District*, issued by the U.S. District Court for the Eastern District of Pennsylvania in 2011. See Box 2.6. *Easton* involves students who were suspended for wearing bracelets with messages similar to your client's message, so it is obviously

Box 2.6   **FEDERAL DISTRICT COURT CASE (Constitutional Rights of Public School Student)**

Case 5:10-cv-06283-MAM   Document 39   Filed 04/12/11   Page 1 of 40

IN THE UNITED STATES DISTRICT COURT
FOR THE EASTERN DISTRICT OF PENNSYLVANIA

H., et al.   :   CIVIL ACTION
                                    :
        v.   :
                                    :
EASTON AREA SCHOOL DISTRICT   :   NO. 10-6283

MEMORANDUM

McLaughlin, J.   April 12, 2011

        This case involves a middle school's ban on breast
cancer awareness bracelets that bear the slogan "I ♥ Boobies!
(Keep A Breast)" and similar statements. These bracelets are
distributed by the Keep A Breast Foundation, which operates
breast cancer education programs and campaigns that are oriented
toward young women. On the school's designated breast cancer
awareness day, two female students defied the school's bracelet
prohibition and both were suspended for a day and a half and
prohibited from attending an upcoming school dance. The
students, by and through their parents, filed this law suit
seeking, among other things, a preliminary injunction to enjoin
the school district from enforcing the ban.

        The plaintiffs argue that the school has violated their
First Amendment right to freedom of speech. The two Supreme
Court cases examining student speech that are most relevant to
this case are Fraser and Tinker. See Bethel Sch. Dist. v.
Fraser, 478 U.S. 675 (1986); Tinker v. Des Moines Indep. Cmty.

Box 2.6   *(continued)*

Case 5:10-cv-06283-MAM   Document 39   Filed 04/12/11   Page 2 of 40

Sch. Dist., 393 U.S. 503 (1969). Fraser allows schools to ban
speech that is lewd or vulgar. If the speech does not meet the
standard of Fraser, Tinker applies. Tinker forbids the
suppression of student expression unless that expression is
reasonably foreseen as a material and substantial disruption of
the work and discipline of the school. The school district
contends that the bracelets are lewd and vulgar under Fraser and
if not, that they caused a substantial disruption of school
operations under Tinker or the School District had a reasonable
expectation of such disruption.

On the Court concludes that these bracelets cannot
reasonably be considered lewd or vulgar under the standard of
Fraser. The bracelets are intended to be and they can reasonably
be viewed as speech designed to raise awareness of breast cancer
and to reduce stigma associated with openly discussing breast
health. Nor has the school district presented evidence of a
well-founded expectation of material and substantial disruption
from wearing these bracelets under Tinker. The Court will
therefore grant the plaintiffs' motion for preliminary
injunction.

I.   Procedural History

On November 15, 2010, the plaintiffs filed this law
suit and a motion for a temporary restraining order and

2

pertinent. *Easton* refers to the First Amendment, which includes the free speech clause of the U.S. Constitution. It relies on two decisions of the U.S. Supreme Court: *Fraser* from 1986 and *Tinker* from 1969.[7] These cases would make your must-read list, if you had not already come across them.

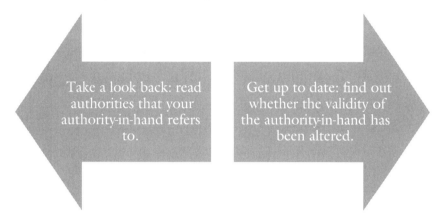

8. GET UP TO DATE

Any legal authority has the potential to lose force through the same processes by which it was created or, in some situations, by those of a different branch. When this happens, the authority is no longer good law. This phenomenon is a strength of our system of government: errors can be corrected, and the law responds to social change. However, it also puts you at serious risk if you do not properly update your research because an authority that is not good law often still appears in legal resources. For example, an older decision that is supplanted by a later decision remains published, as does a statute that has been declared unconstitutional. Thus, updating of primary authorities is essential.

As an example, return to the de la Cruz situation, where the student was suspended from public school. Although the *Easton* case in Box 2.6 was decided by a federal court in 2011, it is not the most authoritative decision in that litigation; to rely on it would be mistaken. A simple updating test reveals that a higher court—the U.S. Court of Appeals for the Third Circuit—issued a decision in the case in 2013, affirming the lower court but using a somewhat different analytical framework and relying on a third Supreme Court case.[8] See Box 2.7.[9]

---

7. The two cases—*Bethel School District v. Fraser*, 478 U.S. 675 (1986), and *Tinker v. Des Moines Independent Community School District*, 393 U.S. 503 (1969)—are significant free speech cases.

8. *Morse v. Frederick*, 551 U.S. 393 (2007).

9. Indeed, the updating test also reveals that the U.S. Supreme Court was asked to review the Third Circuit decision, but it declined. *Easton Area Sch. Dist. v. B.H.*, 134 S. Ct. 1515 (2014). This does not affect the precedential effect of the Third Circuit decision.

Box 2.7   **FEDERAL COURT OF APPEALS DECISION (Constitutional Rights of Public School Student)**

PRECEDENTIAL

UNITED STATES COURT OF APPEALS
FOR THE THIRD CIRCUIT

No. 11-2067

B.H., A MINOR, BY AND THROUGH HER MOTHER;
JENNIFER HAWK; K.M., A MINOR BY AND
THROUGH HER MOTHER;
AMY MCDONALD-MARTINEZ

v.

EASTON AREA SCHOOL DISTRICT,
Appellant

On Appeal from the United States District Court
For the Eastern District of Pennsylvania
(D.C. Civil Action No. 5-10-cv-06283)
District Judge: Honorable Mary A. McLaughlin

Argued on April 10, 2012
Rehearing En Banc Ordered on August 16, 2012
Argued En Banc February 20, 2013

Box 2.7   *(continued)*

OPINION

SMITH, *Circuit Judge*, with whom McKEE, *Chief Judge,* SLOVITER, SCIRICA, RENDELL, AMBRO, FUENTES, FISHER, and VANASKIE, *Circuit Judges* join.

Once again, we are asked to find the balance between a student's right to free speech and a school's need to control its educational environment. In this case, two middle-school students purchased bracelets bearing the slogan "I ♥ boobies! (KEEP A BREAST)" as part of a nationally recognized breast-cancer-awareness campaign. The Easton Area School District banned the bracelets, relying on its authority under *Bethel School District No. 403 v. Fraser*, 478 U.S. 675 (1986), to restrict vulgar, lewd, profane, or plainly offensive speech, and its authority under *Tinker v. Des Moines Independent Community School District*, 393 U.S. 503 (1969), to restrict speech that is reasonably expected to substantially disrupt the school. The District Court held that the ban violated the students' rights to free speech and issued a preliminary injunction against the ban.

We agree with the District Court that neither

5

Box 2.7   *(continued)*

Fraser nor *Tinker* can sustain the bracelet ban. The scope of a school's authority to restrict lewd, vulgar, profane, or plainly offensive speech under *Fraser* is a novel question left open by the Supreme Court, and one which we must now resolve. We hold that *Fraser*, as modified by the Supreme Court's later reasoning in *Morse v. Frederick*, 551 U.S. 393 (2007), sets up the following framework: (1) plainly lewd speech, which offends for the same reasons obscenity offends, may be categorically restricted regardless of whether it comments on political or social issues, (2) speech that does not rise to the level of plainly lewd but that a reasonable observer could interpret as lewd may be categorically restricted as long as it cannot plausibly be interpreted as commenting on political or social issues, and (3) speech that does not rise to the level of plainly lewd and that could plausibly be interpreted as commenting on political or social issues may not be categorically restricted. Because the bracelets here are not plainly lewd and because they comment on a social issue, they may not be categorically banned under *Fraser*. The School District has also failed to show that the bracelets threatened to substantially disrupt the school under *Tinker*. We will therefore affirm the District Court.

6

Updating of secondary sources is similarly a wise step, so as to avoid relying on a discussion that does not take into account more recent developments and thus misstates the rule of law. Furthermore, updating can lead you to later sources that refer to the source you are now reading, permitting you to use one source as a springboard to others.

Fortunately, legal research resources are designed for updating. First, many resources are themselves updated. Although you may not research in books all that often, you should know that many are updated in one of several ways: pocket parts slipped into the back covers, supplemental softcover pamphlets filed at the end of the set of hardcover volumes, or replacement pages placed in various locations in loose-leaf binders. Online resources often are updated more seamlessly; always look for an indication of the currency of every resource in which you research.

In addition, some resources are designed primarily for the purpose of updating those sources that are not themselves updated; these resources alert researchers to changes in the law. A prime example of this is a case citator, the tool we used to figure out that the district court case in Box 2.6 had been superseded by the appellate case in Box 2.7. As another example, commercial publishers of statutes provide notice of bills that may change the statutes, which is useful when counseling clients considering future transactions.

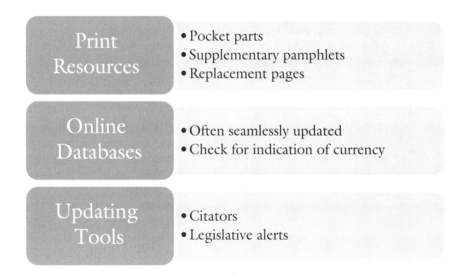

Print Resources	• Pocket parts • Supplementary pamphlets • Replacement pages
Online Databases	• Often seamlessly updated • Check for indication of currency
Updating Tools	• Citators • Legislative alerts

9. Manage Your Information File

By now, you may have surmised that some, if not many, research projects involve a lot of reading — not just a lot of reading of one source, but likely reading many sources found in various resources. For this to work well, you must effectively manage the information you acquire during your research.

First, keep a research log of what you have done. Retracing steps you have already taken not only causes frustration but also impairs cost-effectiveness. An effective log should encompass not only the sources and resources you have covered but also the research terms and search methods that you used along the way—in detail. Include not only what succeeded but also what did not, lest you return to an unsuccessful search later. Describe how you updated your research in each source. Note when you conducted each phase of your research.

Also record the information that you need to properly cite each source you read. When you present your legal analysis in writing to another lawyer—whether your supervisor, opposing counsel, or a judge—you will provide citations to each source, following a particular set of citation rules. Depending on the situation, you may follow a court's rules, or you may follow a citation manual, such as *The Bluebook: A Uniform System of Citation* or the *ALWD Guide to Legal Citation*.[10] Every citation rule both requires certain information about the source and details its style of presentation (in admittedly excruciating detail). Most citation requirements are fairly sensible. For example, a case citation requires the name of the case, information about where to locate it, the deciding court, and the date of the decision.[11]

Second, create a research library with copies of the important sources you have found. Legal analysis requires scrupulous adherence to the exact content of the texts involved, so having the sources at hand when you turn to writing your analysis is wise. At a minimum, include the primary authorities that you have read; you may want to include the most important portions of secondary sources as well. Storing your documents in a searchable electronic format is wise (including scanning print materials), because it permits you to conduct key-word searches in your file.

As you build your library, organize it for maximum utility. A classic approach is to begin by creating folders for various types of authorities (e.g., secondary sources, the statute, cases by court). As you progress into a complex research project involving various topics or tasks, you may alter your organizational scheme accordingly, developing folders according to topics. Another option is to develop a topical index for your library, in which you indicate under each entry which source pertains to that topic.

As you acquire some level of proficiency, you will develop your own preferences for accomplishing these tasks. Certainly, one option is to use the tools provided by one of the major commercial publishers. The advantages are not small: they are likely to be well constructed, and they are readily available when you are researching in the particular resource. However, be mindful that your research should rarely be tied to a single publisher's resources. And it may be

---

10. *The Bluebook* has long been published by a consortium of law schools. The *ALWD Guide*, which is newer, is published by the Association of Legal Writing Directors. To a significant but not complete extent, they call for the same citation practices.

11. For good reasons you may sometimes choose to research in a resource that is not what the citation rule requires you to cite to. You may be able to figure out the proper citation without switching resources, or you may have to switch into a different resource briefly for purposes of perfecting a citation.

more effective in the long run for you to design your own system that suits your preferences more closely.

Above all, develop a system you follow consistently. If some materials are lying on your desk, others are bookmarked on your browser, and still others are attached to e-mails you have sent yourself, you have undermined your efficiency and increased your frustration. Haphazardness does not correlate with professionalism.

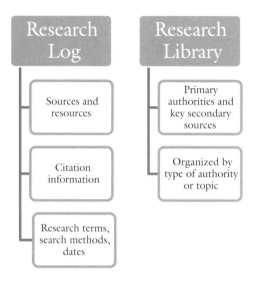

Finally, consider carefully the medium in which you read the major sources on which you will build your analysis. Experts in reading have found that screen reading does not yet replicate reading a printed page; thus, for serious reading, reading the printed page is preferable to screen reading.[12] Furthermore, in the legal setting, you must not only understand a legal rule; you must also parse its precise language, down to its punctuation. Many senior lawyers complain about new lawyers who cut and paste language from online resources into their papers but never fully parse the language themselves — and then miss key steps of the analyses or misconstrue some parts of the rules. To avoid this serious but tempting trap, print out the key language you have stored in your research file and work through it as painstakingly as you can, with your mind fully primed on learning, comprehending, and retaining it.

---

12. There are various explanations for this. For many, screen reading is less conducive to learning than reading a printed page; screen reading is less intuitive, which impairs comprehension; screen reading also drains more mental resources and makes retention more difficult. Thus, a common finding in surveys is that respondents prefer to read text on paper to clearly understand it. Over 100 studies are summarized in Ferris Jabr, *The Reading Brain in the Digital Age: The Science of Paper Versus Screens,* Sci. Am. (Apr. 11, 2013), http://www.scientificamerican.com/article/reading-paper-screens (last visited Dec. 8, 2015).

10. Stop When You're Done

This final practice may seem to be a facile tautology: of course, you would stop when you are done — right? In fact, this practice is one of the most difficult to master. For some (indeed, most) research projects, you will not find an unequivocal answer to your client's legal issue. You could continue pursuing leads, but it will not be cost-efficient or professionally responsible to keep going. So you will have to exercise good judgment in the face of some degree of doubt.[13]

Experienced researchers offer the following tests for knowing when it is time to stop:

- Do you have a firm grasp of the legal framework? Have you explored the pertinent specific rules?
- Have you found controlling primary authorities providing substantial guidance for your analysis? Have you confirmed that they are good law?
- Have you worked through a reasonable number of credible resources, given your client's resources?
- Are you seeing the same points and sources over and over again (the law of diminishing returns)?

Finally, a fine test of your research is to continue preparing the work product — whether a research memo, litigation document, or contract — that relies on your research. It is common to find holes in research at the writing stage. On the other hand, if you find that your research supports your writing effort, you likely have indeed stopped researching when you are done.

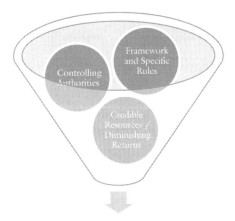

Start Writing

---

13. The highest degree of doubt arises when you research a situation lacking a controlling law. Most of the time, you will be able to discern this by finding the next-closest legal rule. For example, if in the Cassie Collins situation, she were talking on a cell phone and you found a statute banning texting but not talking while driving, you would infer that there was no law covering her situation.

BUILD YOUR UNDERSTANDING

Test Your Knowledge

1. What is the difference between precision and recall in research terms, and why are both important?

2. What are appropriate and inappropriate uses of a legal dictionary?

3. What are the three different dimensions of the content factor to take into account as you assess the available resources for a particular phase of your research?

4. What is the difference between writer-driven access methods and researcher-driven searching? Why should you consider using both?

5. You have found (a) a useful treatise written in 2008 (read in print) and (b) a pertinent case decided in 2012 (read online). Why is it important to update each of these? How would you do so?

Put It into Practice

Recall the situation (detailed in Chapter 1 at pages 20-21): Your client, Emmet Wilson, is a veteran who has developed post-traumatic stress disorder (PTSD). Among other treatments, he has been assigned a therapy dog. Mr. Wilson's landlord has raised concerns because the building is a no-pets building. Indeed, the lease (which is for a year) so specifies, and the landlord says that other tenants have raised the issue. So she has given Mr. Wilson notice that if he does not give up the dog, he will be evicted in a month. Your small firm is handling this case on a pro bono basis. Unless otherwise instructed, research this situation in West Virginia.

---

1. Master your client's situation.
   a. State the answers to the following questions about the real-world facts of your client's situation: who, what, when, where, why, and how.
   b. Identify your client's legal context.
   c. Identify the practical parameters of your research task.

2. Develop your research terms.
   a. Develop at least five fact-based terms. Take two of your best terms and develop at least three alternative ways to phrase each of them.
   b. Develop several legal concepts to use as research terms. Hint: think about the situation from the landlord's point of view; then think about it from Mr. Wilson's point of view.
   c. Look up one legal term both in a thesaurus and in a dictionary. Identify the two sources, and state what you learned from each.
   d. Explain why your set of terms should achieve both recall and precision.

3. Begin to create a research plan.
   a. Note the time frame of your research.

b. Assume that the issues are governed by state law; note the potential lawmakers.

4. Work several access angles. *For the purpose of this question only*, assume that Mr. Wilson's situation is set in Minnesota. Go to the Minnesota Legislature website, www.leg.state.mn.us.

a. Research whether a landlord may indeed discriminate against a tenant based on his mental illness. Use the access methods illustrated in this chapter: (1) table of contents and sections, (2) index, and (3) key-word search. Compare your results.

b. Similarly, research a second issue through the same access methods in the same Minnesota Legislature website: what are the grounds for evicting a tenant who has a lease? Compare your results.

Make Connections

Words are a lawyer's stock-in-trade; lawyers are wordsmiths who use words with great care. How have you used words with special care before? What lessons can you transfer from that setting to legal research?

Answers to Test Your Knowledge Questions

1. The difference is that *precision* refers to finding only pertinent texts and *recall* refers to finding all pertinent texts. Both are important because legal research requires both efficiency (accomplished through precision) and comprehensiveness (accomplished through recall).

2. It is appropriate to use a dictionary to assist you in building your legal research vocabulary, but rarely should it be used as your authority for a point of law.

3. The three different dimensions of the content factor as to resources and their importance are:
   - Jurisdiction — the resource should focus on the law of the client's situation, not that of other jurisdictions
   - Time range — the resource should go back far enough in time but also be current enough to encompass the law when the client's situation occurred or will occur
   - Breadth and depth of materials — the resource should have sufficient material of the type needed for the specific research project, based on the topic and tasks to be performed

4. The difference between writer-driven access methods and researcher-driven searching is that the former are created by the authors and editors of the source (tables of contents and indexes), and the latter is created by the researcher in the context of the specific research project (key-word searching). Using writer-driven access methods piggybacks on the expertise of the writers. Key-word searching comes at the task a different way and is more tailored to the client's situation.

5. (a) A treatise written in 2008 (read in print) could itself be updated through a pocket part, supplemental pamphlet, or replacement pages; these should be read to learn about new developments in the law and newer references. (b) A case decided in 2012 (read online) is not itself updated, so it would be updated by a case citator to determine whether it is still good law and to find new sources citing it.

SECONDARY SOURCES

<table>
<tr><td>SECONDARY SOURCES</td><td>CHAPTER
3</td></tr>
</table>

SECONDARY SOURCES

Secondary sources are so named because they are not the law; rather, they are written by professors, lawyers, and lawmakers acting outside their lawmaking capacity. Even so, secondary sources serve several vital roles in legal research. Thus, using them in research is an excellent way to piggyback on others' work.

First, secondary sources are also called *commentary* because they describe the law. The authors read and knit together primary authorities on a subject and then present a description of the law in a logical framework, sometimes in considerable detail. Often this description is easier to read than the primary authorities themselves. While you should not blindly accept this description as perfect, reading a good secondary source in the beginning can ground your research, and reviewing the source midway through your research can help you make sure that you are covering all needed points.

Second, secondary sources provide references to primary authorities; indeed, some provide an abundance of references. These references can get you started in your search for primary authority. Be mindful, however, that the references will only be as current as the secondary source, and that the references will not be tailored to your jurisdiction if the secondary source is not focused on your jurisdiction.

Third, depending on your research setting, secondary sources can provide helpful material that goes beyond a description of the law. For example, if your client is in litigation and needs to argue for a change in current law, you may turn to certain secondary sources to support your argument before the court. Indeed, some secondary sources provide a text that is useful in and of itself for a specific task. An example of this is a sample policy for a transaction that a client is contemplating.

This chapter first discusses in detail six major secondary sources: treatises, encyclopedias, legal periodical articles, Restatements of the Law, jury instruction guides (JIGs), and *American Law Reports* (ALR) annotations. All six are potentially useful in providing a legal analysis of a client's situation and are citable to varying degrees. This chapter provides guidance on what to draw out of these secondary sources.

Because secondary sources are not law, it is not imperative that you excel in researching in each of them. However, you would do well to become proficient in their use because each is useful in various research contexts. Each of these secondary sources has strengths, and each also has weaknesses. Furthermore, any subject that you are asked to research may be covered well in one type of secondary source but not another. As a preview of this chapter, the chart in Box 3.1 highlights some key advantages and disadvantages for each secondary source and notes a classic use for which it is particularly useful.

Box 3.1   SIX MAJOR SECONDARY SOURCES

Secondary Source	Relative Advantages and Disadvantages	Classic Use
Treatise	Thorough discussion of subject; may not be updated	Obtain solid grounding at outset of research
Encyclopedia	Broad coverage of many topics; very general and low citability; preferred for state law topics	Obtain very general discussion of topic when beginning research in very unfamiliar area
Legal Periodical Article	Very detailed coverage of narrow topic, possibly with arguments for reform; may be too idiosyncratic and will not be updated	Obtain insight into narrow or new topic or obtain argument for law reform, especially if credible author
Restatements of the Law	Highly credible statement of best rule on certain subjects with some supporting material; covers only some areas	Obtain classic statement of widely accepted legal rule
Jury Instruction Guide (JIG)	Highly credible statement of rules on certain legal subjects in your jurisdiction; covers only some areas	Obtain statement of your jurisdiction's rule on specific topic for litigation purposes

Box 3.1   *(continued)*

American Law Reports (ALR) Annotations	In-depth description of cases nationwide on narrow topic, with strong updating; covers only some topics and low citability	Obtain insight into why courts split on specific issues

The chapter concludes with briefer coverage of practice guides, a broad category of secondary sources that encompasses various formats. Practice guides are most useful when your purpose is to obtain guidance on how to carry out a specific task or stay up to date in an area of practice.

TREATISES

A *treatise* is a publication that thoroughly discusses a single legal subject at some length.[1] The subject may be fairly narrow (such as a single tort) or broad (such as the field of torts). Traditionally published in print, a treatise may occupy one volume or many volumes. The typical treatise is divided into chapters and sections or paragraphs, with various tables and indexes to direct you to the pertinent material. The text is supported by footnotes that may run longer than the text that they support. Many classic treatises were written by professors, as are some current ones.[2] Others are written by practicing lawyers and have a stronger practitioner orientation. The most widely respected treatises are considered highly citable.

A strong treatise is a good choice for grounding your research, especially in an area of law in which you do not have much experience. It can provide a framework to work within, ideas for specific topics to pursue, some starting references to primary authorities, and a citable source for basic points of law.

Many researchers prefer to use treatises in print, and you will find a good number of these in law libraries. Online library catalogs generally allow treatises to be located by author, title, key-word, and subject searches.

Treatises are also becoming widely available online. You may find an electronic treatise available through a law library, through one of the services to

---

1. Casebooks and law school study aids are not treatises.
2. Some of the classic treatises are published in abridged form for law students.

which it subscribes. Other options are the collections provided by Westlaw, Lexis, and Bloomberg Law; each of these companies offers different treatises. When you research within these online collections, do so strategically. That is, first browse the sources listed under a practice area or under your jurisdiction's tab to identify potential treatises within which to conduct your research.

As you select a treatise to read, a wise approach is to ask for a recommendation from someone with experience in the area of law or from a librarian. Factors to consider include the credibility of the treatise, the clarity of its organization, the usefulness of its finding tools, the cogency of its text, and the extensiveness of its references. Furthermore, an updated treatise is much more valuable than one that was published some time ago and has not been updated.

Options for finding the pertinent portions of a treatise vary somewhat depending on its medium of publication. If possible, it is wise to use the two writer-driven access methods: its table(s) of contents and its index. For an online treatise, you may also conduct a key-word search in the text and sometimes also in its index. Once you have found a pertinent section, look at where it appears in the overall organization of the treatise, and strongly consider reading adjacent sections as well.

As an example, our client Bower's Bounty, a grocery store in Kansas, has been sued by a former employee for defamation. The employee claims that not only was she fired, but she also suffered harm to her reputation when false statements about her work conduct were made within the company.

To become grounded in the subject of defamation before seeking primary authorities, we turned to a treatise on torts law, *The Law of Torts*.[3] (Defamation is a type of tort.) There, we found a general overview of the requirements of the tort: publication of defamatory material concerning the plaintiff to a third person. See Box 3.2.

Furthermore, we could find more detailed discussions of various subtopics in the treatise as well. To find precisely which section covered a subtopic of interest, we could use the tables of contents, which also served to provide a big-picture overview of defamation. See Box 3.3. Alternatively we could use the index to identify the section covering a specific topic. See Box 3.4. We used both the table of contents and the index to identify section 520 as covering the requirement of publication — a concern raised by our client's situation because the communication was made within the company, not to some third party.

---

3. Dan B. Dobbs, Paul T. Hayden & Ellen M. Bublick, *The Law of Torts* (2d ed., Westlaw database updated June 2015).

Box 3.2   **TREATISE TEXT (Employment Defamation)**

---

§ 519.Elements of defamation—Common law and constitution, Dan B. Dobbs, Paul T....

Dan B. Dobbs, Paul T. Hayden and Ellen M. Bublick, The Law of Torts § 519 (2d ed.)

Dobbs' Law of Torts
Database updated June 2015
Dan B. Dobbs, Paul T. Hayden, and Ellen M. Bublick
Part VII. Dignitary and Economic Torts
Subpart B. Dignitary Torts
Chapter 44. Defamation
Topic B. Common Law Requirements

§ 519. Elements of defamation—Common law and constitution

The Common Law

Traditional common law elements—libel. Defamation by writing and by contemporary means analogous to writing is libel. Defamation communicated orally is slander. Communication in any form can be defamatory, but defamation is most commonly communicated in words, pictorial elements, acts or some combination of these methods. This chapter often uses the term defamation to include any form of communication. In claims for libel, once the plaintiff showed a publication of defamatory material about the plaintiff, the traditional rule permitted courts to presume that the publication was made with malice,[1] that the words were false,[2] and that the plaintiff suffered damages.[3] The upshot was that the plaintiff could recover substantial damages for libel upon proof of three elements: (1) defendant's publication of defamatory material (2) of and concerning the plaintiff (3) to a third person. These rules created a regime of prima facie strict liability, because no proof of the defendant's fault was required. As usual with such extremes, courts then created a limited number of affirmative defenses with the burden on the defendant.[4]

Additional elements required in contemporary law. Many contemporary cases have announced that three non-traditional requirements are now necessary to sustain a libel claim. These cases tend to say the plaintiff must prove, besides the elements listed above, that (4) the defendant was guilty of fault equivalent to negligence or something greater in all cases,[5] (5) the publication was false,[6] and (6) the plaintiff suffered actual damages.[7] Others list only some of these added elements.[8] These added elements came about as courts attempted to integrate federal Constitutional rules of free-speech[9] into the common law of libel. When the Restatement first introduced these additional requirements in 1977,[10] they appeared to reflect the Constitutional requirements. A later Supreme Court decision, however, suggests that the Constitution does not require these added elements where the defendant defames a purely private person on an issue that is not of public concern.[11] Nevertheless, states apparently continue to state these added elements of proof for all cases, not merely those involving public figures or issues of public concern.[12]

Slander, special requirements. In the case of slander, the plaintiff must also prove either (a) special (pecuniary) harm *or* (b) a publication meaning that the plaintiff has committed a serious crime, or that the plaintiff has a character trait or a practice incompatible with her trade, business, or profession, or that the plaintiff suffers an incurable and communicable disease.[13] The requirement of pecuniary harm is significantly more demanding than the requirement of actual harm or damages.[14]

The Constitution

Since 1964, the structure of the common law defamation case has been radically altered by constitutional rulings based upon defendants' rights to free speech. All three of the common law presumptions—fault, falsity, and damages—have been reversed by constitutional decisions governing a substantial number of cases.[15] Although some issues remain undecided, the constitutional rules probably cover the following territory:

(1) If the plaintiff is a public official or a public figure, she must now prove that the defendant published a knowing or reckless falsehood, but states are free to permit recovery of presumed damages if they choose to do so.[16]

(2) If the plaintiff is a private person but the issue involved in the publication is one of public concern, the plaintiff is required to prove falsity of the publication, some fault on the part of the defendant (usually negligence), plus actual injury or damages. Upon such proof, she cannot recover punitive damages, and without such proof she cannot

---

Box 3.2   (continued)

§ 519.Elements of defamation—Common law and constitution, Dan B. Dobbs, Paul T....

recover anything.[17]
(3) If the plaintiff is a private person and the alleged defamation is of no public concern, the states are free to permit
recovery of presumed damages; probably the states are free to invoke common law strict liability rules as well.[18]
Where falsity is required, the effect is to protect opinion statements that cannot be said to be either true or false.[19] Even
where the constitutional limitations may not apply, some states have now adopted some of these constitutional limitations
as a part of their common law.[20] The constitutional rules increased the rationality of defamation law, but they have also
added their own complexity to the existing intricacies of defamation.

Westlaw. © 2015 Thomson Reuters. No Claim to Orig. U.S. Govt. Works.

Footnotes

[1]   See, e.g., Senna v. Florimont, 196 N.J. 469, 958 A.2d 427 (2008) (but holding that fault is now required when the publication
         touches on an issue of public concern); Doss v. Jones, 5 Howard 158 (Miss. 1840) ("the law imputes malice or an evil intention in
         all cases, when words actionable in themselves are spoken")

[2]   See Hepps v. Philadelphia Newspapers, Inc.506 Pa. 304, 485 A.2d 374, 379 (1984) ("falsity of the defamatory words is presumed,"
         truth is an affirmative defense), rev'd, Philadelphia Newspapers, Inc. v. Hepps, 475 U.S. 767, 106 S.Ct. 1558, 89 L.Ed.2d 783
         (1986) (Constitutional rules require the plaintiff to prove falsity, at least in certain cases).

[3]   See Greenmoss Builders, Inc. v. Dun & Bradstreet, Inc., 143 Vt. 66, 76, 461 A.2d 414, 419 (1983), aff'd, Dun & Bradstreet, Inc. v.
         Greenmoss Builders, Inc., 472 U.S. 749, 105 S. Ct. 2939, 86 L. Ed. 2d 593 (1985) ("When the defamation is actionable per se the
         plaintiff can recover general damages without proof of loss or injury, which is conclusively presumed to result from the
         defamation") (Constitutional rules permit presumption of damages in libel cases where the plaintiff is a private person and the
         defamation does not touch issues of public concern); In re Storms v. Action Wisconsin Inc., 309 Wis.2d 704, 748, 750 N.W.2d
         739, 761 (2008) ("Damages are presumed from proof of the defamation by libel"; but holding that Constitutional fault levels were
         required when a public figure sues).

[4]   See generally § 538.

[5]   See Seaton v. TripAdvisor LLC, 728 F.3d 592 (6th Cir. 2013) (applying Tennessee law, defamation requires proof that a party
         published a statement with knowledge that it is false, or with a reckless disregard for the truth of the statement, or with negligence
         in failing to ascertain its truth); Blodgett v. University Club, 930 A.2d 210 (D.C. 2007); Costello v. Hardy, 864 So.2d 129 (La.
         2004); Morgan v. Kooistra, 941 A.2d 447 (Me. 2008); Higginbotham v. Public Service Com'n of Maryland, 412 Md. 112, 985
         A.2d 1183 (2009) ("There can 'be no recovery without fault in any defamation action'"); Smith v. Anonymous Joint Enterprise,
         487 Mich. 102, 793 N.W.2d 533 (Mich. 2010); Boone v. Sunbelt Newspapers, Inc., 347 S.C. 571, 556 S.E.2d 732 (2001); Sullivan
         v. Baptist Mem. Hosp., 995 S.W.2d 569 (Tenn. 1999); Belcher v. Wal-Mart Stores, Inc., 211 W.Va. 712, 568 S.E.2d 19 (2002).

[6]   Eckman v. Cooper Tire & Rubber Co., 893 So.2d 1049 (Miss. 2005); Mark v. Seattle Times, 96 Wash.2d 473, 635 P.2d 1081
         (1981).

[7]   Nazeri v. Missouri Valley College, 860 S.W.2d 303 (Mo. 1993). Traditionally, slander claims required proof of *pecuniary* damages
         while libel cases presumed damages. Under a rule developed in some 19th Century American cases, pecuniary damages must be
         proved in certain libel cases, but not all. See § 535.

[8]   E.g., Hopkins v. O'Connor, 282 Conn. 821, 925 A.2d 1030 (2007) (adding to the traditional common law elements only that the
         plaintiff must show reputational injury resulting from the defendant's publication).

[9]   § 554.

[10]   Restatement Second of Torts § 558 (1977).

[11]   See § 557.

Box 3.3   **TREATISE TABLE OF CONTENTS (Employment Defamation)**

WestlawNext™

Home > Secondary Sources > Texts & Treatises > Torts & Personal Injury Texts & Treatises > Dobbs' Law of Torts > Part VII. Dignitary and
Economic Torts > Subpart B. Dignitary Torts

Chapter 44. Defamation   Add to Favorites

Browse Table of Contents below or search above.

TOOLS & RESOURCES

Dobbs' Law of Torts Index

◉ Search all content   ○ Specify content to search

Topic A. Introducing Defamation

§ 516. Scope of defamation law
§ 517. Historical development of defamation law
§ 518. Defamation's social settings, including international defamation

Topic B. Common Law Requirements

§ 519. Elements of defamation--Common law and constitution
§ 520. Requirement of publication generally
§ 521. Publication--Effects of a repeater's publication
§ 522. Protections for transmitters and internet providers
§ 523. Publication--Compelled self-publication
§ 524. The requirement of defamatory content and its test
§ 525. Examples of defamatory content
§ 526. Interpreting meaning and effect
§ 527. Qualifying as plaintiff in a defamation suit: publication must refer to plaintiff
§ 528. Identification of the plaintiff through evidence and inference
§ 529. Works of fiction
§ 530. Defaming the plaintiff by defaming others
§ 531. Defaming the plaintiff by defaming a group
§ 532. Defamation of corporations, government entities and the dead
§ 533. The requirement of falsity vs. "the truth defense"
§ 534. The slander rules
§ 535. Libel per quod: when special harm is required in libel cases
§ 536. The complex case of "defamatory" credit reports

Topic C. Defenses

§ 537. The truth defense
§ 538. Immunities or absolute privileges generally
§ 539. Absolute privilege for judicial and quasi-judicial proceedings and complaints to police
§ 540. Absolute privilege for legislative business
§ 541. Absolute privilege for executive branch business
§ 542. Absolute privilege of consent
§ 543. Absolute privileges--Internet communications
§ 544. The common law qualified privileges
§ 545. The interest privileges
§ 546. The public interest privilege
§ 547. Self interest, interest of others, and common interest
§ 548. Fair report privilege: reports of public documents and proceedings
§ 549. Reports of news--Neutral reportage
§ 550. Abuse or loss of privilege
§ 551. Revising privileges after the constitutional cases

Topic D. Constitutional Limitations on Recovery

§ 552. Defamation liability under the First Amendment--Religious freedom
§ 553. Right to association and petition for redress and the anti-SLAPP statutes
§ 554. Constitutional fault and damage requirements generally
§ 555. Public official and public figure plaintiffs
§ 556. Private person plaintiffs defamed on issues of public concern
§ 557. Private person plaintiffs defamed on issues of no public concern
§ 558. Bases of the constitutional rules
§ 559. Who are public officials
§ 560. Who are public figures generally
§ 561. Limited purpose public figures
§ 562. All-purpose public figures

Box 3.4   **TREATISE INDEX (Employment Defamation)**

Defamation, DOBBLOT Index

DOBBLOT Index

Dobbs' Law of Torts
Index updated February 2015

Dobbs' Law of Torts
Defamation
Defamation

See also Injurious Falsehood; Privacy
Generally, 516 to 577
abuse or loss of qualified privilege, 550
actual malice, 555
ambiguity
       judge and jury, 526
       libel per quod, 535
association rights, effect on **defamation** claims, 553
bigotry
       group **defamation**, in, 531
       imputations appealing to, 525
       imputations of, 572
burden of proof
       clear and convincing standard, 552, 555, 560 564
       privilege issues, 544, 550
       truth or falsity, 533, 537, 568
civil rights violation, **defamation** not actionable as, 541
clergy, liability for, 552
colloquium, 535
Communism, imputation of, 525
complaint to police, 539
consent to, 542
constitutional rules
       generally, in summary, 519
       actual damages, when required, 556, 558
       actual malice, 555
       bases for, 558
       clear and convincing evidence, 555
       common law privileges, impact on, 551
       expert testimony in, 526
       fault required
           generally, 554, 555
           tests and proof, 564
       First Amendment speech and religion clauses generally, 552
       negligence or some fault requirement, 565
       opinion, see opinion, this topic
       media defendants, constitutional protections limited to, query, 564
       private person plaintiffs
           fault, proving, 565
           issues of no public concern, 557
           issues of public concern, 556, 558

Box 3.4   *(continued)*

Defamation, DOBBLOT Index

          abuse and loss of, 550
          common interest privilege, 547
          consent to **publication**, 542
          constitutional impact on common law privileges, 551
          neutral reportage, 549
          pleadings, report of, 548
          qualified
                    generally, 544
                    fair report of public documents or proceedings, 548
                    interest privileges generally, 545
                    public interest privilege, 546
                    self interest, common interest, others' interest, 547
procedural incidents generally, 573
professional incompetence, imputation of, 534
professional standard of care, 565
public figures
          all-purpose public figures, 562
          knowing or reckless falsehood requirement, 555
          limited-purpose public figures, 561
          retirement from public figure status, 563
          who are, 560
public interest privilege, 546
public officials
          knowing or reckless falsehood requirement, 555
          who are, 559
          ridicule and satire, 572
          truth or falsity, burden of proof, 568
public records and proceedings, privilege to report, 548
publication
          disseminators vs. publishers, 522
          failure to remove, 520
          intent and negligence, 520
          internet communications, 522
          privilege analysis as alternative, 523
          repeaters, 521
          requirement of, 520
          self **publication**, 523
          third person required, 520
          transmitters, 522
punitive damages, 554, 574
racism, appeal to or imputation of, see bigotry, this topic
radio publishers, 522
rape victim, imputation that plaintiff was, 525
reference to the plaintiff
          identification of plaintiff, evidence and inference, 528
          required, 527
reform proposals, 577
remedies
          damages generally, 574
          injunction, 576
          restitution (disgorgement), 576

THE READING AND MINING OF A SECONDARY SOURCE

Once you have found a useful secondary source, you will want to capture its useful content. One option is to highlight and store the document in your research file.[4] It often is wise to take notes too, which prompts you to process the information carefully. What you record from a secondary source will vary from source to source and will depend on the purpose for which you are reading the source. Note-taking on a treatise provides a basic example. See Box 3.5.

First, the most basic information that you should extract from a treatise is the rule of law it presents, with particular regard for its application to your client's situation. Also extract elaborations on the rule that pertain to your client's situation, but avoid elaborations that are not pertinent. Second, record the references that the treatise lists that may merit reading. Note that many references may be outside your jurisdiction; focus on those that are within your jurisdiction. Third,

---

Box 3.5 **TREATISE NOTES (Employment Defamation)**

The Law of Torts § 519

Dan B. Dobbs, Paul T. Hayden, & Ellen M. Bublick
2d ed. 2011 updated June 2015 (Westlaw)

Rules

Defamation by writing = libel.
Defamation communicated orally = slander.
Recovery of substantial damages for libel requires defendant's publication of defamatory material of and concerning plaintiff to third person. Furthermore, some courts say that plaintiff must prove fault equivalent to negligence or something greater, publication was false, and plaintiff suffered actual damages.*
For slander, plaintiff must also prove special (pecuniary) harm or publication, meaning commission of serious crime or trait or practice incompatible with her trade.
*However, with constitutional decisions, states may now presume damages and provide recovery based on strict liability.
Opinion statements cannot be basis of recovery.

References to Other Sources

No Kansas cases
Restatement (Second) of Torts § 558

Found on Westlaw in Secondary Sources / Texts & Treatises / Torts & Personal Injury.

Researched: July 15, 2015.

---

4. You may use the resource's storage option, if you are researching online in a resource with this capability, or you may create your own.

note the citation information for the treatise, should you decide to cite it at some point. This information should include the date, which is critical to your assessment of the currency of the information that you draw from the treatise. Fourth, record how you found the treatise so you can easily find it again if needed. And, finally, note the date you conducted your research.

ENCYCLOPEDIAS

As you might expect, a legal *encyclopedia* presents an alphabetically ordered series of discussions about a wide range of legal subjects. From a research standpoint, this breadth of coverage is its chief advantage. Even though legal encyclopedias are large publications indeed,[5] each subject is not covered in as much depth as it receives in a treatise, and the references are relatively sparse. In general, encyclopedias are updated annually. They are not written by well-known experts, so they generally are not considered as citable as are some other secondary sources.

The two national-scope encyclopedias are *American Jurisprudence 2d* and *Corpus Juris Secundum*; both cover over 400 subjects of federal and state law. If your state has one, a state encyclopedia is generally more useful than a national encyclopedia for subjects controlled by state law, because both the text and the references draw on the specifics of your state's law. Indeed, state encyclopedias are sometimes viewed positively enough to be citable within their respective state courts.

Encyclopedias are most useful at the outset of a research project, especially when you have little idea of what your topic really is. Because an encyclopedia has such a wide range of coverage, it is likely to include information on your topic, and its strong finding tools likely will succeed in getting you to the pertinent portions of the encyclopedia. Although the discussion will be general, it should provide a basic grounding in the subject.

For many researchers, using a print encyclopedia is desirable because it facilitates browsing, which is useful at the beginning stages of research. Both of the national-scope encyclopedias are available online: *American Jurisprudence 2d* in both Lexis and Westlaw, and *Corpus Juris Secundum* in Westlaw. The online availability of state encyclopedias varies.

Researching in an encyclopedia resembles researching in a treatise, but with the added dimension that your first step is to discern which subject — or *topic,* in encyclopedia terminology — to read. Depending on the resource you are using (print or online), good options for finding pertinent topics and sections within a topic are looking in the alphabetical list of topics and then within the table of contents for that topic, using the index for the encyclopedia, or performing a key-word search. Once you have found a pertinent section, look at where it appears in the overall organization of the topic, and read adjacent sections as well.

---

5. In print, the two national-scope encyclopedias run about 150 volumes.

As an example, our client Cassie Collins was ticketed for using her cell phone while driving in California. As she was pulling out of a parking lot and into the street, her car was hit by another car. When the police officer interviewed her about the crash, she confessed to using her cell phone at the time of the accident: she was speaking into her cell phone to find the nearest Starbuck's coffee shop. She was ticketed for this use.

To become grounded in the subject of traffic laws before seeking primary authorities, we turned to a California encyclopedia, *California Jurisprudence 3d*, using it online via Westlaw.[6] We found the specific section on *Wireless telephones* by searching for *telephone* within the *Auotomobiles* topic; alternatively, we could scroll through the table of contents for that topic to find it under *Rules of Road* and then *General Safety Rules*. The brief discussion set out both the legal rules and references to a section of the California Vehicle Code, as well as two California state court cases — information that nicely set up our research in primary authority. See Box 3.6.

---

6. We researched online rather than in print because we were in Minnesota and did not have access to this state encyclopedia in print.

Box 3.6	ENCYCLOPEDIA (Driving While Using Cell Phone)

§ 315.Wireless telephones, 8 Cal. Jur. 3d Automobiles § 315

8 Cal. Jur. 3d Automobiles § 315

California Jurisprudence 3d
Database updated August 2015
Automobiles

Alan J. Jacobs, J.D., Jack K. Levin, J.D., Alys Masek, J.D., Kimberly C. Simmons, J.D. and Jeffrey J. Shampo, J.D.

VIII. Rules of Road
C. General Safety Rules

Topic Summary Correlation Table References

§ 315. Wireless telephones

West's Key Number Digest

West's Key Number Digest, Automobiles ⚷10, 11, 147, 153
West's Key Number Digest, Highways ⚷166

Treatises and Practice Aids

2 Witkin, Cal. Criminal Law (4th ed. 2012), Crimes Against Public Peace and Welfare § 326

A person may not drive a motor vehicle while using a wireless telephone unless that telephone is specifically designed and configured to allow hands-free listening and talking and is used in that manner while driving.[1] This does not apply to a person using a wireless telephone for emergency purposes, including, but not limited to, an emergency call to a law enforcement agency, health care provider, fire department, or other emergency services agency or entity.[2] It also does not apply to an emergency services professional using a wireless telephone while operating an authorized emergency vehicle in the course and scope of his or her duties.[3] Nor does it apply to a person while driving a motor vehicle on private property.[4]

The term "drive," as used in this statute, requires proof of volitional movement, but the phrase "while driving" does not require movement contemporaneous with the prohibited activity at all times. Thus, a defendant's act of listening to messages on a hand-held wireless telephone while stopped at a traffic light was done "while driving" and violated the statute.[5]

CUMULATIVE SUPPLEMENT

Cases:

Defendant who held his cellular telephone in his hand and looked at a map application while driving did not thereby commit the offense of using a wireless telephone while driving. Cal. Veh. Code § 23123(a). People v. Spriggs, 2014 WL 783865 (Cal. App. 5th Dist. 2014).

Box 3.6   *(continued)*

§ 315.Wireless telephones, 8 Cal. Jur. 3d Automobiles § 315

[END OF SUPPLEMENT]

Footnotes

1   Veh. Code, § 23123, subd. (a).

2   Veh. Code, § 23123, subd. (c).

3   Veh. Code, § 23123, subd. (d) (referring to definition of "authorized emergency vehicle" found in Veh. Code, § 165).

4   Veh. Code, § 23123, subd. (f).

5   People v. Nelson, 200 Cal. App. 4th 1083, 132 Cal. Rptr. 3d 856 (1st Dist. 2011), review denied, (Feb. 29, 2012).

End of Document   © 2015 Thomson Reuters. No claim to original U.S. Government Works.

WestlawNext © 2015 Thomson Reuters. No claim to original U.S. Government Works.   2

LEGAL PERIODICAL ARTICLES

Many individuals and organizations generate what you may think of as articles on legal subjects and publish them in a wide variety of publications. But in the legal research world, the term *article* is used to refer to a fairly narrow category of publications. The classic publisher of an article is a law school's law review, which is a scholarly publication edited by upper-level law students.[7] Many law schools publish both a main law review, which includes articles on a wide variety of topics, and one or more law reviews that focus on specific areas of law. The articles in a law review have titles that reflect the identity, and hence the expertise, of their authors: professors, lawmakers, and practitioners write *articles* and *essays*; students write *notes* or *comments*. Other publishers of articles are the journals of bar associations and academic organizations.

A typical article provides a detailed discussion of a narrow subject, along with copious references. An article is often the main secondary source that covers emerging or arcane subjects in depth. The discussion may cover not only current law, but also the evolution of the law, empirical studies in that area, a critique of the law as it stands, and recommendations for law reform. Indeed, some influential articles have paved the way for law reform. On the other

---

7. This is highly unusual for academia, where the standard approach is that faculty edit scholarly publications. In recent years, there has been some movement in legal academia toward faculty-edited journals.

hand, articles are not updated, and some can be idiosyncratic, as a goal of law reviews can be to publish interesting, if not unusual, legal thought.

Thus, law reviews are a less reliably useful secondary source for basic research than other secondary sources, but they are potentially very useful if there is a good one on your topic. Then, an article can provide a wealth of information and indeed may be citable depending on the credibility of the author.

You may find articles through two main approaches.[8] One is to run a key-word search in a database of articles. The major commercial publishers (Lexis, Westlaw, and Bloomberg Law) provide articles with coverages varying by law review, although most do not predate 1980. On the other hand, HeinOnline generally extends to the first volume of a law review, but its coverage may not be as current. Google Scholar is a more recent provider of law reviews that merits consideration as well.

The second approach is to use a legal periodicals index. The major indexes are Legal Resource Index, also known as LegalTrac; Index to Legal Periodicals and Books (ILPB); and Index to Legal Periodicals Retrospective (the predecessor to ILPB).[9] When you use a periodicals index, you take advantage of the indexer's expert categorization of the articles. You also avoid retrieving nonpertinent articles that happen to come up when you run a key-word search in a database of articles.

As an example, our client Daniel de la Cruz was suspended from his Pennsylvania middle school for shaving into his hair the phrase "I [heart] boobies." He shaved it there to support his sister, who was undergoing treatment for breast cancer; this phrase has been used to increase awareness of breast cancer among young women. Some minor disturbances did occur at his school as a result of his unusual hairstyle. Yet he believes that his suspension was not legal because it was a reaction to his exercising his right to free speech.

To become grounded in the subject of the constitutional rights of public school students — a specific legal issue that has arisen in a uniquely current factual context — we elected to look for an article. We went to HeinOnline's Law Journal Library. Because this database contains an enormous number of articles and the broad topic of free speech is probably popular for article authors, we ran an advanced search in the title segment, rather than in the text of the articles, as follows: *(speech OR "first amendment") AND (student* OR school*)*. We displayed the articles with the most recent listed first.

Our search yielded a good handful of useful articles. A 2014 note written by a student describes a case involving similar facts, provides references to the major primary authorities on the topic, and provides her analysis of various ways to look at the issues. Because the author was a student, the note would not be particularly citable, but it provided good leads for our research in primary authority. See Box 3.7. By comparison, we also found a 2009 article by an esteemed constitutional law scholar, whose analysis of the major U.S. Supreme Court cases would prove valuable in helping us understand a complicated area of law and could provide a basis for persuading a court in our favor. See Box 3.8.

---

8. A third option is to explore the materials posted on the Legal Scholarship Network, part of the Social Science Research Network (SSRN). Faculty often post articles on SSRN even before formal publication.

9. Westlaw provides an additional index, Current Index to Legal Periodicals, and Lexis provides Legal Resource Index.

Box 3.7   STUDENT NOTE (Constitutional Rights of Public School Student)

BRACELETS AND THE SCOPE OF STUDENT SPEECH RIGHTS IN *B.H. EX REL. HAWK v. EASTON AREA SCHOOL DISTRICT*

JACQUELYN BURKE[*]

Abstract: The U.S. Court of Appeals for the Third Circuit held that a district wide ban of bracelets containing the word "boobies" was an impermissible restriction of students' First Amendment speech rights. The majority's focus on the bracelets' social message is critical for the preservation of students' rights to discuss social issues, particularly health issues. Alternatively, Judge Hardiman's dissent focused on the bracelets' alleged sexual innuendo and did not give credence to the bracelets' purpose. Judge Hardiman advocated upholding the ban due to the bracelets' supposed sexual nature. Had Judge Hardiman prevailed, knowledge and awareness of a vital health issue would have been wrongly suppressed because of the disease's connection to a sexual body part. It is important that the majority prevailed in order for students to maintain their rights to discuss and be well informed on social issues.

INTRODUCTION

During the 2010–2011 school year, middle school students, B.H. and K.M. wore bracelets with the slogan "I ♥ boobies! (KEEP A BREAST)" to the Easton Area Middle School.[1] These bracelets, made by the Keep a Breast Foundation ("KABF"), were created with the purpose of stimulating dialogue and raising awareness about breast cancer in young women.[2] Although there were no disturbances or disruptions to other students' education as a result of these bracelets, the school and eventually the entire school district banned wearing the bracelets.[3] B.H. and K.M.'s respective mothers filed a lawsuit against the school district challenging the constitutionality of the ban on § 1983 grounds for the infringement of the girls' First Amendment right to free speech.[4] This statute creates a civil cause of action for the deprivation of constitutional rights, privileges, or immunities.[5]

---

* Staff Writer, BOSTON COLLEGE JOURNAL OF LAW AND SOCIAL JUSTICE (2013–2014).
[1] B.H. *ex rel.* Hawk v. Easton Area Sch. Dist., 725 F.3d 293, 299 (3d Cir. 2013).
[2] *See id.* at 298.
[3] *Id.* at 299–300.
[4] 42 U.S.C. § 1983 (2012); *see B.H. ex rel. Hawk*, 725 F.3d at 297, 300.
[5] 42 U.S.C. § 1983.

Box 3.7 *(continued)*

The Third Circuit, siding with the girls and their mothers, held that the ban infringed on the girls' First Amendment speech rights.[6] The court found that because "I ♥ boobies! (KEEP A BREAST)" is not "plainly lewd" and instead advocates for a social issue (breast cancer awareness), wearing the bracelets may not be unconditionally banned.[7] Judge Hardiman wrote a dissent arguing that the bracelets were lewd and an inappropriate discourse in a school setting.[8] Adopting Judge Hardiman's perspective would have narrowed speech as it relates to young women's awareness of vital health issues.[9] The court noted that the fact that this social issue involved breasts did not justify its censorship.[10] The Easton School District's ban highlights the dangers of allowing censorship to prevail over awareness raising dialogue.[11]

Education in schools should go beyond just the curriculum, and extend to learning about how to engage social issues and confront difficult realities.[12] Because preventative care is essential for women in taking control of their health, all young women—including middle school students—should have every right to raise awareness and knowledge of breast cancer.[13]

---

[6] *See B.H. ex rel. Hawk*, 725 F.3d at 323–24.

[7] *Id.* at 302.

[8] *Id.* at 336 (Hardiman, J., dissenting) (espousing the idea that expressions that are overly "sexualized" are inappropriate for young adults).

[9] *See id.* at 324 (majority opinion) (pointing out that "schools cannot avoid teaching our citizens-in-training how to appropriately navigate the 'marketplace of ideas.'" (quoting Tinker v. Des Moines Sch. Dist., 393 U.S. 503, 511 (1969))); Brief of the Keep a Breast Foundation in Support of Appellees and Affirmance at 34, *B.H. ex rel. Hawk*, 725 F.3d 293 (No. 11-2067) [hereinafter Brief of Keep a Breast Foundation]. The bracelets are not intended to be sexual speech, but instead "speech designed to raise awareness of breast cancer and reduce stigma associated with openly discussing breast health." Brief of Keep a Breast Foundation, *supra* at 29. The bracelets carry a message of positive body image and support for breast cancer awareness. *See id.* at 22. The district court rejected the school district's notion that all references to women's breasts are "inherently sexual" and there is nothing offensive about talking about "breasts and breast health, even in a middle school context." Brief of Appellees at 50, *B.H. ex rel. Hawk*, 725 F.3d 293 (No. 11-2067).

[10] *See* Brief of the Student Press Law Center in Support of Appellees B.H. & K.M. et al., and Affirmance at 4–5, *B.H. ex rel.* Hawk, 725 F.3d 293 (3d Cir. 2013) (No. 11-2067) [hereinafter Brief of the Student Press Law Center].

[11] *See id.* at 5–6, 34. (stating that the "social value" of breast cancer awareness is critical to the freedom of expression and ideas). The language of the "boobies" campaign takes aim at negative body images and taboos about self-touching in order to make women comfortable with speaking about their bodies. *See* Brief of Keep a Breast Foundation, *supra* note 9, at 29. B.H. bought the bracelet in order to raise awareness and initiate dialogue on that subject. Brief of Appellees, *supra* note 9, at 7–8 (noting that breast cancer screening helps catch it at its early stages when it is most treatable).

[12] *See* Bethel Sch. Dist. No. 403 v. Fraser, 478 U.S. 675, 681 (1986). Public schools must prepare students to be citizens as well as teach students habits, manners, and values necessary for adult life in this country. *Id.*

[13] *See B.H. ex rel. Hawk*, 725 F.3d at 335 (Hardiman, J., dissenting); Brief of Keep a Breast Foundation, *supra* note 9, at 8.

Box 3.8   ARTICLE (Constitutional Rights of Public School Student)

Teaching that Speech Matters: A Framework for Analyzing Speech Issues in Schools

*Erwin Chemerinsky**

The Supreme Court's recent decision in Morse v. Frederick *continues a pattern of judicial unwillingness to protect student speech. A key flaw in the Court's approach is in failing to draw a distinction between government control over the curriculum (and even student speech in curricular activities) and student speech outside the school's curriculum. Deference to school officials is appropriate in the former, but not in the latter. Unfortunately, the Court's approach, as reflected in its last few decisions concerning student speech, has been uncritical deference to schools and far too little protection of student speech.*

TABLE OF CONTENTS

I.   THE ABANDONMENT OF FREE SPEECH PROTECTION IN
     SCHOOLS 827
II. RESTORING THE FIRST AMENDMENT IN EDUCATIONAL
     INSTITUTIONS 832
III. THE STANDARD FOR REGULATING STUDENT SPEECH 836
CONCLUSION 840

Courts in recent years have provided little protection for student speech, least of all when it is involved in curricular activities.[1] But the distinction between "curricular" and "non-curricular" makes little sense when the speech is a school newspaper, and the censorship has nothing to do with course instruction. Instead, courts should focus on whether the government's choices about speech are in the curricular

---

* Dean and Distinguished Professor of Law, University of California, Irvine, School of Law.

[1] In other words, a sensible approach can be drawn between the need for deference to school officials when regulating speech in curricular activities, but much less deference when it is student speech outside curricular areas.

RESTATEMENTS OF THE LAW

While treatises, encyclopedias, and articles have counterparts in other fields, the *Restatements of the Law* are a distinctly legal phenomenon. In the 1920s, influential legal thinkers, concerned that the myriad decisions coming out of courts around the country were producing a far-too-unruly pattern of law, created the American Law Institute (ALI). The aim of the ALI has been to study critical areas of law on which courts around the country rule and to "restate" the laws on those subjects in credible, concise, and well-explained documents. Now nearly a century old, the ALI, composed of about 4,200 members from elite positions in the legal profession nationwide, continues with this mission.

Each Restatement is created through an elaborate process, including initial drafting by a preeminent scholar in the subject, rounds of review by a panel of experts and the ALI Council, exposure to public comment, and approval by the membership. The format consists of black-letter rules, comments, illustrations, and reporter's notes explaining the history of the rules and providing references. Because of this process, the Restatements are considered a particularly authoritative secondary source, although some would say that some of them are less restatements of existing law than expressions of the drafters' views of what the law should be.

Over the years, some courts have cited and adopted Restatement rules. When a court does so, that rule becomes law in that state — but that is by court action when the court decides a case, not just because it is a Restatement rule. A court may also decline to adopt a Restatement rule, or it may adopt one rule but not another, or indeed adopt just a part of a rule.

Restatements are not often the best place to begin a research project. First, as noted in Box 3.9, the Restatements currently offered by the ALI cover only a limited set of subjects. Second, the format is distinctive and not particularly user-friendly; other secondary sources are easier to read. On the other hand, a Restatement is an excellent source of a well-respected rule on a topic. It thus is useful when you are seeking a standard statement of a rule for an unremarkable point or, conversely, when you are seeking to establish the law in your jurisdiction, perhaps because your jurisdiction has not yet addressed your topic.

Lexis and Westlaw both provide extensive Restatement databases for adopted Restatements, including the rules with supporting materials; the case citations, which are the ALI's periodic compilation of brief descriptions of cases that have cited to each Restatement; and the index (Westlaw only). Both also provide a citator function. A *citator* is a finding tool that lists later sources — *citing sources* — that have cited an earlier source — *the cited source* — that you are now reading. In the context of the Restatement, the Restatement is the cited source, and the citing sources of interest are cases (particularly cases in your jurisdiction).

An alternative approach for Restatements research is HeinOnline, which provides Restatements materials (the rules and supporting materials, tables of contents, index, and case citations) exactly as they are published by the ALI.

Box 3.9   RESTATEMENT OF THE LAW SUBJECTS

Foundational Legal Subjects

Agency (Third)
Conflict of Laws (Second)
Contracts (Second)
Judgments (Second)
Property:
- Landlord and Tenant (Second)
- Mortgages (Third)
- Servitudes (Third)
- Wills and Other Donative Transfers (Third)

Restitution and Unjust Enrichment (Third)
Torts (Second)
Torts:
- Apportionment of Liability (Third)
- Intentional Torts to Persons (Third)
- Liability for Economic Harm (Third)
- Liability for Physical and Emotional Harm (Third)
- Products Liability (Third)

Specialized Areas

Charitable Nonprofit Organizations
Employment Law
Law Governing Lawyers (Third)
Liability Insurance
Suretyship and Guaranty (Third)
Trusts (Third)
Unfair Competition (Third)

Non-Domestic U.S. Law

Law of American Indians
Foreign Relations Law of the United States (Third and Fourth)
U.S. Law of International Commercial Arbitration

Although some early Restatements have been revised, the series designation indicates not whether a Restatement is a revision, but rather when it was created. As an example, a second series Restatement was issued in 1952-1986.

Some of these are not yet final; check the ALI website for details.

You may search these materials via a key-word search, but there is no citator function.[10]

As an example, our client All-Day Wellness, a Minnesota company, operates in the competitive business of providing consultants who help midsized employers provide services to encourage healthy practices among their employees. All-Day Wellness invests quite a bit in training every new employee, and the clients become attached to the employees they work with. Thus, the company would like to deter departing employees from working for its competitors. A covenant not-to-compete in the employment contract would accomplish this purpose.

To confirm our recollection that covenants not-to-compete may be problematic under contract law, we elected to look for the pertinent Restatement rule. We went to the Restatement (Second) of Contracts database on Lexis and worked through the table of contents, from *Unenforceability on Grounds of Public Policy* to *Restraint of Trade*. We found section 188, which covers the situation of an employee being restrained from competing with his or her employer. Comment g provided the reasoning behind the rule, and illustration 6 was a pertinent example. See Box 3.10.

An advantage of researching the Restatement in Lexis is that it can be cited or, in Lexis lingo, *Shepardized*. We wanted to learn whether section 188 had been adopted by the Minnesota courts. When we clicked on the Shepard's link for that section to obtain the report for the detailed materials pertaining to the employment scenario, we learned that they had been cited by many courts, but not in Minnesota. See Box 3.11.

---

10. HeinOnline also publishes preliminary drafts, so it is a strong source for historical research and researching new Restatements.

Box 3.10   RESTATEMENT RULE AND SUPPORTING MATERIALS
(Covenant Not-to-Compete)

Restat 2d of Contracts, § 188

Restatement 2d, Contracts - Rule Sections > *Chapter 8- Unenforceability on Grounds of Public Policy* > *Topic 2- Restraint of Trade*

§ 188 Ancillary Restraints on Competition

(1) A promise to refrain from competition that imposes a restraint that is ancillary to an otherwise valid transaction or relationship is unreasonably in restraint of trade if

(a) the restraint is greater than is needed to protect the promisee's legitimate interest, or

(b) the promisee's need is outweighed by the hardship to the promisor and the likely injury to the public.

(2) Promises imposing restraints that are ancillary to a valid transaction or relationship include the following:

(a) a promise by the seller of a business not to compete with the buyer in such a way as to injure the value of the business sold;

(b) a promise by an employee or other agent not to compete with his employer or other principal;

(c) a promise by a partner not to compete with the partnership.

COMMENTS & ILLUSTRATIONS

Comment:

a. Rule of reason. The rules stated in this Section apply to promises not to compete that, because they impose ancillary restraints, are not necessarily invalid. Subsection (1) restates in more detail the general rule of reason of § 186 as it applies to such promises. Under this formulation the restraint may be unreasonable in either of two situations. The first occurs when the restraint is greater than necessary to protect the legitimate interests of the promisee. The second occurs when, even though the restraint is not greater than necessary to protect those interests, the promisee's need for protection is outweighed by the hardship to the promisor and the likely injury to the public. In the second situation the court may be faced with a particularly difficult task of balancing competing interests. No mathematical formula can be offered for this process.

b. Need of the promisee. If a restraint is not ancillary to some transaction or relationship that gives rise to an interest worthy of protection, the promise is necessarily unreasonable under the rule stated in the preceding Section. In some instances, however, a promise to refrain from competition is a natural and reasonable means of protecting a legitimate interest of the promisee arising out of the transaction to which the restraint is ancillary. In those instances the same reasons argue for its enforceability as in the case of any other promise. For example, competitors who are combining their efforts in a partnership may promise as part of the transaction not to compete with the partnership. Assuming that the combination is not monopolistic, such promises, reasonable in scope, will be upheld in view of the interest of each party as promisee. See Subsection (2)(c) and Comment *h.* (It is assumed in the Illustrations to this Section that the arrangements are not objectionable on grounds other than those that come within its scope.) The extent to which the restraint is needed to protect the promisee's interests will vary with the nature of the transaction. Where a sale of good will is involved, for example, the buyer's interest in what he has acquired cannot be effectively realized unless the seller engages not to act so as unreasonably to diminish the value of what he has sold. The same is true of any other property interest of which exclusive use is part of the value. See Subsection (2)(a) and Comment *f.* In the case of a post-employment restraint, however, the promisee's interest is less clear. Such a restraint, in contrast to one accompanying a sale of good will, is not necessary in order for the employer to get the full value of what he has acquired. Instead, it must usually be justified on the ground that the employer has a legitimate interest in restraining the employee from appropriating valuable trade information and customer relationships to which he has had access in the course of his employment. Arguably the employer

Box 3.10 *(continued)*

Restat 2d of Contracts, § 188

2. The facts being otherwise as stated in Illustration 1, neither A's nor B's business extends to a radius of a hundred miles. The area fixed is more extensive than is necessary for B's protection. A's promise is unreasonably in restraint of trade and is unenforceable on grounds of public policy. As to the possibility of refusal to enforce limited to part of the promise, see § 184(2).

3. A sells his grocery business to B and as part of the agreement promises not to engage in business of any kind within the city for three years. The activity proscribed is more extensive than is necessary for B's protection. A's promise is unreasonably in restraint of trade and is unenforceable on grounds of public policy. As to the possibility of refusal to enforce only part of the promise, see § 184(2).

4. A sells his grocery business to B and as part of the agreement promises not to engage in a business of the same kind within the city for twenty-five years, although B has ample opportunity to make A's former good will his own in a much shorter period of time. The time fixed is longer than is necessary for A's protection. A's promise is unreasonably in restraint of trade and is unenforceable on grounds of public policy. As to the possibility of refusal to enforce only part of the promise, see § 184(2).

5. A, a corporation, sells its business to B. As part of the agreement, C and D, officers and large shareholders of A, promise not to compete with B within the territory in which A did business for three years. Their promises are not unreasonably in restraint of trade and enforcement is not precluded on grounds of public policy.

g. Promise by employee or agent. The employer's interest in exacting from his employee a promise not to compete after termination of the employment is usually explained on the ground that the employee has acquired either confidential trade information relating to some process or method or the means to attract customers away from the employer. Whether the risk that the employee may do injury to the employer is sufficient to justify a promise to refrain from competition after the termination of the employment will depend on the facts of the particular case. Post-employment restraints are scrutinized with particular care because they are often the product of unequal bargaining power and because the employee is likely to give scant attention to the hardship he may later suffer through loss of his livelihood. This is especially so where the restraint is imposed by the employer's standardized printed form. Cf. § 208. A line must be drawn between the general skills and knowledge of the trade and information that is peculiar to the employer's business. If the employer seeks to justify the restraint on the ground of the employee's knowledge of a process or method, the confidentiality of that process or method and its technological life may be critical. The public interest in workable employer-employee relationships with an efficient use of employees must be balanced against the interest in individual economic freedom. The court will take account of any diminution in competition likely to result from slowing down the dissemination of ideas and of any impairment of the function of the market in shifting manpower to areas of greatest productivity. If the employer seeks to justify the restraint on the ground of the employee's ability to attract customers, the nature, extent and locale of the employee's contacts with customers are relevant. A restraint is easier to justify if it is limited to one field of activity among many that are available to the employee. The same is true if the restraint is limited to the taking of his former employer's customers as contrasted with competition in general. A restraint may be ancillary to a relationship although, as in the case of an employment at will, no contract of employment is involved. Analogous rules apply to restraints imposed on agents by their principals. As to the duty of an agent not to compete with his principal during the agency relationship, see *Restatement, Second, Agency §§ 393*, 394.

Illustrations:

6. A employs B as a fitter of contact lenses under a one-year employment contract. As part of the employment agreement, B promises not to work as a fitter of contact lenses in the same town for three years after the termination of his employment. B works for A for five years, during which time he has close relationships with A's customers, who come to rely upon him. B's contacts with A's customers are such as to attract them away from A. B's promise is not unreasonably in restraint of trade and enforcement is not precluded on grounds of public policy.

7. A employs B as advertising manager of his retail clothing store. As part of the employment agreement, B promises not to work in the retail clothing business in the same town for three years after the termination of his

Box 3.11   CITATOR REPORT FOR RESTATEMENT (Covenant Not-to-Compete)

Page 2 of 18

Shepard's®: Contracts Second sec. 188 cmt. g

Citing Decisions (46)

Narrow by: None Applied

Analysis: Cited in Concurring Opinion at (1), Cited in Dissenting Opinion at (1), "Cited by" (44)

Court:1st Circuit (3), 4th Circuit (2), 10th Circuit (1), 11th Circuit (1), 6th Circuit (1), 7th Circuit (1), Tennessee (10), Indiana (4), Massachusetts (4), Illinois (3), Texas (3), Alaska (2), Nebraska (2), New York (2), Colorado (1), Connecticut (1), Delaware (1), Dist. of Columbia (1), Kansas (1), New Hampshire (1), Vermont (1)

1st Circuit - Court of Appeals

1.   **Lanier Professional Servs. v. Ricci** ⚠

192 F.3d 1, 1999 U.S. App. LEXIS 22502, 15 I.E.R. Cas. (BNA) 940, 139 Lab. Cas. (CCH) P58734

Court
1st Cir. Mass.

▪ **Cited by:** 192 F.3d 1 p.5

Date:
1999

... that an ambiguous "post-employment restraint imposed by the employer's standardized form contract" will be construed against the drafter. Sentry Ins. v. Firnstein , 14 Mass. App. Ct. 706 , 442 N.E.2d 46 , 46-47 (Mass. App. Ct. 1982) (citing **Restatement (Second) of Contracts § 188 cmt. g** (1981)). The court's conclusion that Lanier had not demonstrated a substantial likelihood of success on the merits reflected factual findings that are not clearly erroneous and a correct understanding ...

2.   **Ikon Office Solutions, Inc. v. Belanger** ⚠

59 F. Supp. 2d 125, 1999 U.S. Dist. LEXIS 10963

Court
D. Mass.

▪ **Cited by:** 59 F. Supp. 2d 125 p.131

Date:
1999

... whether they are unconscionable, offend public policy, or are unfair under the circumstances. Chase Commercial Corp. v. Owen , 32 Mass. App. Ct. 248 , 588 N.E.2d 705 (Mass. App. Ct. 1992) . See also Sentry , 442 N.E.2d at 47 (citing **Restatement (Second) of Contracts, § 188 cmt. g** (1981)). 2 The Restatement provides as follows: "Such contracts are scrutinized with particular care because they are often the product of unequal bargaining power and because the employee is likely ...

3.   **Home Gas Corp. v. De Blois Oil Co.** ◆

JURY INSTRUCTION GUIDES

Jury instruction guides (JIGs) are both similar to the Restatements in several ways and yet also different. The standard format resembles that of the Restatement: a rule followed by explanatory material with references. Like the Restatements, they are generated through a deliberative process involving drafting by experts, discussion, and final approval. On the other hand, their purpose is to provide a concise statement of the law that a judge may use to instruct a jury as it begins to deliberate on a case. Thus, unlike the Restatements, they are specific to one jurisdiction, such as a single state, and they are designed to accurately and concisely represent that jurisdiction's law. Given this purpose, they generally are regularly updated (unlike the Restatements).

JIGs are most obviously useful when you are preparing for trial and writing your proposed jury instructions for the judge. However, this is not their only application. They can be useful in your research earlier as well, because knowing how a case would be framed should it get to a jury is important when framing or defending it — or indeed when negotiating a dispute. Beyond this, in some jurisdictions, JIGs operate as highly respected summaries of state law on the subjects that they cover. Indeed, you may find them useful as general summaries of state law, especially if your state does not have a strong state encyclopedia.

Various approaches to finding JIGs should prove successful, depending on the jurisdiction. Some jurisdictions post them on their court websites. Lexis provides them under Practice Pages by Jurisdiction, Westlaw under the Secondary Sources tab, and Bloomberg Law under various federal and state law tabs. Some law libraries carry print versions.

As an example, recall our client Bower's Bounty, sued for defamation by a former employee. Our initial research in a treatise provided a big-picture definition of the tort of defamation. To narrow in on the law of Kansas, we then consulted the Pattern Jury Instructions — Civil database within the Westlaw collection of Kansas Secondary Sources. To obtain an overview of all the specific instructions, we looked at the table of contents and selected *Intentional Torts and Negligent Misrepresentation* and then *Defamation*. Eight instructions discussed defamation, covering the basic definition, defenses, and specific situations. In particular, we read the instruction defining defamation. Furthermore, it provided references not only to Kansas cases, but also to the Restatement (Second) of Torts. See Box 3.12.

Box 3.12	**JURY INSTRUCTION GUIDE (Employment Defamation)**

127.51Defamation, Pattern Inst. Kan. Civil 127.51

Pattern Instructions Kansas - Civil
Database updated February 2015

Kansas Judicial Council

Chapter 127.00. Intentional Torts and Negligent Misrepresentations
E. Defamation

127.51 Defamation

Defamation is communication to a person of false information tending to *(expose another living person to public hatred, contempt or ridicule)(deprive another of the benefits of public confidence and social acceptance)(degrade and vilify the memory of one who is dead and to scandalize or provoke [his] [her] surviving relatives and friends).*

Notes on Use

This instruction has been modified to eliminate malice as an element of defamation. If the defendant asserts conditional privilege, malice is considered. See PIK 4th 127.53, Qualified or Conditional Privilege.

Comment

The definition of defamation in the instruction is taken from the definition of criminal defamation in K.S.A. 21-4004 on the basis of a statement in Jerald v. Houston, 124 Kan. 657, 662, 261 P. 851 (1927), that whatever is punishable as libel may be the basis of a civil action of tort and that when taken over into the law of torts, the definition of the criminal statute is merely an authoritative statement of the meaning of the term libel. The criminal statute does not make a distinction between libel and slander. Such common law classification relates only to the manner in which the wrongful act is committed and appears to be unnecessary. The modern concept is that either conduct gives rise to an actionable claim termed defamation, and the same rules of law are applicable to each. Luttrell v. United Telephone System, Inc., 9 Kan. App. 2d 620, 683 P.2d 1292 (1984), *aff'd* 236 Kan. 710, 695 P.2d 1279 (1985).

The instruction accords with Restatement (Second) of Torts § 559, comments b and c (1977).

In Lindemuth v. Goodyear Tire & Rubber Co., 19 Kan. App. 2d 95, 103, 864 P.2d 744 (1993), the court cited PIK 2d 14.51 (1992 Supp.) [PIK 4th 127.51] with approval, noting that malice is not a necessary element of defamation unless it is first decided that such proof is required based upon the particular facts of the case.

"The elements of [defamation] include false and defamatory words (Hein v. Lacy, 228 Kan. 249, 616 P.2d 277 [1980]) communicated to a third person (Schulze v. Coykendall, 218 Kan. 653, 657, 545 P.2d 392 [1976]) which result in harm to the reputation of the person defamed. Gobin v. Globe Publishing Co., 232 Kan. 1, 6, 649 P.2d 1239 (1982) (*Gobin III*.)" Luttrell v. United Telephone System, Inc., 9 Kan. App. 2d 620 at 620–621, 683 P.2d 1292 (1985).

© 2015 Kansas Judicial Council

AMERICAN LAW REPORTS ANNOTATIONS

American Law Reports (ALR) annotations also are uniquely legal publications that exist to provide guidance on the abundance of cases decided by U.S. courts.[11] However, ALR annotations differ from the Restatements and JIGs in that they are written by individual lawyers who are not well-known experts and are published by a commercial publisher, so they have far less credibility. They have a different purpose and format as well. Each ALR annotation focuses on a fairly narrow subject on which a good number of cases have been decided, whether in state courts or in federal courts. The annotation does not distill the cases into a concise rule of law; rather it presents the pattern of the decisions on the subject and provides an exhaustive set of references. Furthermore, an ALR annotation is updated on an ongoing basis as new cases are decided. Issues of state law are covered in the main ALR annotation volumes, which are now in the seventh series; issues of federal law are covered in *American Law Reports Federal,* now in the third series.[12]

Each ALR annotation begins with a scope note setting out its coverage, followed by a summary and practice pointers. The bulk of the ALR annotation consists of legal propositions or statements about legally relevant facts, supported by detailed case descriptions. A typical ALR annotation also has references to other secondary sources, including other ALR annotations, legal periodical articles, and practice guides. Because an ALR annotation can be lengthy, it is supplemented by its own finding tools, including an outline, index, and table of jurisdictions that lists cases covered from each jurisdiction.

ALR annotations are very useful, but only in limited research settings. Because the scope of an ALR annotation is typically quite narrow, it is not a good secondary source to provide an overview of an area of law, so it does not work well for grounding your research at the outset of a project. On the other hand, an ALR annotation is a good choice when you have identified a narrow topic on which an ALR annotation has been written. An ALR annotation can be especially helpful if you are seeking to understand fully how facts may influence court rulings on that topic or if the court in your jurisdiction has yet to rule, so that the pattern of rulings elsewhere could prove informative and perhaps persuasive.

Two main approaches to researching in ALR annotations work well. First, if you have access to a print version, consider researching in print. This approach is free; the index is excellent and should direct you to a pertinent ALR annotation; reading a lengthy ALR annotation in print is an efficient way to browse your way to pertinent information. Second, both Lexis and Westlaw provide ALR annotations, searchable by key words; Westlaw also provides the index.

---

11. ALRs also contain reprints of leading cases on their topics.

12. Initially all topics, federal and state, were covered in the single *American Law Reports.*

As an example, recall again our client Bower's Bounty, sued for defamation by a former employee. The treatise provided the big-picture definition of the tort of defamation, and the JIG provided the Kansas definition. The client's situation raised the specific question of whether the communication of the statement within the company would qualify as a publication. We researched this in the Lexis Secondary Materials ALRs database. Through the search *defamation /10 publication /10 company or corporation*, we found a pertinent ALR annotation discussing intracorporate communication of employee evaluations. The summary explained that courts split on whether such communications qualify as publication for the purposes of defamation; the detailed discussion broke out the cases according to the types of communication. The detailed discussion covered a Kansas case, *Luttrell v. United Telephone System, Inc.*[13] — a strong lead. Furthermore, the ALR annotation provided references to other secondary sources, such as a treatise, the Restatement (Second) of Torts, and *American Jurisprudence 2d*. See the excerpts in Box 3.13.

---

13. 683 P.2d 1292 (Kan. Ct. App. 1984), *aff'd*, 695 P.2d 1279 (Kan. 1985).

Box 3.13   AMERICAN LAW REPORTS (Employment Defamation)

47 A.L.R.4th 674, *1b

Workmen's compensation provision as precluding employee's action against employer for fraud, false imprisonment, defamation, or the like, _46 A.L.R.3d 1279_

What constitutes "publication" of libel in order to start running of period of limitations, _42 A.L.R.3d 807_

Liability of partners or partnership for libel, _88 A.L.R.2d 474_

Rights and remedies of workmen blacklisted by labor union, _46 A.L.R.2d 1124_

Libel and slander: words reflecting upon one in his character as employee as actionable per se, _6 A.L.R.2d 1008_

Libel and slander: Publication of notice of cessation of relationship of principal and agent or employer and employee, or of business or professional relationship, 138 A.L.R. 671

Dissemination of adverse employment references by former employer as unlawful employment practice under Title VII of Civil Rights Act of 1964 _(42 U.S.C.A. § 2000e-2_(a)(1)), _50 A.L.R. Fed. 722_

Torts-Libel and Slander-Communications Between Employees of Company Concerning Company Business Held Sufficient Publication to Subject Company to Liability. 38 Virginia L R 400 (1952)

[*2]   Summary and comment
[*2a]   Generally

The court, in an early and often cited case[10] involving the subject matter of this annotation, resolved the issue by determining that, in regard to an office manager whose performance was not satisfactory to the home office, a libelous communication sent by one corporate agent to another agent or representative of the same corporation could not be a corporate publication of the libel since the corporation was but communicating with itself.[11] In juxtaposition to this pronouncement, the Restatement of the Law of Torts § 577 (Comment i) indicates that when one agent of a corporation communicates, within the scope of his employment, with another agent of the same corporation, there is publication of the communication by both the agent and the corporation. The conflict of views is, apparently, attributable to a confusion between publication and privilege.[12] Indeed, it is obvious that some courts commence their inquiry into corporate defamation of an employee with a definition which focuses primarily on privilege vel non: defamation is "an unprivileged publication of false and defamatory matter of another which is actionable irrespective of special harm, or, if not so actionable, is the legal cause of special harm to the other."[13]

Regardless of the possible muddying of the waters by looking first at the "privileged nature of the occasion" rather than treating it as a defense[14] after publication has been established,[15] it is clear that a number of courts subscribe

---

[10]   _Prins v Holland-North America Mortg. Co. (1919) 107 Wash 206, 181 P 680,_ 5 ALR 451, § 5[b].

[11]   It is to be noted, however, that in the concurring opinion (concurring only on the ground that summary judgment should not have been granted) in _Pate v Tyee Motor Inn, Inc. (1970) 77 Wash 2d 819, 467 P2d 301,_ § 4[a], it was pointed out that in the Prins Case, there was communication of defamatory statements between corporate officials which was also read by other corporate employees, and there could hardly be a doubt that under the facts of Prins there was publication since the letter or memorandum defamatory of the plaintiff was actually read by at least two other employees of the defendant company. The court went on to say that the court had properly held for the defendant corporation under the circumstances but, in doing so, issues of qualified privilege and publication were, unfortunately, intermingled.

[12]   Prosser and Keeton on the Law of Torts, Chapter 19 § 113, note 15.

[13]   _General Motors Corp. v Piskor (1975) 27 Md App 95, 340 A2d 767,_ affd in part and revd in part _277 Md 165, 352 A2d 810,_ later app _281 Md 627, 381 A2d 16, 93 ALR3d 1097,_ § 4[a].

[14]   For a discussion of "privilege" as a defense in an action for defamation, see _Am. Jur. 2d, Libel and Slander §§ 192-200._

[15]   For a discussion of publication, generally, see _Am. Jur. 2d, Libel and Slander §§ 146-168._

Box 3.13   *(continued)*

47 A.L.R.4th 674, *3b

Under Minnesota defamation law, communications between employees of a corporation can constitute defamatory publication. *Krutchen v. Zayo Bandwidth Northeast, LLC, 591 F. Supp. 2d 1002, 28 I.E.R. Cas. (BNA) 1106 (D. Minn. 2008)* (applying Minnesota law).

Preparation of and distribution of letter to personnel file and to other officers may constitute publication sufficient to support cause of action for defamation. *Michaelson v Minnesota Mining & Mfg. Co. (1991, Minn App) 474 NW2d 174, 6 BNA IER Cas 1146.*

Intra-office communications can be published in terms of defamation if the individual who reads the communications is independent of the process by which the communications were produced. *White v. Trew, 720 S.E.2d 713 (N.C. Ct. App. 2011).*

In defamation action brought by former employee against former employer and supervisor who had accused plaintiff of theft, defendants' motion for summary judgment was granted as to plaintiffs' claim of slander due to compelled self-publication to prospective employer where jurisdiction did not recognize claim for slander due to self-publication; defendant's motion for summary judgment was denied as to plaintiffs' claim for slander where, although conditional privilege existed as to statements communicated to plaintiff's supervisors, plaintiff produced evidence which may establish abuse of that privilege by publishing alleged defamatory statement to non-supervisory employees. *Quinn v Limited Express, Inc. (1989, WD Pa) 715 F Supp 127* (applying Pa law).

[*4]   Particular circumstances under which publication has been found or held supportable
[*4a]   Statements by supervisory personnel

In the following cases involving defamation claims based on statements, in regard to an employee's evaluation, by corporate supervisory personnel to other corporate employees, the courts found that such statements constituted publication to a third person as required by the law of defamation.

A statement by a supervisor, an employee of the defendant corporation, acting within the scope of his employment, to the defendant corporation's managing agent to the effect that a former employee who was reapplying for employment had misused company funds, constituted publication, the court ruled in *Kelly v General Telephone Co. (1982, 2d Dist) 136 Cal App 3d 278, 186 Cal Rptr 184,* rejecting the defendant corporation's argument that the plaintiff had not alleged publication of the statements because he had alleged only that the statements were made by one of the defendant corporation's employees to other employees of the defendant. Publication occurs when a statement is communicated to any person other than the party defamed, the court explained, adding that publication might involve internal corporate statements. The order of dismissal was reversed with directions to the trial court to overrule the demurrer to the slander action.

Remarks communicated by one corporate employee to another concerning the job performance of a third employee were publication for the purposes of a defamation action against the employer, the court ruled in *Luttrell v United Tel. System, Inc. (1984) 9 Kan App 2d 620, 683 P2d 1292, 47 ALR4th 669,* affd *236 Kan 710, 695 P2d 1279, 102 CCH LC P 55495.* The court explained that one of the defendant corporation's employees had informed the plaintiff employee's supervisor that the plaintiff had been engaging in illegal activities and the supervisor had communicated this information to two other corporate employees. Noting that this issue of first impression was whether interoffice communications between supervisory employees of a corporation, acting within the scope and course of their employment, regarding the work of another employee of the **corporation**, constituted **publication** to a third person sufficient for a **defamation** action, the court pointed out that damage to one's reputation within a corporate community might be just as devastating as that effected by defamation spread to the outside, and that thus, the injury caused by intracorporate defamation should not be disregarded simply because the corporation could be sued as an individual entity. The defendant corporation had argued that corporate employers must be free to evaluate and comment on their employees' work performance and that this freedom would be unduly restrained if they were liable for intracorporate defamation. Seeing no reason for greater freedom from liability for defamation to be accorded a corporate employer than that already available to all employers through the qualified privilege,

PRACTICE GUIDES

Within the broad category of practice guides fall many other secondary sources that have two common traits: they are less oriented toward explaining the law than the secondary sources already described, and they are more focused on assisting lawyers in accomplishing a specific task. Thus, you generally will turn to these resources when your work on a project has progressed to the point that you have framed your legal analysis and are turning to undertaking a specific task. This section provides a brief introduction to these resources.

One category of practice guide goes by titles such as *Causes of Action, American Jurisprudence Pleading and Practice Forms Annotated,* and *Nichols Cyclopedia of Legal Forms Annotated.* Each such publication focuses on a specific task — whether to frame a lawsuit, write a certain type of pleading, or prepare a document used in a transaction — and provides sample documents, along with concrete advice for executing that task in various legal and factual settings.

With these publications and any others that provide a sample document for your consideration, it is imperative to realize that it is only a sample, prepared by its author without regard to your client's specific situation and based, perhaps, on law that differs in some way from that of your jurisdiction or on law that has since changed. Thus, you must always view samples as a place to start, but never as a place to conclude your drafting efforts.

A second type of practice guide is often called a *looseleaf service* because its standard format for print publication is in looseleaf binders (which facilitate frequent updating through replacement pages). A looseleaf service focuses on a specialized area of legal practice and provides a wide range of materials related to that area, including sophisticated secondary sources. These materials often include not only discussion of the legal rules, but also practical guidance such as checklists and sample documents.

As an example, our client Exact Electronics is considering establishing a social media policy for its employees. This matter has not only legal but also management dimensions; it requires not only legal analysis, but also careful drafting. Thus, we turned to the *CCH Labor & Employment* looseleaf service (available on Westlaw). Our search for *social media policy* yielded two documents that illustrate the usefulness of looseleafs: one was both a checklist and a brief discussion; the other was a sample policy. With these two together, we had a good idea of topics to cover and some language to consider using. See Boxes 3.14 and 3.15.

Box 3.14   LOOSELEAF CHECKLIST (Social Media Policy)

¶ 47,268 CHECKLIST: WHAT TOPICS SHOULD BE..., 2012 WL 5470799...

CCH-HRCL P 47,268 (C.C.H.), 2012 WL 5470799

CCH Human Resources Compliance Library

2015

HR Compliance Library

Employee Relations

Social Networking

Analysis and Guidance

¶ 47,268 CHECKLIST: WHAT TOPICS SHOULD BE COVERED IN A **SOCIAL MEDIA POLICY**?

Checklist: What topics should be covered in a social media policy?

Topics to be covered in a social media policy include:
- Identify and define social media. Specify which sites are included.
- Address when the policy applies. Specify when social media communication outside of the workplace may fall under the social media policy. Specify whether the policy applies to any posting where the poster is identified as a company employee or whether it applies any time the company is mentioned.
- Identify the type of information that is considered proprietary and confidential company information and discuss the importance of nondisclosure.
- Inform employees that they are responsible for what they post on any social media forum. Employees should be notified that even though they have the opportunity to express themselves in social media, they are still required to use common sense and judgment.
- Identify topics not to be discussed, such as: negative statements about a competitor or a client, negative statements about other employees, revealing confidential or proprietary information.
- If employee posts include the name of the employer, employees should specify that their comments are their own opinion and not the opinion of the employer.
- Relate social media policy to the other policies of the organization. Specify that standards of conduct apply whether the conduct is online or in-person.
- Provide a contact person to whom questions about acceptable content can be directed.
- Provide and maintain a list of 'FAQs' with examples as to what content is encouraged.
- Address the consequences for violation of the policy.

The challenge in drafting a social media policy is often doing so in a manner that protects the company while not discouraging employees from posting content that promotes the company's brand. To accomplish this, design a plan that specifies what content is acceptable instead of simply providing a list of prohibited activities. You may want to provide examples of what is considered acceptable content, as well as provide means of support when an employee has questions about a potential post. By providing these resources, employees are encouraged to be creative and their creativity is not stifled by the social media policy.

Box 3.15 LOOSELEAF SAMPLE DOCUMENT (Social Media Policy)

¶ 2429 SAMPLE SOCIAL MEDIA COMMUNICATIONS POLICY, 2011 WL 1830890...

CCH-HRMHRPG P 2429 (C.C.H.), 2011 WL 1830890

Human Resources Management - HR Practices Guide

Copyright (c) 2011 CCH INCORPORATED, A Wolters Kluwer business. All rights reserved.

HR Practices Guide Explanations

Policies

Communication and Training

¶ 2429 SAMPLE **SOCIAL MEDIA** COMMUNICATIONS **POLICY**

Sample **social media** communications **policy**

NOTE: This document is just a sample for educational purposes, and should not be relied on as legal advice [70]. Consult with employment counsel before implementing this **policy**.

{ ABC Company} understands the importance of social computing, networking and **social media** in today's world. **Social media** takes many forms including (Facebook, LinkedIn, MySpace, Twitter, etc), blogs, wikis, file sharing sites, forums, discussion groups and chat rooms. **Social Media** can be an extremely effective way of marketing our company and expanding our interactions with employees, vendors and customers. While embracing new technologies, we also want to make sure that the Company and our employees engage in social networking in a responsible manner.

This **policy** provides guidance on how to engage in social networking in a way to protect yourself and the interests of the Company, its employees, vendors and customers. These guidelines supplement current Company **policies**.
1. **Social networking sites should not be considered private.** Generally, information posted on social networking sites is public and you should expect that even with your use of certain privacy settings what you post on social networking sites will be seen by others and should not be considered private.
2. **Company policies still apply/Monitoring.** Company **policies** still apply when using **social media** sites. Rules against harassment and inappropriate conduct and other rules contained in the Employee Handbook apply to your on-line activities. **Social media** sites should not be used during work times unless for business-related activities. We may monitor employee **social media** communications to ensure compliance with Company **policies**.
3. **Use common sense/Think before you post.** You are responsible for the content you publish on **social media** sites. What you post could be online for a long time. As a representative of the Company, always consider how your comments will be viewed in light of protecting and enhancing both the Company's reputation and your own.
4. **Respect others/Keep gripes and disputes offline.** Be respectful to fellow employees, customers, vendors and competitors. Do not post negative or disparaging comments about the Company or its services, products, management or employees. **Social media** sites should not be used as a platform for employee disputes or other internal Company matters. You can be disciplined or held legally liable for any actions that are unlawful or for information posted that may be defamatory, proprietary, confidential, harassing, pornographic, and libelous or creates a hostile work environment.
5. **Protect confidential information.** Respect the privacy of customers, venders and employees. Do not share or disclose confidential or proprietary information of the Company, or its customers, venders, and employees on **social media** sites. Always ask permission before posting references to customer, vender or employee pictures or other information that was intended to be private.
6. **No phony identities/Be clear about who you are.** Only authorized employees may communicate information on behalf of the Company. Without permission you are not authorized to make statements, comments or press releases on behalf of the Company. Be clear and write in first person. You should make clear that you are speaking for yourself and not on

Box 3.15   *(continued)*

¶ 2429 SAMPLE SOCIAL MEDIA COMMUNICATIONS POLICY, 2011 WL 1830890...

behalf of the Company. In some instances it may be appropriate to add in this language: 'The views expressed on this 'site' are my own and do not reflect the views and opinions of ABC Company.'

7. **Use your own email.** Always use your personal email address (not your ABC.com email) as your primary means of identification. Company, names, logos and trademarks may not be used without the Company's permission.

8. **Respect copyrights and fair use.** Remember to respect the copyrighted materials owned by others, and reference the sources you use. Never distribute copyrighted materials (such as videos, photos, books, etc.) online as copyright infringement and plagiarism laws apply to posts on the Internet.

9. **Stay productive. Social media** participation can be productive and beneficial both personally and professionally. However, ensure that such personal activities do not interfere with your work activities.

10. **Use social networking safely.** Understand which social networking sites you would benefit from most, how each works and what features each offers. Always review the applicable privacy and security settings so that you understand how much or little information you are comfortable sharing.

If you have any questions about this **policy** or any issues surrounding **social media**, please contact:

_____ _____

Telephone number.

Email address.

Footnotes

[70]   Sample **policy** provided by David B. Wilson, Hirsch Roberts Weinstein LLP, Two Park Plaza, Suite 610, Boston, Massachusetts 02116; telephone: 617-348-3415.

End of Document   © 2015 Thomson Reuters. No claim to original U.S. Government Works.

Two other types of publications that fall into the practice guide category, broadly construed, are written to keep lawyers current in their areas of practice. First, most lawyers are required to attend continuing legal education (CLE) courses on a regular basis to maintain their licenses to practice, and the presenters prepare CLE manuals for these courses. Often, these manuals present not only updates on the most recent developments in the law (such as new cases and statutes), but also practical advice and sample documents.

Second, most lawyers who specialize in an area of legal practice subscribe to one or more current-awareness publications, such as newsletters, in their practice areas. Many also monitor social media postings of experts and organizations in their areas. Again, these updating publications often cover not only new legal developments, but also prove practical guidance.[14] Furthermore, most lawyers also subscribe to legal magazines and newspapers to keep abreast of developments in the profession in general.

Consider again, as an example, the interest of Exact Electronics in establishing a social media policy for its employees. Employment law is an area of law that changes rapidly, so current-awareness publications abound. As an example, see the posting from *Practitioner Insight Commentaries: Labor & Employment* in Box 3.16.[15] This posting alerted us to the challenge of not violating the employees' rights under a major federal statute.[16]

---

14. Yet a third way to maintain currency is a database alert. If you find a source that is pertinent to your practice, you may have one of the more sophisticated commercial resources issue an alert to you when it is altered in certain ways.

15. Note that this posting was written by two lawyers in a New York City law firm. Much updating secondary source material is written by lawyers for other lawyers as a way of assuring high standards of practice across the bar.

16. This statute is covered in detail in Chapter 7 on Administrative Agency Materials.

Box 3.16   NEWSLETTER ARTICLE (Social Media Policy)

Balancing Protection of Information With Employee Rights in..., 2015 WL 1883380

Balancing Protection of Information With Employee Rights in Confidentiality Policies

(April 27, 2015) - The developing law on employer confidentiality policies underscores the tension between an employer's ever-increasing need to protect confidential information and an employee's established right to discuss terms and conditions of employment. With the exponential growth of social media, instant communication and theft of confidential information, employers are erecting stronger firewalls and more restrictive employment policies to protect their and their clients' information. These are worthy goals from a business perspective, but they potentially conflict with the legal right of employees to discuss information relating to their wages, hours and working conditions.

The National Labor Relations Board (NLRB) is scrutinizing employers' workplace rules and policies, including those pertaining to confidentiality. In doing so, the NLRB has turned to its well-established principle that an employer violates the National Labor Relations Act (NLRA) by maintaining a rule that "reasonably tends to chill employees in the exercise of their Section 7 rights" under the NLRA to discuss terms and conditions of employment. In this regard, the NLRB first determines whether the rule at issue explicitly restricts employees' rights; if it does, the rule is unlawful and the analysis ends. If the rule survives the first part of the test, the NLRB goes on to determine whether employees would reasonably construe the rule to restrict employee rights, whether the rule was promulgated in response to union activity, or if the rule was applied to restrict employee rights. The rule is unlawful if any of these factors are satisfied. *See Martin Luther Mem'l Home, Inc.*, 343 N.L.R.B. 646 (Case 7-CA-44877 2004).

Lawful vs. Unlawful

A number of NLRB cases following the reasoning above have found confidentiality policies did not violate the NLRA. For example, the NLRB in *K-Mart*, 330 N.L.R.B. 263 (Case 32-CA-15575 et al. 1999), ruled K-Mart's policy prohibiting discussion of "company business and documents" was lawful because employees would reasonably read the rule as protecting private business information rather than prohibiting discussion of terms and conditions of employment. Similarly, in *Burndy, LLC*, 34-CA-65746 (N.L.R.B. July 31, 2013), the NLRB found a rule prohibiting employees from disclosing "employee information" was *not* unlawful because it was included in a broader section of a policy restricting disclosure of intellectual property. The NLRB found a reasonable employee would construe such a rule as prohibiting disclosure of classified company information, not terms and conditions of employment.

In contrast, several cases over the last year have shown that confidentiality policies involving explicit prohibitions on discussing terms or conditions of employment or overly broad prohibitions on discussing personnel and company information may be found to be unlawful. For example, in *Flex Frac Logistics, LLC v. N.L.R.B.*, 746 F.3d 205 (5th Cir. 2014), the Fifth Circuit held a confidentiality policy prohibiting employees from disclosing "company financial information" and "personnel information" violated the NLRA because such information implicitly included wages. Further, in *Fresh & Easy Neighborhood Market*, 361 N.L.R.B. No. 8 (31-CA-077074, 31-CA-080734 July 31, 2014), the NLRB held an employer's confidentiality policy was unlawful where it prohibited disclosure of "customer and employee information" and the provision was not adequately limited by context.

Media Statements and Company Investigations

With respect to media policies, in *DirecTV U.S. DirecTV Holdings, LLC*, 359 N.L.R.B. No. 54 (21-CA-039546 2013), a policy expressly instructing employees not to contact the media was unlawful because such policy could encompass protected communications regarding a labor dispute. To withstand scrutiny, media policies must be tailored to protect the employer's legitimate interest in not having employees hold themselves out as speaking for the company.

Box 3.16   *(continued)*

Balancing Protection of Information With Employee Rights in..., 2015 WL 1883380

Policies forbidding employees from communicating about company investigations also must be carefully drafted and applied. In *Hyundai America Shipping Agency, Inc.* 357 N.L.R.B. No. 80 (28-CA-22892 Aug. 26, 2011), the NLRB held a company's policy broadly barring employees from discussing employee investigations was unlawful because the company failed to engage in individualized reviews of each situation to determine whether there was a substantial justification for prohibiting employees' discussion of investigatory matters, such as the protection of witnesses or evidence. And in *Banner Health System*, 358 N.L.R.B. No. 93 (28-CA-023438 2012), the NLRB held it was unlawful for a company to routinely ask employees making a complaint not to discuss the matter with their coworkers. Both cases demonstrate the employer's need to analyze each situation; proper consideration of factors such as safety, harassment or spoliation of evidence could and should result in a reasonable restriction on communications about the investigation.

'Savings Clauses'

Employers should be aware that a "savings clause" may not cure a defective policy. According to an administrative law judge (ALJ) decision in *American Red Cross Blood Services*, No. 08-CA-090132 (N.L.R.B. June 4, 2013), a clause providing an agreement "does not deny any rights provided under the [NLRA] to engage in concerted activity, including but not limited to collective bargaining" will not make an overly broad confidentiality policy lawful. The ALJ held such a clause would cancel unlawfully broad language only if employees are savvy enough to know the NLRA permits employees to discuss terms and conditions of employment. On the other hand, *Tiffany Co.*, (01-CA-111287 N.L.R.B. Aug. 5, 2014), upheld a savings clause that appeared immediately following an unlawful prohibition on disclosure of compensation information and explicitly provided the policy "does not apply to employees who speak, write or communicate with fellow employees or others about their wages, benefits or other terms of employment."

* * *

As demonstrated by these cases, the application of the law in the area of confidentiality policies is unsettled, and employees and employers face uncertainty as a result. Perhaps some of the uncertainty will be eliminated through the promulgation of model confidentiality policies, as NLRB General Counsel Richard F. Griffin Jr. contemplated in a memorandum analyzing the legality of various policies in employee handbooks. In addition, due to procedural issues relating to President Obama's recess appointments to the NLRB in January 2012, there is a chance certain of these decisions may be changed in the near term. It remains important, however, for employers to take a reasoned approach to confidentiality and protect important business information without overreaching.

By John P. Furfaro and Risa M. Salins

Partner John P. Furfaro and counsel Risa M. Salins are members of Skadden, Arps, Slate, Meagher & Flom's Labor and Employment Law practice in New York.

BUILD YOUR UNDERSTANDING

Test Your Knowledge

1. List at least two differences between secondary sources as a category of research materials and primary authorities as a category of research materials.

2. For each of the secondary sources listed below, state two or three descriptive phrases that distinguish each of them from the others:
   - Treatise
   - Encyclopedia
   - Legal periodical article
   - Restatements of the Law
   - Jury instruction guide (JIG)
   - *American Law Reports* (ALR) annotation

3. For each of the research contexts stated below, identify which one or two of the six secondary sources listed in question 2 that you would consult:
   - You are researching an area of law that is fairly new to you and thus seek a general overview.
   - You are researching a case where your client's legal position is not in accord with current law, so you are looking for arguments in favor of changing the law.
   - You are looking for a concise statement of the legal rule that applies in most states.
   - You are looking for a concise statement of the legal rule that applies in your jurisdiction to frame the lawsuit that you are preparing for your client.
   - You are looking for the different ways that courts around the country have ruled on your narrow legal topic.

4. Citing is the practice of using one source to find new sources, introduced in this chapter through the Restatements of the Law. Fill in the blanks: If I were citing a Restatement rule, the _____ would be the cited source, a _____ would be the citing source, and my purpose would be to determine whether _____.

Put It into Practice

Recall your client's situation (detailed in Chapter 1 at pages 20-21): Your client, Emmet Wilson, is a veteran who has developed post-traumatic stress disorder (PTSD). Among other treatments, he has been assigned a therapy dog. Mr. Wilson's landlord has raised concerns because the building is a no-pets building. Indeed, the lease (which is for a year) so specifies, and the landlord says that other tenants have raised the issue. So she has given Mr. Wilson notice that if he does not give up the dog, he will be evicted in a month.

This scenario is set in West Virginia. As you research, if possible, aim to find law in the state of West Virginia and references to primary authorities from West Virginia.

_____

1. To explore treatises, research this possible dimension of Mr. Wilson's situation: A colleague has suggested that the landlord's actions might be discrimination under the federal Fair Housing Act — that is, if Mr. Wilson comes within the group of people protected under that statute. Find a treatise on discrimination in housing, and research whether psychiatric impairments are protected under the statute.
   a. Provide the title of the treatise you have chosen, its author(s), its date of publication, and its medium (e.g., print, Westlaw).
   b. Use the table of contents to identify the pertinent portion of the treatise; set out the divisions and subdivisions of the treatise.
   c. Now use the index to identify the pertinent portion of the treatise; explain how you did this (e.g., the index topic(s) that worked well).
   d. State the guidance the treatise provided.
   e. Identify at least one primary authority that supports your answer. For a statute, provide the title and section numbers. For a case, list the name, court, and date.

2. To explore encyclopedias, research the point that Mr. Wilson's landlord would make: the lease precludes keeping pets, so the landlord may evict Mr. Wilson if he continues to keep the dog. Research whether this view has legal merit in _American Jurisprudence 2d_.
   a. Identify the topic and section(s) covering this topic.
   b. Explain how you found the section(s).
   c. State the guidance the encyclopedia provided.
   d. Identify at least one primary authority that supports your answer.
   e. Peruse the table of contents to discern the framework into which the section(s) fit. State two or three additional sections that you would go on to read based on that framework.

3. To explore legal periodical articles, research any dimension of the client situation.
   a. First, conduct a key-word search in a database of articles. Indicate which resource you chose to research in (e.g., HeinOnline, Westlaw, Lexis); explain your choice.
   b. State your search; explain exactly what you asked the program to do.
   c. List up to three pertinent articles that your search yielded.
   d. Select the most promising of the articles. State its author, title, law review name and volume, starting page number, and date.
   e. State several useful points that you learned from the article.
   f. Identify at least three primary authorities cited in the article that you would read next.
   g. Finally, search for articles in a legal periodicals index. Identify the index that you used, and at least one useful index topic. Did your index research yield any additional articles? Explain.

4. To explore *American Law Reports* annotations (not *ALR Federal*), research the client's situation with a close factual focus on how state courts have handled cases in which landlords have sought to evict tenants because they are keeping pets.
   a. If you research online, state your search and explain exactly what you asked the program to do. If you research in print, state one or more useful index topic(s).
   b. State the title, citation (volume number, series, and page number), and author of the most pertinent ALR annotation that you found.
   c. State several useful points you learned from the ALR annotation.
   d. If the ALR annotation covers West Virginia cases, provide the following information for each such case: the name, court, and date.

5. To explore Restatements of the Law, research this variation on Mr. Wilson's situation: a standard rule of contract law, known as the *statute of frauds*, is that contracts involving land must be in writing and signed by the party to be charged to be enforced. If there were no written lease, Mr. Wilson might have an argument to make. To determine whether such an argument would apply to a lease, research in the Restatement (Second) of Contracts.
   a. Indicate which resource you chose to research in (e.g., HeinOnline, Lexis, or Westlaw); explain your choice.
   b. Explain how you found the pertinent Restatement section.
   c. Identify the pertinent Restatement section.
   d. Provide your answer to the question posed.

Make Connections

Before you start researching a client's situation, it is almost always a good idea to contemplate for a bit what you think is just, given the situation. This will help you focus on a result that is both fair and legally sound. In this chapter, you have seen some early indications of the controlling law for our client situations; so far, do they accord with your sense of what is just? As you begin to work on Mr. Wilson's situation, what do you think would be a just rule?

Answers to Test Your Knowledge Questions

1. Two differences between secondary sources and primary authorities are that secondary sources are not written by lawmakers acting in a lawmaking capacity and thus do not operate as legal rules, whereas primary authorities are created through lawmaking processes and have the force of law.

2. Key attributes for each of the following secondary sources are:
   - Treatise — deep coverage of a single subject
   - Encyclopedia — general coverage of many subjects
   - Legal periodical article — very detailed coverage of a specific, possibly arcane, topic, which may include arguments for reform
   - Restatements of the Law — best rule of national case law developed by an esteemed group of experts
   - Jury instruction guide — jurisdiction's rule of law, created for litigation purposes
   - *American Law Reports* annotation — detailed analysis of many court rulings on a narrow issue

3. For these situations, good choices would be:
   - You are researching an area of law that is fairly new to you and thus seek a general overview — treatise or encyclopedia
   - You are researching a case where your client's legal position is not in accord with current law, so you are looking for arguments in favor of changing in the law — legal periodical article
   - You are looking for a concise statement of the legal rule that applies in most states — Restatement of the Law
   - You are looking for a concise statement of the legal rule that applies in your jurisdiction to frame the lawsuit that you are preparing for your client — jury instruction guide
   - You are looking for the different ways that courts around the country have ruled on your narrow legal topic — *American Law Reports* annotation

4. If I were citing a Restatement rule, the Restatement rule would be the cited source, a case in my jurisdiction would be the citing source, and my purpose would be to determine whether my jurisdiction has adopted the Restatement as law.

PRIMARY AUTHORITY FROM THE U.S.

Governments in the United States generate a dauntingly large volume of law in a dauntingly wide variety of forms. This phenomenon is traceable in part to the fact that the United States consists of both a federal government and a collection of state governments[1] — and indeed a collection of local governments as well. The other explanation is that ours is a tripartite governing system, with each branch — judiciary, legislature, executive — set up to make law and to interact with the other branches. Thus, a not-small part of the expertise that you will offer your clients is the ability to present a legal analysis that combines the pertinent laws made by these various lawmaking bodies.

Of course, you must be able to find those laws first. In each of the following chapters, we first explain the type of law, its creation, and its relationship to other types of law. Then we discuss and demonstrate several sound approaches for researching that type of law.

- Chapter 4 discusses cases decided by courts.
- Chapter 5 discusses enacted law — chiefly statutes enacted by legislatures, but also constitutions and local laws.
- Chapter 6 discusses the rules of procedure and professional responsibility that govern the operation of legal proceedings and the behavior of lawyers.
- Chapter 7 discusses the various types of law that administrative agencies make while implementing the law that controls a wide range of activities.

---

1. Furthermore, the states are paralleled by U.S. territories and the District of Columbia.

CASE LAW

Many, but not all, of your research projects will take you into cases decided by the judiciary, comprised of the courts. Courts make law through cases in two different settings. First, cases form the *common law*—the law that exists where the legislative and executive branches have not already acted. Second, the judiciary decides cases by interpreting, applying, and reviewing the laws made by the legislative and executive branches.

Thus you must excel in case law research. To reach this level of skill requires an understanding of the operation of the U.S. court system and the common law. Furthermore, you need to understand how to read the cases that you find in your research and how to mine from them leads for further research. This chapter covers these two topics and then covers several recommended approaches to researching case law.

First, a vocabulary note: Lawyers use the word *case* to refer to several things: a client's matter, especially if it involves a dispute; a dispute that has become litigation; and what a court writes when it decides a case. To make things more complicated, the text that sets out a court's outcome and reasoning is also called a *decision* or *opinion*. *Case law* is used for a set of cases that together constitute the law on a topic.

THE U.S. CASE LAW SYSTEM

Hundreds, if not thousands, of courts in the United States decide cases every week on an amazingly wide array of subjects. The large number of such cases is partly because the U.S. legal system is a federal system: not only do we have federal courts, but each state has a set of courts as well.

Round 1: State Courts

To illustrate various topics about state courts and case law in general, consider a case pertinent to the Bower's Bounty situation arising in Kansas, in which our client has been sued by a former employee alleging defamation. That case, *Luttrell v. United Telephone System, Inc.,* appears in Box 4.1. Please read it carefully before proceeding. *Luttrell* provides a basis for discussion of the following topics: subjects handled by state courts, the structure of state courts, resolution of a case by a lower court, the reasons for appeals, precedent and stare decisis, mandatory versus persuasive precedent, and the ways that a case can become bad law.

Luttrell presents a good example of what state courts do in that it involves a tort, an area of law developed in large part through common law adjudication. Other classic subjects of state court adjudication are interpretations of state statutes and state constitutions.

The *Luttrell* case was decided by the Kansas state courts, which exemplify a typical state court structure. The major courts[1] of the State of Kansas are the various district courts based in counties, the Kansas Court of Appeals, and the Kansas Supreme Court. Other states have several courts at the intermediate level or no intermediate-level courts at all. The *Luttrell* case began in the district court for Johnson County; the decision in Box 4.1 was rendered by the Kansas Court of Appeals; the Kansas Supreme Court granted review and, in a brief decision not shown here,[2] affirmed and adopted the decision in Box 4.1.

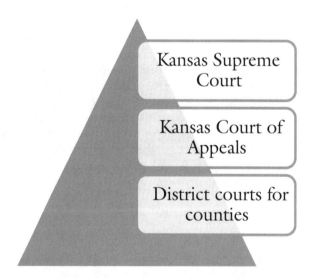

Luttrell illustrates how most cases in litigation are resolved in the lower courts these days. An employee, Marvin Luttrell, as *plaintiff,* sued his employer, alleging that coworkers made defamatory statements about him. The employer, as *defendant,* made a *motion to dismiss,* which is simply a formal request to the court to end the case on the grounds that the claim was legally deficient; the court granted this motion. This means that the judge decided the case based just on the framing of the case by the plaintiff and the legal

---

1. Kansas also has municipal courts that handle minor issues such as traffic offenses.
2. *Luttrell v. United Tele. Sys., Inc.,* 695 P.2d 1279 (Kan. 1985).

Box 4.1   STATE CASE FROM WESTLAW (Employment Defamation)

Luttrell v. United Telephone System, Inc., 9 Kan.App.2d 620 (1984)

683 P.2d 1292, 47 A.L.R.4th 669

---

9 Kan.App.2d 620
Court of Appeals of Kansas.

Marvin G. LUTTRELL, Appellant,
v.
UNITED TELEPHONE SYSTEM, INC., Appellee.

No. 56031. | July 19, 1984. | Review Granted Sept. 6,
1984.

Employee brought action against employer alleging that
statements by managerial employees concerning
employee's job performance constituted defamation. The
District Court, Johnson County, Phillip L. Woodworth, J.,
granted employer's motion to dismiss for failure to state
claim upon which relief may be granted, and employee
appealed. The Court of Appeals, Parks, J., held that
remarks communicated by one corporate employee to
another concerning job performance of third employee are
publication for purposes of defamation against employer;
thus, claim was improperly dismissed.

Reversed and remanded.

West Headnotes (8)

[1]   **Libel and Slander**
        ⟜Nature and elements of defamation in general

        Tort of defamation includes both libel and
        slander.

        8 Cases that cite this headnote

[2]   **Libel and Slander**
        ⟜Nature and elements of defamation in general

        Elements of defamation include false and
        defamatory words communicated to a third
        person which result in harm to the reputation of
        the person defamed.

23 Cases that cite this headnote

[3]   **Corporations and Business Organizations**
        ⟜Defamation

        Corporation may be liable for defamatory
        utterances of its agent which are made while
        acting within scope of his authority.

        2 Cases that cite this headnote

[4]   **Libel and Slander**
        ⟜Injury to reputation

        Laws of libel and slander protect reputation.

        Cases that cite this headnote

[5]   **Libel and Slander**
        ⟜Common business interest

        Communication made within work situation is
        qualifiedly privileged if it is made in good faith
        on any subject matter in which person
        communicating has an interest, or in reference to
        which he has a duty, if it is made to a person
        having corresponding interest or duty.

        11 Cases that cite this headnote

[6]   **Libel and Slander**
        ⟜As to character of employee

        Employer who is evaluating or investigating
        employee in good faith and within bounds of
        employment relationship is protected from threat

Box 4.1   *(continued)*

Luttrell v. United Telephone System, Inc., 9 Kan.App.2d 620 (1984)

683 P.2d 1292, 47 A.L.R.4th 669

of defamation suits by requirement that employee prove that employer acted with knowledge of falsity or reckless disregard for the truth.

14 Cases that cite this headnote

[7] **Libel and Slander**
☞Publication

Remarks made in course and scope of employment by one corporate employee and communicated to second corporate employee concerning job performance of third employee are publication for purposes of defamation action against corporate employer. K.S.A. 60–212(b)(6).

13 Cases that cite this headnote

[8] **Libel and Slander**
☞Form and requisites in general

Allegation by employee that managerial employees of corporate employer had made false statements about his job performance was sufficient to state defamation action.

3 Cases that cite this headnote

*620 **1293 *Syllabus by the Court*

Remarks made in the course and scope of employment by one corporate employee and communicated to a second corporate employee concerning the job performance of a third employee constitute publication for the purposes of a defamation action against the corporate employer.

Attorneys and Law Firms

Richard M. Smith of Smith & Winter-Smith, Mound City, for appellant.

Paul Hasty, Jr. of Wallace, Saunders, Austin, Brown & Enochs, Chartered, Overland Park, for appellee.

Before FOTH, C.J., and PARKS and SWINEHART, JJ.

Opinion

PARKS, Judge:

Plaintiff Marvin G. Luttrell appeals the dismissal of his defamation action against the defendant, United Telephone System, Inc.

Plaintiff alleges in his petition that several managerial employees of defendant maliciously communicated defamatory remarks about him between themselves while acting within the scope of their employment. Particularly, he alleges that on or about April 6 or 7 of 1982, Mr. R.H. Baranek, an employee of defendant, stated to Mr. R.L. Flint, plaintiff's supervisor, that plaintiff was illegally taping telephone conversations on April 1 and that Baranek had requested him to stop but plaintiff persisted in this illegal activity the rest of the afternoon despite the direct order given him to stop by his supervisor. He further alleged that the communication of the same defamatory information was made by Mr. Flint to Mr. T.V. Tregenza and by Mr. Tregenza to Mr. W. Soble, all while acting within the scope of their employment. Defendant filed a motion to dismiss pursuant to K.S.A. 60–212(b)(6) on the grounds that intracorporate communications did not constitute "publication." The trial court sustained the motion to dismiss for failure to state a claim upon which relief may be granted.

[1] [2] [3] The tort of defamation includes both libel and slander. The elements of the wrong include false and defamatory words (*Hein v. Lacy,* 228 Kan. 249, 259, 616 P.2d 277 [1980]) communicated ***621** to a third person (*Schulze v. Coykendall,* 218 Kan. 653, 657, 545 P.2d 392 [1976]) which result in harm to the reputation of the person defamed. *Gobin v. Globe Publishing Co.,* 232 Kan. 1, 6, 649 P.2d 1239 (1982) (*Gobin III*). A corporation may be liable for the defamatory utterances of its agent which are made while acting within the scope of his authority. *Bourn v. State Bank,* 116 Kan. 231, 235, 226 P. 769 (1924).

Box 4.1   *(continued)*

Luttrell v. United Telephone System, Inc., 9 Kan.App.2d 620 (1984)

683 P.2d 1292, 47 A.L.R.4th 669

In this case, the defendant argued and the district court agreed that there can be no communication to a third person, or "publication," when the defamatory words are exchanged by agents of a single corporate defendant. This issue of first impression is more precisely whether interoffice communications between supervisory employees of a corporation, acting within the scope and course of their employment, regarding the work of another employee of the corporation, constitute publication to a third person sufficient for a defamation action.

There is a considerable division of authority concerning this issue. For example, courts recently considering the laws of Nevada, Missouri, Arkansas, Georgia and Louisiana have all accepted the assertion that intracorporate defamation is simply the corporation talking to itself and not publication. See *e.g., Jones v. Golden Spike Corp.,* 97 Nev. 24, 623 P.2d 970 (1981); *Ellis v. Jewish Hospital of St. Louis,* 581 S.W.2d 850 (Mo.App.1979); *Halsell v. Kimberly-Clark Corp.,* 683 F.2d 285 (8th Cir.1982); *Monahan v. Sims,* 163 Ga.App. 354, 294 S.E.2d 548 (1982); *Commercial Union Ins. Co. v. Melikyan,* 424 So.2d 1114 (La.App.1982). The contrary conclusion has been reached in courts applying the laws of Kentucky, Massachusetts, New **1294 York and California. See *e.g., Brewer v. American Nat. Ins. Co.,* 636 F.2d 150 (6th Cir.1980); *Arsenault v. Allegheny Airlines, Inc,* 485 F.Supp. 1373 (D.Mass.), *aff'd* 636 F.2d 1199 (1st Cir.1980); *Pirre v. Printing Developments, Inc.,* 468 F.Supp. 1028 (S.D.N.Y.), *aff'd* 614 F.2d 1290 (2d Cir.1979); *Kelly v. General Telephone Co.,* 136 Cal.App.3d 278, 186 Cal.Rptr. 184 (1982). The latter opinions have held that while communications between supervisory employees of a corporation concerning a third employee may be qualifiedly privileged, they are still publication. Prosser also favors the view that such communications are publication and dismisses those cases holding otherwise as confusing *622 publication with privilege. Prosser, Law of Torts § 113, p. 767 n. 70 (4th ed. 1971).

[4] Undeniably, the district court's holding in this case is not without support or technical appeal; however, we believe it ignores the nature of the civil injury sought to be protected in a defamation action. Damage to one's reputation is the essence and gravamen of an action for defamation. It is reputation which is defamed, reputation which is injured, reputation which is protected by the laws of libel and slander. *Gobin III,* 232 Kan. at 6, 649 P.2d 1239. Certainly, damage to one's reputation within a

corporate community may be just as devastating as that effected by defamation spread to the outside. Thus, the injury caused by intracorporate defamation should not be disregarded simply because the corporation can be sued as an individual entity.

[5] Defendant argues that corporate employers must be free to evaluate and comment on their employees' work performance and that this freedom will be unduly restrained if they are liable for intracorporate defamation. However, the law in this state has already extended protection to comments made within a work situation by means of a qualified privilege. A communication is qualifiedly privileged if it is made in good faith on any subject matter in which the person communicating has an interest, or in reference to which he has a duty, if it is made to a person having a corresponding interest or duty. The essential elements of a qualifiedly privileged communication are good faith, an interest to be upheld, a statement limited in its scope to the upholding of such interest and publication in a proper manner only to proper parties. *Dobbyn v. Nelson,* 2 Kan.App.2d 358, 360, 579 P.2d 721, *aff'd* 225 Kan. 56, 587 P.2d 315 (1978). Thus, in *Dobbyn* the Court held that a letter written by an employee of the Kansas State University library concerning the conduct of another employee and transmitted to the second employee's superior was qualifiedly privileged. *Dobbyn,* 2 Kan.App.2d at 361, 579 P.2d 721. As a result, the plaintiff was required to prove that the defendants acted with knowledge of falsity or reckless disregard for the truth before the privilege could be overcome. See also *Scarpelli v. Jones,* 229 Kan. 210, 216, 626 P.2d 785 (1981).

[6] By virtue of the qualified privilege, the employer who is evaluating or investigating an employee in good faith and within the bounds of the employment relationship is protected from the threat of defamation suits by the enhanced burden of proof *623 which the plaintiff would have to bear. We see no reason for greater freedom from liability for defamation to be accorded the corporate employer than that already available to all employers through the qualified privilege.

[7] [8] We conclude that remarks communicated by one corporate employee to another concerning the job performance of a third employee are publication for the purposes of a defamation action against the employer. Since the dismissal motion was granted in this case prior to the commencement of any discovery, we make no findings concerning the possible application of qualified privilege to the communications alleged.

Box 4.1   *(continued)*

Luttrell v. United Telephone System, Inc., 9 Kan.App.2d 620 (1984)

683 P.2d 1292, 47 A.L.R.4th 669

The dismissal for failure to state a claim upon which relief may be granted is reversed and the case is remanded for further proceedings.

All Citations

9 Kan.App.2d 620, 683 P.2d 1292, 47 A.L.R.4th 669

End of Document   © 2015 Thomson Reuters. No claim to original U.S. Government Works.

arguments of the lawyers; the case did not proceed far enough to get to a jury. Many cases are decided by a judge in this way, on a motion to dismiss or, a bit later in the case, on a *motion for summary judgment*. Very few cases actually go to trial and yield a *jury verdict*; in that rare situation, a group of people from various backgrounds decides what happened and renders a decision.

The *Luttrell* case illustrates the function of appellate courts. If efficiency were the sole concern of a legal system, one decision per dispute would suffice; however, as the existence of appellate courts demonstrates, other concerns are also present. The first of the two appellate courts, which is considered intermediate because it is in the middle of a three-tier structure, focuses on correcting errors that the lower court may have made. The highest court focuses on making law. However, both appellate courts inevitably do some of each. At both levels, the case is heard by a panel, generally consisting of three judges at the intermediate court or seven or nine justices at the highest court. Appellate outcomes vary from affirming the lower court to reversing the lower court. As indicated in the last sentence in *Luttrell*, the lower court ruling was reversed, and the case was remanded (sent back) for further proceedings.

Luttrell also illustrates well the operation of the common law and the importance of the judicial decision. In the common law tradition, judges make law when they render decisions. They pronounce legal rules, and they explain how the rules apply to the facts of the dispute before them. This *ratio decidendi* underlies the legal force, or *precedent*, that the case has in controlling future situations under the legal principle of *stare decisis*. The full Latin phrase is *stare decisis et non quieta movere*—roughly translated, "stand by decisions and not disturb settled matters." Thus, once a dispute with certain features has been decided a particular way, stare decisis dictates that other disputes with those features be decided the same way. This principle promotes both fairness (because similar situations are treated similarly) and predictability (because people and organizations can plan their affairs). As similar disputes with new features arise, the court decides those cases, so that over time, a body of cases accrues and a refined rule of law evolves.

Precedent operates hierarchically within a court system, so each case is controlling only insofar as a court's *jurisdiction*, or power to decide a case, extends. That is, a decision is *binding* or *mandatory* within its jurisdiction; outside its jurisdiction, it is only *persuasive precedent*. Thus, a state supreme court decision binds the courts within its system but generally not those outside that system. A decision of an intermediate court does not bind the highest court. The lowest courts are bound by decisions of both the intermediate court of appeals and the highest courts, but not their fellow lowest courts, although the latter are generally considered strongly persuasive.

Luttrell is a strong example of the creation of common law. The topic is defamation, which is based on the defendant's publication of a false statement about the plaintiff; defamation is a claim that is in large part controlled by state case law.[3] In part, the decision cites to well-established rules of defamation law

---

3. The exception is where there are constitutional free speech implications, but that is not so here.

already created by Kansas courts (in the paragraphs preceded by the numbers 1-3 and 5), as stare decisis requires. Yet the *Luttrell* case raised a new question for the Kansas court: whether there could be defamation based on a communication occurring totally within the defendant corporation. In considering this question, there were no Kansas cases to rely on, so the court turned to cases from other states for guidance (in the paragraph beginning "There is a considerable division of authority") and discussed the general contours and policies of Kansas law. It then pronounced the new rule on this topic (answering the question affirmatively), thereby creating the rule not only for the *Luttrell* case, but other Kansas cases as well.[4]

Closely related to a case as precedent is the critical question of whether a case remains *good law*. A decision that you find in your research may lose force, or become bad law, in several ways. The first is through *subsequent history*: the case is not from the highest court, and it is ruled on adversely or displaced by the decision of a higher court in the same litigation. Second, a case may lose force through *adverse treatment*: a case in different litigation later treats it adversely. Third, a case may become bad law through lawmaking by another branch of government, typically the legislature. It is through these methods that the law created in cases evolves to reflect new insights or social change.

In the *Luttrell* example, you could rely on the court of appeals decision because the supreme court affirmed it and indeed adopted the decision; thus, it is not undermined by subsequent history.[5] But if, for example, the Kansas Supreme Court decided twenty years after *Luttrell* that a communication solely within an organization was no longer a publication for defamation purposes, *Luttrell* would be *overruled* and thus no longer good law. Or if the Kansas Legislature enacted a statute defining defamation to exclude a communication solely within a corporation, *Luttrell* would be legislatively overruled and no longer good law.

---

4. The case may or may not have continued in litigation after the appeal. Often, once the legal issues have been resolved, cases settle.

5. If the Kansas Supreme Court had written a more extensive decision discussing the facts and rule, you would rely on that decision in lieu of the court of appeals decision.

Round 2: Federal Courts

To illustrate various topics about federal courts and additional points about cases in general, consider a case pertinent to the de la Cruz situation, in which our client was suspended from public school in Pennsylvania for shaving a statement into his hair. Portions of the case of *B.H. v. Easton Area School District* appear in Box 4.2. Please review them before proceeding.[6] *Easton* provides a basis for discussion of the following topics: subjects handled by federal courts, the structure of the federal courts, panel and en banc decisions, split opinions, published versus unpublished opinions, and appeal as of right versus discretionary review.

The issue in *Easton* is a matter of free speech, which is a facet of federal constitutional law. Constitutional law and the interpretation of federal statutes are the mainstays of the federal courts.

The federal court system is large: it has nearly 100 district courts (one to four per state or territory), where motions are decided and trials are held; twelve regional circuit courts of appeals (eleven numbered courts, each covering a set of states, and one for the District of Columbia); the U.S. Supreme Court, which is the highest court of the land; and various specialized courts.[7] Thus, as to a topic of federal law, you will rely mostly on U.S. Supreme Court cases and on court of appeals cases from the circuit of your client's situation, which are binding. Cases from other courts of appeals are persuasive, and federal district court cases from the district court where your client's situation is set can be highly persuasive.

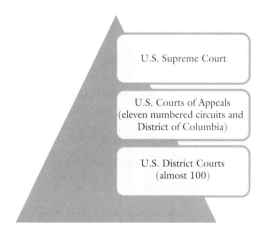

U.S. Supreme Court

U.S. Courts of Appeals (eleven numbered circuits and District of Columbia)

U.S. District Courts (almost 100)

---

6. You will see that the judges of the Third Circuit disagreed on how to rule in a similar case, including on what the legal framework should be. The framework in the second paragraph of the opinion by Judge Smith controls. For purposes of our client's situation, we would likely argue that the statement was not plainly lewd and could be interpreted as commenting on social issues, so it could not be categorically restricted; this would raise the issue of disruption.

7. These courts hear cases on topics such as international trade, claims against the government, and tax matters, at the initial level or on appeal.

Box 4.2   **FEDERAL COURT OF APPEALS CASE FROM LEXIS (Constitutional Rights of Public School Student)**

⚠ Caution
As of: September 16, 2015 10:53 AM EDT

B.H. v. Easton Area Sch. Dist.

United States Court of Appeals for the Third Circuit

April 10, 2012, Argued; August 16, 2012, Rehearing En Banc Ordered; February 20, 2013, Argued En Banc; August 5, 2013, Opinion Filed

No. 11-2067

Reporter
725 F.3d 293; 2013 U.S. App. LEXIS 16087; 2013 WL 3970093

B.H., A MINOR, BY AND THROUGH HER MOTHER; JENNIFER HAWK; K.M., A MINOR BY AND THROUGH HER MOTHER; AMY MCDONALD-MARTINEZ v. EASTON AREA SCHOOL DISTRICT, Appellant

Subsequent History: US Supreme Court certiorari denied by *Easton Area Sch. Dist. v. B. H., 134 S. Ct. 1515, 188 L. Ed. 2d 450, 2014 U.S. LEXIS 1839 (U.S., Mar. 10, 2014)*

Prior History: [**1] On Appeal from the United States District Court For the Eastern District of Pennsylvania. (D.C. Civil Action No. 5-10-cv-06283). District Judge: Honorable Mary A. McLaughlin.
B. H. v. Easton Area Sch. Dist., 827 F. Supp. 2d 392, 2011 U.S. Dist. LEXIS 39483 (E.D. Pa., 2011)

Core Terms

bracelets, lewd, majority opinion, plainly, offensive, boobies, vulgar, concurrence, school district, sexual, ban, schools, obscenity, plausibly, BREAST, social issues, commenting, awareness, categorically, message, illegal drug use, observer, joined, breast cancer, Marks, middle school, disruption, ambiguous, cases, profane

Case Summary

Overview

HOLDINGS: [1]-Plainly lewd speech, which offended for the same reasons obscenity offended, could be categorically restricted regardless of whether it commented on political or social issues; [2]-Speech that did not rise to the level of plainly lewd but that a reasonable observer could interpret as lewd could be categorically restricted as long as it could not plausibly be interpreted as commenting on political or social issues; [3]-Speech that did not rise to the level of plainly lewd and that could plausibly be interpreted as commenting on political or social issues could not be categorically restricted; [4]-Under the *First Amendment*, because the bracelets the students wore that were part of a nationally recognized breast-cancer-awareness campaign were not plainly lewd and because they commented on a social issue, they could not be categorically banned by the school district.

Outcome

Judgment affirmed.

LexisNexis® Headnotes

Constitutional Law > ... > Fundamental Freedoms > Freedom of Speech > Obscenity

Education Law > Students > Freedom of Speech > Political & Symbolic Speech

HN1 The scope of a school's authority to restrict lewd, vulgar, profane, or plainly offensive speech is defined by the following framework: (1) plainly lewd speech, which offends for the same reasons obscenity offends, may be categorically restricted regardless of whether it comments on political or social issues; (2) speech that does not rise to the level of plainly lewd but that a reasonable observer could interpret as lewd may be categorically restricted as long as it cannot plausibly be interpreted as commenting on political or social issues; and (3) speech that does not rise to the level of plainly lewd and that could plausibly be interpreted as commenting on political or social issues may not be categorically restricted.

Civil Procedure > Appeals > Appellate Jurisdiction > Interlocutory Orders

HN2 *28 U.S.C.S. § 1292(a)(1)* grants appellate jurisdiction over interlocutory orders of the district courts

Box 4.2   *(continued)*

725 F.3d 293, *293; 2013 U.S. App. LEXIS 16087, **1

HN37 Student expression may not be suppressed simply because it gives rise to some slight, easily overlooked disruption, including but not limited to a showing of mild curiosity by other students, discussion and comment among students, or even some hostile remarks or discussion outside of the classrooms by other students.

> Education Law > ... > Gender & Sex Discrimination > Title IX > Scope of Title IX

HN38 Under Title IX, students may sue federally-funded schools that act with deliberate indifference to harassment that is so severe, pervasive, and objectively offensive that the victim students are effectively denied equal access to an institution's resources and opportunities.

> Civil Procedure > Appeals > Reviewability of Lower Court Decisions > Preservation for Review

HN39 An appellate court generally refuses to consider issues that the parties have not raised below.

> Constitutional Law > ... > Fundamental Freedoms > Freedom of Speech > Political Speech

HN40 The timeliness of political speech is particularly important.

Counsel: Keely J. Collins, John E. Freund, III [ARGUED],Jeffrey T. Tucker, King, Spry, Herman, Freund & Faul, Bethlehem, PA, Counsel for Appellant.

Seth F. Kreimer, University of Pennsylvania School of Law, Philadelphia, PA; Mary Catherine Roper [ARGUED], American Civil Liberties Union of Pennsylvania, Philadelphia, PA; Molly M. Tack-Hooper, Berger & Montague, Philadelphia, PA; Witold J. Walczak, American Civil Liberties Union, Pittsburgh, PA, Counsel for Appellees.

Sean A. Fields, Pennsylvania School Boards Association, Mechanicsburg, PA, Counsel for Amicus Appellant.

Wilson M. Brown, III, Kathryn E. Deal, Drinker, Biddle & Reath, Philadelphia, PA; Rory Wicks, Gary L. Sirota, Encinitas, CA; Amy R. Arroyo, Carlsbad, CA; Wayne Pollock, Dechert LLP, Philadelphia, PA; Frank D. LoMonte, Laura Napoli, Student Press Law Center, Arlington, VA; Terry L. Fromson, Carol E. Tracey, Women's Law Project, Philadelphia, PA; David L. Cohen, Philadelphia, PA, Counsel for Amici Appellees.

Judges: Before: McKEE, Chief Judge, SLOVITER, SCIRICA, RENDELL, [**2] AMBRO, FUENTES, SMITH, FISHER, CHAGARES, JORDAN, HARDIMAN, GREENAWAY, JR., VANASKIE, and GREENBERG, Circuit Judges. HARDIMAN, Circuit Judge, dissenting with whom CHAGARES, JORDAN, GREENAWAY, JR., and GREENBERG, join. GREENAWAY, JR., Circuit Judge, dissenting, with whom CHAGARES, JORDAN, HARDIMAN and GREENBERG, join.

Opinion by: SMITH

Opinion

[*297] SMITH, *Circuit Judge*, with whom McKEE, *Chief Judge*, SLOVITER, SCIRICA, RENDELL, AMBRO, FUENTES, FISHER, and VANASKIE, *Circuit Judges* join.

Once again, we are asked to find the balance between a student's right to free speech and a school's need to control its educational environment. In this case, two middle-school students purchased bracelets bearing the slogan "I ♥ boobies! [*298] (KEEP A BREAST)" as part of a nationally recognized breast-cancer-awareness campaign. The Easton Area School District banned the bracelets, relying on its authority under *Bethel School District No. 403 v. Fraser, 478 U.S. 675, 106 S. Ct. 3159, 92 L. Ed. 2d 549 (1986),* to restrict vulgar, lewd, profane, or plainly offensive speech, and its authority under *Tinker v. Des Moines Independent Community School District, 393 U.S. 503, 89 S. Ct. 733, 21 L. Ed. 2d 731 (1969),* to restrict speech that is reasonably expected to substantially disrupt the school. The District [**3] Court held that the ban violated the students' rights to free speech and issued a preliminary injunction against the ban.

We agree with the District Court that neither *Fraser* nor *Tinker* can sustain the bracelet ban. The scope of a school's authority to restrict lewd, vulgar, profane, or plainly offensive speech under *Fraser* is a novel question left open by the Supreme Court, and one which we must now resolve. We hold that *Fraser*, as modified by the Supreme Court's later reasoning in *Morse v. Frederick, 551 U.S. 393, 127 S. Ct. 2618, 168 L. Ed. 2d 290 (2007),* sets up *HN1* the following framework: (1) plainly lewd speech, which offends for the same reasons obscenity offends, may be categorically restricted regardless of whether it comments on political or social issues, (2) speech that does not rise to the level of plainly lewd but that a reasonable observer could

725 F.3d 293, *298; 2013 U.S. App. LEXIS 16087, **3

interpret as lewd may be categorically restricted as long as it cannot plausibly be interpreted as commenting on political or social issues, and (3) speech that does not rise to the level of plainly lewd and that could plausibly be interpreted as commenting on political or social issues may not be categorically restricted. Because the bracelets here are not plainly [**4] lewd and because they comment on a social issue, they may not be categorically banned under *Fraser*. The School District has also failed to show that the bracelets threatened to substantially disrupt the school under *Tinker*. We will therefore affirm the District Court.

I.

A. Factual background

As a "leading youth focused global breast cancer organization," the Keep A Breast Foundation tries to educate thirteen- to thirty-year-old women about breast cancer. Br. of Amicus Curiae KABF at 13. To that end, it often partners with other merchants to co-brand products that raise awareness. And because it believes that young women's "negative body image[s]" seriously inhibit their awareness of breast cancer, the Foundation's products often "seek[] to reduce the stigma by speaking to young people in a voice they can relate to." *Id.* at 14-15. If young women see such awareness projects and products as cool and trendy, the thinking goes, then they will be more willing to talk about breast cancer openly.

To "start a conversation about that taboo in a light-hearted way" and to break down inhibitions keeping young women from performing self-examinations, the Foundation began its "I ♥ Boobies!" initiative. [**5] *Id.* at 20-21. Part of the campaign included selling silicone bracelets of assorted colors emblazoned with "I ♥ Boobies! (KEEP A BREAST)" and "check y♥urself! (KEEP A BREAST)." *Id.* at 21-22. The Foundation's website address (www.keep-a-breast.org) and motto ("art. education. awareness. action.") appear on the inside of the bracelet. *Id.*

As intended, the "I ♥ Boobies" initiative was a hit with young women, quickly becoming one of the Foundation's "most successful and high profile educational campaigns." *Id.* at 20-21. Two of the young women drawn to the bracelets were middle-school

students B.H. and K.M. They [*299] purchased the bracelets with their mothers before the 2010-2011 school year—B.H. because she saw "a lot of [her] friends wearing" the bracelets and wanted to learn about them, and K.M. because of the bracelet's popularity and awareness message. App. 72, 92, 106, 442.

But the bracelets were more than just a new fashion trend. K.M.'s purchase prompted her to become educated about breast cancer in young women. The girls wore their bracelets both to commemorate friends and relatives who had suffered from breast cancer and to promote awareness among their friends. Indeed, their bracelets [**6] started conversations about breast cancer and did so far more effectively than the more-traditional pink ribbon. App. 73-74. That made sense to B.H., who observed that "no one really notices" the pink ribbon, whereas the "bracelets are new and . . . more appealing to teenagers." App. 74.

B.H., K.M., and three other students wore the "I ♥ boobies! (KEEP A BREAST)" bracelets at Easton Area Middle School during the 2010-2011 school year. A few teachers, after observing the students wear the bracelets every day for several weeks, considered whether they should take action. The teachers' responses varied: One found the bracelets offensive because they trivialized breast cancer. Others feared that the bracelets might lead to offensive comments or invite inappropriate touching. But school administrators also believed that middle-school boys did not need the bracelets as an excuse to make sexual statements or to engage in inappropriate touching. *See, e.g.*, Viglianti Test., App. 196, 198 (testifying that such incidents "happened before the bracelets" and were "going to happen after the bracelets" because "sexual curiosity between boys and girls in the middle school is . . . a natural and continuing [**7] thing").

In mid- to late September, four or five teachers asked the eighth-grade assistant principal, Amy Braxmeier, whether they should require students to remove the bracelets. The seventh-grade assistant principal, Anthony Viglianti, told the teachers that they should ask students to remove "wristbands that have the word 'boobie' written on them," App. 343, even though there were no reports that the bracelets had caused any in-school disruptions or inappropriate comments.[1]

[1] In mid-October before the ban was publicly announced, school administrators received some unrelated reports of inappropriate touching, but neither the word "boobies" nor the bracelets were considered a cause of these incidents.

Box 4.2   *(continued)*

725 F.3d 293, *299; 2013 U.S. App. LEXIS 16087, **7

With Breast Cancer Awareness Month approaching in October, school administrators anticipated that the "I ♥ boobies! (KEEP A BREAST)" bracelets might reappear.[2] The school was scheduled to observe Breast Cancer Awareness Month on October 28, so the day before, administrators publicly announced, for the first time, the ban on bracelets containing the word "boobies." Using the word "boobies" in his announcement, Viglianti notified students of the ban over the public-address system, and a student [**8] did the same on the school's television station. The Middle School still encouraged students to wear the traditional pink, and it provided teachers who donated to Susan G. Komen for the Cure with either a pin bearing the slogan "Passionately Pink for the Cure" or a T-shirt reading "Real Rovers Wear Pink."

[*300] Later that day, a school security guard noticed B.H. wearing an "I ♥ boobies! (KEEP A BREAST)" bracelet and ordered her to remove it. B.H. refused. After meeting with Braxmeier, B.H. relented, removed her bracelet, and returned to lunch. No disruption occurred at any time that day.

The following day, B.H. and K.M. each wore their "I ♥ boobies! (KEEP A BREAST)" bracelets to observe the Middle School's Breast Cancer Awareness Day. The day was uneventful—until lunchtime. Once in the cafeteria, both girls were instructed by a school security guard to remove their bracelets. Both girls refused. Hearing this encounter, another girl, R.T., stood up and similarly refused to take off her bracelet. Confronted by this act of solidarity, the security guard permitted the girls to finish eating [**9] their lunches before escorting them to Braxmeier's office. Again, the girls' actions caused no disruption in the cafeteria, though R.T. told Braxmeier that one boy had immaturely commented either that he also "love[d] boobies" or that he "love[d] her boobies."

Braxmeier spoke to all three girls, and R.T. agreed to remove her bracelet. B.H. and K.M. stood firm, however, citing their rights to freedom of speech. The Middle School administrators were having none of it. They punished B.H. and K.M. by giving each of them one and a half days of in-school suspension and by forbidding them from attending the Winter Ball. The administrators notified the girls' families, explaining only that B.H. and K.M. were being disciplined for "disrespect," "defiance," and "disruption."

News of the bracelets quickly reached the rest of the Easton Area School District, which instituted a district-wide ban on the "I ♥ boobies! (KEEP A BREAST)" bracelets, effective on November 9, 2010. The only bracelet-related incident reported by school administrators occurred weeks after the district-wide ban: Two girls were talking about their bracelets at lunch when a boy who overheard them interrupted and said something [**10] like "I want boobies." He also made an inappropriate gesture with two red spherical candies. The boy admitted his "rude" comment and was suspended for one day.[3]

This was not the first time the Middle School had banned clothing that it found distasteful. Indeed, the School District's dress-code policy prohibits "clothing imprinted with nudity, vulgarity, obscenity, profanity, and double entendre pictures or slogans."[4] Under the policy, seventh-grade students at the Middle School have been asked to remove clothing promoting Hooters and Big Pecker's Bar & Grill, as well as clothing bearing the phrase "Save the ta-tas" (another breast-cancer-awareness slogan). Typically, students are disciplined only if they actually refuse to remove the offending apparel when asked to do so.

B. Procedural history

Through their mothers, B.H. and K.M. sued the School District under *42 U.S.C. § 1983*.[5] Compl., ECF No. [**11] 1 ¶ 3, B.H. v. [*301] Easton Area Sch. Dist., No. 5:10-CV-06283-MAM (E.D. Pa. Nov. 15, 2010). They sought a temporary restraining order allowing them to attend the Winter Ball and a preliminary injunction against the bracelet ban. *B.H. v. Easton Area Sch. Dist., 827 F. Supp. 2d 392, 394 (E.D. Pa. 2011)*. At the District Court's urging, the School District reversed course and

---

[2] The Middle School permits students to wear the Foundation's "check y♥urself (KEEP A BREAST)" bracelets.

[3] After the district-wide ban was in place, there were several incidents of middle-school boys inappropriately touching girls, but they were unrelated to the "I ♥ boobies! (KEEP A BREAST)" bracelets.

[4] B.H. and K.M. do not assert a facial challenge to the constitutionality of the dress-code policy.

[5] The District Court had both federal-question jurisdiction under *28 U.S.C. § 1331* and *§ 1983* jurisdiction under 28 U.S.C. § 1343(a)(3). *See Max v. Republican Comm. of Lancaster Cnty., 587 F.3d 198, 199 n.1 (3d Cir. 2009)*.

Box 4.2   *(continued)*

725 F.3d 293, *301; 2013 U.S. App. LEXIS 16087, **11

permitted B.H. and K.M. to attend the Winter Ball while retaining the option to impose a comparable punishment if the bracelet ban was upheld. *Id*. The District Court accordingly denied the motion for a temporary restraining order. *Id*.

The District Court conducted an evidentiary hearing on the request for a preliminary injunction. It soon became clear that the School District's rationale for disciplining B.H. and K.M. had shifted. Although B.H.'s and K.M.'s disciplinary letters indicated only that they were being disciplined for "disrespect," "defiance," and "disruption," the School District ultimately based **[**12]** the ban on its dress-code policy[6] together with the bracelets' alleged sexual innuendo. According to the School District's witnesses, the Middle School assistant principals had conferred and concluded that the bracelets "conveyed a sexual double entendre" that could be harmful and confusing to students of different physical and sexual developmental levels. Sch. Dist.'s Br. at 9. And the principals believed that middle-school students, who often have immature views of sex, were particularly likely to interpret the bracelets that way. For its part, the Foundation explained that no one there "ever suggested that the phrase 'I (Heart) Boobies!' is meant to be sexy." App. 150. To that end, the Foundation had denied requests from truck stops, convenience stores, vending machine companies, and pornographers to sell the bracelets.

After the evidentiary hearing, the District Court preliminarily enjoined the School District's bracelet ban. According to the District Court, B.H. and K.M. were likely to succeed on the merits because the bracelets did not contain lewd speech under *Fraser* and did not threaten to substantially disrupt the school environment under *Tinker*. The District Court could find no other basis for regulating the student speech at issue. The School District appealed, and the District Court denied its request to stay the injunction pending this appeal.

II.

Although the District Court's preliminary injunction is not a final order, we have jurisdiction under *HN2* 28

U.S.C. § 1292(a)(1), which grants appellate jurisdiction over "[i]nterlocutory orders of the district courts . . . granting, continuing, modifying, refusing, or dissolving injunctions." *See Sypniewski v. Warren Hills Reg'l Bd. of Educ., 307 F.3d 243, 252 n.10 (3d Cir. 2002)*. **[**14]** *HN3* We review the District Court's factual findings for clear error, its legal conclusions *de novo*, and its ultimate decision to grant the preliminary injunction **[*302]** for abuse of discretion. *Id. at 252*. *HN4* Four factors determine whether a preliminary injunction is appropriate:

> (1) whether the movant has a reasonable probability of success on the merits; (2) whether the movant will be irreparably harmed by denying the injunction; (3) whether there will be greater harm to the nonmoving party if the injunction is granted; and (4) whether granting the injunction is in the public interest.

Id. (quoting *Highmark, Inc. v. UPMC Health Plan, Inc., 276 F.3d 160, 170 (3d Cir. 2001)*). The District Court concluded that all four factors weighed in favor of B.H. and K.M. In school-speech cases, though, the first factor—the likelihood of success on the merits—tends to determine which way the other factors fall. *Id. at 258*. Because the same is true here, we focus first on B.H. and K.M.'s burden to show a likelihood of success on the merits. *Id.*

III.

The School District defends the bracelet ban as an exercise of its authority to restrict lewd, vulgar, profane, or plainly offensive student speech under *Fraser*. As to **[**15]** the novel question of *Fraser*'s scope, jurists seem to agree on one thing: "[t]he mode of analysis employed in *Fraser* is not entirely clear." *Morse, 551 U.S. at 404*.[7] On this point, we think the Supreme Court's student-speech cases are more consistent than they may first appear. As we explain, *Fraser* involved only *plainly* lewd speech. We hold that, under *Fraser*, *HN5* a school may also categorically restrict speech

---

6   Even the Middle School administrators seemed unsure which words would be prohibited by the dress code. When deposed, Viglianti and principal Angela DiVietro testified that the word "breast" (as in apparel stating "keep-a-breast.org" or "breast cancer awareness") would be inappropriate because the word "breast" "can be construed as [having] a sexual connotation." **[**13]** App. 490, 497. At the District Court's evidentiary hearing, they reversed course. Viglianti stated that "keep-a-breast.org" would be appropriate "[i]n the context of Breast Cancer Awareness Month," and DiVeitro no longer believed the phrase "breast cancer awareness" was vulgar to middle-school students.

7   The rest of the Supreme Court's student-speech jurisprudence might fairly be described as opaque. *See Morse, 551 U.S. at 418* (Thomas, J., concurring) ("I am afraid that our jurisprudence now says that students have a right to speak in schools

Box 4.2   *(continued)*

725 F.3d 293, *302; 2013 U.S. App. LEXIS 16087, **15

that—although not *plainly* lewd, vulgar, or profane—could be interpreted by a reasonable observer as lewd, vulgar, or profane so long as it could not also plausibly be interpreted as commenting on a political or social issue. Because the "I ♥ boobies! (KEEP A BREAST)" bracelets are not plainly lewd and express support for a national breast-cancer-awareness campaign—unquestionably an important social issue—they may not be categorically restricted under *Fraser*.

A. The Supreme Court's decision in *Fraser*

HN6 "[A]s a general matter, the *First Amendment* means that government has no power to restrict expression because of its message, its ideas, its subject matter, or its content." *Ashcroft v. ACLU, 535 U.S. 564, 573, 122 S. Ct. 1700, 152 L. Ed. 2d 771 (2002)*. Of course, there are exceptions. *HN7* When acting as sovereign, the government is empowered to impose time, place, and manner restrictions on speech, *see Ward v. Rock Against Racism, 491 U.S. 781, 791, 109 S. Ct. 2746, 105 L. Ed. 2d 661 (1989)*, make reasonable, content-based [**17] decisions about what speech is allowed on government property that is not fully open to the public, *see Ark. Educ. Television Comm'n v. Forbes, 523 U.S. 666, 674-75,* [*303] *118 S. Ct. 1633, 140 L. Ed. 2d 875 (1998)*, decide what viewpoints to espouse in its own speech or speech that might be attributed to it, *see Johanns v. Livestock Mktg. Ass'n, 544 U.S. 550, 560, 125 S. Ct. 2055, 161 L. Ed. 2d 896 (2005)*, and categorically restrict unprotected speech, such as obscenity, *see Miller v. California, 413 U.S. 15, 23, 93 S. Ct. 2607, 37 L. Ed. 2d 419 (1973)*.[8]

HN8 Sometimes, however, the government acts in capacities that go beyond being [**18] sovereign. In

those capacities, it not only retains its sovereign authority over speech but also gains additional flexibility to regulate speech. *See In re Kendall, 712 F.3d 814, 825, 58 V.I. 718 (3d Cir. 2013)* (collecting examples). One of those other capacities is K-12 educator. *HN9* Although "students do not 'shed their constitutional rights to freedom of speech or expression at the schoolhouse gate,'" the *First Amendment* has to be "applied in light of the special characteristics of the school environment" and thus students' rights to freedom of speech "are not automatically coextensive with the rights of adults in other settings." *Morse, 551 U.S. at 396-97* (internal quotation marks and citations omitted).

The Supreme Court first expressed this principle nearly a half century ago. In 1965, the United States deployed over 200,000 troops to Vietnam as part of Operation Rolling Thunder—and thus began the Vietnam War. That war "divided this country as few other issues [e]ver have." *Tinker, 393 U.S. at 524* (Black, J., dissenting). Public opposition to the war made its way into schools, and in one high-profile case, a group of high-school and middle-school students wore black armbands to express their opposition. [**19] *Id. at 504* (majority opinion). School officials adopted a policy prohibiting the armbands and suspending any student who refused to remove it when asked. *Id.* Some students refused and were suspended. *Id.* The Supreme Court upheld their right to wear the armbands. *Id. at 514. Tinker* held that *HN10* school officials may not restrict student speech without a reasonable forecast that the speech would substantially disrupt the school environment or invade the rights of others. *Id. at 513.* As nothing more than the "silent, passive expression of opinion, unaccompanied by any disorder or disturbance on [the students'] part," the students' armbands were protected by the *First Amendment. Id. at 508.*

except when they do not . . . ."); *id. at 430* (Breyer, J., concurring in part and [**16] dissenting in part) ("[C]ourts have described the tests these cases suggest as complex and often difficult to apply."); *see, e.g., Doninger v. Niehoff, 642 F.3d 334, 353 (2d Cir. 2011)* ("The law governing restrictions on student speech can be difficult and confusing, even for lawyers, law professors, and judges. The relevant Supreme Court cases can be hard to reconcile, and courts often struggle with which standard applies in any particular case."); *Guiles ex rel. Guiles v. Marineau, 461 F.3d 320, 326, 331 (2d Cir. 2006)* (acknowledging "some lack of clarity in the Supreme Court's student-speech cases" and stating that the "exact contours of what is plainly offensive [under *Fraser*] is not so clear").

8   Other examples of categorically unprotected speech include child pornography, *see New York v. Ferber, 458 U.S. 747, 764-65, 102 S. Ct. 3348, 73 L. Ed. 2d 1113 (1982)*, advocacy that imminently incites lawless action, *see Brandenburg v. Ohio, 395 U.S. 444, 447-48, 89 S. Ct. 1827, 23 L. Ed. 2d 430 (1969)* (per curiam), fighting words, *see Chaplinsky v. New Hampshire, 315 U.S. 568, 571-72, 62 S. Ct. 766, 86 L. Ed. 1031 (1942)*, true threats, *see Watts v. United States, 394 U.S. 705, 708, 89 S. Ct. 1399, 22 L. Ed. 2d 664 (1969)* (per curiam), commercial speech that is false, misleading, or proposes illegal transactions, *see Cent. Hudson Gas & Elec. Corp. v. Pub. Serv. Comm'n of N.Y., 447 U.S. 557, 562, 566-67, 100 S. Ct. 2343, 65 L. Ed. 2d 341 (1980)*, and some false statements of fact, *see United States v. Alvarez, 132 S. Ct. 2537, 2546-47, 183 L. Ed. 2d 574 (2012)*.

Box 4.2   *(continued)*

725 F.3d 293, *324; 2013 U.S. App. LEXIS 16087, **83

Dissent by: HARDIMAN; GREENAWAY, JR.

Dissent

HARDIMAN, *Circuit Judge*, dissenting with whom CHAGARES, JORDAN, GREENAWAY, JR., and GREENBERG, join.

Today the Court holds that twelve-year-olds have a constitutional right to wear in [*325] school a bracelet that says "I [**84] ♥ boobies! (KEEP A BREAST)." Because this decision is inconsistent with the Supreme Court's *First Amendment* jurisprudence, I respectfully dissent.

I

My colleagues conclude that the Supreme Court's decision in *Bethel School District No. 403 v. Fraser, 478 U.S. 675, 106 S. Ct. 3159, 92 L. Ed. 2d 549 (1986)*, cannot justify the Easton Area School District's bracelet ban "because [the bracelets] comment on a social issue." Maj. Typescript at 6. This limitation on the ability of schools to regulate student speech that could reasonably be deemed lewd, vulgar, plainly offensive, or constituting sexual innuendo finds no support in *Fraser* or its progeny. The Majority's "high value speech" modification of *Fraser* is based on the following two premises it derives from the Supreme Court's decision in *Morse v. Frederick, 551 U.S. 393, 127 S. Ct. 2618, 168 L. Ed. 2d 290 (2007)*: first, that Justice Alito's concurrence in *Morse* is the "controlling" opinion in that case, Maj. Typescript at 21 n.10, 43, 45, 47; and second, that *Morse* "modified" the Supreme Court's decision in *Fraser*, Maj. Typescript at 6, 46-51. Both premises are wrong.

A

I begin with the Majority's first premise, namely, that Justice Alito's concurrence in *Morse* is the "controlling" opinion in that case, despite [**85] the fact that Chief Justice Roberts's majority opinion was joined in full by four other Justices. Maj. Typescript at 36-46. This distinctly minority view is contrary both to the understanding of *Morse* expressed by eight of our sister Courts of Appeals and to what we ourselves have repeatedly articulated to be the Court's holding in *Morse*. By endorsing the Fifth Circuit's mistaken understanding of *Morse*, the Majority applies an incorrect legal standard that leads to the unfortunate result the Court reaches today.

The notion that Justice Alito's concurrence in *Morse* is the controlling opinion flows from a misunderstanding of the Supreme Court's "narrowest grounds" doctrine as established in *Marks v. United States, 430 U.S. 188, 97 S. Ct. 990, 51 L. Ed. 2d 260 (1977)*. In *Marks*, the petitioners had been convicted of distributing obscene materials pursuant to jury instructions that were modeled on the definition of obscenity articulated in *Miller v. California, 413 U.S. 15, 93 S. Ct. 2607, 37 L. Ed. 2d 419 (1973)*. *Marks, 430 U.S. at 190*. Because the petitioners' conduct occurred before the Court had decided *Miller*, they argued that due process entitled them "to jury instructions not under *Miller*, but under the more favorable [obscenity] formulation of *Memoirs* [**86] *v. Massachusetts*." *Id.* That formulation was unclear, however, because the *Memoirs* Court had issued a fractured decision; no more than three of the six Justices who voted for the judgment endorsed any one of three separate opinions, each of which articulated a different standard for obscenity. *See Memoirs v. Massachusetts, 383 U.S. 413, 414, 418, 86 S. Ct. 975, 16 L. Ed. 2d 1 (1966)* (plurality opinion) (Justice Brennan, joined by Chief Justice Warren and Justice Fortas, stating that obscenity may be proscribed if it is "utterly without redeeming social value"); *id. at 421, 424* (Black and Douglas, JJ., concurring in judgment) (concurring separately on the grounds that obscenity cannot be proscribed); *id. at 421* (Stewart, J., concurring in judgment) (concurring on the grounds that only hard-core pornography is proscribable as obscene). The lack of a majority opinion in *Memoirs* [*326] led the Sixth Circuit in *Marks* to reject the petitioners' argument that the plurality's "utterly without redeeming social value" standard was the governing rule. It reasoned that because "the *Memoirs* standards never commanded the assent of more than three Justices at any one time . . . *Memoirs* never became the law." *Marks, 430 U.S. at 192* (describing [**87] the lower court's holding).

On appeal, the Supreme Court rejected the Sixth Circuit's reasoning and articulated the following standard: "When a fragmented Court decides a case and no single rationale explaining the result enjoys the assent of five Justices, 'the holding of the Court may be viewed as that position taken by those members who concurred in the judgments on the narrowest grounds . . . .'" *Id. at 193* (quoting *Gregg v. Georgia, 428 U.S. 153, 169 n.15, 96 S. Ct. 2909, 49 L. Ed. 2d 859 (1976)* (plurality opinion)). Based on this reasoning, the Court concluded that because three Justices joined the plurality opinion and Justices Black and Douglas "concurred on broader grounds," "[t]he view of the

Box 4.2   (continued)

725 F.3d 293, *326; 2013 U.S. App. LEXIS 16087, **87

Memoirs plurality . . . constituted the holding of the Court and provided the governing standards." *Marks, 430 U.S. at 193-94*.

As *Marks* demonstrates, the narrowest grounds rule is a necessary tool for deciphering the holding of the Court when there is no majority opinion. *See, e.g., Grutter v. Bollinger, 539 U.S. 306, 325, 123 S. Ct. 2325, 156 L. Ed. 2d 304 (2003)* (attempting to apply the *Marks* rule to derive a holding in the "fractured decision" *Regents of the University of California v. Bakke, 438 U.S. 265, 98 S. Ct. 2733, 57 L. Ed. 2d 750 (1978))*. Contrary to the Majority's holding today, [**88] neither *Marks* nor other Supreme Court decisions support the "unprecedented argument that a statement of legal opinion joined by five Justices of th[e] Court does not carry the force of law," *Vasquez v. Hillery, 474 U.S. 254, 261 n.4, 106 S. Ct. 617, 88 L. Ed. 2d 598 (1986)*. Rather, the narrowest grounds rule applies only to "discern a single holding of the Court in cases in which no opinion on the issue in question has garnered the support of a majority." *Id.; cf.* Black's Law Dictionary 1201 (9th ed. 2009) (defining a "majority opinion" as "[a]n opinion joined in by more than half the judges considering a given case").

Unable to find persuasive Supreme Court authority to buttress its novel reading of *Marks*, the Majority argues that our Court has "applied the narrowest-grounds approach in circumstances beyond those posed by *Marks*, including to determine holdings in majority opinions." Maj. Typescript at 37-38 (footnotes, citation, and internal quotation marks omitted). For support, the Majority cites our decisions in *Horn v. Thoratec Corp., 376 F.3d 163 (3d Cir. 2004)*, and *United States v. Bishop, 66 F.3d 569 (3d Cir. 1995)*. Maj. Typescript at 39-42. Neither case counsels the Majority's application of the narrowest-grounds [**89] doctrine to interpret *Morse*.

In *Horn*, we looked to Justice Breyer's concurrence in *Medtronic v. Lohr, 518 U.S. 470, 116 S. Ct. 2240, 135 L. Ed. 2d 700 (1996)*, for guidance on how to address an issue central to our case, but that the *Lohr* Court discussed only in dicta. *See Horn, 376 F.3d at 175-76* (comparing Justice Breyer's "more narrow" view on preemption with "Justice Stevens' sweeping pronouncement [in his plurality opinion] that [the statute at issue] almost never preempts a state common law claim"). Likewise, in *Bishop*, we cited Justice Kennedy's concurrence in *United States v. Lopez, 514 U.S. 549, 115 S. Ct. 1624, 131 L. Ed. 2d 626 (1995)*, in order to reinforce the already established principle that [*327]

courts must exercise "'great restraint' before a court finds Congress to have overstepped its commerce power" despite *Lopez's* revolutionary holding. *Bishop, 66 F.3d at 590* (quoting *Lopez, 514 U.S. at 568* (Kennedy, J., concurring)). Critically, in neither of these cases did we indicate a belief that a concurring Justice can create a new rule of law simply by both asking and answering a question left unaddressed by the majority opinion. In fact, we noted that Justice Breyer's concurrence in *Horn* was particularly persuasive because "Justice Breyer did not [**90] discuss issues in his concurring opinion that Justice Stevens, writing on behalf of the four-judge plurality, did not reach." *Horn, 376 F.3d at 175*. That is not the case here.

The Majority concedes that a concurring "justice's opinion 'cannot add to what the majority opinion holds' by 'binding the other four [j]ustices to what they have not said.'" Maj. Typescript at 39 (quoting *McKoy v. North Carolina, 494 U.S. 433, 462 n.3, 110 S. Ct. 1227, 108 L. Ed. 2d 369 (1990)* (Scalia, J., dissenting)). Yet by holding that Justice Alito's concurrence "controls the majority opinion in *Morse*," Maj. Typescript at 36, the Majority violates this very principle. The majority in *Morse* noted that "this is plainly not a case about political debate," *Morse, 551 U.S. at 403*, and refused to address what the result of the case would have been had Frederick's banner been "political." The Majority implies that Justice Alito's concurrence provides a definitive, "controlling" answer to fill the void left by the *Morse* majority opinion, but the Supreme Court has disavowed this approach: "The Court would be in an odd predicament if a concurring minority of the Justices could force the majority to address a point they found it unnecessary (and did [**91] not wish) to address, under compulsion of [the dissent's] new principle that silence implies agreement." *Alexander v. Sandoval, 532 U.S. 275, 285 n.5, 121 S. Ct. 1511, 149 L. Ed. 2d 517 (2001)*. Put another way, a majority "holding is not made coextensive with the concurrence because [the majority] opinion does not expressly preclude (is 'consistent with[]' . . .) the concurrence's approach." *Id.*

Notwithstanding the Majority's statement to the contrary, we have never applied the *Marks* rule to hold that a concurrence may co-opt an opinion joined by at least five Justices. Rather, consistent with *Marks*, "we have looked to the votes of dissenting Justices if they, combined with votes from *plurality or concurring opinions*, establish a majority view on the relevant issue." *United States v. Donovan, 661 F.3d 174, 182 (3d Cir. 2011)* (emphasis added); *see also Student Pub.*

| Box 4.3 | **FEDERAL APPELLATE COURTS MAP** |

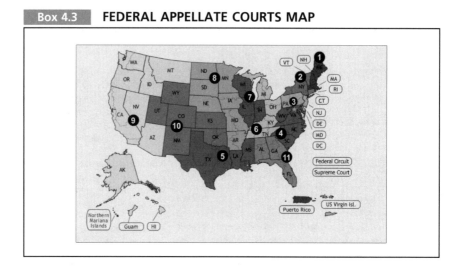

The *Easton* case was first handled by the U.S. District Court for the East-ern District of Pennsylvania. *Easton* is similar to *Luttrell* in that it was decided in the lower court not by jury verdict, but by a motion decided by a judge. This time, the motion was for a *preliminary injunction*, which is an order that certain actions be taken or not taken during the litigation. Often, a prelimin-ary injunction is the major ruling in a case because it reveals the court's view of how the law applies to the facts of the dispute, and the parties settle the case thereafter. The district court decision in *Easton* was published,[8] which is not uncommon for federal district court decisions (but rare for state district court decisions). Federal lower court decisions are sometimes given significant cre-dence, even though as lower court decisions, they are not technically binding.

The decision in Box 4.2 is from the U.S. Court of Appeals for the Third Circuit, which encompasses Pennsylvania. Much of your research in federal case law will include court of appeals cases. We have provided only an excerpt from *Easton* because the main opinion alone ran twenty pages in the version used for Box 4.2. The decision is lengthy because the case raised a close legal question (that is, one that could have been decided either way). *Easton* thus illustrates two features that arise from time to time in close cases.

One feature is that the decision was argued and made en banc. The stan-dard approach at the court of appeals is for a panel of only three judges to handle a case. For more difficult cases, the entire court — in this case, fourteen judges — may rehear and decide the case, potentially giving it more weight than a standard panel decision.

The second feature is the *split decision*, in which there is more than one opinion. Split decisions are most common at the highest court and in en banc situations. The *majority opinion* garners more than half of the votes; it thus states the outcome and reasoning for which the case stands. A *dissenting*

---

8. *H. v. Easton Area Sch. Dist.*, 827 F. Supp. 2d 392 (E.D. Pa. 2011), *aff'd sub nom. B.H. ex rel. Hawk v. Easton Area Sch. Dist.*, 725 F.3d 293 (3d Cir. 2013), *cert. denied*, 134 S. Ct. 1515 (2014).

opinion disagrees with both the outcome and some key portion of the reasoning of the majority. A *concurring opinion* agrees with the outcome of the majority opinion but sets forth some differences in reasoning. On fairly rare occasions, a court can split so significantly that there is no majority opinion; the opinion that garners the largest number of votes is the *plurality opinion*. When you find a split decision in your research, you should focus on the majority opinion, of course. However, do not disregard the views stated in a concurrence or dissent; sometimes these views eventually come to influence other judges in later cases. In *Easton,* nine judges agreed on one approach, the majority opinion; five judges wrote two dissenting opinions.

Majority	• More than half of the votes • Outcome and reasoning govern
Concurrence	• Concurs in outcome of majority • Differs in some facet of reasoning
Dissent	• Disagrees with outcome of majority • Disagrees with reasoning of majority

Easton also provides an example of a case submitted for publication.[9] The distinction between *published opinion* and *unpublished opinion* is something of a misnomer: all decisions are published, at least to the parties, and with court electronic records systems and expansive commercial online resources, most decisions are accessible to the public in some sense as well. The distinction really refers to whether the court intends the decision to be taken as precedential; it reflects whether the court sees the case as raising a new legal issue and the opinion as adding to the law. Although historically courts have been reluctant to permit lawyers to rely on unpublished cases, this reluctance has been easing. For example, the federal courts of appeals today do not restrict the citation of recent unpublished cases, so long as the party citing an unpublished case provides a copy of any decision not available in a publicly accessible database to the other parties.[10]

Finally, *Easton* illustrates a fairly common phenomenon in the federal courts: although the losing party sought review by the U.S. Supreme

---

9. As for state courts, the decisions of the highest court typically are all published. The decisions of the intermediate appeals court may be designated as published or unpublished by that court. The courts or legislature may have a rule governing the citation of unpublished decisions.

10. Fed. R. App. P. 32.1.

Court, the U.S. Supreme Court declined to review the case.[11] In both the state and federal systems, two types of appeals exist. Generally, a party has an *appeal as of right* to the intermediate appeals court (i.e., the circuit court of appeals in the federal system). The highest court (i.e., the U.S. Supreme Court for the federal system) generally exercises *discretionary review*, taking only those cases that are most important to its purposes of making law and harmonizing the case law around the country. When the Supreme Court declines to review a case, its denial of review has no independent significance: the appellate court decision stands, but the denial does not signify that the Supreme Court agrees with the appellate court decision.

Round 3: Selecting Cases

You may well find yourself having to choose which of many cases to focus on. This challenge often arises as to federal case law because of the high volume of federal cases, but it also can arise as to frequently litigated topics under state law.

Obviously, only cases that are good law pertaining to the point of law that you are researching should make it onto your list of cases to consider. Most of the time, you should consider only binding cases. Consider cases from higher courts more seriously than those of lower courts.

When there is little to no precedent in your jurisdiction, you may consider persuasive cases from a sister jurisdiction, which may be followed depending on how dominant the rule is and how well reasoned the case is. As noted earlier with *Luttrell*, a state may look to the law of a sister state; so too may a federal court look to decisions of a different federal court. For example, the de la Cruz situation arose in the Third Circuit, so the *Easton* decision would be binding. Had it been decided by a different circuit, however, it still would be worth consideration because of its factual similarity and extensive discussion, especially if there were no equally strong Third Circuit decision.

Some situations involving persuasive precedent reflect the complexities of our federal system. In *diversity jurisdiction*, federal courts may adjudicate claims arising under state law when the parties are citizens of different states. In *concurrent jurisdiction*, state courts may adjudicate certain claims arising under federal law. One state may adjudicate a claim arising under the law of another state if a contract so provides. In these cases, the deciding court seeks to rule as the court whose law is controlling would rule. For example, if the Bower's Bounty case were to be filed in federal court because the employee and Bower's Bounty were citizens of different states, the federal court would seek to apply the law of

---

11. *Easton Area Sch. Dist. v. B.H. ex rel. Hawk*, 134 S. Ct. 1515 (2014) (petition for writ of certiorari denied). As interesting as *Easton* is, the case did not merit review because the Court had already issued several rulings in the area of free speech rights of public school students.

defamation as set by the Kansas Supreme Court. Decisions rendered in the cases described in this paragraph are not considered weighty.

Beyond these objective factors, various looser factors come into play. Published cases are preferred over unpublished cases, and en banc decisions are considered especially weighty. A newer case represents the court's current thinking, but some older *seminal* cases in which the court first or most thoroughly discusses a rule and on which the law is built also merit attention. The more similar a case is to your client's situation, the better; this is determined from both a factual and a legal standpoint. Finally, the quality of the opinion matters, including its clarity, comprehensiveness, and cogency. The factors influencing which cases to pursue are illustrated here.

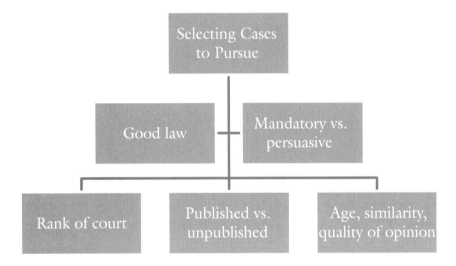

The Reading and Mining of a Case

While reading cases for the purposes of legal analysis is too large a topic to cover in depth in this book, some key points can be made. First, you will want to draw out the legal rules that the court states in the decision or, if there is more than one opinion, in the majority opinion. Second, you also should draw out information about the dispute that was litigated and the court's ratio decidendi, to the extent that the case parallels your client's situation. This is done by writing a case brief with components that follow a certain sequence.

Several additional sets of notes, which reflect a timeline of sorts, will advance your research. You should note how, where, and when you found the case, as covered later in this chapter. Looking back in time, you should mine any leads to older sources that the case provides. Most cases refer to the cases, statutes, or secondary sources on which the court relied in coming to its decision. Some you may already know about, others not; some may be important, others not. Record those that you should consider as your research proceeds. Looking forward in time, you should note newer pertinent sources that refer to the case, which you learn about from citing the case, as covered later in this chapter.

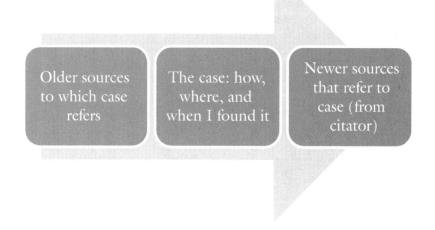

Box 4.4 contains both a case brief for *Luttrell* and a set of research notes for *Luttrell*.

RECOMMENDED APPROACHES TO RESEARCHING CASE LAW

The Backdrop: Case Reporters

Even with this background information on the U.S. courts and case law, there is yet a bit more information to learn before you can read about our recommended approaches to researching case law. This information is about the print method of publishing cases that well served the courts and the legal profession before the advent of online publishing. The print method matters still, not because you are likely to research in print, but because it continues to be reflected in online cases and it is central to some citation systems, particularly *The Bluebook* and the *ALWD Citation Manual*.

For centuries, government printing offices around the country published the precedential decisions of their courts in *official reporters*—hardcover books containing case after case, organized by date of issuance rather than logic. These

Box 4.4   **CASE BRIEF AND RESEARCH NOTES**
              (Employment Defamation)

Case Brief

Luttrell v. United Telephone System, Inc., 683 P.2d 1292 (Kan. Ct. App. 1984)

Decision is affirmed at 695 P.2d 1279 (Kan. 1985).

Facts: P (employee) alleges that another employee told his supervisor he was illegally taping phone conversations, was asked to stop, yet persisted despite being told not to. P's supervisor told another employee, who told yet another employee. P alleges statements were malicious and within scope of employment. Employees were supervisors apparently.

Procedure and outcome: P sued D (employer) for defamation. DC granted D's motion to dismiss for failure to state claim. Here: reversed and remanded.

Issue: When defamatory words are exchanged by agents of same corporation about fellow employee's performance, is there publication required for tort of defamation?

Holding: Communication of remarks by one corporate employee to another concerning job of third employee is publication required for defamation action against employer.

Rules of law: (1) Defamation elements are: false and defamatory words communicated to third person, resulting in harm to reputation of person defamed.

(2) Corporation is liable for defamation by agent made while acting within scope of employment.

(3) Qualified privilege exists when good faith, interest to be upheld, statement limited in scope to interest, publication in proper manner to proper parties. Privilege is defeated if speaker acted with knowledge of falsity or reckless disregard of truth.

Reasoning: Issue of intracorporate communication was issue of first impression. Courts around country split on issue; *Prosser* favors view that such communications are publication. Focus should be on nature of injury in defamation — damage to reputation; this may be as devastating when communication is inside corporation as outside. Employer's need to evaluate and comment on employee work is protected by qualified privilege.

Research Notes

Found via Westlaw search in Kansas State and Federal Cases for *defam /p employ!*

Research conducted June 15, 2015.

<u>Kansas Cases *Luttrell* Refers to</u>

Hein, 616 P.2d 277 (1980)

Schulze, 545 P.2d 392 (1976)

Gobin, 649 P.2d 1239 (1982)

Dobbyn, 579 P.2d 721, 587 P.2d 315 (1978)

Scarpelli, 626 P.2d 785 (1981)

<u>Main Kansas Cases Found by Citing *Luttrell*</u>

Dominguez, 974 P.2d 112 (1999)

Lindemuth, 864 P.2d 744 (1993)

Turner, 722 P.2d 1106 (1986)

Batt, 774 P.2d 371 (1989)

reporters were not all that timely and certainly not well organized.[12] Not surprisingly, private companies decided that they could do a better job.

The West Reporter System, begun in the late 1800s, soon prevailed as the dominant system. Indeed, it became the only reporter for some jurisdictions. Now owned by Thomson Reuters, the West Reporter System continues to provide a vast array of cases in a set of reporters organized by level of court for federal court cases and by geography for state court cases. See Box 4.5.[13] West publishes cases quickly, in softcover pamphlets; after additional editorial work, West consolidates several softcover pamphlets into a hardcover book.

For each case, West editors write a set of summaries of the points of law set out in the case, called *headnotes*. Each summary is assigned to a topic and key number within the vast West outline of U.S. case law known as the *Key Number System*. The Key Number System is comprised of topics, broken down in very fine detail into numbered subtopics, accompanied by a sketch of a key. The headnotes, along with the topics and key numbers, appear near the beginning of a case in a reporter and also are published in a separate source called *digests*. Thus, researching in cases in print proceeds as follows:

1. In the digest —
   a. Discern one or more useful topics and subtopics.
   b. Read the headnotes thereunder to find the ones that most clearly pertain to your client's situation.
   c. From those headnotes, identify the corresponding cases.
2. In the reporters, read the cases identified in the digest.

These days, you probably will not use West print reporters and digests per se in your research. However, as a testimony to its dominance, the West Reporter System underlies the way that cases are presented in other resources. For example, when we found the *Luttrell* case in other resources, it was identified as being located in the *Pacific Reporter 2d*, and when we found *Easton*, it was identified as being located in the *Federal Reporter 3d*. And if you research on Westlaw, you will have the option of using the Key Number System online — a strong option to consider.

Overview

Because it is so crucial to accomplish case law research well, and because a good amount of time in most research projects is indeed spent researching cases, choosing your approach wisely matters. One key to selecting a good approach is to realize that you will research case law in different contexts. For example, sometimes you may already know a good deal — perhaps the identity of a pertinent case (or, indeed, several cases). Other times, you may have only a broad knowledge of the area of law.

---

12. About half of the states no longer publish official reporters.

13. The geographical scheme may not be what you would expect. For example, Kansas cases appear in the *Pacific Reporter*.

Box 4.5   WEST REPORTERS

Cases from These Courts	Appear in These West Reporters (current series)
U.S. Supreme Court	*Supreme Court Reporter*
Federal courts of appeals	*Federal Reporter 3d* *Federal Appendix*
Federal district courts	*Federal Supplement 3d* *Federal Reporter* (until 1932)
Connecticut, Delaware, District of Columbia, Maine, Maryland, New Hampshire, New Jersey, Pennsylvania, Rhode Island, Vermont	*Atlantic Reporter 3d*
Illinois, Indiana, Massachusetts, New York, Ohio	*North Eastern Reporter 2d* (also *New York Supplement 2d*)
Iowa, Michigan, Minnesota, Nebraska, North Dakota, South Dakota, Wisconsin	*North Western Reporter 2d*
Alaska, Arizona, California, Colorado, Hawaii, Idaho, Kansas, Montana, Nevada, New Mexico, Oklahoma, Oregon, Utah, Washington, Wyoming	*Pacific Reporter 3d* (also *California Reporter 3d*)
Georgia, North Carolina, South Carolina, Virginia, West Virginia	*South Eastern Reporter 2d*
Arkansas, Kentucky, Missouri, Tennessee, Texas	*South Western Reporter 3d*
Alabama, Florida, Louisiana, Mississippi	*Southern Reporter 3d*

As you might expect, for case law research in particular, resources abound, each with its advantages and disadvantages. Consider thinking about them as you would about transit options for a journey. Some are best for short and direct trips, when you do not need much assistance; these are court websites. Others are better for longer, more complicated trips, when you need considerable assistance from a tour guide and are willing to pay a fair amount; these are high-end commercial resources. Yet others fill the gap between these two poles; these are the economy-class commercial resources. And for the intrepid traveler, there is Google Scholar. See Box 4.6 for a description of the various approaches.

An important caveat: the protocols of all the resources described in this part change fairly often. The descriptions are general and current as of late 2015. Study the materials for each resource that you use to learn its specific options and details, and expect them to change.

Box 4.6   APPROACHES TO CASE LAW RESEARCH

Resource	Relative Advantages	Relative Disadvantages	Best Uses
Court Websites	Accessibility Provision of the official version of a case (often) No cost	Limited historical coverage Limited search options No editorial enhancements No citator	Retrieval of a known case Monitoring of new cases in your area
High-End Commercial Resources	Comprehensiveness of coverage Currency Editorial enhancements Varied search options Sophisticated citators	Cost Extensiveness that can be overwhelming	High-stakes situations Citing cases
Economy-Class Commercial Resources	Mid-range coverage Varied search options Low cost	Mid-range coverage Few editorial enhancements No true citator	Standard client situations as to stakes, difficulty, resources
Google Scholar	Ease of use No cost	Limited coverage Lower credibility Few editorial enhancements No true citator	Retrieval of known case Collecting handful of cases Preliminary research

Court Websites

When you turn to case law research, you may already know of a leading case (or more than one) from your research in secondary sources. If your goal is simply to obtain a copy — indeed, an authoritative version — of a pertinent case, a good choice is the court's website. Note, however, that the version obtained from a court website will not have the enhancements provided by a commercial publisher. Compare the version of *Easton* in Box 2.7 in Chapter 2 (a court website version) with that in Box 4.2 (a commercial resource's enhanced version). Searching for the two cases featured in this chapter reveals the strengths and weaknesses of court websites.

First, the website of the Kansas State Courts provides decisions of both the Kansas Court of Appeals and the Kansas Supreme Court on a current basis. However, it is not fully or even substantially retrospective, as it begins only in 1996. Thus, as we researched the Bower's Bounty case, we found that it did not include the *Luttrell* case, decided in 1984.

Federal courts increasingly provide access to their recent decisions. Thus, when researching the de la Cruz client situation, we could find both the district court and Third Circuit decisions in the *Easton* litigation on the respective court websites; those decisions date to 2011 and 2013.

A strong alternative to the websites of specific federal courts is at FDsys, the U.S. Government Publishing Office's Federal Digital System website (www.gpo.gov/fdsys). There you will find a collection of United States Courts Opinions, which encompasses decisions from all levels of the federal courts beginning in 2004. The research process entails selecting the court and year of interest and then searching by docket number, name of a party, or other key words.

High-End Commercial Resources

At the opposite end of the spectrum from court websites are the commercial resources Westlaw and Lexis. As noted in Chapter 1, for many decades, both have reliably provided a wide range of primary authorities and secondary sources with strong search capabilities. In the context of case law research, they offer an extraordinarily wide range of cases in exchange for their not-inconsiderable cost, typically from the origins of a court to its most recent decisions, including not only published but also unpublished cases, as well as some lower court cases. Both systems also provide various ways to search for a case. Once you find a case, you will also find many editorial enhancements and be able to link directly to many of the sources cited in it. Most important, you will be able to use a sophisticated citator to determine whether the case is good law, as well as find later sources (including cases) that cite the case.

These two resources thus offer the full range of functions needed to conduct case law research. Because of their expense, they raise issues of cost-effectiveness, however. This expense may well be justified for some projects, including those involving thorny legal issues, factually sensitive topics, an unfamiliar area of law, or significant sums at stake. In other situations, you may use these resources to supplement the other approaches described in this chapter.

Westlaw. This resource provides a wide range of choices for researching in case law. Although its default is to set up a search throughout a wide range of sources, the smarter approach is to research in the database of cases that suits your needs. Similarly, although you may use an unstructured search, you may obtain more certain results by running several carefully constructed searches, especially because you can construct a search based on the West Key Number System. Furthermore, a critical and nearly always fruitful step when using Westlaw is to cite your cases, both to verify that they are good law and to learn about more recent pertinent cases.

As an example, assume that we used Westlaw to research case law for the Bower's Bounty client situation. Our client has been sued for defamation in employment—a serious claim from both a financial and reputational standpoint. The lawsuit has been filed in Kansas state courts.

In our search, we selected the State Materials tab, then Kansas, and then selected a database containing the complete case law from the two appellate courts for the state of Kansas[14] to the present. We ran two different searches. First, we ran a simple terms-and-connectors search for *defam! /p employ!*, which sought cases containing words with the stem *defam* in the same paragraph as words with the stem *employ*.[15] See Box 4.7 for the list of the first ten cases by relevance that we retrieved, as well as the entry for *Luttrell*,

---

| Box 4.7 | **WESTLAW TERMS-AND-CONNECTORS SEARCH (Employment Defamation)** |

First Ten Results

Luttrell (Kansas Court of Appeals decision)
Turner
Lindemuth
Luttrell (Kansas Supreme Court decision)
Riddle
Batt
Hall
Dominguez
Moran
Anderson

---

14. Indeed, it also contained cases from the territorial court beginning in 1858.

15. We reasoned that *defamation* or some version of it is likely to be used these days rather than the more dated terms *libel* and *slander.* The stem *employ!* would capture employee, employer, and employment.

Box 4.7   *(continued)*

List of 20 results for adv: defam! /p employ!

1. Luttrell v. United Telephone System, Inc.
Court of Appeals of Kansas. July 19, 1984 9 Kan.App.2d 620 683 P.2d 1292

Employee brought action against employer alleging that statements by managerial employees concerning employee's job performance constituted **defamation**. The District Court, Johnson County, Phillip L. Woodworth, J., granted **employer's** motion to dismiss for failure to state claim upon which relief may be granted, and employee appealed. ...

...No.56031. July 19, 1984. Review Granted Sept. 6, 1984. **Employee** brought action against **employer** alleging that statements by managerial **employees** concerning **employee's** job performance constituted **defamation**. The District Court, Johnson County, Phillip L. Woodworth, J., granted **employer's** motion to dismiss for failure to state claim upon which relief may be granted, and **employee** appealed. The Court of Appeals, Parks, J., held that remarks communicated by one corporate **employee** to another concerning job performance of third **employee**...
...to Others 237 44(3) k. As to character of **employee**. **Employer** who is evaluating or investigating **employee** in good faith and within bounds of **employment** relationship is protected from threat of **defamation** suits by requirement that **employee** prove that **employer** acted with knowledge of falsity or reckless disregard for the...

2. Turner v. Halliburton Co.
Supreme Court of Kansas. July 30, 1986 240 Kan. 1 722 P.2d 1106

Employee brought action against former employer and supervisor for **defamation** and tortious interference with right to contract, as result of statements accusing employer of theft of company property which served as basis for termination. The Cowley District Court, Robert L. Bishop, J., after dismissing another claim for breach of **employment**...

...COMPANY and William Arend , Appellants. No.58647. July 30, 1986. **Employee** brought action against former **employer** and supervisor for **defamation** and tortious interference with right to contract, as result of statements accusing **employer** of theft of company property which served as basis for...
...L. Bishop, J., after dismissing another claim for breach of **employment** contract, entered judgment in favor of **employee**, and **employer** and supervisor appealed. The Supreme Court, Holmes, J., held that...

3. Lindemuth v. Goodyear Tire and Rubber Co.
Court of Appeals of Kansas. December 10, 1993 19 Kan.App.2d 95 864 P.2d 744

Former employee brought suit against former employer, alleging intentional infliction of emotional distress, **defamation**, outrage and tortious interference with contract. The Shawnee District Court, Fred S. Jackson, J., granted summary judgment for employer, and employee appealed. The Court of Appeals, Gernon, P.J., held that:...

...AND RUBBER COMPANY, Appellee. No.69604. Dec. 10, 1993. Former **employee** brought suit against former **employer**, alleging intentional infliction of emotional distress, **defamation**, outrage and tortious interference with contract. The Shawnee District Court, Fred S. Jackson , J., granted summary judgment for **employer**, and **employee** appealed. The Court of Appeals Gernon , P.J., held that: (1) **employee's** state law claims arising out of actions by **employers** and others prior to any grievance procedure were not preempted...
...by §301 of Labor Management Relations Act (LMRA); (2) **employer's** conduct did not rise to extreme and outrageous level necessary...

which came up first. Our second search was devised by selecting the *Libel and Slander* topic from the list provided under the *Key Numbers* link on the All Content page; then selecting subtopic *Words and Acts Actionable*, then *Publication*; and finally running those key numbers as our search in Kansas cases. See Box 4.8 for the entry for *Luttrell,* which came up third, and the list of the ten cases. Note that our terms-and-connectors search is a researcher-driven search, while the key-number search is a writer-driven search. In addition, note that there is some overlap between the results, but it is not exact.

The case as it appears in Westlaw appears in Box 4.1.[16] Note the eight numbered paragraphs that precede the opinion written by the court; these are the headnotes written by the West editors, each of them matched to a topic and key number.[17] The headnotes are a finding tool (neither a primary authority nor a secondary source); they may not be cited. However, they are useful in several ways. First, before you read the case, you can preview it by reading the headnotes. Second, after you read the case, you can check your understanding of its legal points against the headnotes.

Each pertinent case is a potential springboard to more pertinent sources, especially cases. First, as you read a case, you can link to older sources — especially cases and statutes — that the case refers to by clicking on their citations within the case that you are reading. Thus, while reading *Luttrell* in Westlaw, we could use it to expand our research by linking to the older Kansas cases cited by the court.

Second, you can use a case to find newer sources, especially newer cases, as well. One technique involves the headnotes presented at the beginning of the

---

Box 4.8   WESTLAW KEY-NUMBER SEARCH (Employment Defamation)

Ten Results

Wright
Ruebke
Luttrell (Kansas Court of Appeals decision)
Rockgate Management (listed twice)
Gatlin
Luttrell (Kansas Supreme Court decision)
Wright
Batt
Lyon

---

16. In various places in the opinion itself are bold-faced numbers. These are the page numbers tied to print reporters, including the West *Pacific Reporter 2d* and a Kansas official reporter.

17. Most of them are about defamation, so they are connected to the *Libel and Slander* topic, but one pertains to a different area of law — when a company is legally responsible for its employees' actions. The actual key numbers do not show in this printout.

Box 4.8   *(continued)*

List of 10 headnotes for k23 Publication

⚷⤳**23 Publication** (10)
Jurisdiction: Kansas

237 LIBEL AND SLANDER   709
   237I Words and Acts Actionable, and Liability Therefor   156
     237⚷⤳23 Publication   10
     237⚷⤳23.1 In general.   3

1. Wright v. Bachmurski
Court of Appeals of Kansas.   August 10, 2001   29 Kan.App.2d 595
Headnote: Intentional or negligent communication of the defamatory matter is called "publication," and the person making the communication is called the "publisher." Restatement (Second) of Torts §577(1).

> **Document Summary:** TORTS - Defamation. Accountant's former clients were independent tortfeasors and thus also liable for defamation.

2. Ruebke v. Globe Communications Corp.
Supreme Court of Kansas.   June 12, 1987   241 Kan. 595
Headnote: For there to be liability for defamation there must be publication of matter that is both defamatory and false; where published statements are substantially true, there is no liability and motion for summary judgment is proper.

8 Cases that cite this legal issue

> **Document Summary:** Criminal defendant brought civil libel action against publisher of crime magazine based on publication of article about triple murder of which he was accused. The Reno District Court, William F. Lyle, Jr., J., granted magazine's motion for summary judgment. On appeal, the Supreme Court, Lockett, J., held that truth of statements in article had not been revealed by subject's subsequent convictions and subject was limited public figure and had failed to prove malice. Affirmed.

3. Luttrell v. United Telephone System, Inc.
Court of Appeals of Kansas.   July 19, 1984   9 Kan.App.2d 620
Headnote: Remarks made in course and scope of employment by one corporate employee and communicated to second corporate employee concerning job performance of third employee are publication for purposes of defamation action against corporate employer. K.S.A. 60-212(b)(6).

13 Cases that cite this legal issue

> **Document Summary:** Employee brought action against employer alleging that statements by managerial employees concerning employee's job performance constituted defamation. The District Court, Johnson County, Phillip L. Woodworth, J., granted employer's motion to dismiss for failure to state claim upon which relief may be granted, and employee appealed. The Court of Appeals, Parks, J., held that remarks communicated by one corporate employee to another concerning job performance of third employee are publication for purposes of defamation against employer; thus, claim was improperly dismissed. Reversed and remanded.

case. Below a headnote may be a reference to the number of citing cases that have referred to the case that you are presently reading for the proposition stated in the headnote. Clicking on that link connects to a list of the newer cases, from which you can link to the newer cases themselves.

To find more recent citing cases referring to *Luttrell* while still reading it, we focused on headnote 7 (which is about the publication topic) and clicked on the reference below that headnote to thirteen citing cases. The list included two decisions of the Kansas Court of Appeals that we had already found through our two searches, eight cases from the federal district court sitting in Kansas, and three cases from other jurisdictions.[18]

Third, a critical step in case law research that is accomplished effectively on Westlaw is citing cases, or *KeyCiting* in Westlaw lingo. This step can be done after finding the case in Westlaw. In addition, Westlaw can be used solely for KeyCiting cases found through some other resource.

KeyCite provides three sets of information about a case. The first is its history, which presents in linear and graphic form the various decisions rendered in the litigation. The second is its negative treatment, which encompasses adverse rulings not only in the same litigation, but also adverse treatment in different litigations or proceedings. These two sets of information are imperative to assess as they determine whether the case is good law. KeyCite encapsulates this information using flags of various colors. The third category of KeyCite information is citing references, which includes not only cases with and without precedential force, but also secondary sources and lesser documents[19]; reading this information is less critical. Information about a citing case includes not only its identity, but also a brief description of the case, the depth and nature of the discussion of the cited case, and the headnotes (if any) in the cited case for which the citing case refers to the cited case.[20]

To be sure that *Luttrell* was good law, we checked it through KeyCite. From a subsequent history standpoint, we learned that the Kansas Supreme Court affirmed and adopted the court of appeals decision.[21] See the end of the KeyCite report in Box 4.9. There was no negative history from Kansas courts. The case was given a yellow warning flag by KeyCite because it was not followed by a court outside Kansas, but this was not important to us.

Finally, to wind up our Westlaw research, we also looked at the list of citing references for any additional significant cases. See the beginning of the Key-Cite report in Box 4.9. We concluded that this report confirmed that we were coming to closure on the task of building a list of cases to read, as it did not reveal new cases that merited consideration.

---

18. The last eleven cases would not be precedential. Indeed, a good number were not published.

19. These include trial court orders and materials filed by lawyers.

20. The table of authorities option provides information about the cases that the case you are reading itself refers to (i.e., older cases) and thus does not provide information about newer cases.

21. Completing the research would entail checking the history of this decision as well.

| Box 4.9 | **KEYCITE REPORT (Employment Defamation)** |

List of 20 Citing References for Luttrell v. United Telephone System, Inc.

Citing References (20)

Treatment	Title	Date	Type	Depth	Headnote(s)
Examined by	**1. Naab v. Inland Container Corp.** 1994 WL 70268, *1+ , D.Kan. Ronald Naab worked for Inland Container until he was terminated on the basis of an appraisal completed by his supervisor, Joseph Miller. Naab has sued Inland and Miller alleging...	Feb. 28, 1994	Case	▪▪▪▪	6 7 8 P.2d
Discussed by	**2. Hall v. Kansas Farm Bureau** 50 P.3d 495, 504+ , Kan. BUSINESS ORGANIZATIONS - Association. President of cooperative marketing association could not be removed by vote of board of directors.	July 12, 2002	Case	▪▪▪▪	2 5 6 P.2d
Discussed by	**3. Dominguez v. Davidson** 974 P.2d 112, 117+ , Kan. TORTS - Defamation. Qualified privilege protected supervisor's statement that employee filed false injury claim.	Mar. 05, 1999	Case	▪▪▪	2 5 P.2d
Discussed by	**4. Lindemuth v. Goodyear Tire and Rubber Co.** 864 P.2d 744, 750+ , Kan.App. Former employee brought suit against former employer, alleging intentional infliction of emotional distress, defamation, outrage and tortious interference with contract. The...	Dec. 10, 1993	Case	▪▪▪	5 6 7 P.2d
Discussed by	**5. Gearhart v. Sears, Roebuck & Co., Inc.** 27 F.Supp.2d 1263, 1277+ , D.Kan. Former employee brought action against former employer and supervisor, alleging that they discriminated against her on basis of age, disability, and gender, harassed her on basis...	Oct. 19, 1998	Case	▪▪▪	5 P.2d
Discussed by	**6. Etzel v. Musicland Group, Inc.** 1993 WL 23741, *7+ , D.Kan. Richard Todd Etzel filed this action against his former employer, The Musicland Group, Inc. (Musicland), for outrageous conduct during the events surrounding his termination and...	Jan. 08, 1993	Case	▪▪▪	2 7 8 P.2d

Box 4.9   *(continued)*

List of 20 Citing References for Luttrell v. United Telephone System, Inc.

Treatment	Title	Date	Type	Depth	Headnote(s)
Discussed by	**7. Polson v. Davis** 〞 635 F.Supp. 1130, 1146+ , D.Kan. Former city employee brought action against city and city personnel director alleging sex discrimination retaliatory discharge, deprivation of property and liberty without due...	Apr. 25, 1986	Case	▮▮▮▯	2 6 7 P.2d
Discussed by	**8. Hagebak v. Stone** 〞 61 P.3d 201, 205+ , N.M.App. TORTS - Defamation. Defamatory intracorporate communications have qualified privilege.	Dec. 09, 2002	Case	▮▮▮▯	6 7 P.2d
Declined to Follow by NEGATIVE	**9. Charleswell v. Bank of Nova Scotia** 2001 WL 1464759, *4 , Terr.V.I. Before the Court is Defendant The Bank of Nova Scotia's ("Scotiabank") Motion for Summary Judgment pursuant to Rule 56 of the Federal Rules of Civil Procedure. For the reasons...	May 01, 2001	Case	▮▮▯▯▯	7 P.2d
Cited by	**10. Turner v. Halliburton Co.** 722 P.2d 1106, 1113 , Kan. Employee brought action against former employer and supervisor for defamation and tortious interference with right to contract, as result of statements accusing employer of theft...	July 30, 1986	Case	▮▮▯▯▯	5 6 P.2d
Cited by	**11. Purdum v. Purdum** 301 P.3d 718, 748 , Kan.App. CIVIL RIGHTS - Religion. Establishment clause precluded court's jurisdiction over defamation action based on statements made to Archdiocese Tribunal.	May 17, 2013	Case	▮▮▯▯▯	—
Cited by	**12. Davis v. Hildyard** 113 P.3d 827, 832 , Kan.App. HEALTH - Immunity. Physicians were immune from liability for defamation for statements made during meetings conducted within ambit of peer review.	June 17, 2005	Case	▮▮▯▯▯	1 2 P.2d
Cited by	**13. Richardson v. Dietrich** 105 P.3d 279, 279 , Kan.App. Robert Richardson appeals the district court's order granting summary judgment against him on all claims that his former employer, U.S.D. # 437, violated the Veteran's Preference...	Feb. 04, 2005	Case	▮▮▯▯▯	1 2 P.2d

Box 4.9   *(continued)*

List of 20 Citing References for Luttrell v. United Telephone System, Inc.

Treatment	Title	Date	Type	Depth	Headnote(s)
Cited by	**14. Batt v. Globe Engineering Co., Inc.** 774 P.2d 371, 375+ , Kan.App. Employee brought action against employer and supervisor alleging defamation, breach of employment contract, and tortious interference with employment contract, arising out of...	May 19, 1989	Case		1 2 7 P.2d
Cited by	**15. Stead v. Unified School Dist. No. 259, Sedgwick County, Kan.** 2015 WL 1137746, *13 , D.Kan. EDUCATION - Administrators. Kansas elementary school principal was not deprived of her due process-protected liberty interest in name clearing hearing.	Mar. 13, 2015	Case		1 2 P.2d
Cited by	**16. Michaels v. City of McPherson, Kan.** 2014 WL 3107966, *10 , D.Kan. This matter is before the court on two motions: (1) plaintiff's motion for partial summary judgment (Doc. 72) on Counts I and VIII; and (2) defendants' motion for summary judgment...	July 07, 2014	Case		2 P.2d
Cited by	**17. Haggins v. Liberti** 2011 WL 6740542, *10 , D.Kan. Plaintiff Tyreice Haggins brought the present defamation against his former employer, United Parcel Service, and three UPS supervisors, after he was terminated for falsifying his...	Dec. 22, 2011	Case		—
Cited by	**18. Auld v. Value Place Property Management LLC** 2010 WL 610690, *5 , D.Kan. On December 4, 2006, Plaintiff Stuart Auld received an offer of employment as Director, Development Services from Defendants Value Place Property Management, LLC (VPPM) and/or...	Feb. 19, 2010	Case		7 P.2d
Cited by	**19. Snyder v. American Kennel Club** 661 F.Supp.2d 1219, 1230 , D.Kan. TORTS - Defamation. Professional dog handlers could not sustain libel claim against national organization which regulated showing of purebred dogs.	Oct. 06, 2009	Case		5 6 P.2d

Box 4.9   *(continued)*

List of 20 Citing References for Luttrell v. United Telephone System, Inc.

Treatment	Title	Date	Type	Depth	Headnote(s)
Cited by	**20. D'Souza-Klamath v. Cloud County Health Center, Inc.** 2009 WL 902377, *10+ , D.Kan. This matter comes before the court upon defendant Cloud County Health Center, Inc.'s motion for summary judgment. Plaintiff has filed a response opposing the motion, and...	Mar. 31, 2009	Case	▀▀▘▘▘	8 P.2d

WestlawNext © 2015 Thomson Reuters. No claim to original U.S. Government Works.   4

List of 2 History for Luttrell v. United Telephone System, Inc.

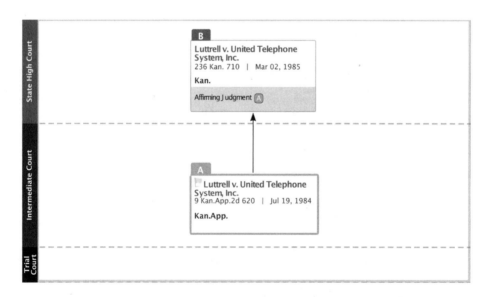

WestlawNext © 2015 Thomson Reuters. No claim to original U.S. Government Works.   1

Two additional points about Westlaw: You may initially tailor a search, for example to find cases written by a particular judge, with a specific party in the title, or from specified dates, through advanced search options. Once you have run a search, you may filter your results by date of decision, status of decision (published only), or key numbers, among other criteria. Using these filters wisely can increase the efficiency of your research considerably.

Lexis. Researching cases in Lexis has strong parallels to researching cases in Westlaw. The default is to research in a wide range of sources, but if you are seeking only cases, focus your search on the cases from your jurisdiction. You may run various types of searches, including natural-language and terms-and-connectors searches. Lexis also offers a Browse function, which entails selecting from a list of topical areas and then selecting more and more detailed subtopics until you reach the Get Documents point, when your topic/sub-topics choice is run as a search. And Lexis provides a strong citator in Shepard's.

As an example, we used Lexis to research case law for the de la Cruz situation. Our client, a student in a public middle school in Pennsylvania, was suspended for a statement that he had shaved into his hair in support of his ill sister. This statement could be protected free speech under the U.S. Constitution. Litigation of this matter (should litigation occur)[22] could take place in the federal courts in the Third Circuit.

We filtered our search at the outset by electing to search in U.S. Supreme Court and Third Circuit cases. We chose two different search strategies. The first was a terms-and-connectors search: *free speech /p public school /p*

---

22. This client situation is an example of work that a firm might handle on a pro bono basis, if a family was unable to pay the attorney's fees.

student;[23] this search yielded thirty-six cases, including several leading cases from the Supreme Court and the *Easton* case from the Third Circuit (appearing eighth on the list). The Lexis results list provides a brief description of the case. See Box 4.10. The second strategy was to use the Topics outline, found at the Browse link. We began with *Constitutional Law* and worked through *Bill of Rights, Fundamental Freedoms, Freedom of Speech*, and *Expressive Conduct*. This search yielded one of the leading Supreme Court cases, which is about students wearing armbands in school.

The *Easton* case as it appears in Lexis is excerpted in Box 4.2 earlier in this chapter. Note that Lexis provides a citation to the West reporter (725 F.3d 293) at the outset of the decision.[24] The opinion by the court is preceded by extensive editorial enhancements: the case's litigation history, both before and after the decision you are reading; core terms (which could be used in further research); a case summary; and headnotes from Lexis. These headnotes are connected to the topical outline of the law in Lexis, and the topics/subtopics are listed at the beginning of each headnote.

After reading the case, we could easily connect to other cases from it. First, we could click on the hyperlinks to sources (including cases) cited within it. Second, once we identified a particularly useful portion of the case and worked back to its corresponding headnote, we could use its topic/subtopic heading to retrieve other cases on that topic.[25]

Shepard's is Lexis's case citator (the equivalent of Westlaw's KeyCite). It may be used either as you are researching cases in Lexis or on its own. Most important, Shepard's provides information permitting you to discern whether a case that you have read is still good law, including the use of colored symbols. Shepard's also facilitates updating by directing you to later sources (especially cases) citing the case that you are currently reading. Information about the citing cases includes both the point for which the citing case turned to the cited case, as captured in Lexis headnotes, and the extent of the discussion.

When we researched the de la Cruz situation, we Shepardized *Easton* and obtained a fourteen-page report. See the excerpt in Box 4.11. The Appellate History report is a strong indicator of whether the case is good law. In the case of *Easton*, it reported prior case history and the fact that the Supreme Court declined to review the Third Circuit decision. The Citing Decisions report listed eight decisions, although none were appellate decisions that merited consideration. Thus, we concluded that *Easton* was good law (even though Lexis gave it a cautionary yellow triangle). Shepard's also provided a list of

---

23. Lexis processes common phrases (such as "free speech") automatically.

24. Within the pages of the opinion appear boldfaced numbers permitting you to track the page numbers in the West print reporters.

25. This is similar to using the Key Number system to construct a search. The Key Numbers in Westlaw are not the same as the topic-subtopics used by Lexis, however.

Box 4.10 **LEXIS SEARCH (Constitutional Rights of Public School Student)**

 LexisNexis®

Results for: **free speech /p public school /p student**

Cases

1. Tinker v. Des Moines Indep. Cmty. Sch. Dist., 393 U.S. 503

A regulation issued by **public school** authorities prohibiting **students** from wearing black armbands during school hours to publicize their ...
... in Vietnam and their support for a truce, violates the **students'** constitutional rights to **free speech** under the First Amendment , where there was no evidence ...
... of the school or impinge upon the rights of other **students** or that the prohibition was necessary to avoid material and ...

Jurisdiction
U.S. Federal

Court
Supreme Court

Date
Feb 24, 1969

Overview: The wearing of armbands by students to public high school in protest of the Vietnam War was entirely divorced from actually or potentially disruptive conduct and, therefore, protected under the First Amendment.

2. Morse v. Frederick, 551 U.S. 393

Public-school officials held not to violate First Amendment **free-speech** guarantee by suspending **student** who refused to take down "BONG HiTS 4 JESUS" banner unfurled by **student** and other **students** at school-sponsored event.
... the First Amendment , as originally understood, does not protect **student** speech in **public schools** . Although colonial schools were exclusively private, public education proliferated ...
... By the time the States ratified the Fourteenth Amendment , **public schools** had become relatively common. W. Reese, America's **Public Schools**: From the Common School to "No Child Left Behind" 11-12 (2005) (hereinafter Reese). If **students** in **public schools** were originally understood as having **free-speech** rights, one would have expected 19th-century **public schools** to have respected those rights and courts to have enforced ...
... simpler reason: As originally understood, the Constitution does not afford **students** a right to **free speech** in **public schools**.

Jurisdiction
U.S. Federal

Court
Supreme Court

Date
Jun 25, 2007

Overview: School officials did not violate First Amendment by suspending student who refused to take down pro-drug banner at school-sponsored event; the student's § 1983 claim failed because school officials were entitled to take steps to safeguard those entrusted to their care from speech that could reasonably be regarded as encouraging illegal drug use.

Box 4.10   *(continued)*

8. ▲ B.H. v. Easton Area Sch. Dist., 725 F.3d 293

... to restrict speech because of the heckler's veto of other **students** ' disruptive reactions. See Appellees' Br. at 35 (emphasis added). ...

... precise interplay between the anti-heckler's veto principle present elsewhere in **free-speech** doctrine and Tinker's substantial-disruption standard in **public schools** . Compare Zamecnik , 636 F.3d at 879 (noting that ...

... veto doctrine and the substantial-disruption test and concluding that other **students** ' harassment of "Zamecnik because of their disapproval of her ...

Jurisdiction
U.S. Federal

Court
3rd Circuit Court of Appeals

Date
Aug 05, 2013

> **Overview:** Under the First Amendment, because the bracelets the students wore that were part of a nationally recognized breast-cancer-awareness campaign were not plainly lewd and because they commented on a social issue, they could not be categorically banned by the school district.

9. ◆ C.H. v. Bridgeton Bd. of Educ., 2010 U.S. Dist. LEXIS 40038

The basic framework for analyzing First Amendment **free speech** cases with **students** in **public schools** arises from four cases: 1) Tinker ; 2) Bethel School ...

... 168 L. Ed. 2d 290 (2007) . In Tinker , **students** protested the Vietnam War by wearing black armbands to school. ...

Jurisdiction
U.S. Federal

Court
New Jersey District Court

Date
Apr 22, 2010

10. ❶ Miller v. Penn Manor Sch. Dist., 588 F. Supp. 2d 606

[A]ny argument for altering the usual **free speech** rules in the **public schools** cannot rest on a theory of delegation but must instead ...

... this case is the threat to the physical safety of **students**. School attendance can expose **students** to threats to their physical safety that they would not ...

Jurisdiction
U.S. Federal

Court
Pennsylvania Eastern District Court

Date
Sep 30, 2008

> **Overview:** School did not have to demonstrate a substantial and material disruption to restrict a student from wearing a T-shirt stating that he had a "Terrorist Hunting Permit" and a "No Bag Limit" with an automatic weapon pictured because the T-shirt was not First Amendment protected political speech but a message advocating violence and vigilante acts.

Box 4.11   SHEPARD'S REPORT (Constitutional Rights of Public School Student)

 LexisNexis®

Shepard's®: Report Content

Appellate History: Requested
Citing Decisions: None Applied

Other Citing Sources: None Applied
Table Of Authorities: Not Requested

Shepard's®:   B.H. v. Easton Area Sch. Dist. 725 F.3d 293,2013 U.S. App. LEXIS 16087,2013 WL 3970093: (3d Cir. Pa. 2013)

No negative subsequent appellate history

Appellate History (5)

Prior

1.   B. H. v. Easton Area Sch. Dist.

827 F. Supp. 2d 392, 2011 U.S. Dist. LEXIS 39483

Court
E.D. Pa.
Date:
2011

2.   **Criticized in:**
K.J. v. Sauk Prairie Sch.Dist. **A**

2012 U.S. Dist. LEXIS 187689

Court
W.D. Wis.
Date:
Feb. 6, 2012

3.   **Later proceeding at:**
B.H. v. Easton Area Sch. Dist. **A**

2012 U.S. App. LEXIS 17201

Court
3d Cir.

Box 4.11   *(continued)*

Shepard's®: B.H. v. Easton Area Sch. Dist., 725 F.3d 293

Date:
Aug. 16, 2012

4.   ♀   Citation you Shepardized™
      Affirmed by:
      B.H. v. Easton Area Sch. Dist. ⚠

      725 F.3d 293, 2013 U.S. App. LEXIS 16087   **Court**
                                                                   3d Cir. Pa.
                                                                   Date:
                                                                   2013

      Subsequent

5.   **B** **Writ of certiorari denied:**
      Easton Area Sch. Dist. v. B.H. **A**

      134 S. Ct. 1515, 188 L. Ed. 2d 450, 2014 U.S. LEXIS 1839, 82 U.S.L.W. 3527   **Court**
                                                                                    U.S.
                                                                                    Date:
                                                                                    2014

Box 4.11   *(continued)*

Shepard's®: B.H. v. Easton Area Sch. Dist., 725 F.3d 293

Citing Decisions (8)

Narrow by: None Applied

Analysis: Distinguished by (1), Followed by (7), "Cited by" (1)

Court:3rd Circuit (7), 7th Circuit (1)

Headnotes:HN4 (5), HN1 (1), HN15 (1), HN17 (1), HN19 (1), HN20 (1), HN21 (1), HN26 (1), HN28 (1), HN32 (1), HN36 (1), HN38 (1), HN5 (1), HN9 (1)

3rd Circuit - U.S. District Courts

1.   Am. Freedom Def. Initiative v. SEPTA Ⓐ

2015 U.S. Dist. LEXIS 29571

Discussion

🔲 **Cited by:**

This fact specific holding does not mark a retreat from the automatic presumption principle enounced in Elrod and the Third Circuit has since reaffirmed the principle's continued validity. See **B.H. ex rel. Hawk v. Easton Area Sch. Dist ., 725 F.3d 293 , 323 (3d Cir. 2013)** (holding that pursuant to Elrod a restriction which prevents the exercise of the right to freedom of speech "unquestionably constitutes irreparable injury.")

Headnotes
HN9

Court
E.D. Pa.

Date:
Mar. 11, 2015

2.   Brandt v. Burwell Ⓐ

2014 U.S. Dist. LEXIS 87395

Discussion

🟦 **Followed by:**

... merits; (2) whether the movant will be irreparably harmed by denying the injunction; (3) whether there will be greater harm to the nonmoving party if the injunction is granted; and (4) whether granting the injunction is in the public interest.'" **B.H. ex rel. Hawk v. Easton Area Sch. Dist. , 725 F.3d 293 , 302 (3d Cir. 2013)** (quoting Sypniewski v. Warren Hills Reg'l Bd. of Educ. , 307 F.3d 243 , 252 (3d Cir. 2002)) (quoting High-mark, Inc. v. UPMC Health Plan, Inc. , 276 F.3d 160 , ...

Headnotes
HN4

Court
W.D. Pa.

Date:
June 20, 2014

3.   Thomas Global Group, LLC v. Watkins ❶

2014 U.S. Dist. LEXIS 48042

Discussion

🟦 **Followed by:**

... merits; (2) whether the movant will be irreparably harmed by denying

Headnotes
HN4

Box 4.11   *(continued)*

Shepard's®: B.H. v. Easton Area Sch. Dist., 725 F.3d 293

Other Citing Sources: (29)

Narrow by: None Applied

Content: Court Documents (12), Law Reviews (12), Treatises (4), Statutes (1)

Annotated Statutes

1. USCS Const. Amend. 1

                                                            Content
                                                            Statutes

Law Reviews and Periodicals

2. ARTICLE: TERRIFYING TRADEMARKS AND A SCANDALOUS DISREGARD
    FOR THE FIRST AMENDMENT: SECTION 2(A)'S UNCONSTITUTIONAL
    PROHIBITION ON SCANDALOUS, IMMORAL, AND DISPARAGING TRADE-
    MARKS

    25 Alb. L.J. Sci. & Tech. 213   **Content**
                                                            Law Reviews
    ... and awareness program "has brought the subject of early onset breast
    cancer to the national media"). The Third Circuit had occasion to   **Date:**
    consider whether a bracelet bearing this mark was protected speech   2015
    when a student wore one in school. 227 **B.H. ex rel Hawk v. Easton
    Area Sch. Dist., 725 F.3d 293 , 297-98 (3d Cir. 2013)**. It held that, even
    if the phrase were vulgar, since it was used in connection to a social
    issue, it would be protected. 228 Id. at 298.

3. COMMENT: BRACELETS AND THE SCOPE OF STUDENT SPEECH RIGHTS
    IN B.H. EX REL. HAWK v. EASTON AREA SCHOOL DISTRICT

    34 B.C. J.L. & Soc. Just. 40   **Content**
                                                            Law Reviews
    During the 2010-2011 school year, middle school students, B.H. and
    K.M. wore bracelets with the slogan "I ♥ boobies! (KEEP A BREAST)" to   **Date:**
    the Easton Area Middle School. 1 B.H. **ex rel. Hawk v. Easton Area   2014
    Sch. Dist., 725 F.3d 293 , 299 (3d Cir. 2013)**. These bracelets, made by
    the Keep a Breast Foundation ("KABF"), were created with the purpose
    of stimulating dialogue and raising awareness about breast cancer in
    young women. 2 See id. at 298. Although there were no disturbances or
    ...

secondary sources citing to *Easton*, including a dozen legal periodical articles, that we could read to further our understanding of the decision.[26]

Here are a few additional points about Lexis: You may filter your search results to certain time periods, sort cases by publication status, or select cases by frequency of citation. Or you may prefilter your search through the Advanced Search function.

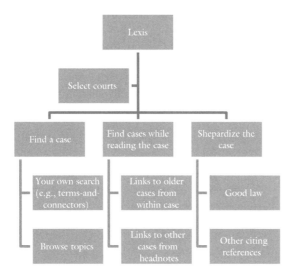

Bloomberg Law. In recent years, Bloomberg Law has sought to enter the market of high-end case law resources (although the Westlaw-Lexis competition already is quite fierce). The basic dimensions of researching in Bloomberg Law parallel those in Westlaw and Lexis. The first is to identify a database, which may be a combination of jurisdiction and practice area. The second step is to search for cases, which is accomplished primarily by terms-and-connectors searching or by citation. Bloomberg Law does not have a full-coverage case summary system akin to the headnotes and key numbers of Westlaw or the topic-subtopic browsing offered by Lexis, so searches of this sort are not available. Nor are the cases accompanied by the editorial enhancements that those resources provide.[27] Third, Bloomberg Law does have a citator, BCite, which provides an indication of the overall status of the case (positive, distinguished, or negative), the direct history of the case, and a list of citing cases and other sources. BCite is less useful than KeyCite and Shepard's, however, because the citing cases are not tied back to headnotes from the cited cases, as Bloomberg Law does not have headnotes.

---

26. Shepard's also has a table-of-authorities function.

27. In certain specialized practice areas, Bloomberg Law offers sophisticated headnotes and organizational outlines.

Economy-Class Commercial Resources

In the context of case law research, economy-class commercial resources offer much more than a court website, yet less than the high-end commercial resources — but at lower prices. This model is exemplified by Fastcase, a resource available as a benefit of membership in many bar associations.[28]

Fastcase provides extensive coverage of published federal cases and fairly extensive coverage of published state cases.[29] It did not begin to cover unreported cases comprehensively until 2010, however. It offers three search options: terms-and-connectors searching, natural-language searching, and retrieving a case by its citation. However, the search results are not enhanced, as they are with the high-end commercial resources. You may link to other sources in Fastcase as you read a case. Finally, although Fasctcase provides a means of tracking citations to a case, this finding tool is not a sophisticated citator.

Thus, for many research projects, Fastcase is a cost-effective alternative to the high-end commercial resources. Compared to the high-end resources, its primary weakness is in the citator function, but this weakness can be offset by targeted use of those resources. A secondary weakness is reduced coverage of certain cases, but many client situations are controlled by the cases existing in its databases.

As an example, we researched the question posed by All-Day Wellness, a Minnesota company, on Fastcase: may it impose a covenant not-to-compete on its new employees?[30] This is a fairly straightforward question, about which we had solid grounding in secondary sources. We first chose Advanced Case Law Search, and then designated Minnesota as our jurisdiction. Our keyword search was *employ* w/20 (covenant /5 compete)*. Fastcase retrieved twenty-six cases, which we reviewed by court hierarchy. The results list provides not only the citation to the case, but also some text from it, an indication of the salience of the search terms (via the relevance percentage), and an indirect indication of the importance of the case by noting how often the case has been cited in cases in the database. One benefit of Fastcase is that it identified

---

28. A similar resource is Casemaker.

29. The federal coverage is co-extensive with *U.S. Reports, Federal Reporter 2d* and *3d*, and *Federal Supplement*. State coverage typically reaches back to 1950.

30. Minnesota is one of the states where lawyers have access to Fastcase as a benefit of membership in the bar association.

several additional decisions that did not actually fit the requirements of the search but that could be pertinent nonetheless.

One case of note was *Walker Employment Service, Inc. v. Parkhurst*, a decision of the Minnesota Supreme Court from 1974,[31] listed second. See the excerpt in Box 4.12. Note that the Fastcase version of the case is preceded by the synopsis (syllabus) written by the court but not the editorial enhancements available from the high-end commercial resources. Even without these enhancements, though, we could derive the rule stated on the last page of the decision: that the covenant must be reasonable in terms of area and time and used to protect confidential relationships with customers. We could link to the cases cited in *Walker* for additional case law as well.

Furthermore, Fastcase provides a useful tool, Authority Check, for using one pertinent case as a springboard to more recent sources. That tool lists later cases that cite the case that you are reading, although it explains that it is not a citator. This explanation is made because Fastcase does not provide editorial guidance on whether the cited case is good law.[32] Rather, Authority Check is an automated system. On the other hand, the list of citing cases includes some brief text from each case.

In our example, the Authority Check report led us to some cases from the Minnesota Supreme Court, as well as unpublished but nonetheless useful cases from the Minnesota Court of Appeals from the 2000s. See Box 4.13.[33] Our reading of these synopses suggested that *Walker* continued to be good law, but a citator check was needed to confirm this conclusion.

---

31. *Walker Emp. Serv., Inc. v. Parkhurst*, 219 N.W.2d 437 (Minn. 1974).

32. Authority Check is augmented by BadLaw Bot, which flags negative signal information stated in a case.

33. It also provided references to law review articles.

Box 4.12   **CASE FROM FASTCASE (Covenant Not-to-Compete)**

Walker Employment Service, Inc. v. Parkhurst, 300 Minn. 264, 219 N.W.2d 437 (Minn., 1974)

Page 437
219 N.W.2d 437
300 Minn. 264
WALKER EMPLOYMENT SERVICE, INC., Appellant,
v.
Harry D. PARKHURST, Jr., et al., Respondents.
No. 44442.
Supreme Court of Minnesota.
June 21, 1974.

Syllabus by the Court

1. A restrictive covenant which was not unreasonable either in terms of area or time, and which was utilized for the obvious reason of protecting the employer's confidential relationships with its customers, is enforceable.

2. Employee willingly entered into the covenant and accepted its terms, and by the nature of his employment he came into knowledge of trade secrets and of customers of employer, which knowledge caused the latter harm when employee used such knowledge and engaged in his own business in direct competition with his former employer. Therefore, although the prayer for injunction is moot, employer has the right to seek damages.

Van Valkenburg, Comaford, Moss, Fassett, Flaherty & Clarkson and Paul Van Valkenburg, Minneapolis, for appellant.

Fredrikson, Byron, Colborn, Bisbee, Hansen & Perlman and Jerome S. Rice and S. Charles Sorenson, Jr., Minneapolis, for respondents.

Heard before OTIS, MacLAUGHLIN, and YETKA, JJ., and considered and decided by the court.

Page 438

YETKA, Justice.

Plaintiff appeals from an order of the Hennepin County District Court, denying its motion for amended findings of fact and conclusions of law or for a new trial. We reverse.

Defendant, Harry D. Parkhurst, Jr., commenced employment as a counselor for plaintiff, Walker Employment Service, Inc., on November 1, 1959. Defendant had previously worked for the Communications Equipment Division of General Electric Company, where he had received considerable technical training. On the first or second day of defendant's employment with plaintiff, the parties executed a written employment contract which contained the following provision:

'In consideration of the foregoing employment, Harry D. Parkhurst, Jr. agrees that upon leaving the employ of Walker Employment Service, Inc., he will not engage in the business of, or accept employment by an employment agency within the County of Hennepin for a period of one (1) year after leaving the employ of Walker Employment Service, Inc. Engaging in or becoming interested in, directly or indirectly, the business of an employment agency as an individual, partner, stockholder, director, officer, employee, or in any other capacity whatsoever, shall be deemed a violation of the foregoing provision.

'This provision applies to a voluntary termination of employment and to termination of employment by Walker Employment Service, Inc. for cause regardless of the duration of employment. If termination of employment is made by Walker Employment Service, Inc. without cause, then this provision shall apply only if at that time employment has continued for a period of at least six (6) months.'

fastcase

Box 4.12   (continued)

Walker Employment Service, Inc. v. Parkhurst, 300 Minn. 264, 219 N.W.2d 437 (Minn., 1974)

relationship that is created, as for example, between a doctor and his patients. Once this relationship is formed, it is beyond question that a doctor's patients will seek his aid regardless of this doctor's employment situation.

In the Bennett case, the employee was deliberately demoted and therefore encouraged, or almost forced, to resign. However, the facts in the Bennett case are not present in the case at bar. In this case not only did Parkhurst have access to the clients and the secrets of his employer, but the restrictive covenant further was not unduly restrictive in that the restrictions only applied for one year after leaving employment and to Hennepin County only. There was no unreasonable restraint in the extent [300 Minn. 272] of time or area, nor does the record indicate that Parkhurst was forced out or relegated to an inferior position. The facts are that Parkhurst testified that in 1963 he and two other employees were orally promised by Walker that they could buy a total of 12 percent of the business, but that this promise was rescinded due to Walker's intention to give his son the business. This occurred almost 9 years before Parkhurst left the business.

There is no indication that Parkhurst ever requested a salary. He was on a commission basis, and while the business and economics of the occupation were good, his income was constantly rising. In fact, it was rising through 1969. It was only when the economy went into a tailspin and the business of his employer dropped considerably that his own income dropped. His loss of income, therefore, was due solely to economic conditions. As a matter of fact, in the year in which Parkhurst left there was an indication his income was once again on

the rise because his income for 9 months was approximately the same as that of the entire 12 months in 1971.

Nor are the facts of Menter present here. In the Menter case the employee had access only to walk-in customers from the general public. In the case at bar, plaintiff had lists of both employers and

Page 442

prospective employees to 'match up.' It had devised forms and methods of operation which Parkhurst adopted in his own business. His situation was similar to a route salesman mentioned in the Menter case. Parkhurst was no simple employee but rather a key man in the Walker operation, given not only commissions but also extra bonuses and profit sharing in years of good return. He was in a unique position to exploit the knowledge he took with him in leaving Walker's employment.

If this particular covenant which was not unreasonable either in terms of area or time, and which was utilized for the obvious reason of protecting the employer's confidential relationships with its customers, is not valid, it is difficult to see what type of covenant could ever be upheld by this court. Therefore, since the evidence is sufficient to establish defendant's breach of the [300 Minn. 273] covenant, we reverse and remand for findings thereon in accordance with this opinion and for a new trial at which plaintiff may prove the damages it suffered as a result of such breach.

Reversed and remanded.

Box 4.13   AUTHORITY CHECK REPORT (Covenant Not-to-Compete)

Fastcase - Authority Check Report   Page 1 of 3

Authority Check Report Generated on August 22, 2015

Walker Employment Service, Inc. v. Parkhurst, 300 Minn. 264, 219 N.W.2d 437 (Minn., 1974)

Authority Check is an automated system that identifies later-citing cases, but it is not a citator, and does not include editorial information telling you whether your case is still good law.

Interactive Timeline

Citation Summary

Total number of times this case has
Cited by federal appellate cases:
Cited by state cases:
Cited by district court cases:
Cited by bankruptcy court cases:
Decision date of most recent cite:

Vertical Axis: Court level

Relevance
Walker Employment Service,...
Vertical Axis: Court level

C of A

F. Dist. & Bankr.

State

1920   1940   1960   1980   2000

Citing Law Reviews

Issue 2 - (Winter 2007): Leadership in Legal Education Symposium VII - Beyond the Dean's Office - Perspectives on Legal Education and Administration Triage in the Trenches of the Legal Writing Course: The Theory and Methodology of Analytical Critique 38 U. Tol. L. Rev. 651 (2006-2007) (University of Toledo Law Review) $
on Minnesota opinions dealing with enforceability of non-competition covenants in employment agreements. See, e.g., Davies & Davies Agency, Inc. v. Davies, 298 N.W.2d 127 (Minn. 1980); Jim W. Miller Constr., Inc. v. Schaefer, 298 N.W.2d 455 (Minn. 1980); Walker Employment Serv. v. Parkhurst, 219 N.W.2d 437 (Minn. 1974); Bennett v. Storz Broad. Co., 134 N.W.2d 892 (Minn. 1965). [Vol. 38 TRIAGE IN THE TRENCHES William BILLINGS V. PARIS FASHIONS, Inc. 316 N.E.4th 100 Supreme Court of Hamilton April 2, 1965 MURPHY, Justice. Factual background Plaintiff...

Issue 2 - (1985): Relationship between Employment Agreements and Trade Secret Litigation in Minnesota: The Evolution of Trade Secret Law from Cherne to Electro-Craft. The 11 Wm. Mitchell L. Rev. 501 (1985) (William Mitchell Law Review) $
...the employer's business .... Id (quoting Bennett v. Storz Broadcasting Co., 270 Minn. 525, 534, 134 N.W.2d 892, 899 (1965)); see also Med- tronic, Inc. v. Gibbons, 527 F. Supp. 1085 (D. Minn. 1981) (restrictive covenant narrowly construed); Walker Employment Serv., Inc. v. Parkhurst, 300 Minn. 264, 219 N.W.2d 437 (1974) (restrictive covenant enforceable if not unreasonable in terms of area or time). 3. See Modern Controls, Inc. v. Andreadakis, 578 F.2d 1264 (8th Cir. 1978). The Modem Controls court recognized that protection of trade secrets is a legitimate interest ...

Issue 3 - (1999): Recent Developments Employment Law 25 Wm. Mitchell L. Rev. 1109 (1999) (William Mitchell Law Review) $
existence of a contract; (2) the alleged wrongdoer's knowledge of the contract; (3) intentional procure- ment of its breach; (4) without justification; and (5) damages."202 196. Id. 197. See Id. at 358. 198. See Id. at 361. The court cited Walker Employment Services, Inc. v. Parkhurst, 300 Minn. 264, 271, 219 N.W.2d 437, 441 (1974), and Bennett v. Ston Broadcasting Co., 270 Minn. 525, 533, 134 N.W.2d 892, 898 (1965), for the proposition that noncompete agreements that serve a legitimate employer interest and are no broader than necessary to protect that interest are...

Issue 2 - (1983): Note Employment Contracts: Covenants Not to Compete in Minnesota 9 Wm. Mitchell L. Rev. 388 (1983) (William Mitchell Law Review) $
... tions of the common law of restrictive covenants in Minnesota. It will 17. See id at 86. 18. Id 19. Id at 86-87. 20. For a discussion of temporal limitations, see tifra notes 113-26 and accompanying text. 21. 278 N.W.2d at 93. 22. See Walker Employment Serv., Inc. v. Parkhurst, 300 Minn. 264, 267, 219 N.W.2d 437, 439 (1974); Eutectic Welding Alloys Corp. v. West, 281 Minn. 13, 17-18 n.6, 160 N.W.2d 566, 569 n.6 (1968). 23. 298 N.W.2d 127 (Minn. 1980). 24. Id at 129. 25. See Id. at 130. 26. See Id at 131-32. 27. See infra notes 106-12 & 153-57 and...

Division II Trademarks &(and) Unfair Competition 1989 ABA Sec. Pat. Trademark & Copyright L. Comm. Rep. 107 (1989) (ABA Section of Patent Trademark and Copyright Law Committee Reports) $
...but are enforceable if reasonable and designed to protect a legitimate interest of the employer. See, e.g., Cherne Industries, Inc. v. Grounds & Associates, Inc. 278 N.W.2d 81 (Minn. 1979); Walker Employment Service, Inc. v. Parkhurst, 300 Minn. 264, 219 N.W.2d 437 (Minn. 1974); Eutectic Welding Alloys Corp. v. West, 281 Minn. 13, 160 N.W.2d 566 (Minn. 1968); Bennett v. Storz Broadcasting Co., 270 Minn. 525, 134 N.W.2d 892 (Minn. 1965); Roth v. Gamble-Skogmo, Inc., 532 F. Supp. 1029, 1031 (D. Minn. 1982). Minnesota makes a clear distinction, however, between contracts...

Show All

All Citing Cases

◄ ◄ 1 to 14 of 14 results ► ►

1. Medtronic, Inc. v. Hedemark, No. A08-0987 (Minn. App. 3/3/2009) (Minn. App., 2009)   March 3, 2009
...required regular personal contact with doctors at approximately 15 hospitals in the Sacramento, California area. Medtronic's concern that Hedemark could manipulate the relationships he developed during his years with Medtronic is reasonable. See Walker Employment Serv., Inc. v. Parkhurst, 300 Minn. 264, 271, 219 N.W.2d 437, 441 (1974) (recognizing that "[e]nforcement of restrictive covenants against professional employees is based on the relationship that is created"); Bennett, 270 Minn. at 534, 134 N.W.2d at 899 (requiring consideration of the "nature and character of...

2. Salon 2000, Inc. v. Dauwalter, No. A06-1227 (Minn. App. 6/5/2007) (Minn. App., 2007)   June 5, 2007
...of the employer; (2) not more restrictive than reasonably necessary to protect the employer's business given the nature of that business and the extent of the duration and the geographic scope of the restraint; and (3) not injurious to the public. Walker Employment Serv. Inc. v. Parkhurst, 300 Minn. 264, 270-71, 219 N.W.2d 437, 441 (1974).   Under the first requirement, Salon 2000 contends, and we agree, that because stylists are in a position to develop a close relationship with the salon's customers, its noncompete agreement is...

Box 4.13 *(continued)*

Fastcase - Authority Check Report

Page 2 of 3

3. IDS Life Ins. Co. v. SunAmerica Life Ins. Co., 136 F.3d 537 (C.A.7 (Ill.), 1998) February 10, 1998
...the employer after termination of the employment unless the covenant is shown to be reasonable, which means tailored in duration and scope to the lawful interest sought to be protected by it. See **Walker Employment Service, Inc. v. Parkhurst**, **300 Minn. 264, 219 N.W.2d 437,** 441 (1974); Bennett v. Storz Broadcasting Co., 270 Minn. 525, 134 N.W.2d 892, 898-99 (1965); Dean Van Horn Consulting Associates, Inc. v. Wold, 367 N.W.2d 556, 560 (Minn.App.1985); Advent Electronics, Inc. v. Buckman, 112 F.3d 267, 274 (7th Cir.1997); Curtis 1000, Inc. v. Suess, 24 F.3d 941, 944 (7th Cir.1994). We...

4. Kallok v. Medtronic, Inc., 573 N.W.2d 356 (Minn., 1998) January 15, 1998
...v. Storz Broadcasting Co., 270 Minn. 525, 533, 134 N.W.2d 892, 898 (1965) (citation omitted). However, noncompete agreements are enforceable if they serve a legitimate employer interest and are not broader than necessary to protect this interest. Walker Employment Serv., Inc. v. Parkhurst, **300 Minn. 264, 219 N.W.2d 437,** 441 (1974); Bennett, 270 Minn. at 533, 134 N.W.2d at 898. In determining whether to enforce a particular noncompete agreement or provision, the court balances the employer's interest in protection from unfair competition against the employee's right to earn a...

5. IDS Financial Services, Inc. v. Smithson, 843 F.Supp. 415 (N.D. Ill., 1994) February 4, 1994
Inc. v. Gibbons, 527 F.Supp. 1085, 1091-92 (D.Minn.1981) (if departing sales representative could immediately call on the same customers on behalf of a competitor, then former employer would be unfairly disadvantaged), aff'd, 684 F.2d 565 (8th Cir.1982); Walker Employment Serv., Inc. v. Parkhurst, **300 Minn. 264, 219 N.W.2d 437,** 441-42 (1974) (restrictive covenant prohibiting former employee from working for competitor for one year in county where he previously worked upheld). Smithson has admitted much of the allegations concerning his contact with IDS clients to inform them that he was...

6. Ecolab, Inc. v. KP Laundry Machinery, Inc., 656 F. Supp. 894 (S.D.N.Y., 1987) March 10, 1987
...interests of the employer which are entitled to contractual protection so long as the protective contracts are of reasonable scope. American Broadcasting Cos., Inc. v. Wolf, 52 N.Y.2d 394, 438 N.Y.S.2d 482, 486, 420 N.E.2d 363, 367 (1981); cf. Walker Employment Services, Inc. v. Parkhurst, **300 Minn. 264, 219 N.W.2d 437,** (1974), quoting Bennett v. Storz Broadcasting Co., 270 Minn. 525, 134 N.W.2d 892, 899 (1965). Overbroad covenants have been struck down when they unreasonably enslaved the employee, tying him to his employer by...

7. Surgidev Corp. v. Eye Technology, Inc., 648 F.Supp. 661 (D. Minn., 1986) November 17, 1986
...and extent of the business, the nature and extent of the service of the employee, and other pertinent conditions. (Footnote omitted.) See also **Walker Employment Service, Inc. v. Parkhurst, 300 Minn. 264, 219 N.W.2d 437** (1974). The reasonableness of the covenant not to compete must be evaluated in the context of the employee's responsibilities and functions, as an employer cannot "unreasonably" extract from its employees commitments which are "far broader" than the employee's "actual functions and status." Eutectic Welding Alloys Corp....

8. Saliterman v. Finney, 361 N.W.2d 175 (Minn. App., 1985) January 22, 1985
...sold. A noncompete covenant in an employment agreement will be enforced when necessary to protect the goodwill of the employer's business. See **Walker Employment Service, Inc. v. Parkhurst, 300 Minn. 264, 219 N.W.2d 437** (1974); Granger v. Craven, 159 Minn. 296, 199 N.W. 10 (1924). Additionally, the Minnesota Supreme Court has long recognized the uniquely vulnerable goodwill of patients which belongs to the owner of a medical practice. Granger, 159 Minn. at 303, 199 N.W. at 13. ...

9. Medtronic, Inc. v. Gibbons, 684 F.2d 565 (C.A.8 (Minn.), 1982) July 23, 1982
...of the employer. Minnesota Mining & Manufacturing Co. v. Kirkevold, 87 F.R.D. 324, 328 (D.Minn.1980), citing Cherne Industrial, Inc. v. Grounds & Assocs., 278 N.W.2d 81, 88 n.2 (Minn.1979); **Walker Employment Service, Inc. v. Parkhurst, 300 Minn. 264, 219 N.W.2d 437** (1974); Eutectic Welding Alloys Corp. v. West, 281 Minn. 13, 160 N.W.2d 566 (1968); and Bennett v. Storz Broadcasting Co., 270 Minn. 525, 534, 134 N.W.2d 892, 899 (1965); see also Modern Controls, Inc. v. Andreadakis, 578 F.2d 1264 (8th Cir. 1978) (Minnesota law). In particular, Minnesota courts have granted injunctive...

10. Roth v. Gamble-Skogmo, Inc., 532 F.Supp. 1029 (D. Minn., 1982) March 4, 1982
...trade. They are to be carefully scrutinized, but are enforceable if they are reasonable in time and geographic area and if they protect a legitimate interest of the employer. E.g., Cherne Industrial, Inc. v. Grounds & Associates, 278 N.W.2d 81 (Minn.1979); Walker Employment Service, Inc. v. Parkhurst, **300 Minn. 264, 219 N.W.2d 437** (1974); Bennett v. Storz Broadcasting Co., 270 Minn. 525, 134 N.W.2d 892 (1965). Minnesota has adopted the "blue pencil doctrine" for restrictive covenants in employment cases. Davies & Davies Agency v. Davies, 298 N.W.2d 127, 131 n. 1 (Minn.1980). Under this doctrine,...

11. Medtronic, Inc. v. Gibbons, 527 F.Supp. 1085 (D. Minn., 1981) December 15, 1981
...covenant is unenforceable if the restraint is not necessary for the protection of the business or goodwill of the employer, or if the restraint imposed upon the employee is broader than necessary to protect the employer's legitimate business interest. E.g., Walker Employment Service v. Parkhurst, **300 Minn. 264, 219 N.W.2d 437,** 441 (1974); Bennett v. Storz Broadcasting Co., 270 Minn. 525, 134 N.W.2d 892, 899 (1965). As discussed earlier, Medtronic has established that it has a legitimate business interest in protecting its goodwill, and that a departing sales representative can transfer this...

12. Modern Controls, Inc. v. Andreadakis, 578 F.2d 1264 (C.A.8 (Minn.), 1978) July 17, 1978
...Minnesota Supreme Court has held that confidential business information which does not rise to the level of a trade secret can be protected by a properly drawn covenant not to compete. **Walker Employment Service v. Parkhurst, 300 Minn. 264, 219 N.W.2d 437** (1974); Bennett v. Storz Broadcasting Co., 270 Minn. 525, 134 N.W.2d 892 (1965). Cf. Equipment Advertiser, Inc. v. Harris, 271 Minn. 451, 458, 136 N.W.2d 302, 306 (1965). See generally Blake, Employee Agreements Not to Compete, supra at 669 n. 146. To require an employer to prove the existence of trade secrets prior to...

13. Harris v. Bolin, 247 N.W.2d 600, 310 Minn. 391 (Minn., 1976) October 1, 1976
...2 On the other hand, this court has upheld covenants not to compete in employment contracts where the restriction is no greater than reasonably necessary to protect the employer's business. **Walker Employment Service, Inc. v. Parkhurst, 300 Minn. 264, 219 N.W.2d 437** (1974). Any analysis of the forfeiture involved here should begin by noting that the employer's contributions to the profit sharing plan are not a gratuity but constitute deferred compensation for services rendered. Van Hosen v. Bankers Trust Co., 200 N.W.2d 504 (Iowa...

14. Alside, Inc. v. Larson, 300 Minn. 285, 220 N.W.2d 274 (Minn., 1974) June 21, 1974
follows the same law as Ohio. We recently had occasion to consider generally the enforceability of restrictive covenants in employment contracts in **Walker Employment Service, Inc. v. Parkhurst,** Minn., **219 N.W.2d 437,** filed herewith. We see no need of repeating what we said there. Under that and previous decisions reviewed in it, we think the restrictive covenant involved in the case now before us is clearly enforceable, at least to the extent of the injunction issued by the court. Applying...

Google Scholar

In recent years, Google Scholar has become an increasingly popular resource for case law research. A major reason is the cost factor: it is free. In addition, it is familiar, it is easy to use, and it offers two fairly refined search functions.

However, it does have some disadvantages. First, its coverage[34] is somewhat limited: as of this writing, it encompassed only "published opinions of US state appellate and supreme court cases since 1950, US federal district [and] appellate . . . courts[35] since 1923, and US Supreme Court cases since 1791." Its coverage is not as current as that of the commercial publishers. Second, because the source of its cases is not clear, it does not yet have the credibility of the other resources. Third, it provides no editorial content with the cases. Fourth, it provides only a limited citator function.

Due to these drawbacks, Google Scholar may be useful to retrieve cases that you already know about — especially those not available from a court website because they are too old. Another good option is to use Google Scholar to obtain a few cases on your topic as you do some preliminary research before researching in a more credible resource. You could turn to Google Scholar for cases when you have a good grounding in your topic already, whether from prior experience or from a strong secondary source. It is not suited for topics of state law in which older cases are important. Most important, you should supplement it with a different resource for citing purposes.

In a general sense, researching in Google Scholar resembles researching in the other resources discussed in this chapter. After selecting case law at the outset, you have a choice of jurisdictions and specific courts to choose from. You may run a standard Google search, which is a natural-language search. Use of the Advanced search option permits you to construct searches that

---

34. Its track record in providing the listed cases is much more limited than that of some other publishers. Thus, Google Scholar has not yet earned the same reputation for reliably exhaustive coverage as, for example, Westlaw and Lexis.

35. It also included tax and bankruptcy court opinions.

include required terms, alternative terms, and phrases. You may also search by party names and limit your search by date.[36] The results list displays cases starting with the most relevant or the most recent (whichever you select) and provides the citation for each case, along with a bit of text containing your search terms.

A case provided by Google Scholar is only minimally enhanced. It has the pagination of the case, as reported in a West reporter, and it has links permitting you to click to other cases available in Google Scholar. However, it does not have any additional editorial content.

As an example, we researched the All-Day Wellness issue involving covenants not-to-compete in Google Scholar. We had a good sense of the topic from secondary source research and were simply seeking some of the major Minnesota cases to provide guidance for a client considering using such a covenant. Therefore, using Google Scholar was a good approach.

For our jurisdiction, we selected Minnesota Supreme Court and Court of Appeals. We used the advanced search *employee covenant compete* (so all three terms were required), which yielded a long list of pertinent cases. We selected the first case in the results list, *Bennett v. Storz Broadcasting Co.*[37] The case as we found it in Google Scholar is excerpted in Box 4.14.

Updating a case found in Google Scholar involves the How Cited function. Clicking on this link provides a display of cases, along with phrases showing how the case that you have read has been cited in later cases. What the display does not provide, however, is the analytical work underlying KeyCite or Shepard's that permits you to conclude that the case is good law.

The How Cited display for the *Bennett* case is excerpted in Box 4.15. We could use this display to identify more recent cases to read — but not to determine conclusively whether *Bennett* was good law.

---

36. Because Google Scholar is also constructed for scholarly articles, the interface is for articles. It takes a bit of interpretation.

37. *Bennett v. Storz Broadcasting Co.*, 134 N.W.2d 892 (Minn. 1965). This is the seminal case in this area in Minnesota.

| Box 4.14 | CASE FROM GOOGLE SCHOLAR (Covenant Not-to-Compete) |

134 N.W.2d 892 (1965)

William BENNETT, Appellant,

v.

STORZ BROADCASTING CO., Respondent.

No. 39538.

Supreme Court of Minnesota.

April 2, 1965.

894   *894 Rice & Efron, and Patrick Murray, Minneapolis, for appellant.

Robins, Davis & Lyons, and Sidney Feinberg, Minneapolis, for respondent.

MURPHY, Justice.

This is an appeal from a judgment entered pursuant to an order granting summary judgment to defendant in an action brought for tortious interference with an employment agreement.

From the record it appears that on January 5, 1960, plaintiff, William Bennett, a radio announcer, entered into a contract with defendant, Storz Broadcasting Company, which operates radio station WDGY, to work as a radio announcer for a salary of $1,083.33 per month, payable semi-monthly. The contract was for a period of one year with two separate options permitting the company to extend the term for one-year periods at a stated increase in monthly salary. The contract included the following restrictive agreement:

> "The Artist further agrees and covenants that upon termination of his employment with the Company for any reason, he shall not directly or indirectly, for a period of 18 months from the date that Artist should cease to be employed by the Company accept employment from, or appear on, or become financially interested in, any radio or television station whose station, offices or antenna is located within a radius of 35 miles of any city in which the Company owns or operates, or has entered into an agreement to purchase or operate a broadcasting station."

At the end of the first year plaintiff was notified that his contract would not be renewed, but that, if he wished, he could remain on as an **employee** at union wages which would amount to a reduction of his salary by one-half. Plaintiff resigned on January 17, 1961, and thereafter entered into contract negotiations with KSTP, another broadcasting station located within a 35-mile radius of defendant's Minneapolis station. This fact came to the attention of defendant, and on February 1, 1961, it wrote the management of KSTP as follows:

895
> "We [attorneys for defendant] are authorized to advise you that if there is any violation of the contract referred to on the part of Mr. Bennett that we *895 will be instructed to institute appropriate legal proceedings."

KSTP thereupon withdrew from further negotiations with plaintiff. Plaintiff contends that by the letter defendant intentionally and wrongfully conspired with its attorneys for the purpose of inducing KSTP not to carry out its declared intention to hire him and that he was thereby deprived of prospective employment to his damage in the sum of $25,000.

Box 4.14   *(continued)*

899   *899 5. It is important to note that courts recognize a distinction between restrictive covenants as they relate to the ordinary commercial transaction involving business or property transfers and those which relate to employment contracts entered into by wage earners. A different measure of reasonableness is used. The test applied is whether or not the restraint is necessary for the protection of the business or good will of the employer, and if so, whether the stipulation has imposed upon the **employee** any greater restraint than is reasonably necessary to protect the employer's business, regard being had to the nature and character of the employment, the time for which the restriction is imposed, and the territorial extent of the locality to which the prohibition extends.[3]

6. Restrictions which are broader than necessary to protect the employer's legitimate interest are generally held to be invalid, and the determination of the necessity for the restriction is dependent upon the nature and extent of the business, the nature and extent of the service of the **employee**, and other pertinent conditions. Arthur Murray Dance Studios v. Witter, supra; Briggs v. Butler, 140 Ohio St. 499, 45 N.E. 2d 757. Restrictive covenants such as are found in the contract before us are proscribed by statute in some states.[4] This court has expressed its views as to such restrictive covenants in several decisions. Our approach has been influenced by a concern for the average individual **employee** who as a result of his unequal bargaining power may be found in oppressive circumstances. We said in Menter Co. v. Brock, 147 Minn. 407, 411, 180 N.W. 553, 555, 20 A.L.R. 857, 859:

> "* * * It may well be surmised that such a **covenant** finds its way into an employment contract not so much to protect the business as to needlessly fetter the **employee**, and prevent him from seeking to better his condition by securing employment with competing concerns. One who has nothing but his labor to sell, and is in urgent need of selling that, cannot well afford to raise any objection to any of the terms in the contract of employment offered him, so long as the wages are acceptable."

In Standard Oil Co. v. Bertelsen, 186 Minn. 483, 487, 243 N.W. 701, 703, it was said:

> "* * * A man's right to labor in any occupation in which he is fit to engage is a valuable right, which should not be taken from him, or limited, by injunction, except in a clear case showing the justice and necessity therefor."

See, also, Heflebower v. Sand (D.Minn.) 71 F.Supp. 607.

Authorities relating to the reasonableness of restrictive covenants as they concern the duration and place of the restriction are found in exhaustive annotations in 41 A.L.R.2d 15 and 43 A.L.R.2d 94. Authorities relating to the subject of liability for wrongfully procuring a breach of contract are fully gathered in Annotation, 26 A.L.R.2d 1227. A further discussion of the legal consensus to be gathered from the innumerable authorities on the subject is unnecessary. It is sufficient to say that the lawfulness of employment contracts containing such covenants depends upon numerous circumstances. It may be fairly said that the merits of a dispute arising from the provisions of a restrictive clause in an employment contract cannot always be determined by an examination of the contract itself. The validity of the contract

900   in each case must be determined on its own facts and a reasonable balance must be *900 maintained between the interests of the employer and the **employee**.

Our decisions with reference to the validity of such restrictive covenants dealt with actions brought for injunctive relief. [5] We have not considered the precise question with reference to damages which might grow out of interference by one whose asserted "superior" right is based on a contract which is invalid or unenforceable. It is true that defendant here has a contract which on its face provides a ground for interference with plaintiff's employment elsewhere, but it is not established that the provision relied on creates an interest or property right which the law will protect. In determining whether it does so, the court must consider not only the nature of the business and character of the employment but all the circumstances of the case, including the situation of the parties, the necessity of the restriction

| Box 4.15 | HOW CITED DISPLAY (Covenant Not-to-Compete) |

Web   Images   More...   Sign in

Bennett v. Storz Broadcasting Co., 134 NW 2d 892 - Minn: Supreme Co...

Read   How cited   **Search**

How this document has been cited

The test applied is whether or not the restraint is necessary for the protection of the business or good will of the employer, and if so, whether the stipulation has imposed upon the **employee** any greater restraint than is reasonably necessary to protect the employer's business, regard being had to the nature and character of the **employment**, the time for which the ...
- in Benfield, Inc. v. Moline, 2004 and 29 similar citations

Under Minnesota law, noncompete agreements in an **employment** setting are "looked upon with disfavor, cautiously considered, and carefully scrutinized."
- in Medtronic, Inc. v. HEDEMARK, 2009 and 16 similar citations

The standard for proving justification is reasonable conduct under all the circumstances of the case.
- in Community Ins. Agency, Inc. v. Kemper, 1988 and 10 similar citations

Specifically, a restraint of **competition** is valid in Minnesota where it is entered into for a just and honest purpose, for the protection of a legitimate business interest of the party in whose favor it is imposed, reasonable as between the parties, and not injurious to the public. Id
- in PRE-PAID LEGAL SERVICES, INC. v. WORRE, 2006 and 11 similar citations

The approach of the Minnesota courts regarding **covenants** such as these has been to evidence a concern for the average individual **employee** who has as a result of his unequal bargaining power may be found in oppressive circumstances.

- in Josten's, Inc. v. Cuquet, 1974 and 8 similar citations

Covenants not to **compete** are agreements in partial restraint of trade that historically have been looked upon with disfavor in Minnesota.
- in Head v. MORRIS VETERINARY CENTER, INC., 2005 and 7 similar citations

They are only enforced if and to the extent that they are reasonably necessary to safeguard a protectable interest of the employer and do not impose unnecessary hardship on the **employee's** livelihood.
- in IDS Life Ins. Co. v. SunAmerica, Inc., 1997 and 7 similar citations

When considering these factors in the context of a summary judgment motion, the court must view the evidence in the light most favorable to the nonmoving party.
- in White v. Minn. Dept. of Natural Resources, 1997 and 8 similar citations

Under Minnesota law, a restrictive **covenant** is unenforceable if the restraint is not necessary for the protection of the business or goodwill of the employer, or if the restraint imposed upon the **employee** is broader than necessary to protect the employer's legitimate business interest
- in Medtronic, Inc. v. Gibbons, 1981 and 6 similar citations

Cited by

≡Pathfinder Communications Corp. v. Macy
795 NE 2d 1103 - Ind: Court of Appeals 2003

≡Sakowitz, Inc. v. Steck
669 SW 2d 105 - Tex: Supreme Court 1984

≡Thiesing v. DENTSPLY INTERN., INC.
748 F. Supp. 2d 932 - Dist. Court, ED Wisconsin 2010

≡STATE OF MINNESOTA BY BURLINGTON NORTHERN RAILROAD CO. v. BIG STONE-GRANT ...
990 F. Supp. 731 - Dist. Court, Minnesota 1997

≡Walker Employment Service, Inc. v. Parkhurst
219 NW 2d 437 - Minn: Supreme Court 1974

all 183 citing documents »

Related documents

Davies & Davies Agcy., Inc. v. Davies
298 NW 2d 127 - Minn: Supreme Court 1980

Walker Employment Service, Inc. v. Parkhurst
219 NW 2d 437 - Minn: Supreme Court 1974

Eutectic Welding Alloys Corporation v. West
160 NW 2d 566 - Minn: Supreme Court 1968

Kallok v. Medtronic, Inc.
573 NW 2d 356 - Minn: Supreme Court 1998

National Recruiters, Inc. v. Cashman
323 NW 2d 736 - Minn: Supreme Court 1982

all related documents »

BUILD YOUR UNDERSTANDING

Test Your Knowledge

1. How are motions and jury verdicts similar? How are they different?
2. The Kansas and federal court systems differ in the number of courts at the intermediate level (the first appellate level). How so? Which does your state court system resemble? Or does it follow yet another model?
3. What is the difference between appeal as of right and discretionary review? Which level of appeals court operates which way, and why?
4. If you were to assert that a case is a strong precedent for your client's situation, what would you be saying about the following?
   - Its ratio decidendi
   - Its jurisdiction
   - Its status as binding or persuasive precedent
   - Its subsequent history
   - Its treatment by later cases
5. You have found an en banc decision from a federal appeals court. How does that case differ from a decision rendered by a panel of judges? Is an en banc or panel decision more weighty?
6. Explain how each of the following opinions in a significantly split decision relates to the others:
   - Concurrence
   - Dissent
   - Majority
7. If the significant difference between a published opinion and an unpublished opinion is not their availability, what is it, and why should you care as a researcher?
8. Assume that you are working on litigation in federal court in the Northern District of Illinois within the Seventh Circuit, which covers Illinois as well as Wisconsin and Indiana. In the following situations, are the specified cases mandatory or persuasive precedent?
   - Your litigation arises under federal law. The case you found in your research is: (a) a U.S. Supreme Court case, (b) a Seventh Circuit case, (c) an Eighth Circuit case, (d) a case from the U.S. District Court for the Northern District of Illinois, (e) a case from the U.S. District Court for the District of Minnesota.
   - The court in your client's litigation is exercising diversity jurisdiction, and the question arises under Illinois state law. The case you found in your research is: (a) a Seventh Circuit case in which the court applied Illinois law, (b) an Illinois Supreme Court case.
9. Assume that you are working on litigation in Chicago that is set in the state courts. In the following situations, are the specified cases mandatory or persuasive precedent?
   - Your litigation arises under Illinois state law. The case you found in your research is: (a) an Illinois Supreme Court case, (b) an Illinois

Appellate Court case, (c) a federal Seventh Circuit case (from diversity jurisdiction litigation).

- The court in your client's litigation is exercising concurrent jurisdiction, and the question arises under a federal statute. The case you found in our research is: (a) an Illinois Supreme Court case, (b) a federal Seventh Circuit case.

10. You have read a pertinent case and are now turning to an online case citator.

- State two examples of information that the citator could provide that would cause you to believe the case is no longer good law.
- As you look for new cases to read from the list of citing cases, what factors would you take into account? State at least four.
- Apply your list to the list of citing cases in Box 4.9 (at pages 135-138) for the *Luttrell* case. Which would you read, and why? Which would you not read, and why?

Put It into Practice

Recall your client's situation (detailed in Chapter 1 at pages 20-21): Your client, Emmet Wilson, is a veteran who has developed post-traumatic stress disorder (PTSD). Among other treatments, he has been assigned a therapy dog. Mr. Wilson's landlord has raised concerns because the building is a no-pets building. Indeed, the lease (which is for a year) so specifies, and the landlord says that other tenants have raised the issue. So she has given Mr. Wilson notice that if he does not give up the dog, he will be evicted in a month.

Although this situation is set in West Virginia, for purposes of this practice set, you will research it in various states, so that you can compare different resources.

Part 1. Begin by researching the legal issue raised by the landlord: that Mr. Wilson's keeping of the dog is a breach of the lease for which she may evict him. As you draft your research terms, keep in mind that this issue could arise not only for dogs, but also for cats and other pets. Realize that the law uses various words to describe segments of a lease, including *terms, clauses, provisions,* and *covenants*. You may want to do some of your own work in generating alternative terms for the idea of *eviction*.

1. Research this issue in Westlaw or Lexis in the state of Indiana. State the following about your research:
   a. The database or set of cases you chose
   b. At least two different searches or types of search methods that yielded useful results
   c. The name and citation of two pertinent cases that you found
   d. The rule of law that you drew from the most useful case you found
   e. An older case that you would link to while reading the most useful case you found

  f. Either a Westlaw topic and key number or a Lexis topic-subtopic from a pertinent headnote that you could use to continue researching

  g. The way that you determined whether the most useful case is still good law and the results

  h. The newer cases citing to the most useful case that you would consider reading (if any)

2. Research this same issue in Fastcase in the state of Missouri. State the following about your research:

  a. The set of cases that you chose

  b. A search that yielded useful results

  c. The name and citation of two pertinent cases that you found

  d. The rule of law that you drew from the most useful case you found

  e. An older case that you would link to while reading the most useful case you found

  f. The information that you learned when you ran the most useful case through Authority Check

3. Research this same issue in Google Scholar in the state of New Jersey. State the following about your research:

  a. The courts that you chose

  b. A search that yielded useful results

  c. The name and citation of two pertinent cases that you found

  d. The rule of law that you drew from the most useful case you found

  e. An older case that you would link to while reading the most useful case you found

  f. The newer cases citing to the most useful case that you would consider reading (if any)

  g. The method that you would use to be sure the case you read is still good law

Part 2. Proceed to researching the legal issue as framed by Mr. Wilson: that evicting him because he needs a dog for therapeutic purposes amounts to discrimination based on his disability. Research this issue as a matter of state law in West Virginia.

4. If you had access to all the resources discussed in this chapter and cost was not an issue, which resource or combinations of resources would you choose for this project, and why?

5. Select one or more of the resources discussed in this chapter (other than court websites). Research this issue.

  a. Write the notes for the leading case on the topic resembling the model in Box 4.4.

  b. Write a narrative of your research process. For example: "I chose X resource to start and selected the . . . database. I used the following search terms. . . ."

  c. Write a critique of your research process. What worked well, and what might you do differently next time?

6. Visit the website of the West Virginia State Courts. If you had been alerted to the leading case only by name, could you have obtained a copy of it from that website? Explain.

Make Connections

You will be conducting case law research in a time of unprecedented abundance — not only of cases, but also of means of access to cases. It is all too easy to be overwhelmed and distracted. What practices will you develop to keep yourself focused and efficient, as you tackle each research project and as you deal with the inevitable evolution in resources?

Answers to Test Your Knowledge Questions

1. Motions and jury verdicts are similar in that both are decisions in cases obtained in the lowest court. They are different in that the former are decided by a judge, sometimes at the early stage of a case, and the latter are rendered by a jury after a trial.

2. The Kansas and federal court systems differ in that there is one appellate court in Kansas and many at the federal level. Consult your state's court website to learn about its system.

3. The term "appeal as of right" means that the appellant has the right to have the case heard by the court; in general, intermediate courts operate in this manner. The highest court in a system exercises discretionary review when it selects most of its cases from many petitions. The two levels of courts have different primary functions: to correct error and make law, respectively.

4. If you were to assert that a case is a strong precedent for your client's situation, you would be saying that:
   - Its ratio decidendi — is pertinent to your client's situation
   - Its jurisdiction — is the same as your client's
   - Its status as precedent — is binding
   - Its subsequent history — is positive or nonexistent (i.e., it is good law)
   - Its treatment by later cases — is positive or nonexistent (i.e., it is good law)

5. An en banc decision from a federal appeals court is decided by the entire court, rather than a panel, and thus is weightier than a decision rendered by a panel.

6. In a significantly split decision:
   - Concurrence — agrees with the result but not all facets of the reasoning of the majority
   - Dissent — disagrees with the result and some facets of the reasoning of the majority
   - Majority — states the result and reasoning of more than half of the judges

7. The difference between a published opinion and an unpublished opinion is that the authors intend the latter not to be precedential, whereas they intend the former to be precedential. A jurisdiction's rules govern how unpublished opinions may be used in litigation. Published opinions should receive more emphasis in research.

8. In litigation in federal court in the Northern District of Illinois:
   - If the litigation arises under federal law: (a) a U.S. Supreme Court case is mandatory, (b) a Seventh Circuit case is mandatory, (c) an Eighth Circuit case is persuasive, (d) a case from the U.S. District Court for the Northern District of Illinois is persuasive (although likely to be taken seriously), and (e) a case from the U.S. District Court for the District of Minnesota is persuasive.

- If the court in your client's litigation is exercising diversity jurisdiction, and the question arises under Illinois state law: (a) a Seventh Circuit case in which the court applied Illinois law is persuasive, and (b) an Illinois Supreme Court case is mandatory.

9. In litigation in Chicago, in the state courts:
   - If your litigation arises under Illinois state law: (a) an Illinois Supreme Court case is mandatory, (b) an Illinois Appellate Court case is mandatory, and (c) a federal Seventh Circuit case (from diversity jurisdiction litigation) is persuasive.
   - If the court in your client's litigation is exercising concurrent jurisdiction, and the question arises under a federal statute: (a) an Illinois Supreme Court case is persuasive, and (b) a federal Seventh Circuit case is mandatory.

10. When you are using a case citator:
    - Information provided by a citator indicating that a case is no longer good law includes that a higher court reversed the decision and that a decision in later litigation overruled the decision.
    - Factors to take into account when looking at a list of citing cases are the topic for which the case is cited; the nature and extensiveness of its discussion of the cited case; and the jurisdiction, publication status, and date of the citing case.
    - The list of cases to read should include the pertinent, reported Kansas appellate cases *Lindemuth* and *Batt*. Cases from D. Kan. are non-precedential federal district court cases, as are the out-of-state cases listed 8 and 9. The D. Kan. cases are decisions of the federal district court and would not merit reading given the existence of Kansas appellate cases.

Enacted Law

Notwithstanding the critical role of case law in the U.S. legal system, most conduct in our country is controlled by statutes. This is due in part to the federal nature of our government: many legislatures operate at the federal, state, and local levels. Furthermore, legislatures may act on their own initiatives to identify issues to address through legislation. Thus, when you undertake a research project, you should assume that it is controlled by a statute until you determine otherwise.

Therefore, you must excel in statutory research. To develop this skill requires an understanding of the legislative process and the interaction of the legislature and the courts in creating a rule of law. Furthermore, you need to understand how to read a statute and how to incorporate the related sources that you should find in your research. This chapter covers these two topics before turning to our recommended approaches to researching statutes.

First, a major note on vocabulary: *Bill* is the word used for a proposed law that has not yet passed. *Law* is the word used for a bill that has been passed. A law passed by the U.S. Congress or state legislature is known as a *statute,* whereas a law passed by a local government is generally called an *ordinance.* For conciseness, this chapter uses *statute* to refer to a law at any level.

When a legislative term concludes, the laws passed are published in chronological order in a publication called *session laws.* Much more important for research purposes, the statutes that are currently in force in a jurisdiction—whenever they are passed—are compiled into a logically organized set called a *code.*[1]

This chapter also covers the documents that create governments in the United States, define the powers and limits of each branch, and establish the most basic rights of citizens relative to the government. At the federal and state level, they are called *constitutions;* at the local level, they typically are known as *charters.* For conciseness, this chapter uses *constitution* to refer to this type of document at any level. Constitutions are created in a process

---

1. A code generally includes only laws of general and permanent application, not laws that pertain to specific individuals or situations or temporary laws.

resembling the enactment of statutes, and they are researched similarly to statutes.

This chapter concludes with an advanced topic in legal research: legislative materials research. Sometimes the language of a statute may be ambiguous when applied to a client's situation, and one option is to research what the legislature intended by the language. Researching the legislature's consideration of the bill as it became law can provide insight into the legislature's intent.

The U.S. Statutory System

Round 1: The Legislative Process and Statute Design

Legislatures make law via a fundamentally different process than courts do, one that involves a series of hearings and debates in which many people participate. Most legislatures (including the U.S. Congress) have two chambers. In such a legislature, the classic process involves introduction of the bill by one or more legislators, hearings on the bill by one or more committees with expertise in the subject matter, deliberation on the bill by these committees, debate in both chambers, passage of the bill, and approval by the chief executive. Both chambers and the chief executive (i.e., the House of Representatives, Senate, and President at the federal level) all must approve a bill in the exact same language for it to become law.[2] The formal process is accompanied by lobbying by constituents and deal-making by legislators.

Out of this lawmaking process come two key principles of statutes as law. First, the statute is not law until the date that the legislature declares it effective. Some statutes contain provisions setting their *effective dates;* others become effective on the standard date for that jurisdiction.[3] Second, the purpose of interpreting a statute is to give meaning to the words chosen by the legislature.

Some statutes are compact; others are dauntingly long. In basic design, many statutes follow a fairly standard sequence. Opening sections state the statute's name and its purpose, both of which provide insight into the legislature's reasons for enacting the statute. A set of *definitions* follow, which apply throughout the statute; note that these definitions may or may not accord with what you would think the words mean in ordinary parlance. The bulk of a statute is its *operative provisions:* first come the *general rules,*

---

2. This process is described in more detail in this chapter's discussion of legislative materials research.

3. For federal statutes, the effective date is the date of the President's approval unless the statute itself states otherwise.

which state what may or may not be done, and then the *exceptions or exemptions*. Nearly every statute represents an accommodation of conflicting policies, and it is in the exceptions that the legislature fits the policies together. *Implementation sections* generally follow the operative provisions; these sections provide the method by which the statute is enforced, whether by government agents or through private litigation. Many statutes close with *technical sections*, such as the effective date.[4]

As with the common law, statutes can evolve. It is not uncommon for a legislature to return to a statute to *amend* it, which may entail refining its expression, adding points, or even changing some rules. When the legislature deems a statute to have been unwise, it may *repeal* the statute, erasing its legal force and removing it from the code. On rare occasions, a legislature enacts a *sunset provision* in a law, calling for the statute to lapse at a specified date.

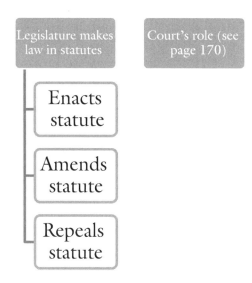

As an example, our client Cassie Collins was ticketed for using a cell phone while driving. More specifically, assume that she was pulling into traffic from the parking lot of a small mall, speaking into her cell phone to find the nearest Starbuck's, when another car ran into her car. This situation occurred in California.

This situation is controlled by section 23123, which is part of the California Vehicle Code. See Box 5.1. Not surprisingly, it is a relatively recent statute, first enacted in 2006. Note the exact words (in italics) chosen by the legislature in section 23123 subdivision (a) to define illegal conduct: driving a motor vehicle while *using a wireless telephone* that is not configured for

---

4. Other possibilities are a severability provision (stating that the statute as a whole stays in force if one provision is declared unconstitutional) and a savings provision (stating that rights or remedies that might otherwise be inferred to be lost due to the enactment of the statute are indeed preserved).

| Box 5.1 | STATUTE MAIN SECTION (Driving While Using Cell Phone) |

§ 23123. Driving a motor vehicle while using a wireless..., CA VEHICLE § 23123

West's Annotated California Codes
   Vehicle Code (Refs & Annos)
      Division 11. Rules of the Road
         Chapter 12. Public Offenses
            Article 1. Driving Offenses (Refs & Annos)

West's Ann.Cal.Vehicle Code § 23123

§ 23123. Driving a motor vehicle while using a wireless telephone; penalty; exceptions

Effective: July 1, 2011

Currentness

(a) A person shall not drive a motor vehicle while using a wireless telephone unless that telephone is specifically designed and configured to allow hands-free listening and talking, and is used in that manner while driving.

(b) A violation of this section is an infraction punishable by a base fine of twenty dollars ($20) for a first offense and fifty dollars ($50) for each subsequent offense.

(c) This section does not apply to a person using a wireless telephone for emergency purposes, including, but not limited to, an emergency call to a law enforcement agency, health care provider, fire department, or other emergency services agency or entity.

(d) This section does not apply to an emergency services professional using a wireless telephone while operating an authorized emergency vehicle, as defined in Section 165, in the course and scope of his or her duties.

(e) This section does not apply to a person driving a schoolbus or transit vehicle that is subject to Section 23125.

(f) This section does not apply to a person while driving a motor vehicle on private property.

(g) This section shall become operative on July 1, 2011.

WestlawNext © 2015 Thomson Reuters. No claim to original U.S. Government Works.   1

Box 5.1   *(continued)*

§ 23123. Driving a motor vehicle while using a wireless..., CA VEHICLE § 23123

Credits

(**Added by** Stats.2006, c. 290 (S.B.1613), § 5, operative July 1, 2011. **Amended by** Stats.2007, c. 214 (S.B.33), § 3, operative July 1, 2011.)

Notes of Decisions (8)

West's Ann. Cal. Vehicle Code § 23123, CA VEHICLE § 23123
Current with urgency legislation through Ch. 132 of 2015 Reg.Sess.

End of Document   © 2015 Thomson Reuters. No claim to original U.S. Government Works.

| Box 5.2 | STATUTE DEFINITION SECTION (Driving While Using Cell Phone) |

VEHICLE CODE - VEH

   DIVISION 1. WORDS AND PHRASES DEFINED [100 - 680] *(Division 1 enacted by Stats. 1959, Ch. 3.)*

    "Private road or driveway" is a way or place in private ownership and used for vehicular travel by the owner and those having express or implied permission from the owner but not by other members of the public.

490.

    (Enacted by Stats. 1959, Ch. 3.)

hands-free listening and talking and is *used in that manner.* Note that there are several exceptions, including for driving a motor vehicle *on private property* in subdivision (f). This term is not defined in section 23123, but there is a pertinent section in the set of definitions for the Vehicle Code as a whole. See Box 5.2. In subdivision (b), section 23123 states the penalty for violation of the statute: fines.

Section 23123 as originally enacted had exemptions for various types of vehicles. The legislature amended the statute to remove those exemptions in 2011.[5]

Round 2: The Legislature and the Courts

If your research yields a statute, the legislature may have chosen to regulate a subject that was not legally regulated before. On the other hand, the legislature may have chosen to act where the courts had already created a common law rule. The U.S. legal system permits the legislature to preempt the courts in this way, whether to codify or indeed modify the common law. As a general principle, when a statute is enacted, it becomes the starting point for the controlling rule.

Often (but not always), a legal topic controlled by statute is also controlled by cases. From a lawmaking standpoint, courts fulfill two roles in such situations.[6]

First, the less common role is to assess the constitutionality of statutes. A legislature may not enact a statute that is beyond its constitutionally authorized powers. A court may invalidate all or a portion of a statute found to be unconstitutional.

Second, the more common judicial role is to interpret the language of statutes. Statutes are often the result of political compromise rathen than precise drafting and are always written about unknown future situations;

---

5. The original statute had a 2011 sunset provision. Most likely, this was intended to prompt the legislature to evaluate the effectiveness of the statute in its early years.

6. They also, of course, resolve the dispute for the litigants — an important role as well.

ambiguity is likely to arise when they are applied to actual, specific situations. The courts not only apply the language to the specific situations but also interpret the statutory language.

Once a court has invalidated or interpreted a statute, the legislature may or may not respond by amending the statute. In these complex situations, it is critical to keep track of the dates of court decisions and legislative enactments relative to that situation, so that you know the precise rule controlling your client's situation.

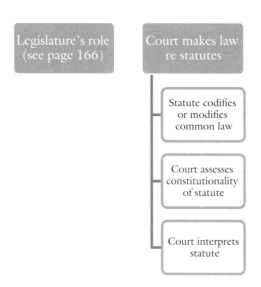

Thus, your research in statutes will involve cases in your jurisdiction inter-preting the statute, if any. If your client's situation raises an ambiguity not resolved by those cases, you will engage in statutory interpretation, a process beyond the scope of this book. However, it merits note that the process involves a variety of research sources; these are *supplemental statutory sources.* Cases predating the statute, as well as legislative history materials, may shed light on the legislature's intent in enacting the statute. Other statutes in your jurisidiction with similar language are useful on the principle that a legislature may intend to use the same language consistently across statutes in its code on the same or nearly the same subject.

Beyond your jurisdiction's primary authority, cases from other jurisdic-tions interpreting similar statutory language can be helpful, especially where the statutes are intended to be interpreted in the same way across jur-isdictions. This is true of laws passed by such organizations as the National Conference of Commissioners on Uniform State Laws and the American Law Institute (ALI), which seek to standardize state laws in areas where uniformity could be beneficial.[7] Dictionaries and secondary sources may provide useful

---

7. The Uniform Commercial Code is one of the best examples of such a law.

insight. Finally, canons of construction are principles about how to read statutes.[8]

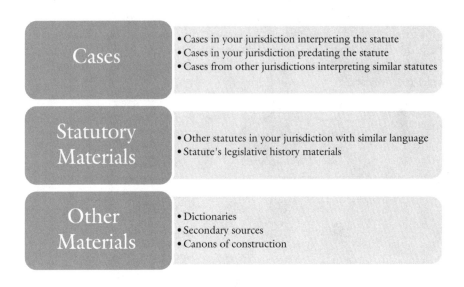

Consider again the Cassie Collins situation. Two ambiguities arise as the statute is applied to her situation: Was she *using* her cell phone (within the meaning of the statute's prohibition)? And was she *on private property* within the statute's exception? Researching beyond the statute itself would yield useful insights into the first question in the form of *People v. Spriggs*,[9] a California Court of Appeals decision. See the opening pages in Box 5.3. There, the court held that a driver who was looking at a map on his cell phone did not violate the statute because he was not using his cell phone, on the grounds that he was not conversing. Among other points, the court examined the language of the statute; reviewed many canons of construction, such as construing all words in context; delved into the legislative history of the statute; and noted that it would be unreasonable to prohibit merely looking at a cell phone.[10] However, the second question in the Cassie Collins situation involves uninterpreted statutory language.

---

8. For example, a provision enacted later prevails over one enacted earlier. Many canons are stated in cases.

9. 168 Cal. Rptr. 3d 347 (Ct. App. 2014).

10. The court also looked at what Governor Arnold Schwarzenegger stated about the law and what later legislation suggested — unusual forms of legislative history.

Box 5.3   STATUTORY INTERPRETATION CASE (Driving While Using Cell Phone)

People v. Spriggs, 224 Cal.App.4th 150 (2014)
168 Cal.Rptr.3d 347, 14 Cal. Daily Op. Serv. 2161, 2014 Daily Journal D.A.R. 2426

224 Cal.App.4th 150
Court of Appeal,
Fifth District, California.

The PEOPLE, Plaintiff and Respondent,
v.
Steven R. SPRIGGS, Defendant and Appellant.

F066927 | Filed February 27, 2014

Synopsis
Background: Defendant was convicted in the Superior Court, Fresno County, No. 002345, Jeffrey Bird, J., of using a wireless telephone while driving. Defendant appealed. The appellate division of the Superior Court affirmed, 215 Cal.App.4th Supp. 1, 154 Cal.Rptr.3d 883. Defendant requested transfer certification and the Court of Appeal granted review.

Holdings: The Court of Appeal, Levy, Acting P.J., held that:

[1] on issue of first impression, statute defining the offense of using a wireless telephone while driving prohibits only the use of a wireless telephone to engage in a conversation, and

[2] holding smartphone in hand and looking at map application while driving did not constitute "using wireless telephone while driving."

Reversed.

West Headnotes (6)

[1]   Statutes
⬠Plain, literal, or clear meaning; ambiguity

Reviewing courts may turn to the legislative history behind even unambiguous statutes when it confirms or bolsters their interpretation.

Cases that cite this headnote

[2]   Statutes
⬠Language and intent, will, purpose, or policy

Court of Appeal must interpret a statute in accord with its legislative intent and where the Legislature expressly declares its intent, Court of Appeal must accept that declaration.

Cases that cite this headnote

[3]   Statutes
⬠Literal, precise, or strict meaning; letter of the law
Statutes
⬠Unintended or unreasonable results; absurdity

Absurd or unjust results will never be ascribed to the Legislature, and a literal construction of a statute will not be followed if it is opposed to its legislative intent.

Cases that cite this headnote

[4]   Automobiles
⬠Equipment in general

The statute defining the offense of using a wireless telephone while driving prohibits only the use of a wireless telephone to engage in a conversation. Cal. Veh. Code § 23123(a).

Cases that cite this headnote

Box 5.3   *(continued)*

People v. Spriggs, 224 Cal.App.4th 150 (2014)

168 Cal.Rptr.3d 347, 14 Cal. Daily Op. Serv. 2161, 2014 Daily Journal D.A.R. 2426

[5]   **Criminal Law**
        ☞Public and private acts and proclamations

In determining whether the statute defining the offense of using a wireless telephone while driving prohibits uses other than engaging in conversation, Court of Appeal would take judicial notice of the legislative history of that statute and the statute prohibiting text-based communication while driving. Cal. Veh. Code §§ 23123(a), 23123.5.

Cases that cite this headnote

[6]   **Automobiles**
        ☞Equipment in general

Defendant who held his cellular telephone in his hand and looked at a map application while driving did not thereby commit the offense of using a wireless telephone while driving. Cal. Veh. Code § 23123(a).

See 2 Witkin & Epstein, Cal. Criminal Law (4th ed. 2012) Crimes Against Public Peace and Welfare, § 326.

Cases that cite this headnote

**348 APPEAL from a judgment of the Superior Court of Fresno County. Jeffrey Bird, Commissioner. (Super.Ct. No. 002345)

Attorneys and Law Firms

McCormick, Barstow, Sheppard, Wayte & Carruth, Scott M. Reddie and Todd W. Baxter, for Defendant and Appellant.

Kamala D. Harris, **Attorney General**, Dane R. Gillette,

Chief Assistant Attorney General, Michael P. Farrell, Assistant Attorney General, Daniel B. Bernstein and Doris A. Calandra, **Deputy Attorneys General**, for Plaintiff and Respondent.

OPINION

LEVY, Acting P.J.

*152 While stopped in heavy traffic, Steven R. Spriggs pulled out his wireless telephone to check a map application for a way around the congestion. A California Highway Patrol officer spotted him holding his telephone, pulled him over, and issued him a traffic citation for violating Vehicle Code section 23123, subdivision (a), which prohibits drivers from "using a wireless telephone unless that telephone is specifically designed and configured to allow hands-free listening and talking, and is used in that manner while driving." Spriggs contends he did not violate the statute because he was not talking on the telephone. We agree. Based on the statute's language, its legislative history, and subsequent legislative enactments, we *153 conclude that the statute means what it says—it prohibits a driver only from holding a wireless telephone while conversing on it. Consequently, we reverse his conviction.

FACTUAL AND PROCEDURAL BACKGROUND

After Spriggs was cited for violating Vehicle Code section 23123, subdivision (a) (hereafter section 23123(a)),¹ he contested the citation. At the trial held before a Fresno County Superior Court traffic commissioner, both Spriggs and the California Highway Patrol officer who issued the citation testified that Spriggs was cited for looking at a map on his cellular telephone while holding the telephone in his hand **349 and driving. The traffic court commissioner subsequently found Spriggs guilty of violating section 23123(a) and ordered him to pay a $165 fine.

Spriggs appealed his conviction to the appellate division of the superior court. There he argued the only use of a wireless telephone section 23123(a) prohibits is listening

Box 5.3   *(continued)*

People v. Spriggs, 224 Cal.App.4th 150 (2014)

168 Cal.Rptr.3d 347, 14 Cal. Daily Op. Serv. 2161, 2014 Daily Journal D.A.R. 2426

and talking on the telephone if the telephone is being used in a manner that requires the driver to hold the telephone in his or her hand. Spriggs asserted the conduct for which he was cited was not a violation of section 23123(a) because he was not listening and talking on the telephone. The People did not file a brief or otherwise appear in connection with the appeal.

The appellate division affirmed Spriggs's conviction in *People v. Spriggs* (2013) 215 Cal.App.4th Supp. 1, 154 Cal.Rptr.3d 883. The appellate division concluded, after reviewing the statute's plain language as well as its legislative history, that the statute was not "designed to prohibit hands-on use of a wireless telephone for conversation only," but instead was "specifically designed to prevent a driver from using a wireless telephone while driving unless the device is being used in a hands-free manner[,]" and "outlawed all 'hands-on' use of a wireless telephone while driving." (*People v. Spriggs, supra,* 215 Cal.App.4th at p. Supp. 5, 6–7, 154 Cal.Rptr.3d 883. italics omitted.)

We subsequently granted review of the matter after the appellate division granted Spriggs's request for transfer certification to this court. We specifically asked the parties to address the following issue: "whether a person driving a motor vehicle, while holding a wireless telephone and looking at or checking a map application on the wireless telephone, violates Vehicle Code section 23123."

*154 On appeal, Spriggs asserts the answer is no, as he was not "using" the wireless telephone within the meaning of the statute because the statute applies only if a driver is listening and talking on a wireless telephone that is not being used in a hands-free mode. The People contend the statute is much broader and applies to all uses of a wireless telephone unless the telephone is used in a hands-free manner.

We agree with Spriggs and conclude, pursuant to the rules of statutory interpretation, including our review of the language and legislative history of section 23123(a), that the Legislature intended the statute to only prohibit the use of a wireless telephone to engage in a conversation while driving unless the telephone is used in a hands-free manner. Therefore, we hold that Spriggs did not violate section 23123(a) and reverse the judgment.

DISCUSSION

I. The applicable principles of statutory construction are well-settled.

The question we must decide, as an issue of first impression, is whether a person violates section 23123(a) by holding a wireless telephone in his or her hand and looking at a map application while driving.[2] This involves statutory interpretation, **350 which we review de novo. (*Bruns v. E–Commerce Exchange, Inc.* (2011) 51 Cal.4th 717, 724, 122 Cal.Rptr.3d 331, 248 P.3d 1185; *California Chamber of Commerce v. Brown* (2011) 196 Cal.App.4th 233, 248, 126 Cal.Rptr.3d 214.)

[1]The principles of statutory construction are clearly established. "Our task is to discern the Legislature's intent. The statutory language itself is the most reliable indicator, so we start with the statute's words, assigning them their usual and ordinary meanings, and construing them in context. If the words themselves are not ambiguous, we presume the Legislature meant what it said, and the statute's plain meaning governs. On the other hand, if the language allows more than one reasonable construction, we may look to such aids as the legislative history of the measure and maxims of statutory construction. In cases of uncertain meaning, we may also consider the consequences of a particular interpretation, including its impact on public *155 policy." (*Wells v. One2One Learning Foundation* (2006) 39 Cal.4th 1164, 1190, 48 Cal.Rptr.3d 108, 141 P.3d 225; see *People v. Smith* (2004) 32 Cal.4th 792, 797–798, 11 Cal.Rptr.3d 290, 86 P.3d 348.) Moreover, "[r]eviewing courts may turn to the legislative history behind even unambiguous statutes when it confirms or bolsters their interpretation." (*In re Gilbert R.* (2012) 211 Cal.App.4th 514, 519, 149 Cal.Rptr.3d 608.)

[2] [3]" 'To resolve [an] ambiguity, we rely upon well-settled rules. "The meaning of a statute may not be determined from a single word or sentence; the words must be construed in context, and provisions relating to the same subject matter must be harmonized to the extent possible. [Citation.] Literal construction should not prevail if it is contrary to the legislative intent apparent in the statute.... An interpretation that renders related provisions nugatory must be avoided [citation]; each sentence must be read not in isolation but in light of the statutory scheme [citation]; and if a statute is amenable to two alternative interpretations, the one that leads to the more reasonable result will be followed [citation]."

Box 5.3   *(continued)*

People v. Spriggs, 224 Cal.App.4th 150 (2014)

168 Cal.Rptr.3d 347, 14 Cal. Daily Op. Serv. 2161, 2014 Daily Journal D.A.R. 2426

[Citations.]' (*People v. Shabazz* (2006) 38 Cal.4th 55, 67–68 [40 Cal.Rptr.3d 750, 130 P.3d 519]; see also *Robert L. v. Superior Court* (2003) 30 Cal.4th 894, 903 [135 Cal.Rptr.2d 30, 69 P.3d 951] [statutory language should not be interpreted in isolation, but must be construed in the context of the entire statute of which it is a part, in order to achieve harmony among the parts].) We must interpret a statute in accord with its legislative intent and where the Legislature expressly declares its intent, we must accept that declaration. (*Tyrone v. Kelley* (1973) 9 Cal.3d 1, 10–11 [106 Cal.Rptr. 761, 507 P.2d 65].) Absurd or unjust results will never be ascribed to the Legislature, and a literal construction of a statute will not be followed if it is opposed to its legislative intent. (*Webster v. Superior Court* (1988) 46 Cal.3d 338, 344 [250 Cal.Rptr. 268, 758 P.2d 596]; *Lungren v. Deukmejian* [(1988)] 45 Cal.3d [727] 735 [248 Cal.Rptr. 115, 755 P.2d 299].)" (*In re J.B.* (2009) 178 Cal.App.4th 751, 756, 100 Cal.Rptr.3d 679.)

2. Section 23123(a) is reasonably construed as only prohibiting a driver from holding a wireless telephone while conversing on it.

a. Statutory language
Section 23123(a) provides: "A person shall not drive a motor vehicle while using a wireless telephone unless that telephone is specifically designed and configured to allow hands-free listening and talking, and is used in that manner while driving." The statute does not define the word "using" or any other term contained therein.

[4] **351** Spriggs contends the statute is clear: "It applies if a person is listening or talking on a wireless telephone while driving and while the wireless telephone is not being used in hands-free mode." He asserts this interpretation is *156 bolstered by the words "telephone" and "hands-free listening and talking[,]" which demonstrate the focus of the statute is on talking on the wireless telephone and not some other use of the telephone, such as looking at a map application.

The People, however, assert the statute clearly prohibits the act of "using a wireless telephone" while driving and, since the word "using" is not ambiguous, it encompasses all uses of the telephone. According to the People, the statute "allows 'using' a wireless 'telephone while driving if the telephone is specifically designed and configured to allow hands-free listening and talking, and is used in that

manner while driving.' Otherwise, using a wireless telephone while driving is prohibited." The People reason that, because under section 23123(a) a "driver may not *use* a cell phone unless it is used in a hands-free manner[,]" that section is violated when a driver holds a wireless telephone and looks at a map application while driving.

While the statute may be interpreted, on its face, as the People assert, we agree with Spriggs that the statute is reasonably construed as only prohibiting engaging in a conversation on a wireless telephone while driving and holding the telephone in one's hand. This is because the statute specifically states the telephone must be used in a manner that allows for "hands-free listening and talking." (§ 23123(a).) It does not state that it must be used in a manner that allows for hands-free looking, hands-free operation or hands-free use, or for anything other than listening and talking. Had the Legislature intended to prohibit drivers from holding the telephone and using it for all purposes, it would not have limited the telephone's required design and configuration to "hands-free listening and talking," but would have used broader language, such as "hands-free operation" or "hands-free use." To interpret section 23123(a) as applying to any use of a wireless telephone renders the "listening and talking" element nonsensical, as not all uses of a wireless telephone involve listening and talking, including looking at a map application.

The appellate division interpreted section 23123(a) as prohibiting all "hands-on use" of a wireless telephone based on its finding that the statute's plain language showed the "primary evil" the Legislature sought to avoid was "the distraction the driver faces when using his or her hands to operate the phone[,]" and "if the Legislature had intended to limit the application of the statute to 'conversing' or 'listening and talking,' as [Spriggs] maintains, it could have done so." (*People v. Spriggs, supra*, 215 Cal.App.4th at pp. Supp. 3–5, 154 Cal.Rptr.3d 883.)While the statute certainly could have been written more clearly, we believe the inclusion of the phrase "hands-free listening and talking" does in fact limit the statute's prohibition to engaging in a conversation while holding a wireless telephone.

157 b. Legislative history
[5]The legislative history of section 23123(a) supports our interpretation.³ **352** Section 23123 was enacted through

Round 3: Federal and State Statutes

Given that much conduct in the United States is controlled by some enacted law, the real question often is which level of legislature has created the law: the U.S. Congress, a state legislature, or a local government. Each operates within a particular sphere set by somewhat abstract principles of constitutional law.[11] Hierarchy does matter; the federal government acting within its proper sphere determines the role of state or local law. The relative roles of the three levels of government are fairly set in many areas of law, while still unresolved in others. In some areas, one level dominates; in other areas, two or even three may interact. Discerning the nature of this interaction is a key step in your research — and an excellent reason to read a strong secondary source early in the research process.

As an example, consider one of the questions posed by Exact Electronics. Exact Electronics has manufacturing plants in small towns in various states. In Oklahoma, an employee is seeking to return from an extended family leave taken after adopting a child, and it turns out that finding an open position for this employee is proving difficult because the plant is fairly small. This topic arises in employment law, which is controlled by a complex web of federal, state, and local laws. The federal Family and Medical Leave Act (FMLA), enacted under Congress's power to regulate interstate commerce, applies only to employers of a certain size and to employees in certain situations (as covered later in this chapter). In some states, statutes cover the same topic for employers and employees in other situations.

THE READING AND BRIEFING OF A STATUTE

While the reading of statutes for purposes of legal analysis is too large a topic to cover in depth in this book, some key points can be made. First, you will want to locate all pertinent language; seeking sections that fit into the segments discussed in the previous part is a wise strategy. Second, you will want to track the precise language — right down to the punctuation — chosen by the legislature. This process is facilitated by writing a *statutory brief.* See Box 5.4.

Additional notes should reflect your research process. You should note how, where, and when you found the statute; also note how current your

---

11. Congress protects national sovereignty and addresses topics assigned to it by the U.S. Constitution. State legislatures address matters of state concern, matters delegated to them by Congress, and matters not expressly assigned to Congress. Local governments, as creatures of the state, exercise only powers explicitly and implicitly granted to them by the state.

| Box 5.4 | STATUTORY BRIEF AND RESEARCH NOTES (Driving While Using Cell Phone) |

Statutory Brief

California Vehicle Code § 23123 (current through ch. 807 of 2015 reg. sess. & ch. 1 of 2015-2016 2d ext. sess.)
General Rule: (a) "A person shall not drive a motor vehicle while using a wireless telephone unless that telephone is specifically designed and configured to allow hands-free listening and talking, and is used in that manner while driving."
Exception: (f) "This section does not apply to a person while driving a motor vehicle on private property."
Definition found in § 490: "'Private road or driveway' is a way or place in private ownership and used for vehicular travel by the owner and those having express or implied permission from the owner but not by other members of the public."
Enforcement: (b) Violation is an infraction punishable by a base fine of $20 for first offense, $50 for subsequent offenses.

Research Notes

Found statute initially via California Legislature website
Switched to Westlaw for additional sources
Researched August 3, 2015

Additional Source
People v. Spriggs, 168 Cal. Rptr. 3d 347 (Ct. App. 2014): Driver reading map on cell phone is not violating statute because not conversing.

statute is. You also should note sources that you may use in your supplemental statutory research — that is, the available sources to use in interpreting the statutory language.

RECOMMENDED APPROACHES TO RESEARCHING STATUTES

Overview

As with case law, strong options abound for researching statutes, and you should choose which to use based on a careful consideration of your context.

One key determinant is the time frame of your research. Most of the time (but not always), your goal is to find the present rule of law because your client's situation occurred recently or will occur soon. However, you may operate in different time frames on occasion. First, if your client's events occurred some time ago and the law has changed, you will need to research the law as of the time of the event in question. Second, if you are counseling a client as to future activities in an area where the law is likely to change, you will be monitoring current legislative activities. These two possibilities are discussed in the last part of this chapter, on researching legislative materials.

A second determinant is the amount of information that you have as you turn to the statutory resources themselves. You may choose differently if you are starting with a good lead from prior knowledge or from research in secondary sources than if you do not have such a solid grounding.

A third determinant is your jurisdiction. Legal publishing does not cover statutory law as uniformly as it covers case law. Thus, the following recommendations are framed somewhat contingently, with the caveat that the actual recommendation depends on the specific publishing situation in your state.

The four major categories of resources are print codes, legislative websites, high-end commercial resources, and economy-class commercial resources. Note that the first category is a print resource. For various reasons, print is well suited to statutes research, as explored in the following discussion. Furthermore, statutory codes began as print publications, and one way to think of the other resources is as online versions of the print codes. Each category has overall advantages and disadvantages, as summarized in Box 5.5.

Print Codes

Many law libraries maintain print copies of the federal code and their home state codes. Compared to a complete set of case reporters, a code is a relatively inexpensive print resource. Furthermore, for many researchers, closely reading a statute in print is preferable to doing so online, and the same is true for browsing potentially pertinent statutes.

Depending on the jurisdiction, you may have a choice between codes. Two different distinctions operate here, with some overlap. First, in general, *official codes* are published by government printing offices; *unoffical codes* are published by commercial publishers. In some states, however, commercial publishers have been designated as the publishers of the official codes. Second, an *unannotated code* provides the text of the statute with few editorial enhancements, while an *annotated code* includes editorial enhancements, such as an explanation of the statute's previous language, citations to and summaries of interpreting cases, and references to secondary sources discussing the statute. An annotated code is, obviously, a richer resource for the researcher.

A typical print code, whether official or unofficial, unannotated or annotated, comes with several editorial tools designed to direct you to the pertinent portion of the code. First, codes are organized topically into chapters or titles, so one logical option is to read the code's list of chapters or titles; from

| Box 5.5 | APPROACHES TO STATUTES RESEARCH |

Resource	Relative Advantages	Relative Disadvantages	Best Uses
Print Codes	Ease of reading and browsing Possibly official version If annotated, fairly current language, legislative references, case summaries, secondary source references Low cost	Not as current as online resources No key-word searching or links Necessity of working with various volumes	Sound resource for most purposes
Legislative Websites	Probably current and authoritative statutory language and legislative references Availability No cost	Only statutory language Limited searching options Challenge of reading codes online	For some jurisdictions, source of current statutory language
High-End Commercial Resources	Current statutory language, legislative references, sophisticated case summaries and links, secondary sources references and links Wide range of access options	Cost Challenge of reading codes online	Follow-up to research in other resources when more information is needed Situations where cost is justified
Economy-Class Commercial Resources	Current statutory language and legislative references, basic case information Various search options Low cost	Less organized case excerpts Fewer secondary source references Challenge of reading codes online	Sound resource for basic situations

that point, peruse the list of sections within the pertinent chapter or title to identify the pertinent sections. Second, check the code's subject matter index, generally found in separate volumes at the end of the set. Third, if the statute of interest has a well-known name, you may look it up by that name in a popular name table.

Once you have identified one or more pertinent sections of a statute through these methods, take some time to explore your surroundings. It is all too easy to focus on the intricacy of the language of the obviously pertinent section and miss the other sections that together form the entire statute. Look for the definitions and implementation sections. In addition, as you read the statute, take note of cross-references to other statutes; where these exist, you must read those statutes too.

After the language of the statute itself, whether in an unannotated code or an annotated code, there very likely will appear a list of the law or laws that created the statute, including their dates of enactment and session law citations. Because you must know whether the language you are reading was in effect at the time of your client's situation, a key step is to check this information.

If the print code that you are working with is an annotated code, the next step is to look at the annotations appearing after the text of the statute itself. If the statute has been amended, you may find a detailed explanation of the statutory language over time. Most useful are the summaries of and citations to cases discussing the statute, organized topically. Binding cases interpreting the statute form part of the controlling law, so checking the annotation for these cases is a key step in your research. Also potentially useful are the citations to secondary sources. Depending on the statute, there may be very little in the way of annotation, or there may be many pages of annotations.[13]

When researching in a print resource, you must always be mindful of the currency of the publications in hand. Print codes are typically updated by pocket parts at the back of the volumes and separate supplementary pamphlets. Because information in these publications can supercede information in the hardcover books, a good practice is to check these publications first.

As an example, recall the question posed by Exact Electronics as to a plant in Minnesota: may it decline to hire an applicant on the grounds that he would be working closely with, although not supervised by, his wife? Minnesota has two print codes: the official, unannotated *Minnesota Statutes* and the unofficial, annotated *Minnesota Statutes Annotated*. We chose to research in the latter because of its substantial annotations. With the prior knowledge that the statute is known as the "Human Rights Act," we found it through the popular names table. See Box 5.6.

As shown in Box 5.7, the Minnesota statute prohibits discrimination in hiring based on marital status, among other reasons. The current language of the operative provision was in the pocket part for 2015 because it was amended in 2014 (to include familial status as a protected class). However, the annotations in the 2012 hardcover volume were still useful in providing the list of laws giving rise to the statute, secondary sources, and case summaries because the rule about marital status discrimination had been in effect for many years. See Box 5.8. Of particular

---

13. Note that these references may not be exhaustive. Rather the editors select the most important and precedential cases, especially as to heavily litigated statutes.

Box 5.6   **PRINT CODE POPULAR NAME TABLE (Employment Discrimination)**

POPULAR NAME TABLE

Human Rights Act, 363A.01 et seq.
Human Services Act, 402.01 et seq.
Human Services Licensing Act, 245A.01 et seq.
Impaired Driving Code, 169A.01
Implied Consent Law, driving under influence of alcohol or drugs, 169A.50
Imprisonment and Exoneration Remedies Act, 611.362 et seq.
Indians, American Indian Language and Culture Education Act, 124D.71
Industrial Hygienist and Safety Professional Title Protection Act, 182A.01
Infectious Waste Control Act, 116.75 et seq.
Insurance Fair Information Reporting Act, 72A.49 et seq.
Insurance Guaranty Association Act, 60C.01 et seq.
Insurance Premium Finance Company Act, 59A.01 et seq.
Insurers Rehabilitation and Liquidation Act, 60B.01 et seq.
Integrated Service Network Act, 62N.01 et seq.
Interagency Services for Children with Disabilities Act, 125A.023, 125A.027
International Student Exchange Law, 5A.01 et seq.
Interstate Banking Act, 48.90 et seq.
Interstate Compact on Industrialized/Modular Buildings, 326B.194
Interstate Corrections Compact, 241.28 et seq.
Invention Services Act, 325A.01 et seq.
Investments, Prudent Investor Act, 501B.151
Isolated Acts Statute, 543.19
Jacob Bill (Sex Offenders Registration), 243.166
Jacobs Law, 518.17, 626.556
Joint Powers Act, governmental units, 471.59
Joint Underwriting Association Act, 62F.01 et seq., 62I.01 et seq.
Journalist Shield Law, 595.024
Junk yards, motor vehicles, construction equipment, agricultural machinery and equipment, 161.242
Juvenile Court Act, 260.011 et seq.
Juvenile protection provisions, Juvenile Court Act, 260C.001 et seq.
Kari Koskinen Manager Background Check Act, 299C.66
Kelsey Smith Act, 237.82 et seq.
Kyles Law, 626.556
Labor Relations Act, 179.01 et seq.
Labor Union Democracy Act, 179.18 et seq.

Lake Improvement District Law, 103B.501 et seq.
Lake Superior Safe Harbors Law, 86A.20 et seq.
Landowners bill of rights, 84.0274, 84.0275
Lead Poisoning Prevention Act, 144.9501 et seq.
Lemon Law, motor vehicles, 325F.665
Leos Law, 10.595
Licenses and permits, Consolidated Food Licensing Act, 28A.01 et seq.
Liens on Personal Property in Self Service Storage Act, 514.970 et seq.
Life and Health Insurance Guaranty Association Act, 61B.18 et seq.
Limited Liability Company Act, 322B.01 et seq., 322C.0101 et seq.
Limited partnerships, Uniform Limited Partnership Act of 2001, 321.0101
Liquor Act, 340A.901 et seq.
Livestock Market Agency and Dealer Licensing Act, 17A.01 et seq.
Living Will Act, 145B.01 et seq.
Local Interim Emergency Succession Act, 1.27
Local Public Health Act, 145A.01 et seq.
Local Water Management Act, 103B.301 et seq.
Local water resources protection and management program, 103B.3361 et seq.
Long Arm Statute, 543.19
Long Term Care Resident Access to Pharmaceuticals Act, 151.415
Lower Saint Croix Wild and Scenic River Act, 103F.351
Management of Institutional Funds Act, 309.73 et seq.
Managing General Agents Act (insurance), 60H.01 et seq.
Manufactured Home Repossession Security Act, 327.61 et seq.
Maternal and Child Nutrition Act, 145.891 et seq.
Maximum Effort School Aid Law, 124C.61
Meat and Poultry Inspection Act, 31A.31
Mediation Act, 572.31 et seq.
Medical Assistance Lien Law, 514.980 et seq.
Medical Practice Act, 147.001 et seq.
Megans Law, sex offenders registration, 243.166
Membership Camping Practices Act, 82A.01 et seq.
Mercury emissions consumer information, 116.925
Metric Implementation and Standards Act, 239.001 et seq.

1322

Box 5.7 PRINT CODE STATUTE TEXT (Employment Discrimination)

§ 363A.04
Note 4

leged personal, emotional, and economic injuries were related to employer's duty to protect her from harassment, discrimination, and retaliation in workplace and fell within MHRA's protections. Radcliffe v. Securian Financial Group, Inc., D.Minn.2012, 906 F.Supp.2d 874. Civil Rights ⟜ 1704

5. Exclusive procedure

Minnesota Human Rights Act (MHRA) exclusivity provision barred employee's claim under Minnesota Whistleblower Act (MWA) prohibiting employer from firing employee because employee, acting in good faith, reported suspected violation of federal or state law. Mudrich v. Wal-Mart Stores, Inc., D.Minn.2013, 955 F.Supp.2d 1001. Civil Rights ⟜ 1704; Labor and Employment ⟜ 852

Exclusive remedy provision of the Minnesota Human Rights Act (MHRA) prohibits an employee from seeking recovery for the same allegedly discriminatory conduct on the same facts under both the MHRA and the state's whistleblower statute. Ewald v. Royal Norwegian Embassy, D.Minn.2012, 902 F.Supp.2d 1208. Civil Rights ⟜ 1704

Employee's defamation claim did not have same factual basis or injuries as claims against employer under the Minnesota Human Rights Act (MHRA), and therefore, defamation claim was not precluded by MHRA exclusivity provision; MHRA did not require a false statement of any kind, statement could be defamatory regardless of race, and defamation claim was based on limited statements, but MHRA claim was premised on a hostile work environment. Walker v. Wanner Engineering, Inc., D.Minn.2012, 867 F.Supp.2d 1050. Libel and Slander ⟜ 68

UNFAIR DISCRIMINATORY PRACTICES

363A.08. Unfair discriminatory practices relating to employment or unfair employment practice

Subdivision 1. Labor organization. Except when based on a bona fide occupational qualification, it is an unfair employment practice for a labor organization, because of race, color, creed, religion, national origin, sex, marital status, status with regard to public assistance, familial status, disability, sexual orientation, or age:

(1) to deny full and equal membership rights to a person seeking membership or to a member;

(2) to expel a member from membership;

(3) to discriminate against a person seeking membership or a member with respect to hiring, apprenticeship, tenure, compensation, terms, upgrading, conditions, facilities, or privileges of employment; or

(4) to fail to classify properly, or refer for employment or otherwise to discriminate against a person or member.

Subd. 2. Employer. Except when based on a bona fide occupational qualification, it is an unfair employment practice for an employer, because of race, color, creed, religion, national origin, sex, marital status, status with regard to public assistance, familial status, membership or activity in a local commission, disability, sexual orientation, or age to:

(1) refuse to hire or to maintain a system of employment which unreasonably excludes a person seeking employment; or

(2) discharge an employee; or

(3) discriminate against a person with respect to hiring, tenure, compensation, terms, upgrading, conditions, facilities, or privileges of employment.

Subd. 3. Employment agency. Except when based on a bona fide occupational qualification, it is an unfair employment practice for an employment agency, because of race, color, creed, religion, national origin, sex, marital status, status with regard to public assistance, familial status, disability, sexual orientation, or age to:

6

Box 5.8   PRINT CODE ANNOTATION (Employment Discrimination)

HUMAN RIGHTS   § 363A.08

Historical and Statutory Notes

Derivation:
St.2002, § 363.03, subds. 1, 9.
Laws 2001, c. 194, § 2.
Laws 2001, c. 186, § 1.
Laws 1997, c. 171, § 1.
Laws 1995, c. 212, art. 2, § 10.
Laws 1994, c. 630, art. 12, § 1.
Laws 1993, c. 277, §§ 5 to 7.
Laws 1993, c. 22, §§ 8 to 15.
Laws 1992, c. 527, §§ 12 to 16.
Laws 1990, c. 567, §§ 3 to 6.
Laws 1989, c. 280, §§ 9 to 14, 21.
Laws 1988, c. 660, § 4.
Laws 1987, c. 245, § 1.
Laws 1987, c. 141, § 2.
Laws 1987, c. 129, § 3.
Laws 1987, c. 23, § 3.
Laws 1986, c. 444.
Laws 1985, c. 248, § 70.
Laws 1984, c. 533, §§ 2, 3.

Laws 1983, c. 276, §§ 7 to 10.
Laws 1983, c. 216, art. 1, § 59.
Laws 1982, c. 517, § 8.
Laws 1981, c. 330, § 1.
Laws 1980, c. 540, §§ 1, 2.
Laws 1980, c. 531, § 4.
Laws 1977, c. 408, § 3.
Laws 1977, c. 351, §§ 5 to 7.
Laws 1975, c. 206, §§ 2 to 5.
Laws 1974, c. 354, § 1.
Laws 1973, c. 296, § 1.
Laws 1973, c. 729, §§ 3, 16.
Laws 1969, c. 9, § 80.
Laws 1969, c. 975, §§ 3 to 5.
Laws 1967, c. 897, §§ 12 to 16.
Laws 1965, c. 586, § 1.
Laws 1965, c. 585, § 2.
Laws 1961, c. 428, § 5.
Laws 1955, c. 516, § 5.

Cross References

Actions, combining allegations of violations under this chapter and of dismissal from employment for age, see § 181.81.
Equal opportunity in athletics, see § 121A.04.
Equal wages for women and men, see § 181.67.
Evidence, use by commissioner of human rights of job evaluation system established under § 471.994 and reports compiled under § 471.995 in actions alleging discrimination, see § 471.997.
Low rent housing, selection of tenants, see § 469.022.
Married women, names on credit cards, see § 325G.041.
Noncompliance with state laws prohibiting discrimination, reduction of special state aid for school districts, see § 127A.42.
Public works contracts, see § 181.59.
Redevelopment projects, use, see § 469.109 et seq.

Law Review and Journal Commentaries

Act against discrimination and the Uniform Law Commissioner's Model Anti-Discrimination Act. Carl A. Auerbach, 55 Minn.L.Rev. 259 (1970).

Antinepotism Rules. 64 Minn.L.Rev. 1183 (1980).

Application of the dynamic approach to statutory interpretation—*Patterson v. McLean Credit Union*, 491 U.S. 164 (1989). 17 Wm.Mitchell L.Rev. 659 (1991).

Arbitration in employment settings: Implications of *Circuit City* and *Waffle House*. Garry Mathiason and George Wood, 59 Bench & B.Minn. 21 (July 2002).

Avoiding a costly mistake: How to successfully handle a sexual harassment investigation. Barbara Jean D'Aguila, 63 Hennepin Law. 8 (Nov.-Dec. 1993).

Consumer protection for Latinos: Overcoming language fraud and English-only in the marketplace. Steven W. Bender, 45 Am.U.L.Rev. 1027 (1996).

The deepening divide: Minnesota and federal employment laws. Sheila Engelmeier and Jonathan J. Hegre, 58 Bench & B.Minn. 21 (April 2001).

The disabled employee and reasonable accommodation under the Minnesota Human Rights Act: Where does absenteeism attributable to the disability fit into the law? Laura Hartman, 19 Wm.Mitchell L.Rev. 905 (1993).

Dutch treats: Lessons the U.S. can learn from how the Netherlands protects lesbians and gays. Astrid A.M. Mattijssen & Charlene L. Smith, 4 Am.U.J. Gender & L. 303 (1996).

Effect of equal rights amendment on Minnesota law. 57 Minn.L.Rev. 771 (1972).

Employment discrimination, case of the Willmar eight. William A. Wines, 1983 Hamline L.Rev. 215.

Equal employment opportunity for women in Minnesota: Prohibition against sexual harassment. Andrew W. Haines, 8 Wm.Mitchell L.Rev. 755 (1982).

Box 5.8   *(continued)*

§ 363A.08

Note 212

D.Minn.1994, 864 F.Supp. 905, affirmed 60 F.3d 423. Civil Rights ⟜ 1231

213. —— Legitimate nondiscriminatory reason, national origin discrimination

Employer articulated legitimate, nondiscriminatory reason for employee's discharge, assuming employee established prima facie case that she had been discriminated against on basis of national origin; employer cited employee's repeated failure to call in absences, repeated failure to respond to inquiries about her medical condition and her return to work date, and her failure to return signed medical authorization form for absences beyond five days. Kovalevsky v. West Pub. Co., D.Minn.1987, 674 F.Supp. 1379. Civil Rights ⟜ 1536; Civil Rights ⟜ 1544

214. —— Pretext, national origin discrimination

Employee's generally positive employment record prior to her placement on performance action plan (PAP) by her supervisor and her eventual termination was not enough evidence on its own to cast doubt that employer's stated reason for the adverse actions, namely employee's job performance, was pretext for national-origin discrimination, in violation of Title VII and the Minnesota Human Rights Act (MHRA); during the six months between the last performance review and the PAP, the scope of employee's job increased, supervisor constantly critiqued her performance, and employee consistently stated her belief she was performing adequately. Guimaraes v. SuperValu, Inc., C.A.8 (Minn.)2012, 674 F.3d 962, rehearing and rehearing en banc denied. Civil Rights ⟜ 1544; Civil Rights ⟜ 1744

Employee failed to establish that employer's legitimate nondiscriminatory reasons for terminating employment were pretext for discrimination on basis of national origin. Kovalevsky v. West Pub. Co., D.Minn.1987, 674 F.Supp. 1379. Civil Rights ⟜ 1544

215. Marital status discrimination—In general

Employer did not discriminate against male employee on basis of marital status, in violation of Minnesota Human Rights Act (MHRA), when it terminated him because of his personal relationship with female subordinate, in that nothing indicated that employer considered his marital status, and termination letter said he was terminated for "business necessity" based on lack of "judgment and professionalism." Freeman v. Ace Telephone Ass'n, D.Minn.2005, 404 F.Supp.2d 1127, affirmed 467 F.3d 695. Civil Rights ⟜ 1197

HUMAN RIGHTS

To prove a claim of marital status discrimination under the Minnesota Human Rights Act (MHRA), a plaintiff must demonstrate that the alleged discrimination was directed at the marital status itself. Freeman v. Ace Telephone Ass'n, D.Minn.2005, 404 F.Supp.2d 1127, affirmed 467 F.3d 695. Civil Rights ⟜ 1196

For marital status discrimination claims under the Minnesota Human Rights Act (MHRA), married, single, and divorced persons are all members of protected groups. Freeman v. Ace Telephone Ass'n, D.Minn.2005, 404 F.Supp.2d 1127, affirmed 467 F.3d 695. Civil Rights ⟜ 1196

The Minnesota Human Rights Act (MHRA) did not require a plaintiff alleging marital status discrimination to allege a direct attack on the institution of marriage; MHRA broadly stated that an employer could not discharge an employee because of marital status, and, reading each term with its plain and ordinary meaning, this language extended protection against marital status discrimination to include the identity of the employee's spouse and the spouse's situation, as well as the spouse's actions and beliefs. Taylor v. LSI Corp. of America, 2011, 796 N.W.2d 153. Civil Rights ⟜ 1196

A plaintiff may make a prima facie showing of marital-status discrimination through either direct evidence of discriminatory intent or circumstantial evidence in accordance with the three-part *McDonnell Douglas* burden-shifting test. Taylor v. LSI Corp. of America, App.2010, 781 N.W.2d 912, review granted, affirmed 796 N.W.2d 153. Civil Rights ⟜ 1744

Employee's claim that employer terminated her based on the identity and situation of her spouse, a co-employee whose forced resignation was occurring at the same time as employee's, in violation of the Minnesota Human Rights Act, fell squarely within the statutory definition of marital status, and did not require a showing that her termination was directed at her marital status itself. Taylor v. LSI Corp. of America, App.2010, 781 N.W.2d 912, review granted, affirmed 796 N.W.2d 153. Civil Rights ⟜ 1197

Alleged marital discrimination must be directed at marital status itself to violate Minnesota Human Rights Act (MHRA); where employer's reason for discharge is not directed at employee's marital status, action under MHRA does not lie. Kepler v. Kordel, Inc., App.1996, 542 N.W.2d 645, review denied. Civil Rights ⟜ 1196

Store manager's wife, who was paid by retail hardware store chain to attend nonbusiness functions at store conventions, was not "employee" under Minnesota Human Rights Act (MHRA) and thus could not claim marital-status discrimination under Act, where purpose of conventions was not business-related, but rather to allow employees opportunity to attend semi-

interest was the reference to *Taylor v. LSI Corp. of America*,[14] a recent Minnesota Supreme Court case, which appears to provide the authoritative interpretation of the statute. Furthermore, both the pocket part and the supplementary pamphlet provided references to additional new cases.

At the federal level, the official code is the *United States Code,* published by the Office of the Law Revision Counsel (OLRC) of the House of Representatives and by the Government Publishing Office on a staggered six-year basis with supplementing publications. Not surprisingly, two strong, unofficial, annotated print codes exist: *United States Code Annotated* (U.S.C.A.), a Thomson Reuters publication (thus connected to Westlaw), and *United States Code Service* (U.S.C.S.), a LexisNexis publication.

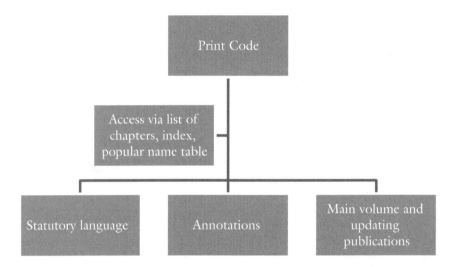

Legislative Websites

Some legislatures maintain a website that provides an up-to-date, official version of their statutes. Other legislatures do not yet do this, or they provide something other than an official current version. If the jurisdiction in which you are researching does provide this resource, and your chief goal is to obtain a copy of the current statute (especially if you already have a citation), a good choice is to use this legislative website, for reasons of cost and credibility. Depending on the website's search options, it may also be a good choice when you believe that a statute is controlling but do not yet have a citation.

---

14. 796 N.W.2d 153 (Minn. 2011).

The first step in researching on a legislature's website is to locate the statutes currently in force, rather than the bills pending before the legislature. The next step is to choose how to search for the pertinent statute, depending on the options offered by the website: keying in the citation, if you already know it; drilling down through the chapters and subchapters (i.e., using the legislature's table of contents); searching the index to the statutes; using the popular name table; or performing a key-word search.

Search by designation	• Key in citation • Use popular name table
Use writer-driven search	• Drill down through divisions (tables of contents) • Search index
Use researcher-driven search	• Key-word search

As an example, we turned to the California Legislature's website[15] to find the statute for the Cassie Collins situation. Finding the pertinent statute was possible without the citation. We drilled down from *Vehicle Code,* to *Division 11. Rules of the Road,* to *Chapter 12. Public Offenses,* to *Article 1. Driving Offenses,* where we found section 23123. We also could have run a search for required and optional terms within a specified code. Note that because of the statute's wording, this search would require use of the word *wireless* — a good example of the necessity of varied search terms. Return to Box 5.2 for a statutory section drawn from the California Legislature's website.

At the federal level, the website of the Office of the Law Revision Counsel of the House of Representatives (OLRC) (uscode.house.gov) offers federal statutes, updated on an ongoing basis.[16] The OLRC website provides the statutory language itself and a limited amount of additional material, including references to laws enacting and amending the statute, effective dates, and general references to regulatory requirements and constitutional litigation, depending on the section. Searching options include keying in statutory

---

15. The FAQ for the site indicated that it is updated with laws that become effective on January 1st of each year and that it is updated as bills are passed and become effective during the session.

16. The website is retrospective only to 1994 legislation, however.

sections by citation, drilling down through the titles and chapters of the code, running searches for key words, and linking to the statute by its name from the popular name tool.

As an example, recall the Exact Electronics question about the employee who has taken a family leave and now seeks to return. We researched this situation initially at the OLRC website. Armed with knowledge that the situation could involve the Family and Medical Leave Act (FMLA), we opted for the popular name tool. See Box 5.9 for the website page. This tool pointed us to 29 U.S.C. § 2601, the first section of the FMLA. After reading through various sections, we determined that § 2612 provided leave for placement of a child through adoption, § 2614 provided for restoration of the employee to an equivalent position upon expiration of the leave — and § 2611 specified which employees are eligible for protection under the FMLA. As for the latter, subsection (2)(B) has an exemption for small work sites, which could be significant depending on the specific attributes of Exact Electronics' workplace. See Box 5.10.

Box 5.9   **LEGISLATIVE WEBSITE POPULAR NAME TOOL (Family Leave Rights)**

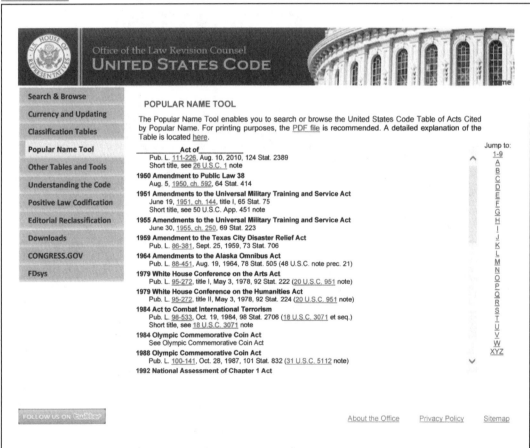

Box 5.10   **LEGISLATIVE WEBSITE STATUTE SECTION (Family Leave Rights)**

---

29 USC 2611: Definitions
Text contains those laws in effect on October 1, 2015

From Title 29-LABOR
　　CHAPTER 28-FAMILY AND MEDICAL LEAVE
　　SUBCHAPTER I-GENERAL REQUIREMENTS FOR LEAVE
Jump To:
　　Source Credit
　　Amendments
　　Effective Date
　　Regulations

---

§2611. Definitions

As used in this subchapter:

(1) Commerce

The terms "commerce" and "industry or activity affecting commerce" mean any activity, business, or industry in commerce or in which a labor dispute would hinder or obstruct commerce or the free flow of commerce, and include "commerce" and any "industry affecting commerce", as defined in paragraphs (1) and (3) of section 142 of this title.

(2) Eligible employee

(A) In general

The term "eligible employee" means an employee who has been employed-
　(i) for at least 12 months by the employer with respect to whom leave is requested under section 2612 of this title; and
　(ii) for at least 1,250 hours of service with such employer during the previous 12-month period.

(B) Exclusions

The term "eligible employee" does not include-
　(i) any Federal officer or employee covered under subchapter V of chapter 63 of title 5; or
　(ii) any employee of an employer who is employed at a worksite at which such employer employs less than 50 employees if the total number of employees employed by that employer within 75 miles of that worksite is less than 50.

(C) Determination

For purposes of determining whether an employee meets the hours of service requirement specified in subparagraph (A)(ii), the legal standards established under section 207 of this title shall apply.

(D) Airline flight crews

(i) Determination

For purposes of determining whether an employee who is a flight attendant or flight crewmember (as such terms are defined in regulations of the Federal Aviation Administration) meets the hours of service requirement specified in subparagraph (A)(ii), the employee will be considered to meet the requirement if-
　(I) the employee has worked or been paid for not less than 60 percent of the applicable total monthly guarantee, or the equivalent, for the previous 12-month period, for or by the employer with respect to whom leave is requested under section 2612 of this title; and
　(II) the employee has worked or been paid for not less than 504 hours (not counting personal commute time or time spent on vacation leave or medical or sick leave) during the previous 12-month period, for or by that employer.

(ii) File

Each employer of an employee described in clause (i) shall maintain on file with the Secretary (in accordance with such regulations as the Secretary may prescribe) containing information specifying

Box 5.10   *(continued)*

itself before or after the member became a veteran.

(19) Veteran

The term "veteran" has the meaning given the term in section 101 of title 38.

(Pub. L. 103–3, title I, §101, Feb. 5, 1993, 107 Stat. 7 ; Pub. L. 104–1, title II, §202(c)(1)(A), Jan. 23, 1995, 109 Stat. 9 ; Pub. L. 108–271, §8(b), July 7, 2004, 118 Stat. 814 ; Pub. L. 110–181, div. A, title V, §585(a)(1), Jan. 28, 2008, 122 Stat. 128 ; Pub. L. 111–84, div. A, title V, §565(a)(1)(A), (2), (3), Oct. 28, 2009, 123 Stat. 2309 , 2310; Pub. L. 111–119, §2(a), Dec. 21, 2009, 123 Stat. 3476 .)

AMENDMENTS

2009-Par. (2)(D). Pub. L. 111–119 added subpar. (D).

Par. (14). Pub. L. 111–84, §565(a)(1)(A)(i), added par. (14) and struck out former par. (14). Prior to amendment, text read as follows: "The term 'active duty' means duty under a call or order to active duty under a provision of law referred to in section 101(a)(13)(B) of title 10."

Par. (15). Pub. L. 111–84, §565(a)(2), amended par. (15) generally. Prior to amendment, text read as follows: "The term 'covered servicemember' means a member of the Armed Forces, including a member of the National Guard or Reserves, who is undergoing medical treatment, recuperation, or therapy, is otherwise in outpatient status, or is otherwise on the temporary disability retired list, for a serious injury or illness."

Pub. L. 111–84, §565(a)(1)(A)(ii), redesignated par. (16) as (15) and struck out former par. (15). Prior to amendment, text read as follows: "The term 'contingency operation' has the same meaning given such term in section 101(a)(13) of title 10."

Pars. (16), (17). Pub. L. 111–84, §565(a)(1)(A)(ii), redesignated pars. (17) and (18) as (16) and (17), respectively. Former par. (16) redesignated (15).

Par. (18). Pub. L. 111–84, §565(a)(3), added par. (18) and struck out former par. (18). Prior to amendment, text read as follows: "The term 'serious injury or illness', in the case of a member of the Armed Forces, including a member of the National Guard or Reserves, means an injury or illness incurred by the member in line of duty on active duty in the Armed Forces that may render the member medically unfit to perform the duties of the member's office, grade, rank, or rating."

Pub. L. 111–84, §565(a)(1)(A)(ii), redesignated par. (19) as (18). Former par. (18) redesignated (17).

Par. (19). Pub. L. 111–84, §565(a)(3), added par. (19).

Pub. L. 111–84, §565(a)(1)(A)(ii), redesignated par. (19) as (18).

2008-Pars. (14) to (19). Pub. L. 110–181 added pars. (14) to (19).

2004-Par. (4)(A)(iv). Pub. L. 108–271 substituted "Government Accountability Office" for "General Accounting Office".

1995-Par. (4)(A)(iv). Pub. L. 104–1 added cl. (iv).

EFFECTIVE DATE OF 1995 AMENDMENT

Amendment by Pub. L. 104–1 effective one year after transmission to Congress of the study under section 1371 of Title 2, The Congress, see section 1312(e)(2) of Title 2. The study required under section 1371 of Title 2, dated Dec. 31, 1996, was transmitted to Congress by the Board of Directors of the Office of Compliance on Dec. 30, 1996.

EFFECTIVE DATE

Subchapter effective 6 months after Feb. 5, 1993, except that, in the case of collective bargaining agreements in effect on that effective date, subchapter applicable on the earlier of (1) the date of termination of such agreement, or (2) the date that occurs 12 months after Feb. 5, 1993, see section 405(b) of Pub. L. 103–3, set out as a note under section 2601 of this title.

REGULATIONS

High-End Commercial Resources

At the opposite end of the spectrum from legislative websites are the online commercial resources Westlaw and Lexis. In the context of statutory research, Westlaw and Lexis offer various advantages in exchange for their not-small cost. As for the statutes themselves, Westlaw and Lexis provide up-to-date language; legislative history notes, indicating when the statute was enacted and became effective; and information about legislative materials.[17] Beyond this, they provide citations and links to (as well as summaries of) cases discussing the statute; references and links to other sources, such as secondary sources, discussing the statute; and statutory citators. Furthermore, they offer various ways to structure a search for the statute, including key-word searching.

One item on the list — a statutory citator — merits a word of explanation. The cited source is the statute, and the citing sources are cases, secondary sources, and other materials. Citing statutes is not as imperative as citing cases. When a statute is changed through the standard method — by amendment — the statutory code reflects the change (unlike case reporters, which continue to carry an obsolete decision). On the other hand, when a statute is ruled unconstitutional by a court decision, it could remain in the statutory code; a citator would be a useful means of discovering this rare event.

Westlaw and Lexis thus offer a desirable range of functions for statutory research, but their cost can raise the concern of cost-effectiveness for some research projects. They thus are best suited to projects involving thorny legal issues, statutes with a fair number of interpreting cases, or situations with significant sums at stake.

As an example, as we proceeded in our research into the Cassie Collins situation, we pulled up section 23123 on Westlaw by keying in its citation in the California Vehicle Code portion of the California Statutes & Court Rules database. Return to Box 5.1. Note the references to the statute's original enactment and amendment, as well as their effective dates, following the statutory language along with the statement of the statute's currency.

The real utility of Westlaw was not so much the statutory language but rather the Notes of Decisions, a set of summaries of interpreting cases deemed significant by the West editors, along with links to the cases. This was how we found the *Spriggs* case, which provided useful insight into one of the issues raised by the statutory language as applied to the Collins situation. See Box 5.11. Furthermore, under the Context & Analysis tab is a list with links to secondary sources available in Westlaw, such as encyclopedias, *American Law Reports* annotations, and treatises. See Box 5.12.[18]

Westlaw alerts you to potential validity problems with a statute through the use of red and yellow flags. Citing section 23123 yielded no concerns, but citing a related statute[19] for purposes of illustration did yield two alerts about pending legislation. See Box 5.13.

---

17. These materials are discussed in the part on researching legislative materials, later in this chapter.

18. Westlaw also provides a list of citing references, which includes less significant decisions and items such as documents filed in court.

19. The related statute pertains to younger drivers. The proposed legislation would amend the penalties.

| Box 5.11 | WESTLAW NOTES OF DECISIONS (Driving While Using Cell Phone) |

List of 8 Notes of Decisions for 23123. Driving a motor vehicle while using a wireless...

Notes Of Decisions (8)

Construction and application

The statute defining the offense of using a wireless telephone while driving prohibits only the use of a wireless telephone to engage in a conversation.   People v. Spriggs (App. 5 Dist. 2014) 168 Cal.Rptr.3d 347, 224 Cal.App.4th 150 .   Statutes   1093   Statutes   1404

In determining whether the statute defining the offense of using a wireless telephone while driving prohibits uses other than engaging in conversation, Court of Appeal would take judicial notice of the legislative history of that statute and the statute prohibiting text-based communication while driving.   People v. Spriggs (App. 5 Dist. 2014) 168 Cal.Rptr.3d 347, 224 Cal.App.4th 150 .   Criminal Law   304(9)

Defendant who held his cellular telephone in his hand and looked at a map application while driving did not thereby commit the offense of using a wireless telephone while driving.   People v. Spriggs (App. 5 Dist. 2014) 168 Cal.Rptr.3d 347, 224 Cal.App.4th 150 .   Automobiles   327

Defendant's act of looking at a map on his cellular phone while holding the phone in his hand was "using a wireless telephone," in violation of the statute prohibiting driving a motor vehicle while using a wireless telephone. People v. Spriggs, 2013, 154 Cal.Rptr.3d 883, 215 Cal.App.4th Supp. 1 , reversed   168 Cal.Rptr.3d 347, 224 Cal.App.4th 150 , ordered not to be officially published, vacated. Automobiles   327

Defendant's act of listening to messages on hand-held wireless telephone while stopped at a traffic light was done "while driving," thus violating the statute prohibiting driving while using a wireless telephone not configured for hands-free use.   People v. Nelson (App. 1 Dist. 2011) 132 Cal.Rptr.3d 856, 200 Cal.App.4th 1083 , review denied. Automobiles   327

In the statute prohibiting driving while using a wireless telephone not configured for hands-free use, the term "drive" requires proof of volitional movement, but the phrase "while driving" does not require movement contemporaneous with the prohibited activity at all times.   People v. Nelson (App. 1 Dist. 2011) 132 Cal.Rptr.3d 856, 200 Cal.App.4th 1083 , review denied. Automobiles   327

The statute prohibiting driving while using a wireless telephone not configured for hands-free use does not prevent a driver from pulling over to the side of the road and parking in order to use a hand-held wireless phone. People v. Nelson (App. 1 Dist. 2011) 132 Cal.Rptr.3d 856, 200 Cal.App.4th 1083 , review denied. Automobiles 327

Admissibility of evidence

In defendant's appeal after conviction of driving while using a wireless telephone not configured for hands-free use, Court of Appeal would take judicial notice of Senate Bill Analysis of the statute creating the offense.   People v. Nelson (App. 1 Dist. 2011) 132 Cal.Rptr.3d 856, 200 Cal.App.4th 1083 , review denied. Criminal Law   304(9)

Box 5.12   WESTLAW CONTEXT & ANALYSIS (Driving While Using Cell Phone)

List of 17 Context & Analysis for § 23123. Driving a motor vehicle while using a wireles...

Context and Analysis (17)

Cross References (2)

Conviction of violation of this section, giving of violation points, see Vehicle Code § 12810.3.
Suspension or revocation of license for driving under the influence or engaging in speed contests or exhibitions of speed, reinstatement conditions, see Vehicle Code § 13352.

Law Review And Journal Commentaries (5)

California roundup: 2014's new civil laws affecting businesses, workplaces, and schools. James S. Azadian and Samuel A Reep, 56 Orange County Law. 28 (June 2014).
Emerging distractions. Diane Curtis, 34 Cal.Law. 6 (May 2014).
Hands-free use of electronic devices. Gordon Eng, 31 L.A. Law. 60 (July/Aug. 2008).
Look Ma, no hands. Tom McNichol, 28 Cal.Law. 33 (Sept. 2008).
Review of Selected 2007 California Legislation (Chapter 290: California's message to hang up and pay attention). Erin Barmby, 38 McGeorge L. Rev. 342 (2007).

Library References (3)

Automobiles ⬡324, 327.
Westlaw Topic No. 48A.
C.J.S. Motor Vehicles §§ 1504 to 1505, 1508 to 1510, 1639, 1659, 1728 to 1731, 1750 to 1751.

ALR Library (1)

36 ALR 6th 443, Civil Liability Arising from Use Of Cell Phone While Driving.

Encyclopedias (4)

Cal. Jur. 3d Automobiles § 315, Wireless Telephones.
Cal. Jur. 3d Automobiles § 316, Wireless Telephones--School Buses or Transit Vehicles.
Cal. Jur. 3d Automobiles § 317, Wireless Telephones--Minor Drivers.
Cal. Jur. 3d Evidence § 28, Legislative History.

Treatises and Practice Aids (2)

35 Causes of Action 2d 151, Causes Of Action Arising Out Of Cell Phone Use While Operating a Motor Vehicle.
2 Witkin, California Criminal Law 4th Crimes Against Public Peace and Welfare § 326, (S 326) Using Wireless Communication Devices.

Box 5.13   **STATUTORY KEYCITE REPORT (Driving While Using Cell Phone)**

List of 2 Validity for § 23123.5. Driving motor vehicle while writing, sending or reading...

Validity (2)

Proposed Legislation (2)

    2015 CA S.B. 737 (NS)
    2015 California Senate Bill No. 737, California 2015-2016 Regular Session, (Apr. 30, 2015), VERSION:
    Amended/Substituted, PROPOSED ACTION: Amended
    2015 CA S.B. 737 (NS)

    2015 California Senate Bill No. 737, California 2015-2016 Regular Session, (Feb. 27, 2015), VERSION:
    Introduced, PROPOSED ACTION: Amended

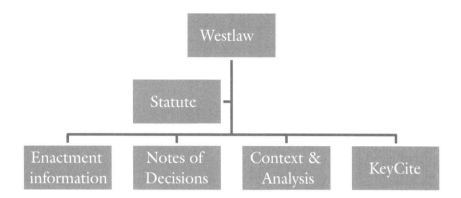

As another example, we continued our research into the Exact Electronics question about returning an employee to work under the FMLA. Section 2611 exempts an employer that employs fewer than fifty employees at a work site, so long as the employer employs fewer than fifty employees within seventy-five miles of the work site. The latter point could be viewed two ways — by road miles or by air miles — so we needed to research further.

For more sources, we turned to Lexis. We could find the statute many ways, such as by keying in the citation or by running a key-word search within an appropriate database. We keyed in the citation for the specific section. Lexis provided, of course, the current statutory language, along with direct links to cross-referenced statutes. Lexis provided currency information for the statutory language and also provided background on the statute's enactments and effective dates following the statutory language. See Box 5.14.

As with Westlaw, Lexis's chief advantage over legislative websites are the annotations: the references, descriptions, and links to supplemental sources. These begin with Case Notes, which are preceded by an outline, and proceed to Research References & Practice Aids, which include statutes that connect in some way to the present section and various types of secondary sources available through Lexis. Perusing the list of cases, we saw that some looked promising on our issue of the small work site, including a Tenth Circuit decision.[20] That case applies a regulation on the topic and holds that the statutory language means surface (not linear) miles.[21]

---

20. *Hackworth v. Progressive Cas. Ins. Co.*, 468 F.3d 722 (10th Cir. 2006). This case is summarized at the bottom of page 199, although its citation is not shown.

21. Regulations are covered in Chapter 7.

Box 5.14   **LEXIS STATUTE WITH ANNOTATIONS (Family Leave Rights)**

29 USCS § 2611

Current through PL 114-51, approved 9/24/15

United States Code Service - Titles 1 through 54 > *TITLE 29. LABOR* > *CHAPTER 28. FAMILY AND MEDICAL LEAVE* > *GENERAL REQUIREMENTS FOR LEAVE*

§ 2611. Definitions

As used in this *title [29 USCS §§ 2611* et seq.]:

(1) Commerce. The terms "commerce" and "industry or activity affecting commerce" mean any activity, business, or industry in commerce or in which a labor dispute would hinder or obstruct commerce or the free flow of commerce, and include "commerce" and any "industry affecting commerce", as defined in paragraphs (1) and (3) of section 501 of the Labor Management Relations Act, 1947 (*29 U.S.C. 142 (1)* and (3)).

(2) Eligible employee.

    (A) In general. The term "eligible employee" means an employee who has been employed--

        (i) for at least 12 months by the employer with respect to whom leave is requested under section 102 [*29 USCS § 2612*]; and

        (ii) for at least 1,250 hours of service with such employer during the previous 12-month period.

    (B) Exclusions. The term "eligible employee" does not include--

        (i) any Federal officer or employee covered under subchapter V of chapter 63 of title 5, United States Code [*5 USCS §§ 6381* et seq.] (as added by title II of this Act); or

        (ii) any employee of an employer who is employed at a worksite at which such employer employs less than 50 employees if the total number of employees employed by that employer within 75 miles of that worksite is less than 50.

    (C) Determination. For purposes of determining whether an employee meets the hours of service requirement specified in subparagraph (A)(ii), the legal standards established under section 7 of the Fair Labor Standards Act of 1938 (*29 U.S.C. 207*) shall apply.

    (D) Airline flight crews.

        (i) Determination. For purposes of determining whether an employee who is a flight attendant or flight crewmember (as such terms are defined in regulations of the Federal Aviation Administration) meets the hours of service requirement specified in subparagraph (A)(ii), the employee will be considered to meet the requirement if--

            (I) the employee has worked or been paid for not less than 60 percent of the applicable total monthly guarantee, or the equivalent, for the previous 12-month period, for or by the employer with respect to whom leave is requested under section 102 [*29 USCS § 2612*]; and

            (II) the employee has worked or been paid for not less than 504 hours (not counting personal commute time or time spent on vacation leave or medical or sick leave) during the previous 12-month period, for or by that employer.

        (ii) File. Each employer of an employee described in clause (i) shall maintain on file with the Secretary (in accordance with such regulations as the Secretary may prescribe) containing information specifying the applicable monthly guarantee with respect to each category of employee to which such guarantee applies.

        (iii) Definition. In this subparagraph, the term "applicable monthly guarantee" means--

Box 5.14 *(continued)*

29 USCS § 2611

(19) Veteran. The term "veteran" has the meaning given the term in *section 101 of title 38, United States Code*.

History

(Feb. 5, 1993,*P.L. 103-3*, Title I, § 101, *107 Stat. 7*; Jan. 23, 1995, *P.L. 104-1*, Title II, Part A, § 202(c)(1)(A), *109 Stat. 9*.)

(As amended Jan. 28, 2008,*P.L. 110-181*, Div A, Title V, Subtitle H, § 585(a)(1), *122 Stat. 128*; Oct. 28, 2009, *P.L. 111-84*, Div A, Title V, Subtitle G, § 565(a)(1)(A), (2), (3), *123 Stat. 2309*, 2310; Dec. 21, 2009, *P.L. 111-119*, § 2(a), *123 Stat. 3476*.)

Annotations

Notes

Explanatory notes:

"Government Accountability Office" has been inserted in brackets in para. (4) on the authority of § 8 of Act July 7, 2004, *P.L. 108-271* (*31 USCS § 702* note), which redesignated the General Accounting Office as the Government Accountability Office, and provided that any reference to the General Accounting Office in any law in force on July 7, 2004, shall be considered to refer and apply to the Government Accountability Office.

Amendments:

1995 . Act Jan. 23, 1995 (effective one year after transmission to Congress of the study under *2 USCS § 1371*, as provided by § 202(e)(2) of such Act, which appears as *2 USCS § 1312(e)(2)*), in para. (4)(A), in cl. (ii)(II), deleted "and" after the concluding semicolon, in cl (iii), substituted "; and" for a concluding period, and added cl. (iv).

2008 . Act Jan. 28, 2008, added paras. (14)-(19).

2009 . Act Oct. 28, 2009, substituted para. (14) for one which read: "(14) Active duty. The term 'active duty' means duty under a call or order to active duty under a provision of law referred to in *section 101(a)(13)(B) of title 10, United States Code*.", deleted para. (15), which read: "(15) Contingency operation. The term 'contingency operation' has the same meaning given such term in *section 101(a)(13) of title 10, United States Code*.", redesignated paras. (16)-(19) as paras. (15)-(18), respectively, substituted para. (15) for one which, as redesignated, read: "(15) Covered servicemember. The term 'covered servicemember' means a member of the Armed Forces, including a member of the National Guard or Reserves, who is undergoing medical treatment, recuperation, or therapy, is otherwise in outpatient status, or is otherwise on the temporary disability retired list, for a serious injury or illness.", substituted para. (18) for one which, as redesignated, read: "(18) Serious injury or illness. The term 'serious injury or illness', in the case of a member of the Armed Forces, including a member of the National Guard or Reserves, means an injury or illness incurred by the member in line of duty on active duty in the Armed Forces that may render the member medically unfit to perform the duties of the member's office, grade, rank, or rating.", and added para. (19).

Act Dec. 21, 2009, in para. (2), added subpara. (D).

Other provisions:

Effective date and applicability of section. Act Feb. 5, 1993, *P.L. 103-3*, Title IV, § 405(b), *107 Stat. 26*, provides:

"(1) In general. Except as provided in paragraph (2), titles I, II, and V and this *title [29 USCS §§ 2611* et seq., *5 USCS §§ 6381* et seq. generally, *2 USCS §§ 60m*, *60n*, and *29 USCS §§ 2651* et seq. generally; for full classification, consult USCS Tables volumes] shall take effect 6 months after the date of the enactment of this Act.

Box 5.14   *(continued)*

29 USCS § 2611

"(2) Collective bargaining agreements. In the case of a collective bargaining agreement in effect on the effective date prescribed by paragraph (1), title I [*29 USCS §§ 2611* et seq.] shall apply on the earlier of--
  "(A) the date of the termination of such agreement; or

  "(B) the date that occurs 12 months after the date of the enactment of this Act.".

Regulations. Act Oct. 28, 2009, *P.L. 111-84*, Div A, Title V, Subtitle G, § 565(a)(5), *123 Stat. 2311*, provides: "In prescribing regulations to carry out the amendments made by this subsection [amending *29 USCS §§ 2611-2613*], the Secretary of Labor shall consult with the Secretary of Defense and the Secretary of Veterans Affairs, as applicable.".

Case Notes

1. "Eligible employee"
2. --Requisite hours of service
3. "Employer"
4. "Serious health condition"
5. --Particular circumstances
6. Miscellaneous

1. "Eligible employee"

Former employee, who alleges that his former employer retaliated against him by refusing to rehire him based on his past use of FMLA leave, qualifies as "employee" under FMLA, and therefore, has private right of action against former employer. *Smith v BellSouth Telecomms., Inc. (2001, CA11 Ala) 273 F3d 1303, 7 BNA WH Cas 2d 801, 81 CCH EPD P 40814, 145 CCH LC P 34411, 15 FLW Fed C 118.*

Dismissal of employee's Family and Medical Leave Act (FMLA), *29 USCS §§ 2601* et seq., claim for lack of subject matter jurisdiction under Fed. R. Civ. Proc. 12(b)(1) because employee was not "eligible employee" under *29 USCS § 2611* was reversed because claim implicated both jurisdiction and underlying merits of FMLA claim; therefore, proper course was to resolve attack under summary judgment standards set forth in Fed. R. Civ. Proc. 56. *Morrison v Amway Corp. (2003, CA11 Fla) 323 F3d 920, 8 BNA WH Cas 2d 865, 16 FLW Fed C 487.*

Airline employee was properly terminated for taking unauthorized leave to care for ill parent since employee was ineligible for leave under *29 USCS § 2611(2)(B)(ii)*; airline was not joint employer of employees of companies which provided ground services for airline's sole daily flight, and thus airline had fewer than requisite number of employees to require it to grant leave. *Moreau v Air Fr. (2003, CA9 Cal) 343 F3d 1179, 2003 CDOS 8421, 2003 Daily Journal DAR 10531, 8 BNA WH Cas 2d 1806, 84* CCH EPD P 41484, 148 CCH LC P 34748, amd, reh den, reh, en banc, den (2004, CA9 Cal) *2004 US App LEXIS 1390* and reprinted as amd (2004, CA9 Cal) *356 F3d 942.*

Employee's discharge for absence violated Family and Medical Act (FMLA), as jury could reasonably find that employee, having 12 months of employment, was "eligible employee" under FMLA where employee's eight-day absence was on employer-authorized short term disability leave, where subsequent two-week absence was unexcused, during which period employee's one-year anniversary of employment occurred, and where employee requested FMLA leave during such time and prior to employee's discharge; district court thus appropriately denied employer's renewed motion for judgment as matter of law. *Babcock v BellSouth Adver. & Publ'g Corp. (2003, CA4 SC) 348 F3d 73, 9 BNA WH Cas 2d 78, 84* CCH EPD P 41508, 149 CCH LC P 34764.

Summary judgment was properly granted in favor of several former employers in case under Family and Medical Leave Act (FMLA), *29 USCS §§ 2601-2654* because ineligible employee's request for maternity leave beginning prior to 12 months of service was not protected under *FMLA. Walker v Elmore County Bd. of Educ. (2004, CA11 Ala) 379 F3d 1249, 9 BNA WH Cas 2d 1441, 85 CCH EPD P 41771, 150 CCH LC P 34895, 17 FLW Fed C 898.*

Box 5.14   *(continued)*

29 USCS § 2611

Even though public agencies fell within Family and Medical Leave Act of 1993 (FMLA), *29 USCS §§ 2601* et seq., regardless of number of employees, those employees could not seek FMLA benefits unless agency employed at least 50 employees within 75 mile area and, because there was nothing in state law that definitively resolved issue of whether auditor's office was separate public agency rather than part of county, court had to turn to Census, which supported employee's position that auditor's office was part of county; therefore, because county employed more than 50 employees, employee was "eligible employee" under *FMLA. Fain v Wayne County Auditor's Office (2004, CA7 Ind) 388 F3d 257, 10 BNA WH Cas 2d 4,* reh den (2004, CA7 Ind) *2004 US App LEXIS 24235.*

Employee's claim of retaliation in violation of Family and Medical Leave Act (FMLA), *29 USCS § 2601* et seq., failed because employee was not eligible employee, entitled to rights under FMLA, since employer employed fewer than 50 employees within 75 miles of employee's workplace. *Humenny v Genex Corp. (2004, CA6 Mich) 390 F3d 901, 10 BNA WH Cas 2d 244, 2004 FED App 422P.*

District court erred when it found in favor of employee on her claim against employer under Family and Medical Leave Act (FMLA), *29 USCS §§ 2601* et seq.; district court applied *29 C.F.R. § 825.111(a)(3)* to define "worksite" as employer's regional office, to identify employee as jointly employed, and to define employer as "primary employer;" however, § 825.111(a)(3), as applied to employees with fixed worksite yet subject to joint employers, was arbitrary, capricious, and manifestly contrary to *29 USCS § 2611(2)(B)(ii),* part of *FMLA. Harbert v Healthcare Servs. Group, Inc. (2004, CA10 Colo) 391 F3d 1140, 10 BNA WH Cas 2d 225.*

29 C.F.R. § 825.111(a)(3), as applied to employee with fixed worksite yet subject to joint employers, is arbitrary, capricious, and manifestly contrary to *29 USCS § 2611(2)(B)(ii),* part of Family and Medical Leave Act (FMLA), *29 USCS §§ 2601* et seq.; common meaning of "worksite," legislative purpose of FMLA, and arbitrary distinction between sole and joint employers militate against deference to agency's construction of *FMLA. Harbert v Healthcare Servs. Group, Inc. (2004, CA10 Colo) 391 F3d 1140, 10 BNA WH Cas 2d 225.*

Since former employee did not qualify as eligible employee for purposes of Family and Medical Leave Act, *29 USCS §§ 2601-2654,* because she was employee of public office holder, district court should have granted chancery clerk's motion for summary judgment based on qualified immunity. *Rutland v Pepper (2005, CA5 Miss) 404 F3d 921, 10 BNA WH Cas 2d 739.*

In context of Family and Medical Leave Act, *29 USCS §§ 2601-2654,* exception for personal staff members of public officer holders, Fifth Circuit provides non exhaustive list of factors to determine whether plaintiff is member of defendant's personal staff: (1) whether elected official has plenary powers of appointment and removal, (2) whether person in position at issue is personally accountable to only that elected official, (3) whether person in position at issue represent selected official in eyes of public, (4) whether elected official exercises considerable amount of control over position, (5) level of position within organization's chain of command, and (6) actual intimacy of working relationship between elected official and person filling position. *Rutland v Pepper (2005, CA5 Miss) 404 F3d 921, 10 BNA WH Cas 2d 739.*

Exception under *29 USCS § 2611(2)(B)(ii)* applied because employer's headquarters, as measured over public roads, was more than 75 miles from employee's worksite, and regulation, *29 C.F.R. § 825.111(b),* which was promulgated by Secretary of Labor, and which set forth method of calculating distance, advanced rather than impaired remedial purpose of Family and Medical Leave Act, *29 USCS § 2601* et seq. *Bellum v PCE Constructors Inc. (2005, CA5 Miss) 407 F3d 734, 10 BNA WH Cas 2d 877, 86* CCH EPD P 41921, 150 CCH LC P 34976.

In Family and Medical Leave Act (FMLA) case, court found that employee-numerosity requirement of FMLA is element of plaintiff's claim, not limit upon federal-court's subject matter jurisdiction; 50-employee threshold appears in definitions section, separate from jurisdictional section, and does not speak in jurisdictional terms or refer in any way to jurisdiction of district courts; thus, plaintiff's case which was dismissed by district court due to lack of subject matter jurisdiction, was remanded for further proceedings. *Minard v ITC Deltacom Communs., Inc. (2006, CA5 La) 447 F3d 352, 11 BNA WH Cas 2d 609, 152* CCH LC P 35123.

Department of Labor's regulation, 29 C.F.R. § 825.11, which measured 75-mile proximity between worksites for purposes of *29 USCS § 2611(2)(B)(ii)* in surface miles rather than in linear miles, was reasonable and consistent

| Box 5.15 | STATUTORY SHEPARD'S REPORT (Family Leave Rights) |

 LexisNexis®

Shepard's®: Report Content

> **Legislative History:**Requested
> ⚠ **Citing Decisions:**Narrowed By:Analysis:Unconstitutional by
>
> **Other Citing Sources:**None Applied

Shepard's®: ⚠ Comprehensive Report for 29 U.S.C. sec. 2611

> ⚓ Pending Legislation
> Subsection reports by specific court citation

Legislative History (1)

1. (Feb. 5, 1993,P.L. 103-3, Title I, § 101, 107 Stat. 7; Jan. 23, 1995, P.L. 104-1, Title II, Part A, § 202(c)(1)(A), 109 Stat. 9.)(As amended Jan. 28, 2008,P.L. 110-181, Div A, Title V, Subtitle H, § 585(a)(1), 122 Stat. 128; Oct. 28, 2009, P.L. 111-84, Div A, Title V, Subtitle G, § 565(a)(1)(A), (2), (3), 123 Stat. 2309, 2310; Dec. 21, 2009, P.L. 111-119, § 2(a), 123 Stat. 3476.)

As with Westlaw, Lexis provides a statutory citator, in this case Shepard's. Indeed, as appropriate, Lexis alerts you to Shepardize the statute. In the case of the FMLA, Lexis alerted us to pending legislation that would amend the FMLA.[22] See Box 5.15. Shepard's also provided a lengthy list of citing cases. The case analysis indicated that one had ruled that the statute was unconstitutional; however, when we followed up on that case,[23] we learned both that it focused on a concern not raised in our case and that it was no longer good law, as reflected in its red stop sign. Again, see Box 5.15.

---

22. The legislation would expand the FMLA to provide rights to families in same-sex situations.

23. *Sims v. Univ. of Cincinnati*, 219 F.3d 559 (6th Cir. 2000) (addressing the statute's application to a public employer).

Box 5.15 *(continued)*

Shepard's®: 29 U.S.C. sec. 2611

Citing Decisions (1)

Narrow by: Analysis: Unconstitutional by

Analysis: Unconstitutional by (1), "Cited by" (1)

Court: 6th Circuit (1)

6th Circuit - Court of Appeals

1. Sims v. University of Cincinnati

    219 F.3d 559, 2000 U.S. App. LEXIS 16677, 2000 FED App. 0231P (6th Cir.), 78 Empl.
    Prac. Dec. (CCH) P40114, 24 Employee Benefits Cas. (BNA) 2853, 141 Lab. Cas.
    (CCH) P34102, 6 Wage & Hour Cas. 2d (BNA) 289

    Court
    6th Cir. Ohio

    Date:
    2000

    R **Unconstitutional by:** 219 F.3d 559 p.562

    LB **Cited by:** 219 F.3d 559 p.561

    ... of the position of such employee. 29 U.S.C.S. § 2612(a)(1) . Eligible
    employees are those who have been employed for a minimum of 12
    months by the employer from whom leave is requested and who have
    performed a threshold 1250 hours of service. **29 U.S.C.S. § 2611(2)(A)(i)**
    , (ii) . The FMLA entitles eligible employees to take leave for a total of
    twelve weeks per calendar year:

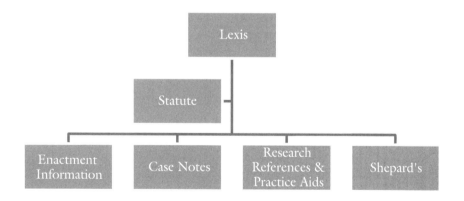

Bloomberg Law, as a newer entrant to the market, provides some similar but not identical advantages to Westlaw and Lexis in the area of statutory research. Bloomberg Law provides federal and state statutes, which are obtained by citation, browsing a table of contents, or key-word searching. For federal and some state statutes, you may also find summaries of interpreting court decisions under the Case Analysis tab, either using filters to sort them by court, date, prelisted topics, strength of discussion, or using key-word searching to identify pertinent cases. Furthermore, Bloomberg Law plans to provide links to its secondary sources for statutes.

Economy-Class Commercial Resources

As in the context of case law research, economy-class commercial resources afford you more than a legislature's website but less than the high-end commercial resources — at lower prices. Fastcase provides a good illustration.

Fastcase provides the *United States Code* and the codes of all fifty states. [24] The statutory language is followed by information about the law's enactment. In addition, it provides excerpts from (not summaries of) and links to cases interpreting the statutes; these excerpts are not as well sorted or categorized as they are by the high-end resources. The statutory databases are searchable by citation, key words, and natural language.

As an example, after researching the FMLA for the Exact Electronics question about returning to work after family leave, we wondered whether a state version might exist in Oklahoma. We selected the Statutes option, then Oklahoma, and then ran a terms-and-connectors search for *(child* OR family) /20 employ* /20 leave*. We obtained[25] an unemployment compensation statute providing for benefits when a parent is terminated because he or she needs to care for a child longer than an employer is willing to provide leave. See Box 5.16.

---

24. Fastcase also provides past codes for some jurisdictions.

25. To confirm that Oklahoma does not have a family leave statute for the private sector, we checked the website of the National Conference of State Legislatures, which did not list one.

Box 5.16   FASTCASE STATUTE WITH CASE EXCERPT (Family Leave Rights)

Fastcase Document - Okla. Stat. tit. 40 Sec. 2-210

In addition to the eligibility provisions provided by this act, an individual shall be eligible to receive unemployment benefits, if monetarily and otherwise eligible, if the claimant was separated from work due to compelling family circumstances. For purposes of this section:

1. "Immediate family member" means the claimant's spouse, parents and dependent children;

2. "Illness" means a verified illness which necessitates the care of the ill person for a period of time longer than the employer is willing to grant paid or unpaid leave;

3. "Disability" means a verified disability which necessitates the care of the disabled person for a period of time longer than the employer is willing to grant paid or unpaid leave. Disability encompasses all types of disability, including:

a. mental and physical disabilities,

b. permanent and temporary disabilities, and

c. partial and total disabilities; and

4. "Compelling family circumstances" means:

a. if the claimant was separated from employment with the employer because of the illness or disability of the claimant and, based on available information, the Oklahoma Employment Security Commission finds that it was medically necessary for the claimant to stop working or change occupations,

b. the claimant was separated from work due to the illness or disability of an immediate family member,

c. if the spouse of the claimant was transferred or obtained employment in another city or state, and the family is required to move to the location of that job that is outside of commuting distance from the prior employment of the claimant, and the claimant separates from employment in order to move to the new employment location of the spouse,

d. if the claimant separated from employment due to domestic violence or abuse, verified by any reasonable evidence, which causes the individual to reasonably believe that the individual's continued employment would jeopardize the safety of the individual or of any member of the individual's immediate family, or

e. if the claimant separated from employment to move with the claimant's spouse to a new location, and if the spouse of the claimant:

(1) was a member of the U.S. Military, the U.S. Military Reserve, or the National Guard,

Box 5.16   *(continued)*

(2) was on active duty within ninety (90) days of the date of discharge,

(3) has a service-connected disability,

(4) was discharged under honorable conditions from the military service, and

(5) takes up residence at a location more than fifty (50) miles away from the claimant's former employer for the purpose of reentering civilian life.

Historical Data

Laws 2009, SB 1175, c. 460, § 2, eff. November 1, 2009; Amended by Laws 2014, HB 2505, c. 220, § 5, eff. November 1, 2014 (superseded document available).

Annotations

⏮ ◀ 1 to 1 of 1 results ▶ ⏭ Authority Check
<u>Case</u> <u>Decision Date</u>   <u>Entire Database</u>

1. <u>Oklahoma Goodwill Industries, Inc. v. State ex rel. Oklahoma Employment</u>   May 20,   0
<u>Security Commission, 2008 OK 48 (Okla. 5/20/2008), 2008 OK 48 (Okla., 2008)</u>   2008
...theory;" and 3) "the record has not been fully developed below." These statements, in and of themselves, prohibit the Court from consideration of an administrative construction of the statute as there is nothing in the record to support exploring the public policy exception. 4. **Title 40 O.S. Supp. 2006 §2-210(7)(d**), see note 2, supra. 5. Id. 6. Title 40 O.S. Supp. 2006 §1-210(7)(d), see note 2, supra. 7. Tyler v. Smith, 472 F.Supp.2d 818 (M.D.La. 2006). 8. See, 20 C.F.R. §416.110. 9. Title 42 U.S.C. §1382; Calef v. Barnhart, 309 F.Supp.2d 425 (E.D.N.Y. 425). 10. White v...

CONSTITUTIONS

Constitutions at the federal and state level create their respective governments, setting out the roles of the various branches and the rights of the citizens as against the government. The U.S. Constitution, as the highest form of law in the United States, also creates our federal system. In some ways, state constitutions parallel the U.S. Constitution, but some also address matters not covered in the U.S. Constitution.

Although constitutions resemble statutes, there are differences. First, while the creation of a constitutional provision begins through the legislative process, it proceeds through the additional process of ratification. For a federal constitutional amendment, this entails ratification by the states; for a state constitutional amendment, this entails a referendum of the electorate.

Second, the language of a constitutional provision typically is abstract and sweeping, reading more like a legal principle than a legal rule. Thus, much of constitutional law consists of the case law interpreting the language of the constitution. Both federal and state courts apply the U.S. Constitution, with the U.S. Supreme Court issuing the authoritative precedents. On the other hand, as to a state constitutional provision, the state's highest court issues the authoritative decisions. For an example of research into federal constitutional cases, return to Chapter 4's discussion of the free speech rights of a public school student.

Third, as to the U.S. Constitution, although many issues of constitutional law are well settled, others remain deeply controversial, and indeed the best approach to reading the Constitution is debated. For example, some favor reliance on the views of the writers of the text far more than do others. Thus, legal scholarship plays a critical role when you are researching these thorny areas of constitutional law.

CHARTERS AND ORDINANCES

A surprising amount of law is neither federal nor state in origin, but local, created by such bodies as city councils and commissions. Local law includes charters (parallel to constitutions) and ordinances, codes, or regulations (parallel to statutes). Historically, a standard means of finding a local law has been to visit the office of the local government. Now many local governments post their laws on their websites. Lexis also has a strong collection of municipal codes.

As an example, return to the Cassie Collins situation, in which our client pulled into traffic from a small, private parking lot. Had she been driving in the city of Santa Barbara, California, in addition to the California law regarding driving while using a cell phone, the Santa Barbara Stop and Yield Regulations would have applied as well. We found them on the city's website. See Box 5.17.

Box 5.17 **CITY ORDINANCE (Driving Regulation)**

Chapter 10.16

STOP AND YIELD REGULATIONS

Sections:

10.16.010	Stop Signs - Transportation Engineer to Erect.
10.16.020	Obedience to Stop Signs at Intersections.
10.16.030	Exceptions to Stops at Intersections.
10.16.040	Emerging from Alley or Private Driveway.
10.16.050	Obedience to Signal Indicating Approach of Railroad Train.
10.16.060	Yield Right-of-Way Signs.
10.16.070	Obedience to Yield Signs.

10.16.010   Stop Signs - Transportation Engineer to Erect.

The Transportation Engineer shall erect or cause to be erected, boulevard stop signs complying with provisions of the Vehicle Code at the entrance to every intersection of two (2) or more streets which he has determined is an intersection at which there is special hazard to life or property by reason of the volume of traffic upon such street, or at such intersections, or because of the number of reported accidents or the apparent probability thereof, or by reason of physical conditions which render any such streets or intersections exceptionally dangerous or hazardous to life or property, and where the factors creating the special hazard are such that according to the principles and experience of traffic engineering the installation of stop signs is reasonably calculated to reduce the expectancy of accidents, and that the use of warning signs would be inadequate. (Ord. 2713 §1(part), 1959; prior Code §31.35.)

10.16.020   Obedience to Stop Signs at Intersections.

When stop signs are erected as provided, at the entrance to any intersection, every driver of a vehicle shall stop at every such sign, before entering the intersection. (Ord. 2713 §1(part), 1959; prior Code §31.36.)

10.16.030   Exceptions to Stops at Intersections.

No stop need be made at any such intersection where:
(1)   A Police Officer is on duty and directs traffic to proceed.
(2)   A traffic signal is in operation and indicates that traffic may proceed.
(3)   The operator turns right into a highway from a separate right turn lane which lane is delineated by buttons, markers, or channelization, and no stop sign is in place at the intersection of such separate right turn lane and such highway. (Ord. 2713 §1(part), 1959; prior Code §31.37.)

10.16.040   Emerging from Alley or Private Driveway.

The driver of a vehicle emerging from an alley, driveway or building shall stop such vehicle immediately prior to driving onto a sidewalk or into the sidewalk area extending across any alley-way, yielding the right-of-way to any pedestrian as may be necessary to avoid collision, and upon entering the roadway shall yield the right-of-way to all vehicles approaching on said roadway. (Ord. 2713 §1(part), 1959; prior Code §31.38.)

10.16.050   Obedience to Signal Indicating Approach of Railroad Train.

Whenever any person driving a vehicle approaches a railroad grade crossing under any of the following circumstances stated in this section, the driver of such vehicle shall stop within fifty feet (50') but not less than ten feet (10') from the nearest rail of such railroad, and shall not proceed until he can do so safely. The foregoing requirements shall apply when:
(1)   A clearly visible electric or mechanical signal device gives a warning of the immediate approach of a railroad train.
(2)   A crossing gate is lowered or when a human flagman gives or continues to give signal of the approach or passage of a railroad train.
(3)   An approaching railroad train is plainly visible and is in hazardous proximity to such crossing.
(4)   No person shall drive any vehicle through, around, or under any crossing gate or barrier at a railroad grade crossing while such gate or barrier is closed or is being opened or closed. (Ord. 2713 §1(part), 1959; prior Code §31.39.)

LEGISLATIVE MATERIALS

Situations for Researching in Legislative Materials

As noted previously, you will research legislative materials in several situations. First, you will research statutory language that is not presently in effect. You may do so in several situations. First, your client's situation may have occurred in the past, under a previous version of the statute, so you need to find *outdated statutory language.*

A second situation arises more often: the language of a statute is ambiguous when applied to your client's situation, and there are no cases providing an authoritative interpretation. One way to resolve this ambiguity is by looking to the legislature's intent in drafting the statutory language. The premise is that statutes are to be interpreted according to what the legislature intended and that this intent can be drawn from the documents created during the statute's creation, that is, the statute's *legislative history.*[26]

Third, in a quite different situation, your client may be contemplating future conduct in an area where the legislature is considering legislation. Then you will be tracking potential (or indeed probable) changes by following *pending legislation.*

The Legislative Process and Documents

To understand which of the many documents created during a statute's legislative history are considered the most authoritative requires a brief overview of the legislative process, with a focus on the federal process as a typical process.[27] What follows is a general description; there are many details and variations from law to law.

The process begins with introduction of a *bill,*[28] which is then referred to a committee with expertise in the area for consideration. The committee, or a subcommittee, may hold a *hearing,* at which the bill's sponsors, experts, representatives of the executive branch, and people likely to be affected by the bill testify and submit written materials. Ultimately, a committee discusses the bill, prepares a *committee report* with its analysis and recommendations, and sends the bill to its parent body.

The bill then goes to the floor of the House of Representatives or Senate for *floor debate.* Members may offer arguments for and against it. *Amendments*

---

26. Certainly one can argue whether a legislature has a single intent, and often it is possible to find conflicting views stated. Nonetheless, this premise holds.

27. The major variation is that of a single-chamber state legislature.

28. Sometimes parallel bills are introduced in both chambers.

may be offered and passed or defeated. Congressional activity including floor debate is recorded in the *Congressional Record*.

Once the bill passes one chamber, it proceeds to the other chamber. The second chamber may pass it without change or amend it and return it to the first chamber. The first may accept the amendments or request a *conference committee*. In the latter situation, members of both chambers confer until they reach agreement, create a *conference committee report* for the compromise bill, and report it to both chambers.

Once a bill does pass both chambers, it is sent to the President. The President has ten days (Sundays excepted) in which to sign the bill, veto it, or permit it to become law by not signing it. If the President vetos the bill, Congress may override the veto by a two-thirds vote of each chamber. Once some version of *presidential approval* occurs, the bill becomes *law*.

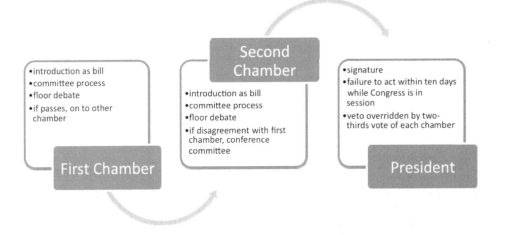

The legislative process can run smoothly and quickly, or it can take years and entail not only many hours of public proceedings but also considerable lobbying behind the scenes. For major legislation, the process can yield hundreds of pages of documents. The categories of documents are summarized in Box 5.18.

The various categories of documents vary in their utility in establishing legislative intent. Most useful are the various versions of the bill, along with proposed and rejected amendments; these provide strong insight into legislative intent because they relate directly to statutory language. Second, committee reports are considered influential because they are prepared and adopted by the committee with expertise and responsibility in the area. In addition, conference committee reports are important because they arise as the bill nears completion and reveal the final compromises. Third, courts sometimes do rely on floor debates, especially if the comments are made by the bill's sponsors. Finally, statements made at hearings and documents provided to legislators can be useful in showing what legislators considered,

| Box 5.18 | **LEGISLATIVE DOCUMENTS** | |

Document	Stage of Process	Weightiness
Bills and successful and unsuccessful amendments	Various stages — for example, introduced, reported out of committee, and passed by a chamber	Very weighty
Committee hearing transcript (witness statements, committee questions and answers, exhibits, supplemental materials)	Consideration by a subcommittee or committee of one chamber	Influential
Committee prints (research reports)	Varies, depending on purpose	Potentially useful for factual information
House or Senate documents (e.g., messages from an executive agency)	Consideration by a subcommittee or committee of one chamber	Potentially useful for factual information
Committee report (text of bill, factual findings, analysis of bill, recommendation, minority views)	Conclusion of a deliberation; conclusion of a conference committee process	Very weighty
Floor debates and proceedings (semi-verbatim transcript of comments, votes, amendments, messages to Congress)[29]	Chamber debate	Potentially weighty
Presidential messages	Signing or veto statements	Indirect evidence

---

29. Members of Congress may revise their remarks and add extended remarks to what is published in the *Congressional Record*, the official record of proceedings and debates in Congress.

although they are not themselves statements of the legislators' intent as they passed the bill.

Furthermore, once a bill becomes law, it is published in the *session laws* for that legislative session, a chronological repository of all laws passed during a session. Session laws thus facilitate research into the language of a statute as of a specific past date, including versions that have been superseded by amendments passed by more recent sessions.[30] *Statutes at Large* is the session law publication for federal statutes.

As an example, consider again the issue posed by Exact Electronics about the employee seeking to return to work after family leave. Our research revealed that Congress passed an exemption for small employers, which could be interpreted in two ways, so legislative history could be instructive. Documents from the enactment of FMLA in 1993 bearing on the exemption for small employers appear in Boxes 5.19 through 5.24: the House Bill, a proposed amendment, testimony from a hearing transcript, the report of the Senate Labor and Human Resources Committee, an excerpt from the floor debate, and President Bill Clinton's signing statement. The most telling statement appears in the committee report, referring to a requirement that the employer must employ fifty people within a seventy-five-mile "radius of the employee's worksite."

Researching Legislative History

Researching legislative history entails two closely linked tasks: (1) identifying the particular law to research and the steps that that law took en route to enactment and (2) obtaining and reading the documents created at the various steps.

This part of the chapter discusses five options for researching federal[31] legislative history: (1) using statutory codes, (2) using the *United States Code Congressional and Administrative News* (U.S.C.C.A.N.), (3) finding a

---

30. Another option is to find an out-of-date code for the pertinent year. Some libraries archive outdated print codes, as do some legislatures' websites and high-end commercial resources.

31. For guidance researching state legislative history, consult a state-specific legal research guide or a law librarian. Another option for some statutes is Westlaw's Graphical Statute's program, discussed later in this chapter in the context of federal statutes.

Box 5.19   **BILL (Family Leave Rights)**

I

103D CONGRESS
1ST SESSION   # H. R. 1

To grant family and temporary medical leave under certain circumstances.

IN THE HOUSE OF REPRESENTATIVES

JANUARY 5, 1993

Mr. FORD of Michigan (for himself, Mr. CLAY, Mr. MILLER of California, Mr. MURPHY, Mr. KILDEE, Mr. WILLIAMS, Mr. MARTINEZ, Mr. OWENS, Mr. SAWYER, Mr. PAYNE of New Jersey, Ms. UNSOELD, Ms. MINK, Mr. ANDREWS of New Jersey, Mr. REED, Mr. ROEMER, Mr. ENGEL, Mr. BECERRA, Mr. SCOTT, Mr. GENE GREEN of Texas, Ms. WOOLSEY, Mr. ROMERO-BARCELO, Mr. KLINK, Ms. ENGLISH of Arizona, Mr. STRICKLAND, Mrs. SCHROEDER, Mrs. ROUKEMA, Ms. SNOWE, Mr. SWETT, Mr. FORD of Tennessee, Mr. MATSUI, Mr. BONIOR, Mr. SANDERS, Mrs. KENNELLY, Mr. GORDON, and Mr. WELDON) introduced the following bill; which was referred jointly to the Committees on Education and Labor, Post Office and Civil Service, and House Administration

JANUARY 21, 1993

Additional sponsors: Mr. GEPHARDT, Mr. ACKERMAN, Mr. BACCHUS of Florida, Mr. BAESLER, Mr. BARRETT of Wisconsin, Mr. BERMAN, Mr. BILBRAY, Mr. BORSKI, Mr. BROWN of California, Ms. BYRNE, Mr. CHAPMAN, Mr. CLYBURN, Mr. CONYERS, Mr. COSTELLO, Mr. DeFAZIO, Ms. DeLAURO, Mr. DELLUMS, Mr. de LUGO, Ms. ESHOO, Mr. ESPY, Mr. FALEOMAVAEGA, Mr. FAZIO, Mr. FLAKE, Mr. FOGLIETTA, Mr. FRANK of Massachusetts, Mr. GIBBONS, Ms. HARMAN, Mr. HINCHEY, Mr. HOLDEN, Mr. HYDE, Mr. JOHNSTON of Florida, Mr. KOPETSKI, Mr. LEHMAN, Ms. LONG, Mr. McCLOSKEY, Mr. McDERMOTT, Mr. MACHTLEY, Ms. MALONEY, Mr. MANTON, Mr. MARKEY, Mr. MAZZOLI, Mr. MEEHAN, Mr. MINETA, Mrs. MORELLA, Mr. MURTHA, Ms. NORTON, Mr. OLVER, Mr. PANETTA, Mr. PASTOR, Ms. PELOSI, Mr. PETERSON of Minnesota, Mr. PETERSON of Florida, Mr. POMEROY, Mr. RAHALL, Mr. REYNOLDS, Ms. SCHENK, Mr. SCHUMER, Mr. SHAYS, Mr. STARK, Mr. STUDDS, Mr. STUPAK, Mr. SWIFT, Mr. VENTO, Mr. WASHINGTON, Mr. WAXMAN, Mr. WISE, Mr. WYNN, Ms. BROWN of Florida, Mr. BLACKWELL, Mr. DOOLEY, Mr. COLEMAN, Mrs. COLLINS of Illinois, Mr. EVANS, Mr. FISH, Mr. LEVIN, Ms. MOLINARI, Mr. NEAL of Massachusetts, Mr. OBERSTAR, Mr. POSHARD, Mr. SABO, Ms. SLAUGHTER, Mr. SMITH of New Jersey, Ms. WATERS, Mr. WHEAT, Mr. DIXON, Mr. SERRANO, Mr. RANGEL, Mr. PALLONE, Mr. TRAFICANT, Mr. CARDIN,

Box 5.19   *(continued)*

2

Mr. ANDREWS of Maine, Mr. SANGMEISTER, Mr. WILSON, Mr. EDWARDS of California, Mr. RAVENEL, Mr. KLECZKA, and Mr. DURBIN

A BILL

To grant family and temporary medical leave under certain circumstances.

1   *Be it enacted by the Senate and House of Representa-*

2   *tives of the United States of America in Congress assembled,*

3   **SECTION 1. SHORT TITLE; TABLE OF CONTENTS.**

4   (a) SHORT TITLE.—This Act may be cited as the

5   "Family and Medical Leave Act of 1993".

6   (b) TABLE OF CONTENTS.—The table of contents is

7   as follows:

Sec. 1. Short title; table of contents.
Sec. 2. Findings and purposes.

TITLE I—GENERAL REQUIREMENTS FOR LEAVE

Sec. 101. Definitions.
Sec. 102. Leave requirement.
Sec. 103. Certification.
Sec. 104. Employment and benefits protection.
Sec. 105. Prohibited acts.
Sec. 106. Investigative authority.
Sec. 107. Enforcement.
Sec. 108. Special rules concerning employees of local educational agencies.
Sec. 109. Notice.
Sec. 110. Regulations.

TITLE II—LEAVE FOR CIVIL SERVICE EMPLOYEES

Sec. 201. Leave requirement.

TITLE III—COMMISSION ON LEAVE

Sec. 301. Establishment.
Sec. 302. Duties.
Sec. 303. Membership.
Sec. 304. Compensation.
Sec. 305. Powers.
Sec. 306. Termination.

•HR 1 SC

Box 5.20   PROPOSED AMENDMENT (Family Leave Rights)

Under the rule, it is now in order for the gentleman from Pennsylvania <Mr. GOODLING> to offer his second **amendment**.

AMENDMENT OFFERED BY MR. GOODLING

Mr. **GOODLING**.

Madam Chairman, I offer an **amendment**.

The CHAIRMAN.

The Clerk will designate the **amendment**.

The text of the **amendment** is as follows:

Amendment offered by Mr. GOODLING: Amend section 101(2)(B) to add a new clause as follows:

(iii) any employee of an employer whose absence during leave would clearly result in substantial and grievous economic injury to the operations of the employer or substantial endangerment to the health and safety of other employees of the employer or the public.

Amend section 101(2)(C) to read as follows:

(c) DETERMINATION.-

(A) CLAUSE (ii).-For purposes of determining whether an employee meets the hours of service requirement specified in subparagraph (A)(ii), the legal standards established under section 7 of the Fair Labor Standards Act of 1938 (29 U.S.C. 207) shall apply.

(B) CLAUSE (iii).-The exception in subparagraph (A)(iii) shall apply only if-

(i) the employer notices the employee of intent of the employer to deny leave on such basis at the time the employer determines that such injury or endangerment would occur; and

(ii) in any case in which the leave has commenced, the employee elects not to return to employment after receiving such notice.

In section 104, strike out subsection (b) and redesignate subsection (c) as subsection (b).

The CHAIRMAN.

The gentleman from Pennsylvania <Mr. GOODLING> will be recognized for 10 minutes, and the gentleman from Michigan <Mr. FORD> will be recognized for 10 minutes.

The Chair recognizes the gentleman from Pennsylvania <Mr. GOODLING>.

Mr. **GOODLING**.

Madam Chairman, I yield myself such time as I may consume.

Madam Chairman, I would like to take some time on this one, because it is a very important **amendment** if we are going to try to improve the bill at all.

What we are talking about here is allowing the employer to deny leave in very critical, limited circumstances when the employee in question is crucial to the ongoing operation of the employer, but only in those circumstances. Again, it is very tightly drawn so that it cannot be abused.

H.R. 1 appears to recognize an employer's right to deny leave in such a situation, but let us look at it carefully. If we turn to section 104(b) of the bill where the so-called key employee exemption is to be found, first the employee must be in the top-paid 10 percent of the employer's work force at the worksite in question, or within 75 miles thereof. Then if the employee's reinstatement would cause substantial and grievous economic harm, the employer need not reinstate the employee.

Note that the focus, strangely, is not on the impact of the employee's absence, but on the reinstatement. Let us read the text of the bill and then the Members will understand what it is all about. Maybe if he or she was making $500,000 a year, reinstatement might lead to grievous harm but when else?

I realize this is strange language that is in this bill, and it may have been structured this way in order to require

Box 5.21   **HEARING TESTIMONY (Family Leave Rights)**

71

TESTIMONY OF MICHAEL R. LOSEY, SPHR

Dear Mr. Chairman:

Good morning. My name is Mike Losey, and I am President and CEO
of the Society for Human Resource Management (SHRM). I am
pleased to be here today to present testimony on behalf of the
Society on the subject of family and medical leave legislation.
SHRM is the leading voice of the human resource profession,
representing the interests of more than 50,000 individual
professional and student members from around the world. SHRM
provides its membership with education and information services,
conferences and seminars, government and media representation,
and publications that equip human resource professionals to
become leaders and decision makers within their organizations.

As you know, the family and medical leave issue has been before
Congress for the last eight years. Throughout that time, SHRM
has expressed concerns over specific provisions of the
legislation. We have also expressed our concern that government
mandates of workforce policies which were previously arranged
between employers and employees will result in administrative,
statutory and competitiveness challenges. Throughout this long
debate on this issue, our nation has experienced changes. We
have witnessed changes in the composition of the workforce,
changes in employment practices and, now, even political change.

1

Box 5.22   **COMMITTEE REPORT (Family Leave Rights)**

FAMILY AND MEDICAL LEAVE ACT OF 1993

P.L. 103–3, see page 107 Stat. 6

DATES OF CONSIDERATION AND PASSAGE

House: February 3, 4, 1993

Senate: February 4, 1993

Cong. Record Vol. 139 (1993)

**House Report (Education and Labor Committee) No. 103–8(I),
Feb. 2, 1993
[To accompany H.R.1]**

**House Report (Post Office and Civil Service Committee) No.
103–8(II), Feb. 2, 1993
[To accompany H.R.1]**

**Senate Report (Labor and Human Resources Committee) No.
103–3, Jan. 27, 1993
[To accompany S.5]**

*The House bill was passed in lieu of the Senate bill after amending
its language to contain the text of the Senate bill. The Senate Report
(this page) is set out below and the President's Signing Statement
(page 54) follows.*

SENATE REPORT NO. 103–3

[page 1]

The Committee on Labor and Human Resources, to which was
referred the bill (S. 5) to entitle employees to family and medical
leave in certain cases involving a birth, an adoption, or a serious
health condition of an employee, a child, a spouse or a parent, with
adequate protection of the employees' employment and health benefit rights, having considered the same, reports favorably thereon
and recommends that the bill do pass.

CONTENTS

		Page
I.	Summary of the bill	1
II.	Background and need for legislation	4
III.	History of legislation	21
IV.	Committee views	21
V.	Cost estimate	39
VI.	Regulatory impact statement	41
VII.	Section-by-section analysis	43
VIII.	Committee action	47
IX.	Minority views	49
X.	Changes in existing law	52

3

Box 5.22   *(continued)*

LEGISLATIVE HISTORY
SENATE REPORT NO. 103–3

I. SUMMARY OF THE BILL

Title I of S. 5, the Family and Medical Leave Act of 1993, makes available to eligible employees up to 12 weeks of unpaid leave per

[page 2]

year under particular circumstances that are critical to the life of a family. Leave may be taken (1) upon the birth of the employee's child, (2) upon the placement of a child with the employee for adoption or foster care, (3) when the employee is needed to care for a child, spouse or parent who has a serious health condition, or (4) when the employee is unable to perform the functions of his or her position because of a serious health condition.

The act exempts small businesses and limits coverage of private employers to employers who employ 50 or more employees for each working day during 20 or more calendar weeks in the current or preceding calendar year. To be eligible for leave, an employee of a covered employer must have been employed by the employer for at least 12 months and must have worked at least 1,250 hours during the 12-month period proceeding the commencement of the leave. The employer must, in addition, employ at least 50 people within a 75-mile radius of the employee's worksite.

If the employer provides paid leave for which the employee is eligible, the employee may elect or the employer may require the employee to substitute the paid leave for any part of the 12 weeks of leave to which the employee is entitled under the act. When the need for leave is foreseeable, the employee must provide reasonable prior notice, and make efforts to schedule leave so as not to disrupt unduly the employer's operations. An employer may also require an employee to report periodically during the leave period on the employee's leave status and intention to return to work. Spouses employed by the same employer are limited to a total of 12 weeks of leave for the birth or adoption of a child or for the care of a sick parent.

An employer may require medical certification to support a claim for leave for an employee's own serious health condition or to care for a seriously ill child, spouse or parent. For the employee's own medical leave, the certification must include a statement that the employee is unable to perform the functions of his or her position. For leave to care for a seriously ill child, spouse or parent, the certification must include an estimate of the amount of time the employee is needed to care for the child or parent. An employer may require a second medical opinion and periodic recertification at its own expense. If the first and second opinions differ, the employer, again at its own expense, may require the binding opinion of a third health care provider, approved jointly by the employee and the employer.

An employee needing leave because of his or her own serious health condition or the serious health condition of a child or parent may, if medically necessary, take leave intermittently or on a reduced leave schedule that reduces the employee's usual number of hours per workweek or per workday. However, if an employee requests leave on such a basis, the employer may require the employee to transfer temporarily to an alternative position which better

4

| Box 5.23 | **FLOOR DEBATE (Family Leave Rights)** |

Page 29

In fact, the United States is the only industrial country without it.

Taxpayers will be better off. Why? Because they do not have to pay unemployment or welfare for workers who have been fired.

But let us put the emphasis where it belongs, on the benefit that makes this bill not just good policy and sound politics, but a compelling moral issue.

Families will be better off. That is what this is about, making families better off. After all, do we really want an America where workers can be fired because they need to take cancer-ridden children for chemotherapy? Do we really want an America where workers can be fired because they need some time off to care for an aging parent who may have Alzheimer's disease? Is that the kind of America that we want, an America that gives lip service to family values but turns it back at the very moment they are the most vulnerable?

For 7 years, this bill has been blocked. Now the roadblocks are removed. The road is clear. Thanks to the likes of the gentleman from Michigan <Mr. FORD>, the gentleman from Missouri <Mr. CLAY>, the gentlewoman from New Jersey <Mrs. ROUKEMA>, and the gentleman from the other body, CHRIS DODD, who have worked tirelessly to make sure this bill hits the President's desk.

Let us get it to the President's desk this week, to the President who not only believes in family values but who values families. Let us move together on this bill that keeps families together.

Mr. MYERS of Indiana.

Madam Chairman, I yield 3 minutes to the gentleman from Kentucky <Mr. BUNNING>.

Mr. BUNNING.

Madam Chairman, I rise in opposition to H.R. 1, the Federal Government-Knows-Best-Act of 1993.

I have nine kids. I know the importance of spending time with newborn infants and children when they are seriously ill. We all understand that. But this bill is not the way to do it.

This bill basically says that the U.S. Congress knows better than the marketplace. This bill says that Congress knows better than the Nation's employers and employees about what kind of benefits our Nation's workers want and need.

It plucks a magic number of 12 weeks a year out of a hat, and says this is what we need.

This kind of one-size-fits-all mandate from on high just does not make sense. It does not matter if your employees want it. It does not matter if it damages your business. This is the one benefit that Congress is going to single out and insist that you provide.

Not only does it reduce flexibility in the kind of benefit programs employers can offer, but like any Government mandate, it also imposes very real costs on small business.

It is another layer of regulation that does nothing to promote economic growth. It will actually destroy job opportunities and damage productivity.

Just yesterday, the owners of a small business in my district explained to me that, if this bill passes, they will just make sure that they do not grow to the point that they have 50 employees. They will hire part-time workers. They will contract out. They will do what is necessary to stay under the 50-employee trigger.

So, this bill-compassionate as it may sound-is going to create a ceiling-a very artificial ceiling that limits growth and slows job creation. And anything that slows job growth is not compassionate in my book. The first and foremost need of American families-any family-is a job. And this bill destroys jobs.

Make no mistake about it, if this bill was as harmless and as inexpensive as its supporters pretend, they would not have had to exempt 95 percent of all businesses from its coverage to get it to the floor.

But, what is even more frightening is that we all know what happens to small business exemptions. They tend to erode over the years. We know that this bill is just the beginning. We know that if we enact this bill, it is just the first step to paid leave and other mandated benefits for all American businesses, large and small alike.

Madam Chairman, this is a bad bill. It is a bad precedent. It is bad economic policy. And it should be rejected.

Box 5.24   **PRESIDENTIAL SIGNING STATEMENT (Family Leave Rights)**

SIGNING STATEMENT
P.L. 103–3

STATEMENT BY PRESIDENT OF THE UNITED STATES

STATEMENT BY PRESIDENT WILLIAM J. CLINTON
UPON SIGNING H.R. 1

29 Weekly Compilation of Presidential Documents 144,
February 8, 1993

Today, I am pleased to sign into law H.R. 1, the "Family and Medical
Leave Act of 1993." I believe that this legislation is a response to a
compelling need—the need of the American family for flexibility in the
workplace. American workers will no longer have to choose between the job
they need and the family they love.

This legislation mandates that public and private employers with at least
fifty workers provide their employees with family and medical leave. At its
core is the provision for employees to take up to 12 weeks of unpaid leave
for the care of a newborn or newly adopted child, for the care of a family
member with a serious medical condition, or for their own illness. It also
requires employers to maintain health insurance coverage and job protection
for the duration of the leave. It sets minimum length of service and hours
of work requirements before employees become eligible.

The need for this legislation is clear. The American workforce has
changed dramatically in recent years. These changes have created a substantial and growing need for family and medical leave for working Americans.

In 1965, about 35 percent of mothers with children under 18 were labor
force participants. By 1992, that figure had reached 67 percent. By the
year 2005, one of every two people entering the workforce will be women.

The rising cost of living has also made two incomes a necessity in many
areas of this country, with both parents working or looking for work in 48
percent, or nearly half, of all two parent families with children in the United
States.

Single parent families have also grown rapidly, from 16 percent of all
families with children in 1975 to 27 percent in 1992. Finally, with America's
population aging, more working Americans have to take time off from work
to attend to the medical needs of elderly parents.

As a rising number of American workers must deal with the dual pres-
sures of family and job, the failure to accommodate these workers with
adequate family and medical leave policies has forced too many Americans to
choose between their job security and family emergencies. It has also
resulted in inadequate job protection for working parents and other employees who have serious health conditions that temporarily prevent them from
working. It is neither fair nor necessary to ask working Americans to

54

compiled legislative history, (4) researching in a government website, and (5) researching in a commercial resource. Some of these options point you to the documents that you need, some contain the documents, and still others do both. Some options are available only for relatively recent laws. For a summary, see Box 5.25.

Box 5.25	APPROACHES TO LEGISLATIVE MATERIALS RESEARCH	
Resource	Advantages and Disadvantages	Comments
Statutory Codes	Text of statute and history information. No legislative history documents.	Only U.S.C.A. provides a reference to U.S.C.C.A.N.
U.S.C.C.A.N.	Committee report, possibly a presidential signing statement. Some citation information to other documents.	Use the print version, if available, for a cost-effective start.
Compiled Legislative Histories	Not available for all statutes. Range of documents varies, but typically very comprehensive. Legislative Insight is particularly comprehensive; HeinOnline is very useful for laws that it covers; Lexis and Westlaw may be cost-effective. Online options afford features such as key-word searching, and some highlight search terms.	Use multiple approaches, as different ones will provide different leads.
Congress.gov	Comprehensive bill tracking for post-1972 bills. Full-text coverage of documents very limited before 1995. Good source for amendments but does not provide hearings. Linking and key-word options. Free.	Use for references and to obtain documents that you cannot research cost-effectively elsewhere.
ProQuest Congressional	Comprehensive bill tracking, which can include sessions before the one in which the bill passed. Best source for tracking hearings, committee prints, and House and Senate documents; good source for those documents. Best bet for older legislation if your coverage includes it.	Standard source when a compiled legislative history is not available.

Box 5.25   *(continued)*

Resource	Advantages and Disadvantages	Comments
Bloomberg Law	Some bills, limited hearing testimony, *Congressional Record*, and committee reports.	Use primarily if it provides a cost-effective option for obtaining a particular document.
Lexis	Some compiled legislative histories, bills, hearing testimony, *Congressional Record*, and committee reports. Limited coverage. Some contracts include Congressional Information Service (CIS) legislative histories.	Use primarily for a compiled legislative history.
Westlaw	Some compiled legislative histories, bills, hearing testimony, *Congressional Record*, and committee reports. Limited coverage. Graphical Statutes tool.	Use primarily for a compiled legislative history.
HeinOnline	U.S. Federal Legislative History library contains many compiled legislative histories. U.S. Congressional Documents library with *Congressional Record. U.S. Statutes at Large* library.	Available by specific subscription. Cost-effective source for compiled legislative histories and for *Congressional Record* volumes not available on Congress.gov.

As you work with legislative materials, keep in mind that the legislative process can be lengthy and involve many participants. Thus, to research the legislative intent behind a law properly, you must read a law's full legislative history. Otherwise, you risk relying on unrepresentative fragments.

Statutory Codes.   A statutory code is a good beginning point for legislative history research because it should contain the text of the current statute, useful historical information, and sometimes a reference to another resource.

First, check for a purpose provision, which is typically in the first or second section of the statute. Because this provision is part of the statute, it is highly authoritative as to legislative intent.

Next, examine the statutory history citations immediately following the text of the statutory section on which you are focusing. Also, read the history information following the citations to learn which of the various laws creating the statute gave rise to which parts of the statute, so you can focus on those that pertain to your client's situation.

If you are researching in U.S.C.A., you will find a reference to one or more documents printed in U.S.C.C.A.N., a basic legislative history resource described below.

As an example, when we researched the Exact Electronics issue involving the FMLA, we started in U.S.C.A. We read § 2601, which provided that the purposes of the FMLA included "balanc[ing] the demands of the workplace with the needs of families" and "accomplish[ing] the purposes . . . in a manner that accommodates the legitimate interests of employers." According to the history information for the FMLA section exempting small employers (§ 2611), the key language was passed as part of Public Law 103-3 in 1993 and had not been amended since then. The law could be found in volume 107 of *Statutes at Large* (the federal session laws) at page 7. The Historical and Statutory Notes also provided a reference to the Senate Report and the signing statement by the President found at 1993 U.S. Code Cong. and Adm. News, p. 3. See Box 5.26.

U.S.C.C.A.N.   Because it is so accessible, U.S.C.C.A.N. often is a good first resource for obtaining some legislative history documents. Each set of bound U.S.C.C.A.N. volumes covers one session of Congress in two sections: one for *Statutes at Large* reprints (the laws themselves) and another for selected legislative history documents. Both sections are arranged by public law number.

You can locate the legislative history material for a law by using its public law number, a reference from U.S.C.A., or a set's subject index. The legislative history section for a law begins with a wealth of information about the law, including, as available: (1) its public law number and *Statutes at Large* citation; (2) the dates of consideration and passage of the legislation by both chambers; (3) the numbers of the House and Senate bills; (4) the committees to which the bills were assigned; (5) the numbers and dates of committee and conference committee reports; and (6) the volumes and years of the *Congressional Record* in which debate and action on the bills occurred. This information is useful if you continue your research in other sources. Review Box 5.22, earlier in this chapter. U.S.C.C.A.N. then typically reprints one or more committee reports and perhaps a presidential signing statement for the law.[32]

Researching the Exact Electronics issue, we found both the committee report and the presidential signing statement through U.S.C.C.A.N. Review Boxes 5.22 and 5.24 earlier in this chapter.

Compiled Legislative Histories.   If your research project merits further consideration of a law's legislative materials, a good next step is to determine whether someone has compiled a legislative history for it. A *compiled legislative history* is a collection of legislative materials created during a

---

32. The committee reports are edited to remove duplicative or less helpful information.

Box 5.26   **ANNOTATED CODE HISTORY INFORMATION (Family Leave Rights)**

29 § 2611   LABOR   Ch. 28

(B) a unit established for the purpose of providing command and control of members of the Armed Forces receiving medical care as outpatients.

(18) Next of kin

The term "next of kin", used with respect to an individual, means the nearest blood relative of that individual.

(19) Serious injury or illness

The term "serious injury or illness", in the case of a member of the Armed Forces, including a member of the National Guard or Reserves, means an injury or illness incurred by the member in line of duty on active duty in the Armed Forces that may render the member medically unfit to perform the duties of the member's office, grade, rank, or rating.

(Pub.L. 103–3, Title I, § 101, Feb. 5, 1993, 107 Stat. 7; Pub.L. 104–1, Title II, § 202(c)(1)(A), Jan. 23, 1995, 109 Stat. 9; Pub.L. 108–271, § 8(b), July 7, 2004, 118 Stat. 814; Pub.L. 110–181, Div. A, Title V, § 585(a)(1), Jan. 28, 2008, 122 Stat. 128.)

HISTORICAL AND STATUTORY NOTES

Revision Notes and Legislative Reports
1993 Acts. Senate Report No. 103–3 and Statement by President, see 1993 U.S. Code Cong. and Adm. News, p. 3.
1995 Acts. Related House Report No. 104–650(Parts I and II) and Related Senate Report No. 104–397, see 1995 U.S. Code Cong. and Adm. News, p. 3.
2008 Acts. Statement by President, see 2008 U.S. Code Cong. and Adm. News, p. S3.

Amendments
2008 Amendments. Pars. (14) to (19). Pub.L. 110–181, § 585(a)(1), added pars. (14) to (19).
2004 Amendments. Par. (4)(A)(iv). Pub.L. 108–271, § 8(b), substituted "Government Accountability Office" for "General Accounting Office".
1995 Amendments. Subsec. (4)(A). Pub.L. 104–1, § 202(c)(1)(A), struck "and" at the end of cl. (ii), struck the

period at the end of cl. (iii), and inserted "; and", and added cl. (iv).

Effective and Applicability Provisions
1995 Acts. Amendment by P.L.104-1 effective 1 year after transmission to Congress of the study under section 1371 of Title 2, The Congress, see section 1312(e)(2) of Title 2. The study required under section 1371 of Title 2, dated Dec. 31, 1996, was transmitted to Congress by the Board of Directors of the Office of Compliance on Dec. 30, 1996.

1993 Acts. Section effective 6 months after Feb. 5, 1993, except that, in the case of collective bargaining agreements in effect on that effective date, this section to apply on the earlier of (1) the date of the termination of such agreement, or (2) the date that occurs 12 months after Feb. 5, 1993, see section 405 of Pub.L. 103–3, set out as a note under section 2601 of this title.

CROSS REFERENCES

Congressional accountability and administrative and judicial dispute-resolution procedures including judicial branch coverage study, see 2 USCA § 1434.
Family and medical leave rights and protections provided to Presidential offices, see 3 USCA § 412.
Participants in private, State, local and Federal community service projects, service sponsors, see 42 USCA § 12631.

262

law's enactment or citations to those materials. Compiled legislative histories exist for many laws.

You have several options for finding a compiled legislative history. First, you may search an online library catalog or a discovery tool[33] provided by your library using a key-word or subject search. These searches sometimes lead you to compilations of documents.

Second, you may consult a bibliography of compiled histories, such as Nancy P. Johnson, *Sources of Compiled Legislative Histories: A Bibliography of Government Documents, Periodical Articles and Books*, a version of which appears in HeinOnline's U.S. Federal Legislative History library. These sources provide citations to compiled legislative histories or other legislative history information for many laws.

Finally, various resources provide collections of compiled legislative histories. For example, HeinOnline provides a large number of compiled legislative histories in its U.S. Federal Legislative History Library, and Westlaw and Lexis each offer some compiled legislative histories.[34] The newest — and by far the most comprehensive — of these resources is ProQuest's Legislative Insight, which includes compiled legislative histories, with citations and links to documents, for more than 27,000 laws enacted from 1789 to 2012, as well as additional legislative histories for laws enacted more recently. If you have access to Legislative Insight, you should use it (though likely not as your only source).[35]

Researching the FMLA's legislative history for the Exact Electronics situation, we expected to find a compiled legislative history, given the prominence of the FMLA. We first checked the Johnson bibliography in HeinOnline, using the FMLA's public law number. We found two citations to comprehensive collections of documents: a legislative history compiled by the law firm of Arnold and Porter, available on Westlaw, and a history compiled by the law firm of Covington and Burling, available on HeinOnline.

Next we turned to HeinOnline's U.S. Federal Legislative History collection and retrieved the six-volume legislative history prepared by Covington and Burling (a reputable law firm). We browsed the cumulative table of contents for the volumes, finding bills, hearings, committee reports, and floor debates and actions as reported in the *Congressional Record*, for the law that passed and for related bills from as far back as the 99th Congress (1985–1986). We searched the compilation using *"75 mile" OR "75 miles"* and retrieved thirty-eight documents. We found many uses of our terms, but the discussions did not offer guidance on our specific question.

---

33. Examples include Summon, Ebsco Discovery Service, Primo, and WorldCat Discovery.

34. The Law Librarians Society of Washington, D.C., maintains a list of those legislative histories at http://www.llsdc.org/lh-of-us-laws-on-the-internet-commercial-sources. It also provides at that site a link to free legislative histories on the Internet at http://www.llsdc.org/legislative-histories. The lists are selective.

35. One downside of this resource is that it does not highlight your search terms in all documents. Thus, reviewing some of them can be very tedious.

Congress.gov. If you do not find a useful compiled legislative history, a free government website is often your next step. Congress.gov, the Library of Congress website, is the official website for U.S. federal legislative information. Congress.gov is replacing the THOMAS website, which will remain available until the transition is complete.

Congress.gov tracks the history of bills, beginning with bills introduced in 1973. It also provides some materials, beginning in 1995 for the *Congressional Record* and for committee reports. Congress.gov does not include the full text of committee hearings.[36] A particular strength of Congress.gov is its coverage of amendments.

Congress.gov provides several search options. The easiest is to search first for the law, then to focus on the bill that became law. Congress.gov provides the following information: (1) summaries of the bill, (2) bill text, (3) actions on the bill, (4) names given to the bill, (5) information about proposed amendments, (6) cosponsors, (7) committees that considered the bill and committee actions, and (8) related bills. You may choose to review only the categories of information that interest you, or you may review all information on the bill. If Congress.gov contains the summary or text of a document that interests you, the site provides a link to it.

Researching the Exact Electronics issue, we searched for "*pl 103-3*" and retrieved the summary report for H.R. 1, the bill that became the FMLA. The first page of the full report provided an overview of the bill and actions on it, tabs for retrieving various types of information about the bill, and a link to "all bill information." See Box 5.27. We selected "all bill information." We found some references to the *Congressional Record* that we had not previously noted. Because Congress.gov had not yet added the *Congressional Record* for the 103rd Congress to its database, we moved to THOMAS. We retrieved nineteen documents meeting our search for discussions of seventy-five mile(s) but, again, found nothing illuminating.

Commercial Online Resources. If you have not found a compiled legislative history for your statute and seek to read legislative history documents beyond those you would obtain through the resources described thus far, various commercial publishers offer online collections of legislative documents.

ProQuest Congressional is the most comprehensive online resource focused solely on providing legislative materials.[37] The basic ProQuest subscription includes a legislative history report for all public laws since 1969; abstracts (descriptions) and indexing for published hearings, committee prints, committee reports, House and Senate documents, and miscellaneous

---

36. A committee's website may contain the transcript of a relevant hearing. The Government Publishing Office's Federal Digital System, which includes selective hearings, is another option for finding and searching legislative history documents. It is available at http://www.gpo.gov/fdsys/.

37. It is derived in part from CIS, an extensive print and microforms resource, which was for many years the gold standard in legislative history research and remains a useful resource for those without access to ProQuest Congressional.

Box 5.27 CONGRESS.GOV INFORMATION (Family Leave Rights)

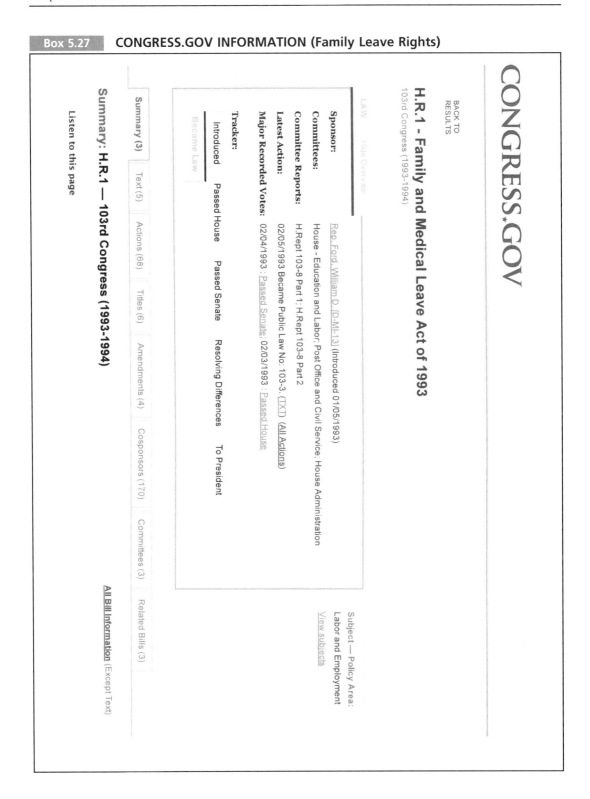

CONGRESS·GOV

BACK TO
RESULTS

H.R.1 - Family and Medical Leave Act of 1993
103rd Congress (1993-1994)

LAW   Hide Overview

Subject — Policy Area:
Labor and Employment
View subjects

Sponsor: Rep. Ford, William D. [D-MI-13] (Introduced 01/05/1993)

Committees: House - Education and Labor; Post Office and Civil Service; House Administration

Committee Reports: H.Rept 103-8 Part 1; H.Rept 103-8 Part 2

Latest Action: 02/05/1993 Became Public Law No: 103-3. (TXT) (All Actions)

Major Recorded Votes: 02/04/1993 : Passed Senate; 02/03/1993 : Passed House

Tracker:

| Introduced | Passed House | Passed Senate | Resolving Differences | To President | Became Law |

| Summary (3) | Text (5) | Actions (68) | Titles (6) | Amendments (4) | Cosponsors (170) | Committees (3) | Related Bills (3) |

Summary: H.R.1 — 103rd Congress (1993-1994)

All Bill Information (Except Text)

Listen to this page

Congressional publications from 1970; some full text documents; and the *Congressional Record* (daily edition)[38] from 1985. The most complete collection includes searchable Portable Document Format (PDF) files of hearings from 1824, committee prints from 1817, committee reports and House and Senate documents from 1789, and more.

An Advanced Search in ProQuest Congressional by public law number in the Legislative Histories category will bring you to the law's legislative history report. The report includes the law's title and summary; bill numbers for enacted and related bills; references to debates and actions as reported in the *Congressional Record*; titles, dates, and numbers for committee prints, hearings, and reports; and references to House and Senate documents — along with links to the available documents. The legislative history report for major laws covers not only the session in which the law was enacted but also previous sessions, if any, in which Congress considered related legislation. See Box 5.28. The Advanced Search option also allows you to select other categories of documents to search, and you may search a single category or multiple categories simultaneously.

Lexis, Westlaw, and Bloomberg Law all provide databases with some bills, limited hearing testimony, the *Congressional Record*, and committee reports, although generally only for relatively recent laws. Lexis offers the same legislative histories found in ProQuest Congressional. First, retrieve the public law and then select CIS Legislative History.

Westlaw also offers Graphical Statutes, an interactive timeline that alerts you to the effective dates for various versions of a statute. For each time period during which a different version was in effect, Graphical Statutes provides links to the text of the statute at that time, the law enacting that version, and citations and links to legislative history documents for that law. Graphical Statutes covers federal laws from 1996 forward. It is available from the History tab on a statutory section.

HeinOnline offers a U.S. Congressional Documents library, which is a good resource for the permanent and daily editions of the *Congressional Record* and for some congressional hearings and committee prints. It also offers a *U.S. Statutes at Large* library.

Researching the Exact Electronics issue, we decided to search ProQuest Congressional's hearings, committee prints and reports, and debate documents as a double-check of our earlier work in the compiled legislative history of the FMLA. We conducted a full-text search for *"75 mile" OR "75 miles" AND "Family and Medical Leave Act,"* ultimately researching documents pertaining to earlier versions of FMLA that had passed but been vetoed.

---

38. The *Congressional Record* is published in both daily and permanent editions. The permanent edition reflects editing and re-arrangement, and the daily edition's two-fold numbering scheme ("S" for Senate and "H" for House of Representatives) yields to a single numbering scheme.

Box 5.28 **PROQUEST CONGRESSIONAL LEGISLATIVE HISTORY REPORT
(Family Leave Rights)**

Legislative History

Title Info

Legislative History of:	PL103-3
Title:	Family and Medical Leave Act of 1993
Date:	February 05, 1993
Length:	24 p.
Enacted Bill:	103 H.R. 1 ; Retrieve Bill Profile Report (/profiles/gis/search/linking /linking?doctype=Bill Tracking&subdoctype=null&pubdate=1993-01-05& docid=billtracking/103_hr_1&searchtype=doc&src=/app-gis/billtracking /103_hr_1&exists=true)
Congress Session:	103- 1
CIS-Number:	93-PL103-3
PL Number:	P.L. 103-3
Statute at Large:	107 Stat. 6
Bills:	99 H.R. 2020; 99 H.R. 4300; 99 S. 2278; 100 H.R. 284; 100 H.R. 925; 100 S. 249; 100 S. 2488; 101 H.R. 770; 101 S. 345; 102 H.R. 2; 102 S. 5; 102 S. 418; 102 S. 688; 103 H.R. 1; 103 S. 5
Permalink:	HTTP.//congressional.proquest.com/congressional/docview /t33.d34.103_pl_3?accountid=147005 (HTTP.//congressional.proquest.com /congressional/docview/t33.d34.103_pl_3?accountid=147005)

Summary

"To grant family and temporary medical leave under certain circumstances."

Entitles eligible private sector and government employees to up to 12 weeks of unpaid medical leave for a serious health condition, and up to 12 weeks of unpaid family leaves of absence for childbirth, adoption, and care of infants or seriously ill children, spouses, or parents.

Exempts from leave requirements small businesses with fewer than 50 employees.

Requires that employees who return from family or medical leave be restored to the positions they held before taking leave or to equivalent positions.

Requires employers to continue health benefits for employees during family and medical leave, and provides that other accrued benefits shall not be lost because of such leave.

Authorizes DOL to enforce worker rights with regard to family and medical leave.

Establishes special rules for employees of local educational agencies and other requirements for civil service employees and Congressional employees.

Establishes a Commission on Leave to study existing and proposed family and medical leave policies.

Box 5.28   *(continued)*

> September 30, House consideration of the Presidential veto message on 102 S. 5 p. H9930

139 Congressional Record, 103 Congress, 1 session - 1993

> February 02, Senate consideration of 103 S. 5 p. S985
>
> February 03, House consideration and passage of 103 H.R. 1 p. H379
>
> February 03, Senate consideration of 103 S. 5 p. S1090
>
> February 04, Senate consideration and passage of 103 H.R. 1 with an amendment, and indefinite postponement of 103 S. 5 p. S1254
>
> February 04, House concurrence in the Senate amendment to 103 H.R. 1 p. H557

Bills Versions

99 H.R. 2020

> INTRODUCED

99 H.R. 4300

> March 04, 1986, INTRODUCED
>
> July 21, 1986, REPORTED, House Post Office and Civil Service Committee
>
> August 08, 1986, REPORTED, House Education and Labor Committee

99 S. 2278

> INTRODUCED

100 H.R. 284

> INTRODUCED

100 H.R. 925

> February 03, 1987, INTRODUCED
>
> March 08, 1988, REPORTED, House Post Office and Civil Service Committee
>
> March 09, 1988, REPORTED, House Education and Labor Committee

100 S. 249

> INTRODUCED

100 S. 2488

> June 08, 1988, INTRODUCED
>
> August 03, 1988, REPORTED, Senate Labor and Human Resources Committee

101 H.R. 770

> February 02, 1989, INTRODUCED

Box 5.28   (continued)

Content Notation

Employee leave of absence for parental and medical reasons

Subjects

Pregnancy; Families; Adoption; Federal employees; Children; Small business; Government and business; Employee benefit plans; Health insurance; Department of Labor; Congressional employees; Aged and aging; Federal advisory bodies

Descriptors

Family and Medical Leave Act; Commission on Leave

Debates

136 Congressional Record, 101 Congress, 2 session - 1990

> May 09, House consideration of 101 H.R. 770 p. H2157
>
> May 10, House consideration and passage of 101 H.R. 770 p. H2198
>
> June 14, Senate consideration and passage of 101 H.R. 770 p. S8006
>
> July 25, House consideration of the Presidential veto message on 101 H.R. 770 p. H5484

137 Congressional Record, 102 Congress, 1 session - 1991

> October 02, Senate consideration and passage of 102 S. 5 p. S14125
>
> November 13, House consideration of 102 H.R. 2, consideration and passage of 102 S. 5 with an amendment, and tabling of 102 H.R. 2 p. H9722

138 Congressional Record, 102 Congress, 2 session - 1992

> July 28, Senate disagreement to the House amendment to 102 S. 5, request for a conference, and appointment of conferees p. S10485
>
> August 04, House insistence on its amendment to 102 S. 5, agreement to a conference, and appointment of conferees p. H7273
>
> August 10, Submission in the House of the conference report on 102 S. 5 p. H7740
>
> August 11, Senate agreement to the conference report on 102 S. 5 p. S12093
>
> September 10, House agreement to the conference report on 102 S. 5 p. H8238
>
> September 24, Senate consideration of the Presidential veto message and passage of 102 S. 5 p. S14841

Box 5.28   *(continued)*

Reports

99 -2 Congress Session - July 21, 1986

"Parental and Medical Leave Act of 1986"

Committee:	Committee on Post Office and Civil Service. House
Bill Number.	99 H.R. 4300

Congressional Publication: 13704 H.rp.699/1 (/profiles/gis/search/linking/linking?doctype=Serial Set 2&subdoctype=House and Senate Reports,Reports on Public Bill&pubdate=1986-07-21&docid=serialset/13704_h.rp.699_1&searchtype=doc& src=/app-gis/serialset/13704_h.rp.699_1&exists=true)

CIS Number.	1986-H623-9
Length:	21 p.
Sudoc:	Y1.1/8:99-699/pt.1

99 -2 Congress Session - August 08, 1986

"Family and Medical Leave Act of 1986"

Committee:	Committee on Education and Labor. House
Bill Number.	99 H.R. 4300

Congressional Publication: 13704 H.rp.699/2 (/profiles/gis/search/linking/linking?doctype=Serial Set 2&subdoctype=House and Senate Reports,Reports on Public Bill&pubdate=1986-08-08&docid=serialset/13704_h.rp.699_2&searchtype=doc& src=/app-gis/serialset/13704_h.rp.699_2&exists=true)

CIS Number.	1986-H343-19
Length:	57 p.
Sudoc:	Y1.1/8:99-699/pt.2

100 -2 Congress Session - March 08, 1988

"Family and Medical Leave Act"

Committee:	Committee on Post Office and Civil Service. House
Bill Number.	100 H.R. 925

Congressional Publication: 13890 H.rp.511/1 (/profiles/gis/search/linking/linking?doctype=Serial Set 2&subdoctype=House and Senate Reports,Reports on Public Bill&pubdate=1988-03-08&docid=serialset/13890_h.rp.511_1&searchtype=doc& src=/app-gis/serialset/13890_h.rp.511_1&exists=true)

We found House hearings on H.R. 770, with testimony from John J. Motley, director of federal government relations for the National Federation of Independent Businesses. With some foresight, he said: "The 75-mile-radius definition to determine the number of employees for eligibility purposes is difficult to conceptualize, difficult to ensure compliance [with], and will lead to greater uncertainties."

As we ended our research, we concluded that although the purpose of the relevant exemption was clear, the legislative history materials, as is often the case, did not provide a definitive answer to the precise meaning of the statutory term.

Researching Pending Legislation

Legislative materials are used not only to research the legislative history of enacted laws for purposes of establishing legislative intent, but also to track the status of pending legislation. Lawyers track pending legislation to help clients plan ahead by taking into account the provisions of probable new laws and, sometimes, to influence the introduction, defeat, modification, or passage of a bill through lobbying.

On the federal side,[39] Congress.gov and ProQuest Congressional offer much the same materials for bills as they do for laws. You can use a bill number (or key-word searching to find bills that you may not know about) to obtain the text and status report for a bill. Congress.gov also allows you to track current legislation by policy area (that is, by subject). See Box 5.29, which is the report for a bill before Congress in 2015 that would amend the FMLA to entitle an eligible employee to up to twelve workweeks of leave during any twelve-month period because of the death of a son or daughter.

Westlaw, Lexis, and Bloomberg Law provide the text of bills and a bill-tracking function. Furthermore, when you read a statute on Lexis or Westlaw, the systems alert you to proposed legislation affecting the statute and lead you to it, through Shepard's on Lexis and through KeyCite and Graphical Statutes on Westlaw.

---

39. A good option for bill tracking at the state level is the legislature's website. More costly options are Lexis and Westlaw; the Shepard's and Graphical Statutes options that provide alerts to pending legislation operate for both state statutes and federal statutes.

Box 5.29   CONGRESS.GOV BILL TRACKING REPORT (Family Leave Rights)

CONGRESS★GOV

BACK TO
RESULTS

S.1302 - Sarah Grace-Farley-Kluger Act

114th Congress (2015-2016) | Get alerts

BILL   Hide Overview

Sponsor: Sen. Tester, Jon [D-MT] (Introduced 05/12/2015)

Committees: Senate - Health, Education, Labor, and Pensions

Latest Action: 05/12/2015 Read twice and referred to the Committee on Health, Education, Labor, and Pensions. (All Actions)

Tracker:

Introduced   Passed Senate   Passed House   To President

Became Law

Subject —
Policy Area:
Labor and
Employment

View subjects

| Summary (1) | Text (1) | Actions (1) | Titles (3) | Amendments (0) | Cosponsors (11) | Committees (|

Summary: S.1302 — 114th Congress (2015-2016)   All Bill Information (Except Text)

Listen to this page

There is one summary for S.1302. Bill summaries are authored by CRS.

Shown Here:
Introduced in Senate (05/12/2015)

Parental Bereavement Act of 2015 or the Sarah Grace-Farley-Kluger Act

Amends the Family and Medical Leave Act of 1993 to entitle an eligible employee to up to 12 workweeks of leave during any 12-month period because of the death of a son or daughter.

Allows such an employee to substitute any available paid leave for any leave without pay.

BUILD YOUR UNDERSTANDING

Test Your Knowledge

1. Define the following terms so that their relationships to each other are clear.
   - Bill
   - Charter
   - Constitution
   - Law
   - Ordinance
   - Statute
2. What is a statute's effective date? Why must you attend to that when you research a statute?
3. The following three verbs are all legislative actions: amend, enact, repeal. Place them in typical chronological sequence, and explain how they differ from each other.
4. What are the two ways in which courts make law where the legislature has enacted a statute? Which is more common, and why?
5. Here is a timeline of events in the life of a statute controlling your client's situation:
   - 1900 Common law rule created
   - 1998 Statute enacted, with effective date of January 1, 2000
   - 2002 Court decides *Alvarez*, declaring statute unconstitutional
   - 2004 Legislature amends statute to resolve *Alvarez* problem
   - 2006 Court interprets statute in *Buckley*
   - 2008 Legislature amends statute to reverse *Buckley* interpretation
     Identify the rule that controls if your client's situation arose in each of the following years: 1999, 2003, 2005, 2007, and 2009. With each answer, provide an explanation.
6. You are representing one side in a negotiation, and you have found a controlling statute. The statute could be read either of two ways — one benefiting your client, the other benefiting the other side. What do you do now?
7. List the common components of a lengthy statute in the order in which they typically appear. Why is each important to read?
8. Statutes appear in various publications. Explain how the items in each pair differ from each other from a research standpoint:
   - Session laws and codes
   - Official and unofficial codes
   - Unannotated and annotated codes
9. Legislative materials are useful when you are either researching a law that was enacted or monitoring pending legislation. For what reasons would you conduct these types of research on a client's behalf?

10. Order the following legislative history materials from most to least influential in revealing the legislature's intent in passing a statute, and explain why your top three are so influential:
    • Amendments
    • Conference committee report
    • Floor debate
    • Hearing testimony
    • Presidential signing statement
    • Report from the committee that first considered the bill
11. Why is a statutory code often the starting point in legislative materials research?
12. What is a compiled legislative history, and why is it an ideal legislative history resource?

Put It into Practice

Recall your client's situation (detailed in Chapter 1 at pages 20-21): Your client, Emmet Wilson, is a veteran who has developed post-traumatic stress disorder (PTSD). Among other treatments, he has been assigned a therapy dog. Mr. Wilson's landlord has raised concerns because the building is a no-pets building. Indeed, the lease (which is for a year) so specifies, and the landlord says that other tenants have raised the issue. So she has given Mr. Wilson notice that if he does not give up the dog, he will be evicted in a month.

Part 1. Statutory Research. Research the legal issue raised by Mr. Wilson, that the landlord's actions in evicting him because he needs a dog for therapeutic purposes amount to discrimination based on his disability in both federal and state law, as directed.

1. A colleague has told you that the situation could be covered by the federal Fair Housing Act. The issue to research is whether a mental impairment is covered by that statute, which is discussed in the statute's definition section. Begin with the OLRC website at uscode.house.gov. State the following:
   a. The method that you used to find the pertinent statute (note that we have provided the name of the statute)
   b. The citation of the definition section, which includes the title number and section number
   c. The language of the pertinent section
   d. The year that language was enacted

2. To find additional sources, turn to either of the print annotated federal codes, U.S.C.A. or U.S.C.S.
   a. State the nature (e.g., hardcover or pocket part) and date of the volume in which you found in print the language of the definition section of the Fair Housing Act.
   b. Read the case summaries to identify cases on the issue of whether mental impairments are covered by the statute. Select one case that

you would go on to read. State the following about that case: its name, citation (reporter, volume, and page number), court, date, and legal point as stated in the summary.

   c. Read the references to secondary sources. Provide the citation to one that you would read (if any), if you were to continue your research.

3. Now turn to the possibility that this issue is covered by a West Virginia statute. Research this issue in Westlaw or Lexis.
   a. State how you found the pertinent statute.
   b. Write a brief of the statute, following the sample in Box 5.4.
   c. Note the statute's effective date.
   d. Read the case summaries to identify cases pertinent to your client's situation; select one case that you would go on to read. State the following about that case: its name, citation, court, date, and legal point as stated in the summary.
   e. Read the references to secondary sources. Provide the citation to one that you would read (if any), if you were to continue your research.

4. For comparison, research the same issue in your own state in Fastcase. State the following about your research:
   a. State the methods that you used to search for a pertinent statute.
   b. Indicate whether your state prohibits discrimination in rental housing based on mental impairment.
   c. Provide the citation to the pertinent statute (if any).

5. If you had access to all resources discussed in this chapter and cost were not an issue, which resource or resources would you use for this project, and why?

Part Two. Legislative Materials Research. Return to researching the federal Fair Housing Act.

6. Find § 3601 in one of the annotated federal codes (print or online). List the public law or laws that make up this section by number and year of enactment.

7. Examine the legislative history materials in U.S.C.C.A.N. for the 1988 public law (the Fair Housing Amendments Act) giving rise to the language pertaining to Mr. Wilson's situation.
   a. State the steps that law took en route to becoming law.
   b. Read the legislative history documents provided in U.S.C.C.A.N., and list here anything you learned about the intent behind the language addressing Mr. Wilson's situation.

8. Now research in the resources identified by your professor. Find two documents (ideally of two different types), other than what you read for question 7.
   a. State how you searched for pertinent information within the resource that you used.
   b. For each of the two documents you read, state the name of the document and state what it had to say about the issue in Mr. Wilson's situation.

9. To determine whether there is any proposed legislation that would change who is protected under the Fair Housing Act, research on either Congress.gov, Lexis, or Westlaw.
   a. Describe how you conducted your research.
   b. If you found no pending legislation, state this.
   c. If you found that there is legislation currently pending that would amend the statute, provide its bill number, give details on what it would do, and state its current status. (If there is more than one bill, select the most recent one.)

Make Connections

1. In many countries, the law is made by the legislatures, not by courts. Our system uses a complex blend of lawmaking processes, which creates significant challenges in research. From what you can tell, is our system a wise one? Explain your answer.

2. Some observers, including legislators, believe that enacted laws should speak for themselves and that legislative materials should not be considered when interpreting a statute. If this were so, what would be used instead? Would this be a wise change? Explain your answer.

Answers to Test Your Knowledge Questions

1. Definitions of the following terms are:
   - Bill — a proposal for a law
   - Charter — a local law that creates a government
   - Constitution — a federal or state law that creates a government and defines the rights of the citizens relative to the government
   - Law — a legal rule that has been passed by a legislature and approved by the executive
   - Ordinance — a law at the local level
   - Statute — a federal or state law

2. A statute's effective date is the date on which it controls people's conduct. A statute is often passed well before it becomes effective, so the fact that is appears in a legal resource does not mean that it is in effect yet.

3. A statute is initially enacted. It may be amended, or changed, to include new sections or have some existing language altered. When a statute is repealed, it is no longer in legal effect.

4. More common is interpreting statutory language in light of specific situations when the court applies it to resolve disputes, which may entail resolving ambiguities. Less common is addressing issues of constitutionality, which may entail declaring a statute unconstitutional; this is relatively rare because legislatures generally act within constitutional bounds.

5. Under the following timeline, the listed sources applied to the client situations arising in the listed years:
   - 1900 Common law rule created — applies to 1999 client situation (1998 statute is not yet effective); also applies to 2003 client situation (1998 statute does not apply, due to *Alvarez*)
   - 2004 Legislature amends statute to resolve *Alvarez* problem — applies to 2005 client situation (statute now is constitutional)
   - 2006 Court interprets statute in *Buckley* — applies along with 2004 statute to 2007 client situation (court interpretation adds to statutory language)
   - 2008 Legislature amends statute to reverse *Buckley* interpretation — applies to 2009 client situation (legislature may counter court interpretation)

6. When representing one side in a negotiation controlled by a statute that could be read two ways, you should research at least the interpreting cases to see whether there is an authoritative ruling. If so, that ruling resolves the matter. If not, the other tools of statutory interpretation are to be explored, including canons of construction and legislative history.

7. The common components of a lengthy statute are the name and purpose, definitions, general rules, exceptions or exemptions, implementation sections, and technical sections. Every part either contributes to the rule or has some impact, such as determining whether the statute is in effect.

8. The distinctions between the following pairs are:
   - Session laws and codes—Session laws contain all laws passed during a session of a legislature, whereas codes contain the laws of general and permanent applicability currently in force for a jurisdiction, whenever they are passed.
   - Official and unofficial codes—Official codes are the authoritative versions, published by the legislature or under its auspices, whereas unofficial versions are not the authoritative versions and are published by someone else.
   - Unannotated and annotated codes—Unannotated codes provide the language of the statute, whereas annotated codes also provide editorial enhancements, including information about interpreting cases and secondary sources.

9. Lawyers research an enacted law's (statute's) legislative history to find outdated language and to determine legislative intent as a means of statutory interpretation. They monitor pending legislation to help a client plan future conduct or to influence law that may affect a client's future interests (lobbying).

10. The legislative history materials are listed from most to least influential in revealing a legislature's intent in passing a statute:
    - Amendments—These provide direct insight into language that the legislature chose and rejected.
    - Conference committee report—This report reflects compromises made at the end stage of the process.
    - Report from the committee that first considered the bill—This report reflects the views of the committee with expertise in the law's subject matter and the initial impetus for the law.
    - Floor debate
    - Hearing testimony
    - Presidential signing statement

11. A statutory code is a good starting point because it provides the public law numbers of the laws that gave rise to the statute, which is key information for legislative history research. An online statutory code links to information about pending legislation for bill-tracking purposes.

12. A compiled legislative history is a collection of the various documents created by the legislature during the consideration of a statute (or a compilation of citations to the documents). Using it is efficient because otherwise, research would entail working in multiple different resources.

RULES OF PROCEDURE AND PROFESSIONAL RESPONSIBILITY

One role of a legal system is to create the rules of law that control the conduct of people and organizations in a society; lawyers call these rules *substantive law*. The issues discussed in other chapters — whether an employer may constrain an employee from working for a competitor, whether a public school may suspend a student for a statement shaved into his hair, whether a driver may be ticketed for using a cell phone, and so on — are controlled by rules of substantive law.

Another role of a legal system is to provide forums through which substantive laws are enforced or, stated another way, disputes are resolved. *Procedural law* exists to ensure that these forums operate in a manner that is seen as fair by participants. Some procedural law is a matter of statute; two examples are under what circumstances you may bring a case in federal court (i.e., federal jurisdiction statutes)[1] and how soon you must bring a lawsuit (i.e., statutes of limitation).

This chapter focuses on a different type of procedural law: rules of procedure. Rules of procedure set out the moves that the parties to a type of litigation may or must take as they litigate a case. This chapter also focuses on rules of legal ethics: the standards by which lawyers' conduct is measured for purposes of professional discipline. Needless to say, deep knowledge of both sets of rules is critical to the professional practice of law.

---

1. *E.g.*, 28 U.S.C. § 1332 (2012) (providing for jurisdiction of cases where the parties are citizens of different states).

RULES OF PROCEDURE

Understanding the Rules and Related Sources

Rules of procedure are primary authority, created by some lawmaking body acting in a lawmaking capacity. Typically, the highest court in a jurisdiction creates its rules of procedure.[2]

Reflecting our federal system, separate sets of rules of procedure exist for different court systems. That is, the federal courts have a set of rules; each state's court system has its own set of rules. Certainly, there are similarities, but you should never assume that what occurs in one court system operates the same way in another court system. This chapter focuses on the federal court rules because they are the most widely applicable and because many state court rules are modeled after the federal rules to some extent.

The rules applicable to litigation in federal court depend on the type of litigation involved. Thus, if your case involves a civil claim in a district court, where cases receive their initial hearing and trial (if any), your focus would be on the Federal Rules of Civil Procedure, along with the Federal Rules of Evidence. On the other hand, if your case involves a criminal prosecution, your focus would be on the Federal Rules of Criminal Procedure, along with the Federal Rules of Evidence. If your case proceeds to appeal, you would be concerned with the Federal Rules of Appellate Procedure.[3]

Each of these main sets of rules provides a road map for the particular type of litigation it covers, setting out the moves the parties may or must take. Failure to follow the rules can have mild to dramatic consequences, depending on the situation. In serious situations, the client may lose the case,[4] and the lawyer may be fined.[5]

As a general matter, the organization of a set of rules is roughly chronological. For example, the Federal Rules of Civil Procedure cover the following topics: introductory matters, commencing an action, pleadings, parties, disclosures and discovery (the process by which lawyers exchange factual information about the case), trials, judgment, remedies, and general matters. Some of the rules are quite detailed (e.g., stating a specific number of days in which a pleading must be served), while others are more general (e.g., specifying the standard that a court is to use in making a decision). See Box 6.1.

---

2. The U.S. Constitution is not clear whether the power to create the rules for the federal courts resides in the Congress or the Supreme Court. Congress delegated the task to the Court in the Rules Enabling Act of 1934, but the rules are subject to Congressional review.

3. Specialized proceedings, such as admiralty, bankruptcy, and multidistrict litigation, have their own rules.

4. For example, failure to respond to a complaint may lead to a default judgment under Federal Rule of Civil Procedure 55.

5. See Federal Rule of Civil Procedure 11.

Box 6.1   **FEDERAL RULE OF CIVIL PROCEDURE (Preliminary Injunction)**

PROVISIONAL AND FINAL REMEDIES   **Rule 65**

commenced if filed in federal court, and from the time of removal if removed from state court. These provisions are deleted as redundant. Rule 1 establishes that the Civil Rules apply to all actions in a district court, and Rule 81(c)(1) adds reassurance that the Civil Rules apply to a removed action "after it is removed."

Rule 65. Injunctions and Restraining Orders

(a) **Preliminary Injunction.**

(1) *Notice.* The court may issue a preliminary injunction only on notice to the adverse party.

(2) *Consolidating the Hearing with the Trial on the Merits.* Before or after beginning the hearing on a motion for a preliminary injunction, the court may advance the trial on the merits and consolidate it with the hearing. Even when consolidation is not ordered, evidence that is received on the motion and that would be admissible at trial becomes part of the trial record and need not be repeated at trial. But the court must preserve any party's right to a jury trial.

(b) **Temporary Restraining Order.**

(1) *Issuing Without Notice.* The court may issue a temporary restraining order without written or oral notice to the adverse party or its attorney only if:

(A) specific facts in an affidavit or a verified complaint clearly show that immediate and irreparable injury, loss, or damage will result to the movant before the adverse party can be heard in opposition; and

(B) the movant's attorney certifies in writing any efforts made to give notice and the reasons why it should not be required.

(2) *Contents; Expiration.* Every temporary restraining order issued without notice must state the date and hour it was issued; describe the injury and state why it is irreparable; state why the order was issued without notice; and be promptly filed in the clerk's office and entered in the record. The order expires at the time after entry—not to exceed 14 days—that the court sets, unless before that time the court, for good cause, extends it for a like period or the adverse party consents to a longer extension. The reasons for an extension must be entered in the record.

(3) *Expediting the Preliminary–Injunction Hearing.* If the order is issued without notice, the motion for a preliminary injunction must be set for hearing at the earliest possible time, taking precedence over all other matters except hearings on older matters of the same character. At the hearing, the party who obtained the order must proceed with the mo-

tion; if the party does not, the court must dissolve the order.

(4) *Motion to Dissolve.* On 2 days' notice to the party who obtained the order without notice—or on shorter notice set by the court—the adverse party may appear and move to dissolve or modify the order. The court must then hear and decide the motion as promptly as justice requires.

(c) **Security.** The court may issue a preliminary injunction or a temporary restraining order only if the movant gives security in an amount that the court considers proper to pay the costs and damages sustained by any party found to have been wrongfully enjoined or restrained. The United States, its officers, and its agencies are not required to give security.

(d) **Contents and Scope of Every Injunction and Restraining Order.**

(1) *Contents.* Every order granting an injunction and every restraining order must:

(A) state the reasons why it issued;

(B) state its terms specifically; and

(C) describe in reasonable detail—and not by referring to the complaint or other document—the act or acts restrained or required.

(2) *Persons Bound.* The order binds only the following who receive actual notice of it by personal service or otherwise:

(A) the parties;

(B) the parties' officers, agents, servants, employees, and attorneys; and

(C) other persons who are in active concert or participation with anyone described in Rule 65(d)(2)(A) or (B).

(e) **Other Laws Not Modified.** These rules do not modify the following:

(1) any federal statute relating to temporary restraining orders or preliminary injunctions in actions affecting employer and employee;

(2) 28 U.S.C. § 2361, which relates to preliminary injunctions in actions of interpleader or in the nature of interpleader; or

(3) 28 U.S.C. § 2284, which relates to actions that must be heard and decided by a three-judge district court.

(f) **Copyright Impoundment.** This rule applies to copyright-impoundment proceedings.

(Amended December 27, 1946, effective March 19, 1948; December 29, 1948, effective October 20, 1949; February 28, 1966, effective July 1, 1966; March 2, 1987, effective August 1, 1987; April 23, 2001, effective December 1, 2001; April 30,

For Complete Annotation Materials, see United States Code Annotated
283

Box 6.1   *(continued)*

Rule 65   RULES OF CIVIL PROCEDURE

2007, effective December 1, 2007; March 26, 2009, effective December 1, 2009.)

ADVISORY COMMITTEE NOTES
1937 Adoption

Note to Subdivisions (a) and (b). These are taken from U.S.C., Title 28, [former] § 381 (Injunctions; preliminary injunctions and temporary restraining orders).

Note to Subdivision (c). Except for the last sentence, this is substantially U.S.C., Title 28, [former] § 382 (Injunctions; security on issuance of). The last sentence continues the following and similar statutes which expressly except the United States or an officer or agency thereof from such security requirements: U.S.C. Title 15, §§ 77t(b), 78u(e), and 79r(f) (Securities and Exchange Commission). It also excepts the United States or an officer or agency thereof from such security requirements in any action in which a restraining order or interlocutory judgment of injunction issues in its favor whether there is an express statutory exception from such security requirements or not.

See U.S.C., [former] Title 6 (Official and Penal Bonds) for bonds by surety companies.

Note to Subdivision (d). This is substantially U.S.C., Title 28, [former] § 383 (Injunctions; requisites of order; binding effect).

Note to Subdivision (e). The words "relating to temporary restraining orders and preliminary injunctions in actions affecting employer and employee" are words of description and not of limitation.

Compare [former] Equity Rule 73 (Preliminary Injunctions and Temporary Restraining Orders) which is substantially equivalent to the statutes.

For other statutes dealing with injunctions which are continued, see e.g.:

U.S.C., Title 28 former:

§ 46 [now 2324] (Suits to enjoin orders of Interstate Commerce Commission to be against United States)

§ 47 [now 2325] (Injunctions as to orders of Interstate Commerce Commission; appeal to Supreme Court; time for taking)

§ 378 [former] (Injunctions; when granted)

§ 379 [now 2283] (Injunctions; stay in State courts)

§ 380 [now 1253, 2101, 2281, 2284] (Injunctions; alleged unconstitutionality of State statutes; appeal to Supreme Court)

§ 380a [now 1253, 2101, 2281, 2284] (Injunctions; constitutionality of Federal statute; application for hearing; appeal to Supreme Court)

U.S.C., Title 7:

§ 216 (Court proceedings to enforce orders; injunction)

§ 217 (Proceedings for suspension of orders)

U.S.C., Title 15:

§ 4 (Jurisdiction of courts; duty of district attorney; procedure)

§ 25 (Restraining violations; procedure)

§ 26 (Injunctive relief for private parties; exceptions)

§ 77t(b) (Injunctions and prosecution of offenses)

1946 Amendment

Note. It has been held that in actions on preliminary injunction bonds the district court has discretion to grant relief in the same proceeding or to require the institution of a new action on the bond. *Russell v. Farley,* 1881, 105 U.S. 433, 466. It is believed, however, that in all cases the litigant should have a right to proceed on the bond in the same proceeding, in the manner provided in Rule 73(f) for a similar situation. The paragraph added to Rule 65(c) insures this result and is in the interest of efficiency. There is no reason why Rules 65(c) and 73(f) should operate differently. Compare § 50, sub. n of the Bankruptcy Act, 11 U.S.C. § 78, sub. n, under which actions on all bonds furnished pursuant to the Act may be proceeded upon summarily in the bankruptcy court. See 2 *Collier on Bankruptcy,* 14th ed. by Moore and Oglebay, 1853–1854.

1948 Amendment

The amendment effective October 1949, changed subdivision (e) in the following respects: in the first clause the amendment substituted the words "any statute of the United States" for the words "the Act of October 15, 1914, c. 323, §§ 1 and 20 (38 Stat. 730), U.S.C., Title 29, §§ 52 and 53, or the Act of March 23, 1932, c. 90 (47 Stat. 70), U.S.C., Title 29, c. 6"; in the second clause of subdivision (e) the amendment substituted the reference to "Title 28, U.S.C., § 2361" for the reference to "Section 24(26) of the Judicial Code as amended, U.S.C., Title 28, § 41(26)"; and the third clause was amended to read "Title 28, U.S.C., § 2284," etc., as at present, instead of "the Act of August 24, 1937, c. 754, § 3, relating to actions to enjoin the enforcement of acts of Congress."

1966 Amendment

Subdivision (a)(2). This new subdivision provides express authority for consolidating the hearing of an application for a preliminary injunction with the trial on the merits. The authority can be exercised with particular profit when it appears that a substantial part of the evidence offered on the application will be relevant to the merits and will be presented in such form as to qualify for admission on the trial proper. Repetition of evidence is thereby avoided. The fact that the proceedings have been consolidated should cause no delay in the disposition of the application for the preliminary injunction, for the evidence will be directed in the first instance to that relief, and the preliminary injunction, if justified by the proof, may be issued in the course of the consolidated proceedings. Furthermore, to consolidate the proceedings will tend to expedite the final disposition of the action. It is believed that consolidation can be usefully availed of in many cases.

The subdivision further provides that even when consolidation is not ordered, evidence received in connection with an application for a preliminary injunction which would be admissible on the trial on the merits forms part of the trial record. This evidence need not be repeated on the trial. On the other hand, repetition is not altogether prohibited. That would be impractical and unwise. For example, a witness testifying comprehensively on the trial who has previously testified upon the application for a preliminary injunction might sometimes be hamstrung in telling his story if he could not go over some part of his prior testimony to connect it with his present testimony. So also, some repetition of testimony may be called for where the trial is conducted by a judge who did not hear the application for the preliminary injunction. In general, however, repetition can be avoided with an increase of efficiency in the conduct of the case and without any distortion of the presentation of evidence by the parties.

Many individual rules interact with other rules because together they specify how the elaborate process of litigation is to operate. Thus, once you have read the rule that most obviously pertains to your client's situation, you should take care to look for related rules as well. One good practice is to scan the rules in the same part of the rules as the one you have read. Another is to check whether any introductory rules may apply (e.g., whether any rules setting out timing or filing requirements apply).

When researching an issue involving a rule of procedure, you will anchor your research in the rule but rarely will stop there. Rules of procedure — particularly the federal rules — are applied over and over as courts use them in litigation. Every decided case has not only a substantive law topic but also a procedural posture. For some rules of procedure, the courts have provided significant additional meaning to the language of the rule itself. The same rules of case selection apply for purposes of procedural law as they do for substantive law. Thus, U.S. Supreme Court cases are the most authoritative cases on issues arising under federal rules. It is preferable to find a case from the circuit in which your client's situation is located. If possible, it is preferable (but not necessary) to find a case in the same substantive law setting as your client's situation.

A second source is the notes of the advisory committee. The federal rules, which are adopted by the U.S. Supreme Court, are initially developed for consideration by an advisory committee, a panel of experts, typically judges and professors. They write *notes of the advisory committee,* which are not themselves authority but nonetheless provide useful insight into the thinking behind the language of the rules and thus constitute quasi-authority.

Third, litigation occurs through documents in which lawyers state a case (pleadings), ask for information from the other side (discovery documents), ask the court to make certain rulings on their client's behalf (motions), ask the jury to render its decision (verdict form), and more. Because there is a certain degree of similarity in how these documents should read from case to case, another step in procedural research is seeking out examples to work from, generically known as *sample forms.* In the case of the federal rules, an appendix of sample forms has long accompanied them, but the sample forms were abrogated December 1, 2015. This action was based on the premise that many alternatives exist, including those provided by the Administrative Office of the United States Courts. You should view all sample forms from whatever source as a starting point for your drafting; keep in mind that you will need to tailor them to fit your client's situation.

Finally, it is common for an individual court to have its own *local rules* supplementing the main rules of procedure. The idea behind local rules is to cover matters of detail that make for the smooth operation of a court. Local rules are often less visible and may seem less important, but compliance with them is nonetheless an important dimension of professionalism.

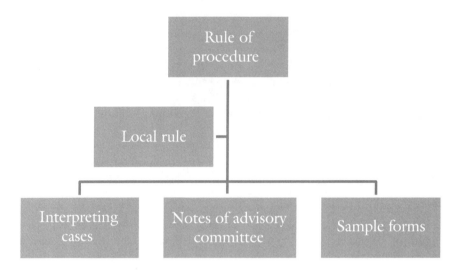

Researching Rules of Procedure

Given the centrality of rules of procedure in the U.S. legal system, resources for researching the rules abound. Most of the time, you will begin your research fairly well informed based on your study of the rules in various courses in law school.

For many lawyers, research in rules of procedure resembles starting in the middle of a target and working outwards. They start with a resource that focuses on the rules themselves, then turn to a source that provides elaboration, then turn to a resource that provides even more information if the situation warrants it. These resources are deskbooks, court websites, treatises, and annotated rules. For a summary of their relative advantages and disadvantages, see Box 6.2.

Deskbooks. Rules of procedure for a jurisdiction are published in their most compact form in deskbooks. A deskbook is an annual publication with the rules currently in force, along with notes of advisory committees and, as applicable, sample forms. Finding a pertinent rule is facilitated by tables of contents and indexes.

As an example, consider the Daniel de la Cruz situation, in which our client was suspended from school in Pennsylvania for shaving a message into his hair that the school considered problematic. Having decided that he has a credible claim grounded in constitutional law, we wanted to use some mechanism of federal procedural law to get him back into school as quickly as possible. We hoped to move the court to order the school to reinstate Daniel while the litigation is pending.

We started with *Federal Civil Judicial Procedure and Rules*, a deskbook, and found Rule 65, regarding preliminary injunctions and temporary restraining orders (TROs). Return to Box 6.1. The rule provides for a preliminary

Box 6.2	APPROACHES TO RULES OF PROCEDURE RESEARCH	
Source	**Information**	**Advantages and Disadvantages**
Deskbook	Rules and notes of advisory committee; sometimes sample forms	Ease of use, but limited information
Court Website	Varies by court: typically includes rules, including local rules, and sample forms; may include notes of advisory committee	Range of rules and authoritative source, but limited information
Treatise	Discussion of rules and leading cases; references to, if not full quotations of, rules and notes of advisory committee	Synthesizes legal framework from various sources, and can be highly authoritative
Annotated Rules	Rules and probably notes of advisory committee; descriptions of and references to cases; references to secondary sources	Extensiveness of references, but less analytical presentation than treatises

injunction with notice to the adverse party; the court may consolidate the trial with the hearing on the motion for the injunction. The TRO is issued without notice to the adverse party when there is a clear showing of immediate and irreparable injury. The rule provides more guidance about procedures than it does about the standard that the court should apply in ruling on these motions. Perhaps the most interesting information in the advisory committee notes concerns the discussion of the 1966 amendment, which explains consolidating the trial with the hearing.

Treatises. Given the richness of texts involved in rules of procedure research (the rules themselves, advisory committee notes, and many cases), secondary sources abound in the area of federal procedure. Two multivolume treatises carry particular weight: *Federal Practice and Procedure*—written by Charles Alan Wright, Arthur R. Miller, and others and often called "Wright and Miller" for short—and *Moore's Federal Practice*.[6] Both cover various types of procedure and are so well regarded that they are cited by courts from time to time for either routine points or points on which there is no case law yet. Westlaw carries Wright and Miller; Lexis carries Moore's.

Consulting a treatise after reading the rule and its supplementing materials is wise for several reasons. First, a highly credible treatise provides an expert's

---

6. Similarly, in some states, a leading treatise plays the same role as to state rules of procedure.

analysis of the text of the rule, along with its relationship to other rules. Second, the treatise also provides a summary of and references to the leading cases interpreting the rule; given the potentially enormous number of cases interpreting the federal rules, this insight can help you focus your case law research and save time. Third, some rules of procedure have changed over time, and case law may have evolved over time as well; a treatise can explain this for you, thereby helping you avoid relying on an out-of-date case.

We turned to Wright and Miller to continue our research into the options of requesting a TRO or preliminary injunction for the de la Cruz situation. We read the discussion of the TRO to determine whether it or the preliminary injunction was more suitable. The treatise explained that a TRO is designed to preserve the status quo until a preliminary injunction hearing can be held and preserves the status quo so that the court can provide effective relief. While the treatise provides the example of keeping property from being destroyed, it also refers to TROs being granted in cases of deprivation of constitutional rights. See Box 6.3.

Annotated Rules. As already noted, authoritative cases interpreting the rule combine with the rule itself to form the entire rule of law. A treatise should flag the leading cases. But you may be interested in finding even more cases (e.g., cases from your circuit, or cases in situations with similar substantive legal issues as your client's situation). Any of the means of finding cases described in Chapter 4 are viable.

Rules of procedure are typically found in a jurisdiction's code. Thus, a strong approach is to think of the rule of procedure as being parallel to a statute and use the jurisdiction's annotated statutes, as described in Chapter 5. At the federal level, this entails researching in the print codes *United States Code Annotated* or *United States Code Service*; their online analogues in Westlaw and Lexis, respectively;[7] or in the *United States Code* on Bloomberg Law.

Researching the de la Cruz situation, we searched for Rule 65 by citation in the USCS Federal Rules Annotated database in Lexis. Lexis provided the rule, notes of the various advisory committees, and an enormous annotation with case descriptions listed under finely framed topics. Focusing this time on the preliminary injunction, we observed that Lexis's topics identified elements of the showing required to obtain a preliminary injunction: *Irreparable Injury, Balance of Hardships,* and *Likelihood of Success on Merits.* One sub-subtopic as to likelihood of success on the merits was *Constitutional cases*; under that sub-subtopic, we found descriptions of cases involving both grants and denials of preliminary injunctions in cases raising constitutional claims. See Box 6.4.

---

7. You may find that you are directed to *Federal Rules Decisions*, the West reporter that specializes in cases that are significant primarily for their procedural points. Cases in *Federal Rules Decisions* are digested in the West's *Federal Practice Digest*.

| Box 6.3 | **TREATISE DISCUSSION (Preliminary Injunction)** |

§ 2951Temporary Restraining Orders—In General, 11A Fed. Prac. & Proc. Civ. §...

11A Fed. Prac. & Proc. Civ. § 2951 (3d ed.)

Federal Practice & Procedure
Federal Rules Of Civil Procedure
Database updated April 2015
The Late Charles Alan Wright[145], Arthur R. Miller[146], Mary Kay Kane[147], Richard L. Marcus[148], Adam N. Steinman[149]
Federal Rules of Civil Procedure
Chapter 9. Provisional and Final Remedies and Special Proceedings
Mary Kay Kane[409]
Rule 65. Injunctions and Restraining Orders
C. Temporary Restraining Orders

Link to Monthly Supplemental Service

§ 2951 Temporary Restraining Orders—In General

Applicants for injunctive relief occasionally are faced with the possibility that irreparable injury will occur before the hearing for a preliminary injunction required by Rule 65(a) can be held.[1] In that event a temporary restraining order may be available under Rule 65(b). The order is designed to preserve the status quo until there is an opportunity to hold a hearing on the application for a preliminary injunction and may be issued with or without notice to the adverse party.[2]

Any temporary restraining order granted without notice must comply with the provisions of Rule 65(b) in order to assure the restrained party some measure of protection in lieu of receiving formal notice and the opportunity to participate in a hearing.[3] Moreover, the restrained party must be informed of the issuance of the order as soon as possible,[4] and it will remain in effect only for 14 days or until an adversary hearing is held to determine the propriety of continuing the injunction pendente lite,[5] whichever period is shorter.[6]

When the opposing party actually receives notice of the application for a restraining order, the procedure that is followed does not differ functionally from that on an application for a preliminary injunction and the proceeding is not subject to any special requirements.[7] Indeed, even if a court denominates an order as a "temporary restraining order" in this situation,[8] Rule 65(b) may not apply and, if there is an adversary hearing or the order is entered for an indeterminate length of time, the "temporary restraining order" may be treated as a preliminary injunction.[9]

By its terms Rule 65(b) only governs restraining orders issued without notice or a hearing. But, as is discussed more fully elsewhere, it has been argued that its provisions, at least with regard to the duration of a restraining order, apply even to an order granted when notice has been given to the adverse party but there has been no hearing.[10] This appears to be a sound exercise of judicial discretion, particularly in those situations in which simply giving notice should not justify treating the order as a preliminary injunction because the time constraints do not allow the parties to prepare adequately for a hearing.[11] The issuance of an ex parte temporary restraining order is an emergency procedure[12] and is appropriate only when the applicant is in need of immediate relief.[13] As described by one commentator:

> The ex parte temporary restraining order is indispensable to the commencement of an action when it is the sole method of preserving a state of affairs in which the court can provide effective final relief. Immediate action is vital when imminent destruction of the disputed property, its removal beyond the confines of the state, or its sale to an innocent third party is threatened. In these situations, giving the defendant notice of the application for an injunction could result in an inability to provide any relief at all.[14]

Thus, Rule 65(b), which continues the pre-federal rule practice of the federal courts,[15] requires that in order to obtain an ex parte restraining order the applicant must show that "immediate and irreparable injury, loss, or damage will result to the

Box 6.3   *(continued)*

§ 2951Temporary Restraining Orders—In General, 11A Fed. Prac. & Proc. Civ. §...

movant before the adverse party can be heard in opposition ....” A demonstration of irreparable injury by the party seeking relief is an essential prerequisite to a temporary restraining order.[16] Some illustrative cases finding irreparable injury in actions challenging threats to plaintiff's constitutional rights,[17] in suits seeking to prevent the disclosure of confidential information,[18] in actions in which there are risks that the assets in dispute will be dissipated,[19] and in a variety of other circumstances[20] are set out in the notes below. Other illustrative cases finding no irreparable injury are set out in the notes below.[21] In some of these cases, for example, plaintiff's delay in seeking a temporary restraining order is held as an indication that there is no immediate threat,[22] and in others courts have found that there is insufficient evidence that defendant intends to engage immediately in the challenged conduct.[23]

An illustration of the type of situation in which a temporary restraining order is especially appropriate is provided by United States v. Little Beaver Theatre, Incorporated,[24] which involved defendant theatre's exhibition of what the government alleged was an obscene motion picture. The United States applied for and received a temporary restraining order that prevented all parties from “disposing of, relinquishing possession of, or in any matter cutting, altering, splicing, destroying, or mutilating” the allegedly obscene film.[25] On a motion for the return of the “seized” film, the court held that “the Temporary Restraining Order ... did not amount to a seizure prior to the adversary hearing, but was properly entered to maintain the status quo.”[26]

Illustrative of cases in which the court has denied a temporary restraining order is Ahmad v. Long Island University.[27] Plaintiff sought a temporary restraining order to prevent his imminent termination as a professor as a result of the university's denial of tenure. The court held that he had failed to establish the requisite level of irreparable harm to justify an order enjoining his termination. It specifically noted that the professor was not precluded from seeking other employment and had not alleged that unemployment would cause a financial strain. Further, the loss of reputation and interruption of his research did not amount to irreparable harm and a monetary award would provide a full remedy if he ultimately prevailed on his underlying discrimination claim.

Another case worth noting is Belknap v. Leary,[28] in which plaintiff requested and received a temporary restraining order from the Southern District of New York that prohibited the New York City police from failing to assure that plaintiffs and other members of their class would be protected while engaged in a forthcoming peaceful assembly and protest. The irreparable injury perceived by the district judge was the physical harm to the demonstrators that was likely to occur if the police were as negligent as they had been earlier in the month when construction workers assaulted anti-war demonstrators in downtown New York. Judge Friendly, in an opinion for the Second Circuit vacating the lower court's order, noted that there was no reason to believe that police measures would be ineffective because corrective procedures had been undertaken since the earlier disturbance. This case is particularly interesting because it illustrates the fact that although they are rare, temporary restraining orders can be framed to require affirmative action on the part of the “restrained” party.[29]

More generally, a court should consider whether damages and other legal remedies are adequate to compensate plaintiff.[30] Only if they are not will the potential injury be considered irreparable for purposes of a restraining order. This point was made clear in Youngstown Sheet & Tube Company v. Sawyer,[31] when the court refused to issue a temporary restraining order against the seizure of the steel mills by the President because plaintiffs had an adequate damage remedy under the Federal Tort Claims Act[32] if the seizure proved to be illegal.

The Supreme Court has rendered a number of decisions, most notably those in Sniadach v. Family Finance Corporation of Bay View,[33] Boddie v. Connecticut,[34] Fuentes v. Shevin,[35] Mitchell v. W.T. Grant Company,[36] and Connecticut v. Doehr,[37] emphasizing the importance of satisfying the procedural due-process requirements of notice and a hearing before a person may be deprived of the use of his property.[38] The philosophy of the first three cases was articulated by Justice Harlan in Boddie as follows:

> That the hearing required by due process is subject to waiver, and is not fixed in form does not affect its root requirement that an individual be given an opportunity for a hearing before he is deprived of any significant property interest, except for extraordinary situations where some valid governmental interest is at stake that justifies postponing the hearing until after the event.[39]

These opinions seem to cast doubt on the validity of the Rule 65(b) procedure because it enables a party to procure an ex parte temporary restraining order that may well inhibit defendant's use of his property on the basis of an affidavit instead of a hearing. However, Justice Stewart's opinion in Fuentes indicates that notice and a hearing may not be required in every case. It suggests the possibility that “there may be cases in which a creditor could make a showing of immediate danger that a debtor will destroy or conceal disputed goods. But the statutes before us are not ‘narrowly drawn to meet any

Box 6.3 *(continued)*

§ 2951Temporary Restraining Orders—In General, 11A Fed. Prac. & Proc. Civ. §...

12

Emergency procedure
Little Tor Auto Center v. Exxon Co., USA, 822 F. Supp. 141 (S.D. N.Y. 1993).

13

Immediate relief required
District court may proceed ex parte on a motion for a temporary restraining order if notice to defendant would render fruitless further prosecution of action. First Technology Safety Systems, Inc. v. Depinet, 11 F.3d 641 (6th Cir. 1993).
Prisoner was not entitled to a temporary restraining order prohibiting prison officials from retaliating against him for having brought a civil-rights action, by threatening to move him to another prison and not allowing him to take materials with him; the threat did not have the degree of immediacy required for granting a temporary restraining order, as it had been made ten months before the petition was filed, there were no particulars as to the threats and no indication that transfer would be undertaken, and the order would not be granted to prevent officials from doing something in the future that was entirely speculative. Bieros v. Nicola, 857 F. Supp. 445 (E.D. Pa. 1994).
Ex parte procedures are permitted in connection with applications for temporary restraining orders when advance contact with the adversary would itself be likely to trigger irreparable injury, such as when appointment of a receiver is needed to preserve property or discovery of contraband which might be destroyed as soon as notice is given. Little Tor Auto Center v. Exxon Co., USA, 822 F. Supp. 141 (S.D. N.Y. 1993).

14

Commentator
Developments in the Law—Injunctions, 78 Harv.L.Rev. 994, 1060 (1965).

15

Pre-rule practice
Houghton v. Cortelyou, 208 U.S. 149, 28 S. Ct. 234, 52 L. Ed. 432 (1908).
United R.Rs. of San Francisco v. City & County of San Francisco, 180 Fed. 948 (C.C.D.Cal. 1910).
Cumberland Tel. & Tel. Co. v. Railroad Comm'n of Louisiana, 156 Fed. 834 (C.C.D.La. 1907).

16

Required showing
Applicant seeking an ex parte order based upon the assertion that defendant would have disregarded a court order and disposed of evidence within the time it would have taken for a hearing, must show that defendant had a history of disposing of evidence or violating court orders or that persons similar to the adverse party had such a history. Showing that the adverse party would have the opportunity to conceal evidence is insufficient to justify proceeding on a motion for a temporary restraining order ex parte. First Technology Safety Systems, Inc. v. Depinet, 11 F.3d 641 (6th Cir. 1993).

But compare
Ordinarily, grant or denial of a temporary restraining order or preliminary injunction in the Eighth Circuit is determined upon consideration of the threat of irreparable harm to the movant, the state of balance between harm and injury that granting an injunction will inflict on the other parties involved in the litigation, the probability that the movant will succeed on the merits, and the public interest; however, when considering the merits of a motion for a TRO or injunction to preclude a party from proceeding with a duplicative, second-filed lawsuit in another forum, the applicable standard is that, in the absence of compelling circumstances, the first court in which jurisdiction attaches has priority to consider the case. Terra Intern., Inc. v. Mississippi Chemical Corp., 896 F. Supp. 1468 (N.D. Iowa 1995).

17

Constitutional rights threatened
Convenience-store owners presented a showing of potential irreparable injury absent a temporary-restraining order preventing the city from enforcing an ordinance requiring them to own and maintain surveillance cameras and allowing for the seizure of surveillance tapes made by the stores on the ground that the ordinance violated the Fourth Amendment. Midwest Retailer Associated, Ltd. v. City of Toledo, 563 F. Supp. 2d 796 (N.D. Ohio 2008).
Residents were entitled to a temporary-restraining order in an action challenging the constitutionality of two city ordinances, one requiring the occupants of all rental units to obtain an occupancy permit by showing proof of legal citizenship or residence, and one preventing businesses from employing illegal aliens; the residents were likely to suffer irreparable harm, through eviction or loss of business, the city failed to demonstrate that it would suffer greater potential harm in the form of higher costs for social services to illegal immigrants or increased crime, as those claims were not

Box 6.3   *(continued)*

§ 2951 Temporary Restraining Orders—In General, 11A Fed. Prac. & Proc. Civ. §...

supported by evidence, the public interest favored protection of the residents' access to homes and jobs and delaying of the enforcement of the ordinances for consideration of constitutional issues, and the residents raised serious claims regarding the constitutionality of the ordinances, under the due-process clause, and the equal-protection clause. Lozano v. City of Hazleton, 459 F. Supp. 2d 332 (M.D. Pa. 2006).

Registrants would suffer irreparable injury in the absence of a temporary-restraining order against hearings regarding pre-election challenges to their voter registrations; the challenged actions threatened or impaired registrants' constitutional rights to due process and to vote. Miller v. Blackwell, 348 F. Supp. 2d 916 (S.D. Ohio 2004).

High-school teacher who was instructed by school district to "cease and desist" from using her video camera to document health and safety problems on school property, and not to release the video to anyone without permission, was entitled to a temporary restraining order enjoining the school district from denying her access to school property for that purpose, and from interfering with or restricting release of the videotapes; the teacher fulfilled the requirement of irreparable injury by demonstrating that her First Amendment rights very likely had been violated. Cirelli v. Town of Johnston School Dist., 888 F. Supp. 13 (D.R.I. 1995).

In an action by an association of prisoners against a state official who had banned meetings of the association in prison, deprivation of the First Amendment rights of the members of the organization and the danger that the organization or its attempts at racial harmony would not survive the ban constituted sufficient irreparable injury to support the issuance of a temporary restraining order. National Prisoners Reform Ass'n v. Sharkey, 347 F. Supp. 1234 (D.R.I. 1972).

18

Confidential information at risk

In view of the affidavits of government officials asserting that the continued publication by the newspaper of articles derived from classified Defense Department documents recounting the history of United States Vietnam policy would result in irreparable harm to the national defense and security, the issuance of a temporary restraining order was warranted to prevent further publication pending the determination of the government's request for a preliminary injunction. U.S. v. Washington Post Co., 446 F.2d 1322 (D.C. Cir. 1971).

Vodka producer was likely to suffer irreparable harm absent a temporary restraining order enjoining its former employee and a competitor from using its trade secret vodka formulation, given that public disclosure of the exclusive formula would deprive the producer of a property interest and allow the competitor to reproduce its work without an equivalent investment of time and money. V'Guara Inc. v. Dec, 925 F. Supp. 2d 1120 (D. Nev. 2013).

National Muslim advocacy organization would likely suffer irreparable injury by further disclosure of its proprietary, confidential, and privileged information by a former intern with the organization and his father, as supported the issuance of a temporary restraining order enjoining the intern and his father from further using, disclosing, or publishing, for a ten-day period, any of the organization's internal documents and any audio and/or video recordings taken of meetings and conversations with organization officials and employees, and requiring the intern and his father to return any materials obtained from the organization that contained attorney-client privileged information, proprietary donor information, and confidential employee personal information. Council on American-Islamic Relations v. Gaubatz, 667 F. Supp. 2d 67 (D.D.C. 2009).

Employer was entitled to a temporary restraining order directing a former employee to return to the employer any and all information pertaining to the employer's customers and to refrain from further using or disclosing that information; continuing use and disclosure of those records by the employee would cause injury to the employer, as well as to the employer's protected clients, for which there was no adequate remedy at law. Merrill Lynch, Pierce, Fenner & Smith v. Bennert, 980 F. Supp. 73 (D. Me. 1997).

For purposes of a temporary restraining order against a former employee's disclosing client records of a brokerage firm in violation of an employment agreement, the firm made a showing of irreparable injury, as it contracted for the performance of a nondisclosure covenant in order to ensure the confidentiality of the clients, and if the information was disclosed, there was no way to recapture and remove it from the knowledge of others. Merrill Lynch, Pierce, Fenner & Smith, Inc. v. Bishop, 839 F. Supp. 68 (D. Me. 1993).

19

Risk of asset dissipation

Produce supplier alleging that the buyer failed to pay for shipped goods would suffer irreparable harm if a temporary restraining order were not issued preventing the buyer from dissipating trust assets created under the Perishable Agricultural Commodities Act; the supplier produced evidence that the trust assets were being dissipated and would continue to be dissipated absent an injunction, and if the trust assets were completely dissipated, the supplier would have virtually no chance for recovery. Sanzone Brokerage, Inc. v. J&M Produce Sales, Inc., 547 F. Supp. 2d 599 (N.D. Tex. 2008).

Box 6.4   **ANNOTATED RULES (Preliminary Injunction)**

USCS Fed Rules Civ Proc R 65

Current through changes received September 28, 2015

United States Code Service - Federal Rules Annotated > *FEDERAL RULES OF CIVIL PROCEDURE* > *TITLE VIII. PROVISIONAL AND FINAL REMEDIES*

Notice

▶ *Part 1 of 2.* You are viewing a very large document that has been divided into parts.

Rule 65. Injunctions and Restraining Orders

(a) Preliminary Injunction.

    (1) *Notice.* The court may issue a preliminary injunction only on notice to the adverse party.

    (2) *Consolidating the Hearing with the Trial on the Merits.* Before or after beginning a hearing on a motion for a preliminary injunction, the court may advance the trial on the merits and consolidate it with the hearing. Even when consolidation is not ordered, evidence that is received on the motion and that would be admissible at trial becomes part of the trial record and need not be repeated at trial. But the court must preserve any party's right to a jury trial.

(b) Temporary Restraining Order.

    (1) *Issuing Without Notice.* The court may issue a temporary restraining order without written or oral notice to the adverse party or its attorney only if:

        (A) specific facts in an affidavit or a verified complaint clearly show that immediate and irreparable injury, loss, or damage will result to the movant before the adverse party can be heard in opposition; and

        (B) the movant's attorney certifies in writing any efforts made to give notice and the reasons why it should not be required.

    (2) *Contents; Expiration.* Every temporary restraining order issued without notice must state the date and hour it was issued; describe the injury and state why it is irreparable; state why the order was issued without notice; and be promptly filed in the clerk's office and entered in the record. The order expires at the time after entry--not to exceed 14 days--that the court sets, unless before that time the court, for good cause, extends it for a like period or the adverse party consents to a longer extension. The reasons for an extension must be entered in the record.

    (3) *Expediting the Preliminary-Injunction Hearing.* If the order is issued without notice, the motion for a preliminary injunction must be set for hearing at the earliest possible time, taking precedence over all other matters except hearings on older matters of the same character. At the hearing, the party who obtained the order must proceed with the motion; if the party does not, the court must dissolve the order.

    (4) *Motion to Dissolve.* On 2 days' notice to the party who obtained the order without notice--or on shorter notice set by the court--the adverse party may appear and move to dissolve or modify the order. The court must then hear and decide the motion as promptly as justice requires.

(c) Security. The court may issue a preliminary injunction or a temporary restraining order only if the movant gives security in an amount that the court considers proper to pay the costs and damages sustained by any party found to have been wrongfully enjoined or restrained. The United States, its officers, and its agencies are not required to give security.

(d) Contents and Scope of Every Injunction and Restraining Order.

Box 6.4 *(continued)*

USCS Fed Rules Civ Proc R 65

(1) ***Contents.*** Every order granting an injunction and every restraining order must:

   (A) state the reasons why it issued;

   (B) state its terms specifically; and

   (C) describe in reasonable detail--and not by referring to the complaint or other document--the act or acts restrained or required.

(2) ***Persons Bound.*** The order binds only the following who receive actual notice of it by personal service or otherwise:

   (A) the parties;

   (B) the parties' officers, agents, servants, employees, and attorneys; and

   (C) other persons who are in active concert or participation with anyone described in Rule 65(d)(2)(A) or (B).

(e) Other Laws Not Modified. These rules do not modify the following:

   (1) any federal statute relating to temporary restraining orders or preliminary injunctions in actions affecting employer and employee;

   (2) *28 U.S.C. § 2361*, which relates to preliminary injunctions in actions of interpleader or in the nature of interpleader; or

   (3) *28 U.S.C. § 2284*, which relates to actions that must be heard and decided by a three-judge district court.

(f) Copyright Impoundment. This rule applies to copyright-impoundment proceedings.

History

(Amended March 19, 1948; Oct. 20, 1949; July 1, 1966; Aug. 1, 1987; Dec. 1, 2001; Dec. 1, 2007.)
(As amended Dec. 1, 2009.)

Annotations

Notes

Other provisions:

Notes of Advisory Committee. *Note to Subdivisions (a) and (b).* These are taken from U.S.C., Title 28, former § 381 (Injunctions; preliminary injunctions and temporary restraining orders).

Note to Subdivision (c). Except for the last sentence, this is substantially U.S.C., Title 28, former § 382 (Injunctions; security on issuance of). The last sentence continues the following and similar statutes which expressly except the United States or an officer or agency thereof from such security requirements: *U.S.C., Title 15, §§ 77t(b)*, *78u(e)*, and *79r(f)* (Securities and Exchange Commission). It also excepts the United States or an officer or agency thereof from such security requirements in any action in which a restraining order or interlocutory judgment of injunction issues in its favor whether there is an express statutory exception from such security requirements or not.

See U.S.C., Title 6 (Official and Penal Bonds) for bonds by surety companies.

Note to Subdivision (d). This is substantially U.S.C., Title 28, former § 383 (Injunctions; requisites of order; binding effect).

Note to Subdivision (e). The words "relating to temporary restraining orders and preliminary injunctions in actions affecting employer and employee" are words of description and not of limitation.

Box 6.4 *(continued)*

USCS Fed Rules Civ Proc R 65

68. Relationship to inadequate legal remedy
69. Impossibility of ascertaining extent of loss
70. Inability to redress injury through monetary award
71. Violation of constitutional right
72. Delay in seeking injunction
73. Physical pain, injury or health risk
74. Retaliation
75. Irreparable injury shown
76. Irreparable injury not shown
(3). Balance of Hardships
77. Generally
78. Preliminary injunction granted
79. Preliminary injunction denied
(4). Likelihood of Success on Merits
80. Generally
81. Degree of certainty required
82. Standard of proof if irreparable injury deficient
(5). Particular Cases of Likelihood of Success on Merits
83. Particular cases
84. Arbitration
85. Civil rights
86. Constitutional cases
87. Environmental cases
88. Intellectual property
89. Labor relations
90. RICO
91. Tax cases
92. Voting rights cases
c. Sufficiency of Evidence
(1). Copyright and Trademark Infringement
93. Generally
94. Preliminary injunction granted
95. Preliminary injunction denied
(2). Employment and Labor Relations
96. Generally
97. Preliminary injunction granted
98. Preliminary injunction denied
(3). Free Speech and Association
99. Generally
100. Preliminary injunction granted
101. Preliminary injunction denied
(4). Other Issues
102. Antitrust
103. Arbitration
104. Campaign financing
105. Constitutional claims
106. Criminal matters; prisons
107. Debtors and creditors
108. --Letter of credit
109. Disability claims
110. Distributorship and franchise agreements
111. Education

Box 6.4   *(continued)*

USCS Fed Rules Civ Proc R 65

company or by treating company as class of one differently than other similarly situated businesses, and even if company had property interest in continuation of conditional zoning permit, which was questionable, city's proposed pre-deprivation hearing procedure coupled with opportunity for post-hearing judicial review provided ample procedural protection to satisfy Due Process Clause; further, other factors also did not favor preliminary injunction. *Systematic Recycling, LLC v City of Detroit (2010, ED Mich) 685 F Supp 2d 663.*

Former state prisoners who claimed that imposition of post-release supervision (PRS) by administrators rather than by judge violated Due Process Clause were not entitled to preliminary injunction because their claims were not cognizable under *42 USCS § 1983*; their challenges to validity and duration of their PRS had to be brought through habeas corpus. *Hardy v Fischer (2010, SD NY) 701 F Supp 2d 614.*

Homeless people living in Skid Row area of Los Angeles were entitled to *Fed. R. Civ. P. 65* preliminary injunction where they established likelihood of success on their claims that city violated *U.S. Const. amends. IV*, *XIV* and Cal. Const. art. I, §§ 7, 13 by seizing and destroying property that city knew was not abandoned with no pre- or post-deprivation opportunities to be heard. *Lavan v City of L.A. (2011, CD Cal) 797 F Supp 2d 1005.*

In suit regarding management of certain church, injunction was not warranted because plaintiff church members failed to show that they were likely to succeed on merits of their First Amendment free exercise of religion claim. *Ram v Lal (2012, ED NY) 906 F Supp 2d 59, 84 FR Serv 3d 187.*

86. Constitutional cases

In action in which student appealed from order denying his motion for preliminary injunction seeking to enjoin enforcement of portion of middle school's 2002-2003 dress code, court found that district court abused its discretion when it concluded that student had not satisfied test governing preliminary injunctions with regard to his claim that challenged portion of school dress code was unconstitutionally overbroad; student had demonstrated strong likelihood of success on merits on his overbreadth claim where dress code excluded broad range and scope of symbols, images, and political messages that were entirely legitimate and even laudatory. *Newsom v Albemarle County Sch. Bd. (2003, CA4 Va) 354 F3d 249* (criticized in *Griggs v Fort Wayne Sch. Bd. (2005, ND Ind) 359 F Supp 2d 731).*

Preliminary injunction on basis of plaintiffs' First Amendment claims was affirmed; there was no abuse of discretion in ruling that plaintiffs were likely to prevail on their First Amendment claims because, given New York City, N.Y., Admin. Code § 10-117(c)'s hindering of young adults' access to materials they needed for their lawful artistic expression and § 10-117(c-1)'s blanket prohibition against young adults' public possession of graffiti implements, encompassing possession for purely lawful purposes, challenged subsections appeared to burden substantially more speech than was necessary to achieve city's legitimate interest in preventing illegal graffiti. *Vincenty v Bloomberg (2007, CA2 NY) 476 F3d 74.*

Where former employee of city department of education asserted First Amendment retaliation claim arising out of statements employee made to reporter, employee was not entitled to preliminary injunction because city department of education's press officer instructed employee to participate in interview and statements that employee made during interview were made in employee's official capacity and therefore were not constitutionally protected. *Almontaser v N.Y. City Dep't of Educ. (2008, CA2 NY) 519 F3d 505, 27 BNA IER Cas 639.*

Students' failed to show fair chance of prevailing on their facial challenge to defendant college's drug testing policy; need to prevent and deter substantial harm that could arise from student under influence of drugs while engaging in safety-sensitive program provided necessary immediacy for college's testing policy. *Barrett v Claycomb (2013, CA8 Mo) 705 F3d 315.*

District court granted preliminary injunction to stay enforcement of city ordinance that required contractors to employ 50 percent of city residents on public projects, finding that contractors would prevail on their claim that

Court Websites. In recent years, litigation in the United States has become increasingly electronic. Much of litigation today operates through electronic filing. From a research standpoint, this has meant that many courts now have websites at which you may find not only the main rules of procedure but also the local rules that the courts employ to make courts run more smoothly.

To continue with our example of the de la Cruz situation, assume that we were to proceed with a lawsuit in federal court and to move for a preliminary injunction. We would need to determine how to begin the lawsuit. If we were in the U.S. District Court for the Middle District of Pennsylvania, we would find on that court's website its Electronic Case Filing Policies and Procedures document, which generally calls for electronic filing of documents with the court. This policy raised the question of whether we could serve the summons and complaint on the school district electronically. The answer appears in clause 12.1; service may not be accomplished electronically. See Box 6.5.

While on the court's website, we also checked for sample forms that would be helpful as we began to draft the documents. There, we found the sample summons for a civil action, which is the one provided by the Administrative Office of the United States Courts. See Box 6.6.

Box 6.5   LOCAL RULES (Electronic Filing)

endorsement by the other parties no later than three business days after filing; or (4) in any other manner approved by the court.

12.   Service of Documents by Electronic Means.

12.1   Service of Process

Fed.R.Civ.P. 5(b) and Fed.R.Crim.P. 49(b) do **not** permit electronic service of process for purposes of obtaining personal jurisdiction, i.e., Rule 4 service. Therefore, service of process must be effected in the traditional manner.

12.2   Other Types of Service:

12.2.1 Filing User

Upon the electronic filing of a pleading or other document, the court's ECF System will automatically generate and send a Notice of Electronic Filing to all Filing Users associated with that case. Transmission of the Notice of Electronic Filing constitutes service of the filed document.

The Notice of Electronic Filing must include the time of filing, the name of the party and attorney filing the document, the type of document, the text of the docket entry, and an electronic link (hyperlink) to the filed document, allowing anyone receiving the notice by e-mail to retrieve the document automatically. If the Filing User becomes aware that the Notice of Electronic Filing was not transmitted successfully to a party, or that the notice is deficient, i.e. the electronic link to the document is defective, the filer shall serve the electronically filed document by e-mail, hand, facsimile, or by first-class mail postage prepaid immediately upon notification of the deficiency of the Notice of Electronic Filing.

12.2.2 Individual who is not a Filing User

A Non-Filing User is entitled to receive a paper copy of any electronically filed document from the party making such filing. Service of such paper copy must be made according to the Federal Rules of Civil Procedure, the Federal Rules of Criminal Procedure and the Local Rules.

12.3   Time to Respond Under Electronic Service

In accordance with Rule 6(e) of the Federal Rules of Civil Procedure and Rule 45(c) of the Federal Rules of Criminal Procedure, service by electronic means is treated the same as service by mail for the purposes of adding three (3) days to the prescribed period to respond.

| Box 6.6 | SAMPLE FORM (Preliminary Injunction) |

AO 440 (Rev. 06/12) Summons in a Civil Action

UNITED STATES DISTRICT COURT
for the

	)	
	)	
	)	
	)	
_____	)	
Plaintiff(s)	)	
v.	)	Civil Action No.
	)	
	)	
	)	
_____	)	
Defendant(s)	)	

SUMMONS IN A CIVIL ACTION

To: *(Defendant's name and address)*

A lawsuit has been filed against you.

Within 21 days after service of this summons on you (not counting the day you received it) — or 60 days if you are the United States or a United States agency, or an officer or employee of the United States described in Fed. R. Civ. P. 12 (a)(2) or (3) — you must serve on the plaintiff an answer to the attached complaint or a motion under Rule 12 of the Federal Rules of Civil Procedure. The answer or motion must be served on the plaintiff or plaintiff's attorney, whose name and address are:

If you fail to respond, judgment by default will be entered against you for the relief demanded in the complaint. You also must file your answer or motion with the court.

CLERK OF COURT

Date: _____

_____
Signature of Clerk or Deputy Clerk

Rules of Professional Responsibility

Understanding the Rules and Related Sources

The effective and just functioning of our legal system depends on the ethical conduct of lawyers, who not only represent clients but also serve as "officer[s] of the legal system and . . . [as] public citizen[s] having special responsibility for the quality of justice." These words come from the preamble to the American Bar Association (ABA) Model Rules of Professional Conduct.

The ABA is the major national professional association of lawyers. Its Model Rules, which date to 1983 and have been revised periodically (including the last major revision in 2002), is the most significant professional responsibility code for lawyers.[8] The codes that actually control lawyers' conduct are adopted on a state-by-state level, typically by a state supreme court or bar association. Most are based on the ABA Model Rules.

These codes focus on the various relationships that lawyers have, as shown in the titles of the main parts of the ABA Model Rules: client-lawyer relationship, counselor, advocate, transactions with persons other than clients, law firms and associations, public service, information about legal services, and maintaining the integrity of the profession. The typical rule states what a lawyer may or must do and is followed by commentary, whether from the ABA or the state drafting committee or both. The rule is primary authority, whereas the commentary operates as quasi-authority. See Box 6.7.

Professional responsibility rules differ from rules of procedure in their mode of operation. In a typical model, a disciplinary committee or board investigates a complaint of unprofessional conduct, holds a hearing, and issues a recommendation as to whether the lawyer should be found to have engaged in misconduct and if so, what the sanction should be. The state supreme court reviews the case and imposes the discipline (which can range from private censure to disbarment). In some places, local bar associations serve some of these functions. It is important to note that other legal proceedings can also involve lawyer misconduct, such as a civil suit for legal malpractice and (in the most serious cases) criminal prosecution for an offense such as fraud. Thus, in addition to the rules and their commentary, professional responsibility law consists of case law.

Professional responsibility law also includes a distinctive source: ethics opinions. The application of professional responsibility rules to the myriad situations that arise in the practice of law often is murky, so various ABA, state, and local bar associations, as well as disciplinary committees, issue ethics opinions. These opinions are not full-fledged adjudications, so they fall into the category of quasi-authority. See Box 6.8.

As with rules of procedure, secondary sources abound in the area of professional responsibility. Of particular note is the Restatement (Third) of

---

8. Its predecessors are the 1908 Canons of Professional Ethics and the 1969 Model Code of Professional Responsibility.

Box 6.7   **RULE OF PROFESSIONAL RESPONSIBILITY (Client Confidentiality)**

[5] An agreement may not be made whose terms might induce the lawyer improperly to curtail services for the client or perform them in a way contrary to the client's interest. For example, a lawyer should not enter into an agreement whereby services are to be provided only up to a stated amount when it is foreseeable that more extensive services probably will be required, unless the situation is adequately explained to the client. Otherwise, the client might have to bargain for further assistance in the midst of a proceeding or transaction. However, it is proper to define the extent of services in light of the client's ability to pay. A lawyer should not exploit a fee arrangement based primarily on hourly charges by using wasteful procedures.

Prohibited Contingent Fees

[6] Paragraph (d) prohibits a lawyer from charging a contingent fee in a domestic relations matter when payment is contingent upon the securing of a divorce or upon the amount of alimony or support or property settlement to be obtained. This provision does not preclude a contract for a contingent fee for legal representation in connection with the recovery of post-judgment balances due under support, alimony, or other financial orders because such contracts do not implicate the same policy concerns.

Division of Fee

[7] A division of fee is a single billing to a client covering the fee of two or more lawyers who are not in the same firm. A division of fee facilitates association of more than one lawyer in a matter in which neither alone could serve the client as well, and most often is used when the fee is contingent and the division is between a referring lawyer and a trial specialist. Paragraph (e) permits the lawyers to divide a fee either on the basis of the proportion of services they render or if each lawyer assumes responsibility for the representation as a whole. In addition, the client must agree to the arrangement, including the share that each lawyer is to receive, and the agreement must be confirmed in writing. Contingent fee agreements must be in a writing signed by the client and must otherwise comply with paragraph (c) of this rule. Joint responsibility for the representation entails financial and ethical responsibility for the representation as if the lawyers were associated in a partnership. A lawyer should only refer a matter to a lawyer whom the referring lawyer reasonably believes is competent to handle the matter. See Rule 1.1.

[8] Paragraph (e) does not prohibit or regulate division of fees to be received in the future for work done when lawyers were previously associated in a law firm.

Disputes over Fees

[9] If a procedure has been established for resolution of fee disputes, such as an arbitration or mediation procedure established by the bar, the lawyer must comply with the procedure when it is mandatory, and, even when it is voluntary, the lawyer should conscientiously consider submitting to it. Law may prescribe a procedure for determining a lawyer's fee, for example, in representation of an executor or administrator, a class or a person entitled to a reasonable fee as part of the measure of damages. The lawyer entitled to such a fee and a lawyer representing another party concerned with the fee should comply with the prescribed procedure.

RULE 1.6: CONFIDENTIALITY OF INFORMATION

(a) Except when permitted under paragraph (b), a lawyer shall not knowingly reveal information relating to the representation of a client.

(b) A lawyer may reveal information relating to the representation of a client if:

Box 6.7   *(continued)*

(11) the lawyer reasonably believes the disclosure is necessary to detect and resolve conflicts of interest arising from the lawyer's change of employment or from changes in the composition or ownership of a firm, but only if the revealed information would not compromise the attorney-client privilege or otherwise prejudice the client.

(c) A lawyer shall make reasonable efforts to prevent the inadvertent or unauthorized disclosure of, or unauthorized access to, information relating to the representation of a client.

Comment

[1] This rule governs the disclosure by a lawyer of information relating to the representation of a client during the lawyer's representation of the client. See Rule 1.18 for the lawyer's duties with respect to information provided to the lawyer by a prospective client, Rule 1.9(c)(2) for the lawyer's duty not to reveal information relating to the lawyer's prior representation of a former client and Rules 1.8(b) and 1.9(c)(1) for the lawyer's duties with respect to the use of such information to the disadvantage of clients and former clients.

[2] A fundamental principle in the client-lawyer relationship is that, in the absence of the client's informed consent, the lawyer must not reveal information relating to the representation. See Rule 1.0(f) for the definition of informed consent. This contributes to the trust that is the hallmark of the client-lawyer relationship. The client is thereby encouraged to seek legal assistance and to communicate fully and frankly with the lawyer even as to embarrassing or legally damaging subject matter. The lawyer needs this information to represent the client effectively and, if necessary, to advise the client to refrain from wrongful conduct. Almost without exception, clients come to lawyers in order to determine their rights and what is, in the complex of laws and regulations, deemed to be legal and correct. Based upon experience, lawyers know that almost all clients follow the advice given, and the law is upheld.

[3] The principle of client-lawyer confidentiality is given effect by related bodies of law: the attorney-client privilege, the work-product doctrine and the rule of confidentiality established in professional ethics. The attorney-client privilege and work-product doctrine apply in judicial and other proceedings in which a lawyer may be called as a witness or otherwise required to produce evidence concerning a client. The rule of client-lawyer confidentiality applies in situations other than those where evidence is sought from the lawyer through compulsion of law. The confidentiality rule, for example, applies not only to matters communicated in confidence by the client but also to all information relating to the representation, whatever its source. A lawyer may not disclose such information except as authorized or required by the Rules of Professional Conduct or other law. See also Scope.

[4] Paragraph (a) prohibits a lawyer from revealing information relating to the representation of a client. This prohibition also applies to disclosures by a lawyer that do not in themselves reveal protected information but could reasonably lead to the discovery of such information by a third person. A lawyer's use of a hypothetical to discuss issues relating to the representation is permissible so long as there is no reasonable likelihood that the listener will be able to ascertain the identity of the client or the situation involved.

Box 6.7   *(continued)*

[15] Paragraph (b) permits but does not require the disclosure of information relating to a client's representation to accomplish the purposes specified in paragraphs (b)(1) through (b)(11). In exercising the discretion conferred by this rule, the lawyer may consider such factors as the nature of the lawyer's relationship with the client and with those who might be injured by the client, the lawyer's own involvement in the transaction and factors that may extenuate the conduct in question. A lawyer's decision not to disclose as permitted by paragraph (b) does not violate this rule. Disclosure may be required, however, by other rules. Some rules require disclosure only if such disclosure would be permitted by paragraph (b). See Rules 8.1 and 8.3. Rule 3.3, on the other hand, requires disclosure in some circumstances regardless of whether such disclosure is permitted by this rule. See Rule 3.3(c).

Withdrawal

[16] If the lawyer's services will be used by the client in materially furthering a course of criminal or fraudulent conduct, the lawyer must withdraw, as stated in Rule 1.16(a)(1). After withdrawal the lawyer is required to refrain from making disclosure of the client's confidences, except as otherwise permitted in Rule 1.6. Neither this rule nor Rule 1.8(b) nor Rule 1.16(d) prevents the lawyer from giving notice of the fact of withdrawal, and the lawyer may also withdraw or disaffirm any opinion, document, affirmation, or the like. Where the client is an organization, the lawyer may be in doubt whether contemplated conduct will actually be carried out by the organization. Where necessary to guide conduct in connection with this rule, the lawyer may make inquiry within the organization as indicated in Rule 1.13(b).

Acting Competently to Preserve Confidentiality

[17] Paragraph (c) requires a lawyer to act competently to safeguard information relating to the representation of a client against unauthorized access by third parties and against inadvertent or unauthorized disclosure by the lawyer or other persons who are participating in the representation of the client or who are subject to the lawyer's supervision. See Rules 1.1, 5.1 and 5.3. The unauthorized access to, or the inadvertent or unauthorized disclosure of, information relating to the representation of a client does not constitute a violation of paragraph (c) if the lawyer has made reasonable efforts to prevent the access or disclosure. Factors to be considered in determining the reasonableness of the lawyer's efforts include, but are not limited to, the sensitivity of the information, the likelihood of disclosure if additional safeguards are not employed, the cost of employing additional safeguards, the difficulty of implementing the safeguards, and the extent to which the safeguards adversely affect the lawyer's ability to represent clients (e.g., by making a device or important piece of software excessively difficult to use). A client may require the lawyer to implement special security measures not required by this Rule or may give informed consent to forgo security measures that would otherwise be required by this Rule. Whether a lawyer may be required to take additional steps to safeguard a client's information in order to comply with other law, such as state and federal laws that govern data privacy or that impose notification requirements upon the loss of, or unauthorized access to, electronic information, is beyond the scope of these Rules. For a lawyer's duties when sharing information with nonlawyers outside the lawyer's own firm, see Rule 5.3, Comments [3]-[4].

[18] When transmitting a communication that includes information relating to the representation of a client, the lawyer must take reasonable precautions to prevent the information from coming into the hands of unintended recipients. This duty, however, does not require that the lawyer use special security measures if the method of communication affords a reasonable expectation of privacy. Special circumstances, however, may warrant special precautions. Factors to be considered in determining the reasonableness of the lawyer's expectation of confidentiality include the sensitivity of the information and the extent to which the privacy of the communication is protected by law or by a confidentiality

Box 6.7   *(continued)*

agreement. A client may require the lawyer to implement special security measures not required by this rule or may give informed consent to the use of a means of communication that would otherwise be prohibited by this rule. Whether a lawyer may be required to take additional steps in order to comply with other law, such as state and federal laws that govern data privacy, is beyond the scope of these Rules.

Former Client

[19] The duty of confidentiality continues after the client-lawyer relationship has terminated. See Rule 1.9(c)(2). See Rule 1.9(c)(1) for the prohibition against using such information to the disadvantage of the former client.

RULE 1.7: CONFLICT OF INTEREST: CURRENT CLIENTS

(a) Except as provided in paragraph (b), a lawyer shall not represent a client if the representation involves a concurrent conflict of interest. A concurrent conflict of interest exists if:

(1) the representation of one client will be directly adverse to another client; or

(2) there is a significant risk that the representation of one or more clients will be materially limited by the lawyer's responsibilities to another client, a former client, or a third person or by a personal interest of the lawyer.

(b) Notwithstanding the existence of a concurrent conflict of interest under paragraph (a), a lawyer may represent a client if:

(1) the lawyer reasonably believes that the lawyer will be able to provide competent and diligent representation to each affected client;

(2) the representation is not prohibited by law;

(3) the representation does not involve the assertion of a claim by one client against another client represented by the lawyer in the same litigation or other proceeding before a tribunal; and

(4) each affected client gives informed consent, confirmed in writing.

Comment

General Principles

[1] Loyalty and independent judgment are essential elements in the lawyer's relationship to a client. Concurrent conflicts of interest can arise from the lawyer's responsibilities to another client, a former client or a third person or from the lawyer's own interests. For specific rules regarding certain concurrent conflicts of interest, see Rule 1.8. For former client conflicts of interest, see Rule 1.9. For

| Box 6.8 | **ETHICS OPINION (Client Confidentiality)** |

OPINION NO. 19

USING TECHNOLOGY TO COMMUNICATE
CONFIDENTIAL INFORMATION TO CLIENTS

A lawyer may use technological means such as electronic mail (e-mail) and cordless and cellular telephones to communicate confidential client information without violating Rule 1.6, Minnesota Rules of Professional Conduct (MRPC). Such use is subject to the following conditions:

1.   E-mail without encryption may be used to transmit and receive confidential client information;

2.   Digital cordless and cellular telephones may be used by a lawyer to transmit and receive confidential client information when used within a digital service area;

3.   When the lawyer knows, or reasonably should know, that a client or other person is using an insecure means to communicate with the lawyer about confidential client information, the lawyer shall consult with the client about the confidentiality risks associated with inadvertent interception and obtain the client's consent.

Adopted: January 22, 1999.
Amended: January 22, 2010.

the Law Governing Lawyers, promulgated in 1998, based not only on the ABA Model Rules, but also on case law, including legal malpractice cases. The Restatement diverges from the current Model Rules on some topics.

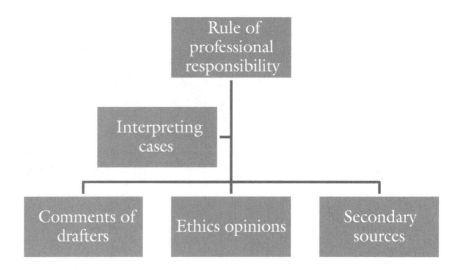

Researching Rules of Professional Responsibility

To a great extent, researching professional responsibility rules parallels researching rules of procedure. For example, state rules deskbooks contain rules of professional responsibility, and state annotated codes are a good resource for finding interpreting cases.

In addition, a leading resource is the website of the ABA Center for Professional Responsibility (CPR).[9] There, the CPR has posted its Model Rules, links to state ethics rules, and a list of states adopting the Model Rules. The most recent opinions of the ABA Standing Committee on Ethics and Professional Responsibility appear in full text. Older opinions, which are indexed by subject and listed by date of issuance, may be ordered.[10]

Resources for state and local ethics opinions include the website of the appropriate organization, *ABA/BNA Lawyers' Manual on Professional Conduct*, and the Lexis and Westlaw legal ethics databases. The *Current Reports* section of the *ABA/BNA Lawyers' Manual on Professional Conduct* is available on Bloomberg Law.

As an example, recall that All-Day Wellness, a Minnesota company, has sought advice on implementing a covenant not-to-compete in its contracts with its employees. The president of All-Day Wellness, who has been our contact throughout our work on this matter, has asked that we send our opinion letter to her family's e-mail address rather than her work e-mail. She thinks that she would rather keep the idea secret from anyone at work for now, because she is not yet sure she will go through with it. It appears that the

---

9. The site is at www.americanbar.org/groups/professional_responsibility.html.

10. The cost depends on the recency of the opinion and your membership in the ABA and the CPR.

family's e-mail address may be a shared one, so there is a risk someone other than the client may read the e-mail.

Our concern arises under the requirement that a lawyer keep information relating to the representation of a client confidential. We began by searching on the Minnesota Supreme Court website, where we found Minnesota Rule of Professional Conduct 1.6. The opening provision (a) states that a lawyer shall not "knowingly" reveal such information.[11] The final provision (c) states that a lawyer shall make "reasonable efforts" to prevent the "inadvertent or unauthorized disclosure of, or unauthorized access to, information relating to the representation." There, we also found comments (particularly comment 18) addressing the situation, albeit in general terminology. These comments are from the ABA Model Rules. Return to Box 6.7.

Our research in Minnesota cases in the annotated code revealed about a dozen cases interpreting other provisions of Rule 1.6, but none addressing the issue of lawyer use of e-mail to communicate with clients. On the other hand, on the website of the Minnesota Lawyers Professional Responsibility Board, we did find a pertinent opinion. This was not surprising, given the widespread debate that arose within the profession in the 1990s when e-mail became a prevalent mode of business communication. This opinion provided much more specific guidance: first, that unencrypted e-mail is permissible as a general matter; second, that insecure e-mail communication raises an obligation to consult with the client about confidentiality risks and to obtain consent before transmitting information about the client in an e-mail.[12] Return to Box 6.8.

---

11. The opening language does not quite track the ABA Model Rules, which specifically exclude situations where a client has given consent and where disclosure is impliedly authorized to carry out the representation. The latter provision does track the Model Rule.

12. The ABA has also addressed this topic in Formal Opinion 11-459 (requiring a warning to a client when there is a significant risk of third-party access).

BUILD YOUR UNDERSTANDING

Test Your Knowledge

1. How do substantive law and procedural law differ? If you were going to bring a lawsuit alleging breach of contract and the tort of fraud, would you need to know substantive law, procedural law, or both? Explain.

2. Define each of the following sources that you may read in the course of rules of procedure research, and indicate in which category — primary authority, quasi-authority, secondary source, or resource — each belongs:
   - Annotated rules
   - Deskbook
   - Local rule
   - Notes of advisory committee
   - Rule of procedure
   - Sample form
   - Treatise

3. Identify several factors that you would consider as you select cases to read from among the many cases interpreting the rule controlling your client's situation.

4. Define each of the following sources that you may read in the course of professional responsibility research, and indicate which category — primary authority, quasi-authority, or secondary source — each belongs in:
   - ABA Model Rules of Professional Responsibility
   - Comments of drafters
   - Ethics opinions
   - Restatement (Third) of the Law Governing Lawyers
   - State rules of professional responsibility

Put It into Practice

Recall your client's situation (detailed in Chapter 1 at pages 20-21): Your client, Emmet Wilson, is a veteran who has developed post-traumatic stress disorder (PTSD). Among other treatments, he has been assigned a therapy dog. Mr. Wilson's landlord has raised concerns because the building is a no-pets building. Indeed, the lease (which is for a year) so specifies, and the landlord says that other tenants have raised the issue. So she has given Mr. Wilson notice that if he does not give up the dog, he will be evicted in a month.

Some time has now passed. Despite your best efforts, the landlord did evict Mr. Wilson, and you have decided to sue on his behalf under the federal Fair Housing Act in the U.S. District Court for the Southern District of West Virginia.

Part 1. Local Rules

1. Locate the local rules for the U.S. District Court for the Southern District of West Virginia on its website. The local rule requires, on the cover sheet filed with the complaint, a citation to a source; what is that source?

Part 2. Rules of Civil Procedure You have received the answer from the lawyer for the landlord and immediately noticed that it does not bear the signature of either the client or the lawyer. Research the legal significance of this omission.

2. In a deskbook or on a website, find the Federal Rule of Civil Procedure, along with the notes of the advisory committee, covering the requirement that pleadings be signed.
    a. Identify the resource you used, and explain how you found the rule.
    b. State what the rule requires, and describe the consequence(s) of failing to follow the rule.
    c. Read the notes to that rule. If you find anything in the notes that pertains to this issue, provide that information and the year of the useful notes.

3. Read a treatise discussion on this topic.
    a. Provide the name of the treatise that you read and the specific section covering this issue.
    b. State the insight that it provided on this issue.
    c. State the name of at least one pertinent case to which it referred.

4. Turn to an annotated rules resource to look for additional pertinent cases. (The case need not be from your jurisdiction.)
    a. Indicate which annotated rules resource you used.
    b. Explain how you researched for pertinent cases.
    c. Identify two more cases that appear to be pertinent; for each case, list its name, court, and date.

5. In light of what you have read, what appears to be the action that you should take at this point to address your opponent's failure to sign the answer?

Part 3. Rules of Professional Responsibility

6. At either the ABA Center for Professional Responsibility's website or the website containing your own state's professional responsibility rules, locate the rules addressing the role of the lawyer as advocate. Identify the rule(s) addressing question 5.
    a. Provide the number(s) of the pertinent rule(s).
    b. State the guidance provided by the rule(s).
    c. State any pertinent elaboration provided by the commentary to the rule(s), along with citations to that commentary.

Make Connections

Rule 3.2 of the ABA Model Rules speaks broadly of making reasonable efforts to expedite litigation. The comment explains that delay "bring[s] the administration of justice into disrepute." The standard is that of a "competent lawyer acting in good faith." The comment lists reasons that generally do not justify delay, including the convenience of the lawyers, frustration of the opposing party, and financial gain. In your view, what reasons would justify extending litigation?

Answers to Test Your Knowledge Questions

1. Substantive law provides standards for the conduct of people and organizations, whereas procedural law controls the conduct of legal proceedings. Bringing the lawsuit would require knowledge of the substantive law of contract and fraud as well as the procedural law stated in the rules of civil procedure.

2. The sources are defined and categorized as follows:
   - Annotated rules—a source containing the rules (primary authority) and descriptions and references to cases (finding tools)
   - Deskbook—a compact volume containing the rules (primary authority) along with notes of the advisory committee and possibly sample forms (quasi-authorities)
   - Local rule—a second-level rule that addresses less significant matters of detail for one court (primary authority)
   - Notes of advisory committee—explanation of the rule by experts who drafted it (quasi-authority)
   - Rule of procedure—a law, typically created by a court, that governs how some type of court proceeding is to occur by setting out what the litigants may and must do (primary authority)
   - Sample form—a model that lawyers may use as they create their litigation documents (quasi-authority if created by lawmaking body, otherwise secondary source)
   - Treatise—a source that is highly authoritative in rules of procedure research and that contains discussion (along with citations to) the rules, comments, and leading cases (secondary source)

3. Factors to consider in selecting cases are the jurisdiction, the level of court, and the similarity of the substantive law issue (in addition to the same procedural law issue).

4. The sources are defined and categorized as follows:
   - ABA Model Rules of Professional Responsibility—a set of model rules created by the major professional organization of lawyers (secondary source)
   - Comments of drafters—views of those who created either the model rules or the state rules (quasi-authority, to the extent that they support state rules)
   - Ethics opinions—opinions issued by disciplinary committees or bar associations not based on full adjudications (quasi-authority)
   - Restatement (Third) of the Law Governing Lawyers—discussion of cases and professional responsibility rules (secondary source)
   - State rules of professional responsibility—rules adopted to control lawyers' conduct (primary authority)

ADMINISTRATIVE AGENCY MATERIALS

The conventional understanding of the U.S. government is that the U.S. Congress (the legislative branch) makes the laws (that is, statutes), the executive branch enforces them, and the judicial branch interprets them. But there is more to the story when it comes to many diverse areas of law, including environmental protection, consumer safety, and employment conditions. In these and other extensively regulated areas, legislatures often adopt broad statutes and then create administrative agencies in the executive branch to fill in the details using their scientific and policy expertise. In so acting, an agency may create law that is every bit as binding as statutes and cases. Furthermore, the courts are involved in reviewing the work of administrative agencies. Thus, practitioners in these areas must be adept at researching the interplay of statutes, case law, and administrative law.

This chapter examines the three most important kinds of administrative materials that lawyers should consult to get a complete picture of the law:

- Legislative regulations, the legally binding regulatory codes adopted and enforced by agencies;
- Decisions and orders, the legally binding conclusions of agencies acting in a quasi-judicial capacity; and
- Interpretive and guidance materials, which are not law but provide insight into how the agency interprets and applies the law.

Although this chapter focuses on federal law, states and many counties and cities have their own administrative agencies that produce their own regulations, decisions and orders, and interpretive and guidance materials. State and local administrative laws are often variations on the federal theme, and courts confronting state and local administrative law issues often look to federal law as persuasive authority.

Recall the question posed by our client Exact Electronics, which wants to establish a policy to govern employee use of social media. Crafting a lawful policy involves employees' legal rights under the law administered by the National Labor Relations Board (NLRB), a major federal agency implementing labor law. The first part of our discussion in this chapter uses the NLRB's regulations on how unions are chosen to represent an employer's workers to illustrate how to research federal regulations. The following parts address issues that a social media policy might raise first under decisions and orders and then under interpretive and guidance documents published by the NLRB.

REGULATIONS

Understanding Regulations

In practice, the terms *rule* and *regulation* are used interchangeably to refer to the codified law promulgated by administrative agencies. Regulations are often referred to as *quasi-legislative* because of their similarities to statutes. Like statutes, regulations usually consist of statements spelling out legal requirements or prohibitions that apply generally and prospectively. Some are long, complex, and very technical. A set of regulations is typically organized into titles, chapters, subchapters, parts, subparts, and sections. Like statutes, regulations emerge from fairly well defined procedures that generate paper trails that can be useful in understanding the law. Regulations are law: they are as binding on a client's situation as a statute.[1]

Regulations are different from statutes in one key respect: Congress makes laws under the authority of the U.S. Constitution, whereas an agency's authority to make law depends on Congress. Generally, administrative agencies are created by Congress to regulate within particular fields; by statute, Congress creates the agency, defines its subject matter, and may authorize it to adopt regulations that carry the force of law. This statute is the agency's *organic statute*.

Supplementing the organic statute is the Administrative Procedures Act (APA), which is regarded as the constitution for federal agencies because it governs so much of what agencies are allowed to do. The APA defines a rule as "the whole or a part of an agency statement of general or particular applicability and future effect designed to implement, interpret, or prescribe law or policy or describing the organization, procedure, or practice requirements of an agency."[2]

Box 7.1 shows a regulation of the NLRB that relates to employee electronic data. It requires employers to provide the Board with contact information, including available personal e-mail addresses and cell-phone numbers, for employees eligible to vote on union representation questions.[3]

---

1. This discussion refers to regulations that an agency creates in its lawmaking capacity, which are thus considered legislative regulations. Other regulations, labeled *interpretive regulations,* have less legal force. Interpretive regulations do not make new law but rather clarify the law and advise the public of the agency's construction of the statute it interprets.

2. 5 U.S.C. § 551(4) (2012).

3. Interestingly, the rule does not explicitly address whether an employer must disclose other online-based contact information for its employees, such as user names in social media.

Box 7.1   REGULATION (Employee Data)

§ 102.62   29 CFR Ch. I (7-1-15 Edition)

(f) *Provision of original signatures.* Evidence filed pursuant to paragraphs (a)(7), (b)(8), or (c)(8) of this section together with a petition that is filed by facsimile or electronically, which includes original signatures that cannot be transmitted in their original form by the method of filing of the petition, may be filed by facsimile or in electronic form provided that the original documents are received by the regional director no later than 2 days after the facsimile or electronic filing.

[79 FR 74478, Dec. 15, 2014]

§ 102.62   Election agreements; voter list; Notice of Election.

(a) *Consent election agreements with final regional director determinations of post-election disputes.* Where a petition has been duly filed, the employer and any individual or labor organizations representing a substantial number of employees involved may, with the approval of the regional director, enter into an agreement providing for the waiver of a hearing and for an election and further providing that post-election disputes will be resolved by the regional director. Such agreement, referred to as a consent election agreement, shall include a description of the appropriate unit, the time and place of holding the election, and the payroll period to be used in determining what employees within the appropriate unit shall be eligible to vote. Such election shall be conducted under the direction and supervision of the regional director. The method of conducting such election shall be consistent with the method followed by the regional director in conducting elections pursuant to §§ 102.69 and 102.70 except that the rulings and determinations by the regional director of the results thereof shall be final, and the regional director shall issue to the parties a certification of the results of the election, including certifications of representative where appropriate, with the same force and effect, in that case, as if issued by the Board, and except that rulings or determinations by the regional director in respect to any amendment of such certification shall also be final.

(b) *Stipulated election agreements with discretionary Board review.* Where a petition has been duly filed, the employer and any individuals or labor organizations representing a substantial number of the employees involved may, with the approval of the regional director, enter into an agreement providing for the waiver of a hearing and for an election as described in paragraph (a) of this section and further providing that the parties may request Board review of the regional director's resolution of post-election disputes. Such agreement, referred to as a stipulated election agreement, shall also include a description of the appropriate bargaining unit, the time and place of holding the election, and the payroll period to be used in determining which employees within the appropriate unit shall be eligible to vote. Such election shall be conducted under the direction and supervision of the regional director. The method of conducting such election and the post-election procedure shall be consistent with that followed by the regional director in conducting elections pursuant to §§ 102.69 and 102.70.

(c) *Full consent election agreements with final regional director determinations of pre- and post-election disputes.* Where a petition has been duly filed, the employer and any individual or labor organizations representing a substantial number of the employees involved may, with the approval of the regional director, enter into an agreement, referred to as a full consent election agreement, providing that pre- and post-election disputes will be resolved by the regional director. Such agreement provides for a hearing pursuant to §§ 102.63, 102.64, 102.65, 102.66 and 102.67 to determine if a question of representation exists. Upon the conclusion of such a hearing, the regional director shall issue a decision. The rulings and determinations by the regional director thereunder shall be final, with the same force and effect, in that case, as if issued by the Board. Any election ordered by the regional director shall be conducted under the direction and supervision of the regional director. The method of conducting such election shall be consistent with the method followed by the regional director in conducting elections pursuant to §§ 102.69 and

60

Box 7.1   *(continued)*

National Labor Relations Board   **§ 102.63**

102.70, except that the rulings and determinations by the regional director of the results thereof shall be final, and the regional director shall issue to the parties a certification of the results of the election, including certifications of representative where appropriate, with the same force and effect, in that case, as if issued by the Board, and except that rulings or determinations by the regional director in respect to any amendment of such certification shall also be final.

(d) *Voter list.* Absent agreement of the parties to the contrary specified in the election agreement or extraordinary circumstances specified in the direction of election, within 2 business days after the approval of an election agreement pursuant to paragraphs (a) or (b) of this section, or issuance of a direction of election pursuant to paragraph (c) of this section, the employer shall provide to the regional director and the parties named in the agreement or direction a list of the full names, work locations, shifts, job classifications, and contact information (including home addresses, available personal email addresses, and available home and personal cellular ("cell") telephone numbers) of all eligible voters. The employer shall also include in a separate section of that list the same information for those individuals whom the parties have agreed should be permitted to vote subject to challenge or those individuals who, according to the direction of election, will be permitted to vote subject to challenge, including, for example, individuals in the classifications or other groupings that will be permitted to vote subject to challenge. In order to be timely filed and served, the list must be received by the regional director and the parties named in the agreement or direction respectively within 2 business days after the approval of the agreement or issuance of the direction unless a longer time is specified in the agreement or direction. The list of names shall be alphabetized (overall or by department) and be in an electronic format approved by the General Counsel unless the employer certifies that it does not possess the capacity to produce the list in the required form. When feasible, the list shall be filed

electronically with the regional director and served electronically on the other parties named in the agreement or direction. A certificate of service on all parties shall be filed with the regional director when the voter list is filed. The employer's failure to file or serve the list within the specified time or in proper format shall be grounds for setting aside the election whenever proper and timely objections are filed under the provisions of § 102.69(a). The employer shall be estopped from objecting to the failure to file or serve the list within the specified time or in the proper format if it is responsible for the failure. The parties shall not use the list for purposes other than the representation proceeding, Board proceedings arising from it, and related matters.

(e) *Notice of election.* Upon approval of the election agreement pursuant to paragraphs (a) or (b) of this section or with the direction of election pursuant to paragraph (c) of this section, the regional director shall promptly transmit the Board's Notice of Election to the parties and their designated representatives by email, facsimile, or by overnight mail (if neither an email address nor facsimile number was provided). The employer shall post and distribute the Notice of Election in accordance with § 102.67(k). The employer's failure properly to post or distribute the election notices as required herein shall be grounds for setting aside the election whenever proper and timely objections are filed under the provisions of § 102.69(a). A party shall be estopped from objecting to the nonposting of notices if it is responsible for the nonposting, and likewise shall be estopped from objecting to the nondistribution of notices if it is responsible for the nondistribution.

[79 FR 74479, Dec. 15, 2014]

§ 102.63 Investigation of petition by regional director; notice of hearing; service of notice; Notice of Petition for Election; Statement of Position; withdrawal of notice of hearing.

(a) *Investigation; notice of hearing; Notice of Petition for Election.* (1) After a petition has been filed under § 102.61(a), (b), or (c), if no agreement such as that provided in § 102.62 is entered into and

Understanding the procedural steps in rulemaking is important because at each step, documents are created that may be helpful in understanding, complying with, or challenging the final rule. Under the APA, most federal regulations are adopted through *informal rulemaking*, also called *notice and comment rulemaking*. This process includes three major steps: (1) notice of a proposed rulemaking, (2) an opportunity for public comment on the proposed rule, and (3) publication of the final rule, along with the agency's explanation.[4]

The process begins with notice that the agency intends to adopt a rule. Typically, a notice of a proposed rulemaking (NPRM) is published in the *Federal Register*, a voluminous official U.S. government publication available in print and online formats. The NPRM usually includes a draft of the proposed regulation, some explanation of the necessity and authority for adopting the regulation, and information about how the public may comment on the proposal. Reading the NPRM can be useful in some cases, especially when there are differences between the proposed regulation and the final regulation. For example, if the final regulation is more lenient than the proposed regulation, one might be able to use that fact to contest a strict interpretation of the final regulation.

During the second phase of rulemaking, the public is invited to submit written comments on the proposed regulation. Comments often are a mix of praise and criticism of the proposed regulation. They may address the proposed regulation's underlying scientific or other empirical justifications, the policy solution that the agency developed, or related topics that should be considered during rulemaking. Comments typically are not published verbatim in the *Federal Register*; rather, they are held by the proposing agency as part of the rulemaking record. The record becomes important if there is a court challenge to the agency's rulemaking choices.

At the end of the comment period, the agency takes one of three paths: (1) adopts the regulation as proposed, (2) adopts a regulation with changes reflecting comments received and other newly developed information, or (3) declines to adopt any regulation. If the agency decides to adopt a final regulation, it usually publishes, in the *Federal Register*, both the text of the final regulation and some explanation of the policy choices made by the agency in arriving at the final language. The latter includes a summary of the comments along with the agency's responses. This explanation is a bit like the legislative history of a statute, although in some ways it is more definitive than a statute's legislative history because regulations are generally adopted by a single agency speaking with a single voice.

In addition to being published in the *Federal Register*, the new regulation is published in the *Code of Federal Regulations* (C.F.R.), which is a codification of federal administrative regulations. If this dual publication seems confusing, an analogy to statutes may be helpful. Statutes are published

---

4. There is a different process as well: *formal rulemaking* is akin to a trial and entails testimony and cross-examination, written proposed findings and conclusions, and the opportunity to file exceptions to the recommended regulations. This process is less commonly used.

chronologically as session laws (such as the federal *Statutes at Large*); similarly, the *Federal Register* serves as the chronological record of administrative actions of different kinds. Statutes also are codified topically in a code that contains all general and permanent public statutes currently in effect, whenever enacted (such as the *United States Code*); the C.F.R. is a codification of regulations currently in effect that is organized by topic. The organization of the C.F.R. roughly parallels the organization of the federal statutory code; for example, labor statutes appear in Title 29 of the U.S.C., and labor regulations appear in Title 29 of the C.F.R.

Notice of Proposed Rulemaking	• Draft of proposed regulation and explanation • Published in *Federal Register*
Public Comments	• Public's view of proposal's justification or policy solution • Comments are held by agency in record; summarized with final regulations
Adoption of Final Regulation	• Regulation and explanation in *Federal Register* • Regulation in *Code of Federal Regulations*

Researching Regulations

When you research regulations, think in terms of reversing the chronology of rulemaking. Start by locating the final regulations pertinent to your client's situation; the regulations are the law. Then consider whether it makes sense to dig deeper into the backstory of the pertinent regulations by looking into their history and the statutory authority of the agency to adopt regulations. For each step of regulations research, various options exist, as summarized in Box 7.2.

Researching the regulation.   The *Code of Federal Regulations* is published in print, but you will most likely do your regulations research online. You can, in fact, accomplish much of your research using two free online resources offered by the U.S. Government Publishing Office: (1) the Federal Digital System, or FDsys (at www.gpo.gov/fdsys), and (2) e-CFR (at www.ecfr.gov). FDsys is an official source supplying PDF versions of the printed C.F.R. pages; these are updated annually (just like the print version), whereas e-CFR is unofficial but has more search options and is within a few days of being current.

| Box 7.2 | APPROACHES TO REGULATIONS RESEARCH |

Source	Full-Text Resources and Finding Tools
Agency Organic Statute	Statutory codes
Regulation	C.F.R. online via FDsys, e-CFR, agency website Commercial databases (Bloomberg Law, HeinOnline, Lexis, Westlaw) C.F.R. in print Finding tool: *CFR Index and Finding Aids*
New Regulatory Action	e-CFR and online *Federal Register*
Case Law	Case law reporters, online databases, court websites Finding tools: annotated codes, citators for regulations
Regulatory History	*Federal Register* in FDsys, Bloomberg Law, HeinOnline, Lexis, Westlaw

Researchers typically use these websites in tandem, starting with e-CFR for its stronger research tools and then moving to FDsys to obtain the official, authoritative materials. HeinOnline also offers a federal regulations database, as do Lexis, Westlaw, and Bloomberg Law.

There are several ways to identify a pertinent regulation. Of course, good secondary sources (discussed in Chapter 3) will provide references to pertinent regulations. Often, you will already be aware of the organic statute creating the agency and setting its rulemaking authority. If so, a good strategy is to examine the annotations in an annotated code (discussed in Chapter 5) for references to the pertinent regulations.

If you come to one of the C.F.R. resources without a citation already in hand, you have several options for locating the pertinent regulation. First, if you have the statutory citation, a good option is to use the Parallel Table of Authorities and Rules that accompanies the print, HeinOnline, and FDsys versions of the C.F.R.[5] By looking up your statute in that table, you will find references to corresponding regulations. Second, you may use the subject index that accompanies the print C.F.R. and the electronic versions on HeinOnline and Westlaw. Using the name of the agency as your search term is a good strategy. Third, you may use a key-word search in online resources. Fourth, you may skim through the titles, chapters, subchapters, parts, and

---

5. In the print and HeinOnline versions, you will find it in the *CFR Index and Finding Aids* volume.

sections of the C.F.R. and browse those sections that seem promising. One of these methods may be more effective than the others, so be flexible. In general, through these tools, you should be able to identify a pertinent title and part, but you may not always locate a specific section immediately.

Once you have identified and located a potentially pertinent section or part, you should examine the material carefully, of course. Examine the table of contents for the unit—whether this is a chapter, subchapter, or part—containing the pertinent material so that you identify all pertinent sections. Be sure to look for definitions, which may appear at the beginning of and apply throughout a unit. Read through all sections within a pertinent unit because they are likely to be interconnected. Then take note of the Source and Authority material in small print at the end of a section or the outline for a unit. You may find a reference to the regulation's statutory authority, as well as the regulation's date of final adoption and citation to the *Federal Register*. As with statutes, a good practice is to brief the regulation.

In the case of the NLRB regulation shown in Box 7.1, we located the NLRB's general rulemaking authority in section 6 of the National Labor Relations Act (codified as 29 U.S.C. § 156). When we researched in Westlaw, the annotations for that section pointed us to the title and chapter of the regulations in the C.F.R. that include the regulation relating to union representation matters. See Box 7.3. With the lead from this annotation, we easily located the regulation in FDsys.

An alternative approach to the C.F.R. in some situations is to work through the website of the agency that you have identified as regulating your client's situation. The level of difficulty of this task depends, of course, on the complexity of the agency involved and the quality of its website. If you know the name of the office within the agency and the name of the specific law or program of interest to you, this may be a fairly direct path. Another possibility is to click on a regulations or similar tab.

When we visited the NLRB website for comparison purposes, we found the same regulation. We also obtained the type of additional insight that an agency website may provide. The NLRB posted information about a switch in 2015 from one set of regulations to another and provided a helpful, redlined version of the older regulations. See Box 7.4.

Box 7.3   **ANNOTATED CODE (Employee Data)**

List of 5 Context & Analysis for § 156. Rules and regulations

Context and Analysis (27)

Code Of Federal Regulations (5)

Construction of rules, see 29 CFR § 102.121.
Issuance, amendment or repeal of rules, see 29 CFR §§ 102.124 and 102.125.
Jurisdictional standards of National Labor Relations Board, see 29 CFR § 103.1 et seq.
Rules and regulations, Series 8, see 29 CFR § 102.1 et seq.
Statements of procedure, see 29 CFR § 101.1.

| Box 7.4 | AGENCY WEBSITE POSTING (Employee Data) |

Find Your Regional Office | Directory | 1-866-667-NLRB | Español

Search

Search Tools

Home   Rights We Protect   What We Do   Who We Are   Cases & Decisions   News & Outreach   Reports & Guidance

Home » Reports & Guidance   Sign up for NLRB Updates

Rules & Regulations

On December 15, 2014, the National Labor Relations Board adopted changes to its representation case procedures.
Those changes became effective April 14, 2015 and are being applied to all petitions filed on or after April 14, 2015.
Petitions filed before April 14, 2015 are being processed under the representation case procedures that were in effect
when the petition was filed and do not include the changes that became effective April 14, 2015. Accordingly, the Rules
with and without the changes appear below.

Rules and Regulations *with* Representation case changes effective April 14, 2015

- Final Rule (Including Discussion of Reasons for Board's Actions) effective April 14, 2015
- Text of Amended Rules
- Red-line Comparison of Amended Rules to Rules before Changes

Rules and Regulations *without* Representation case changes effective April 14, 2015

- NLRB Rules and Regulations - Part 101
- NLRB Rules and Regulations - Part 102
- NLRB Rules and Regulations - Part 103

NLRB Organization and Functions (currently under revision)

Delegation of Authority and Assigned Responsibilities of the General Counsel

You can view the National Labor Relations Act here.

Resources

Download the Mobile App

The NLRB Process

E-File Documents

E-File Charge / Petition

Fact Sheets

Graphs & Data

FAQs

Site Feedback

Forms

National Labor Relations Act (NLRA)

Related Agencies

SHARE

Site Map   Policies   Feedback   FOIA   OpenGov   Inspector General
Accessibility   No Fear Act   USA.gov   PDF Viewer   Download App

Updating the regulation.   Another way that regulations resemble statutes
is that they can be amended and repealed by the agencies that promulgate
them. So once you have located a pertinent regulation, you must make
sure that it is up to date. You can do this most quickly and cost-effectively
using the federal government's free online tools. Updating in this way
involves two steps. First, locate the current version of the regulation in the
e-CFR database, and then look for any changes that may have occurred in the
interim by using the *Federal Register* at FDsys.

In our example, we located the NLRB's employee contact information
regulation, 29 C.F.R. § 102.63, on e-CFR on January 29. That document
was current as of January 27, 2016. See Box 7.5. Although it seemed unlikely
that there would have been any changes to the regulation in that brief period

Box 7.5   **REGULATION IN e-CFR (Employee Data)**

ELECTRONIC CODE OF FEDERAL REGULATIONS

e-CFR data is current as of January 27, 2016

Title 29 → Subtitle B → Chapter I → Part 102 → Subpart C → §102.62

Title 29: Labor
PART 102—RULES AND REGULATIONS, SERIES 8
Subpart C—Procedure Under Section 9(c) of the Act for the Determination of Questions Concerning Representation of Employees and for Clarification of Bargaining Units and for Amendment of Certifications Under Section 9(b) of the Act

§102.62   Election agreements; voter list; Notice of Election.

(a) *Consent election agreements with final regional director determinations of post-election disputes.* Where a petition has been duly filed, the employer and any individual or labor organizations representing a substantial number of employees involved may, with the approval of the regional director, enter into an agreement providing for the waiver of a hearing and for an election and further providing that post-election disputes will be resolved by the regional director. Such agreement, referred to as a consent election agreement, shall include a description of the appropriate unit, the time and place of holding the election, and the payroll period to be used in determining what employees within the appropriate unit shall be eligible to vote. Such election shall be conducted under the direction and supervision of the regional director. The method of conducting such election shall be consistent with the method followed by the regional director in conducting elections pursuant to §§102.69 and 102.70 except that the rulings and determinations by the regional director of the results thereof shall be final, and the regional director shall issue to the parties a certification of the results of the election, including certifications of representative where appropriate, with the same force and effect, in that case, as if issued by the Board, and except that rulings or determinations by the regional director in respect to any amendment of such certification shall also be final.

(b) *Stipulated election agreements with discretionary Board review.* Where a petition has been duly filed, the employer and any individuals or labor organizations representing a substantial number of the employees involved may, with the approval of the regional director, enter into an agreement providing for the waiver of a hearing and for an election as described in paragraph (a) of this section and further providing that the parties may request Board review of the regional director's resolution of post-election disputes. Such agreement, referred to as a stipulated election agreement, shall also include a description of the appropriate bargaining unit, the time and place of holding the election, and the payroll period to be used in determining which employees within the appropriate unit shall be eligible to vote. Such election shall be conducted under the direction and supervision of the regional director. The method of conducting such election and the post-election procedure shall be consistent with that followed by the regional director in conducting elections pursuant to §§102.69 and 102.70.

(c) *Full consent election agreements with final regional director determinations of pre- and post-election disputes.* Where a petition has been duly filed, the employer and any individual or labor organizations representing a substantial number of the employees involved may, with the approval of the regional director, enter into an agreement, referred to as a full consent election agreement, providing that pre- and post-election disputes will be resolved by the regional director. Such agreement provides for a hearing pursuant to §§102.63, 102.64, 102.65, 102.66 and 102.67 to determine if a question of representation exists. Upon the conclusion of such a hearing, the regional director shall issue a decision. The rulings and determinations by the regional director thereunder shall be final, with the same force and effect, in that case, as if issued by the Board. Any election ordered by the regional director shall be conducted under the direction and supervision of the regional director. The method of conducting such election shall be consistent with the method followed by the regional director in conducting elections pursuant to §§102.69 and 102.70, except that the rulings and determinations by the regional director of the results thereof shall be final, and the regional director shall issue to the parties a certification of the results of the election, including certifications of representative where appropriate, with the same force and effect, in that case, as if issued by the Board, and except that rulings or determinations by the regional director in respect to any amendment of such certification shall also be final.

(d) *Voter list.* Absent agreement of the parties to the contrary specified in the election agreement or extraordinary circumstances specified in the direction of election, within 2 business days after the approval of an election agreement pursuant to paragraphs (a) or (b) of this section, or issuance of a direction of election pursuant to paragraph (c) of this section, the employer shall provide to the regional director and the parties named in the agreement or direction a list of the full names, work locations, shifts, job classifications, and contact information (including home addresses, available

Box 7.5   *(continued)*

personal email addresses, and available home and personal cellular ("cell") telephone numbers) of all eligible voters. The employer shall also include in a separate section of that list the same information for those individuals whom the parties have agreed should be permitted to vote subject to challenge or those individuals who, according to the direction of election, will be permitted to vote subject to challenge, including, for example, individuals in the classifications or other groupings that will be permitted to vote subject to challenge. In order to be timely filed and served, the list must be received by the regional director and the parties named in the agreement or direction respectively within 2 business days after the approval of the agreement or issuance of the direction unless a longer time is specified in the agreement or direction. The list of names shall be alphabetized (overall or by department) and be in an electronic format approved by the General Counsel unless the employer certifies that it does not possess the capacity to produce the list in the required form. When feasible, the list shall be filed electronically with the regional director and served electronically on the other parties named in the agreement or direction. A certificate of service on all parties shall be filed with the regional director when the voter list is filed. The employer's failure to file or serve the list within the specified time or in proper format shall be grounds for setting aside the election whenever proper and timely objections are filed under the provisions of §102.69 (a). The employer shall be estopped from objecting to the failure to file or serve the list within the specified time or in the proper format if it is responsible for the failure. The parties shall not use the list for purposes other than the representation proceeding, Board proceedings arising from it, and related matters.

(e) *Notice of election.* Upon approval of the election agreement pursuant to paragraphs (a) or (b) of this section or with the direction of election pursuant to paragraph (c) of this section, the regional director shall promptly transmit the Board's Notice of Election to the parties and their designated representatives by email, facsimile, or by overnight mail (if neither an email address nor facsimile number was provided). The employer shall post and distribute the Notice of Election in accordance with §102.67(k). The employer's failure properly to post or distribute the election notices as required herein shall be grounds for setting aside the election whenever proper and timely objections are filed under the provisions of §102.69(a). A party shall be estopped from objecting to the nonposting of notices if it is responsible for the nonposting, and likewise shall be estopped from objecting to the nondistribution of notices if it is responsible for the nondistribution.

[79 FR 74479, Dec. 15, 2014]

Need assistance?

---

of time, we still needed to be sure. So we went to FDsys, which makes the *Federal Register* available online. Updating entails clicking into the Table of Contents for each issue for the days since the e-CFR currency date. Each Table of Contents lists agency actions alphabetically. See Box 7.6, the entry for January 29, which showed no action for the NLRB.

Regulations, like statutes, are applied and interpreted by the courts to specific situations. In some cases, the court's opinion includes judicial gloss on the regulatory language. Not infrequently, the party subject to the regulation challenges it as, essentially, not in accord with the statute that led to the regulation or not supported by the evidence gathered in the rulemaking process. Thus, researching case law is a necessary next step in updating your regulation research. Along with the various means of researching case law (discussed in Chapter 4) and use of an annotated code (discussed in Chapter 5), citing a regulation through KeyCite or Shepard's is a sound means of locating cases that may undermine a regulation's validity. See Box 7.7.

| Box 7.6 | *FEDERAL REGISTER* DAILY EDITION (Employee Data) |

Table of Contents
Federal Register Vol. 81, Issue 19, Friday, January 29, 2016
More Information
CENTERS FOR MEDICARE & MEDICAID SERVICES

NOTICES
Agency Information Collection Activities: Proposed Collection; Comment Request

Pages 5014-5015 [FR DOC# 2016-01688]   PDF | Text |
                                                                             More

Agency Information Collection Activities: Submission for OMB Review; Comment
Request

Pages 5015-5016 [FR DOC# 2016-01689]   PDF | Text |
                                                                             More

COMMITTEE FOR PURCHASE FROM PEOPLE WHO ARE BLIND OR SEVERELY
DISABLED

NOTICES
Procurement List; Proposed Additions

Page 5009 [FR DOC# 2016-01704]   PDF | Text |
                                                                             More

Procurement List; Deletions

Page 5009 [FR DOC# 2016-01705]   PDF | Text |
                                                                             More

CONSUMER PRODUCT SAFETY COMMISSION

NOTICES
Agency Information Collection Activities; Proposals, Submissions, and Approvals:
Agency Information Collection Activities; Proposed Collection; Comment Request;
Third Party Testing of Children's Products

Pages 5010-5013 [FR DOC# 2016-01699]   PDF | Text |
                                                                             More

DEFENSE DEPARTMENT

NOTICES

Box 7.6   *(continued)*

NATIONAL INSTITUTES OF HEALTH

NOTICES
Meetings:
National Institute on Aging; Notice of Closed Meeting

Page 5016 [FR DOC# 2016-01697]   PDF | Text |
                                                                  More

National Cancer Institute; Notice of Closed Meetings

Page 5016 [FR DOC# 2016-01696]   PDF | Text |
                                                                  More

Center for Scientific Review; Notice of Closed Meetings

Pages 5016-5017 [FR DOC# 2016-01693]   PDF | Text |
                                                                  More

Center for Scientific Review; Notice of Closed Meetings

Pages 5017-5018 [FR DOC# 2016-01694]   PDF | Text |
                                                                  More

NATIONAL SCIENCE FOUNDATION

NOTICES
Sunshine Act Meetings; National Science Board

Pages 5025-5027 [FR DOC# 2016-01757]   PDF | Text |
                                                                  More

POSTAL SERVICE

NOTICES
Temporary Emergency Committee of the Board of Governors; Sunshine Act Meeting

Page 5027 [FR DOC# 2016-01776]   PDF | Text |
                                                                  More

SECURITIES AND EXCHANGE COMMISSION

NOTICES
Self-Regulatory Organizations; Proposed Rule Changes:

Box 7.7   KEYCITE REPORT FOR REGULATION (Employee Data)

List of 20 Citing References for § 102.62 Election agreements; voter list; Notice of Elect...

Citing References (20)

Title	Date	NOD Topics	Type	Depth
1. Salem Hosp. Corp. v. N.L.R.B. 808 F.3d 59, 63 , D.C.Cir. LABOR AND EMPLOYMENT - Unions. Hearing officer's premature closing of record in representation hearing did not prejudice hospital.	Dec. 15, 2015	—	Case	—
2. Chamber of Commerce of United States of America v. National Labor Relations Board 2015 WL 4572948, *28+ , D.D.C. Background: Groups representing employers filed suit against National Labor Relations Board (NLRB) challenging newly enacted regulations governing union elections, claiming the...	July 29, 2015	—	Case	—
3. Associated Builders and Contractors of Texas, Inc. v. N.L.R.B. 2015 WL 3609116, *8+ , W.D.Tex. Before the Court are Plaintiffs' Motion for Expedited Summary Judgment, filed February 9, 2015 (Clerk's Dkt. # 12); Defendant National Labor Relations Board's Partial Motion to...	June 01, 2015	—	Case	—
4. Warren Unilube, Inc. v. N.L.R.B. 690 F.3d 969, 971 , 8th Cir. LABOR AND EMPLOYMENT - Unfair Labor Practices. Substantial evidence supported National Labor Relations Board's determination that union's charge was not baseless.	Aug. 28, 2012	—	Case	—
5. Chamber of Commerce of U.S. v. N.L.R.B. 879 F.Supp.2d 18, 20 , D.D.C. ADMINISTRATIVE PRACTICE - Rulemaking. Rule amending procedure for determining whether majority of employees wanted union representation was adopted without quorum.	May 14, 2012	—	Case	—
6. N.L.R.B. v. MEMC Electronic Materials, Inc. 363 F.3d 705, 706+ , 8th Cir. LABOR AND EMPLOYMENT - Unions. Employer did not show unusual circumstances that would allow it to withdraw from election agreement.	Apr. 09, 2004	In general	Case	—

1

Researching the regulation's history and statutory basis. If significant questions arise about how to interpret or apply a regulation, or if your client is considering whether to challenge a regulation, you will want to dig deeper into the regulation's backstory. In particular, you will want to locate the rule's regulatory history (from notice to adoption) as documented in the *Federal Register* and the statute outlining the agency's authority to adopt the regulation.

The place to start is with the publication of the final rule. In the C.F.R., you can find a reference for the publication of the final rule in the *Federal Register* after the outline of the unit containing the regulation or after an individual rule, depending on how the regulation came to be promulgated. Accompanying the regulation in the *Federal Register* should be explanatory material, which may include descriptions of the overall purpose of the rule, examples of concerns raised in public comments on the rule before it was adopted and the agency's response to these comments, and discussions of previous rules or other agency actions on the same topic. In addition, the regulation's effective date is stated. Tracing back through key events as published in the *Federal Register*, such as the notice of proposed rulemaking, can also be revealing.

In the example for this chapter, we learned that the most recent amendment to the regulation was published in the *Federal Register* on December 15, 2014, in volume 74 beginning on page 74480. The final rules were preceded in the *Federal Register* by more than 170 pages of explanatory material written by the agency. This includes a summary of the comments made by members of the public during the comment period, which traditionally is a fruitful source of interpretive and advocacy points. Interestingly, this explanatory material shows that the NLRB wrestled with public comments about data such as e-mail addresses, cell-phone numbers, and other employee contact information that employees are required to disclose in union voting cases. In response, the NLRB explained that for the time being, it would not require the disclosure of social media user names because currently, few employers would have social media contact information for their employees — although this might change in the future. See Box 7.8.

A final step in mapping out the rule's backstory is to read (or reread) the statute[6] that authorized the agency to adopt the regulation at issue. This may include a general provision in the agency's organic statute, a more specific command by Congress to make rules on a specific topic, or both. As you review the statute, look for the legal standard that the legislature has set for the conduct that you are concerned with, as well as indications of the agency's authority to promulgate regulations regarding that conduct. These may help clarify the rule or may open avenues to questioning the rule's validity if the agency appears to have misread the statute or overstepped its statutory authority. You will find a reference to the statutory authority for a regulation in the C.F.R., as well as in the *Federal Register*.

---

6. On occasion, more than one statute may be involved.

Box 7.8   **EXPLANATION OF REGULATION (Employee Data)**

Federal Register / Vol. 79, No. 240 / Monday, December 15, 2014 / Rules   74337

In *Excelsior,* the Board explained the primary rationale for requiring production of an eligibility list:

[W]e regard it as the Board's function to conduct elections in which employees have the opportunity to cast their ballots for or against representation under circumstances that are free not only from interference, restraint, or coercion violative of the Act, but also free from other elements that prevent or impede a free and reasoned choice. Among the factors that undoubtedly tend to impede such a choice is a lack of information with respect to one of the choices available. In other words, an employee who has had an effective opportunity to hear the arguments concerning representation is in a better position to make a more fully informed and reasonable choice . . . .
As a practical matter, an employer, through his possession of employee names and home addresses as well as his ability to communicate with employees on plant premises, is assured of the continuing opportunity to inform the entire electorate of his views with respect to union representation. On the other hand, without a list of employee names and addresses, a labor organization, whose organizers normally have no right of access to plant premises, has no method by which it can be certain of reaching all the employees with its arguments in favor of representation, and, as a result, employees are often completely unaware of that point of view. This is not, of course, to deny the existence of various means by which a party *might* be able to communicate with a substantial portion of the electorate even without possessing their names and addresses. It is rather to say what seems to us obvious—that the access of *all* employees to such communications can be insured only if all parties have the names and addresses of all the voters. In other words, by providing all parties with employees' names and addresses, we maximize the likelihood that all the voters will be exposed to the arguments for, as well as against, union representation

156 NLRB at 1240–41 (footnotes omitted). The Supreme Court endorsed this rationale in *Wyman-Gordon,* 394 U.S. at 767, stating that:

The disclosure requirement furthers this objective [to ensure the fair and free choice of bargaining representatives] by encouraging an informed employee electorate and by allowing unions the right of access to employees that management already possesses. It is for the Board and not for this Court to weigh against this interest the problems that union solicitation may present.

Since *Excelsior* was decided almost 50 years ago, the Board has not significantly altered its requirements despite transformative changes in communications technology, including that used in representation election campaigns. Fifty years ago, email did not exist; and communication by United States mail was the norm. For example, the union in *Excelsior* requested a list of

names and home addresses to answer campaign propaganda that the employer had mailed to its employees. See *Excelsior,* 156 NLRB at 1246–47. Indeed, if a union wanted to reach employees with its arguments in favor of representation, it frequently resorted to the United States mail or visited employees at their homes because, as the Board recognized in *Excelsior,* the union, unlike the employer, "normally ha[s] no right of access to plant premises" to communicate with the employees. *Id.* at 1240. However, as SEIU points out, in 2010, nearly all working adults used email, and indeed, 39.6 billion emails were being sent every day—more than 80 times the number of letters being sent through the U.S. Postal Service.[138] The AFL–CIO II cites to a study released during the 2014 comment period suggesting that up to 87% of U.S. adults have an email address and use the internet.[139] Other comments likewise assert that the voter list requirements should be updated to include email addresses in recognition of how individuals, employees, employers, and institutions now communicate with one another.[140]

The Board believes that the provision of only a physical home address no longer serves the primary purpose of the *Excelsior* list. Communications technology and campaign communications have evolved far beyond the face-to-face conversation on the doorstep imagined by the Board in *Excelsior.* As Justice Kennedy observed in *Denver Area Educational Telecommunications Consortium, Inc. v. FTC,* 518 U.S. 727, 802–803 (1996) (Kennedy, J., dissenting) (internal citation omitted):

Minds are not changed in streets and parks as they once were. To an increasing degree, the most significant interchanges of ideas and shaping of public consciousness occur in mass and electronic media. The extent of public entitlement to participate in those means of communication may be changed as technologies change.

Similarly, in *J. Picini Flooring,* 356 NLRB No. 9, slip op. at 2–3 (2010) (footnotes omitted), the Board recently observed,

---

[138] See "Email vs. snail mail (infographic)" (Sept. 29, 2010), *http://royal.pingdom.com/2010/09/29/email-vs-snail-mail-infographic.*
[139] Susannah Fox & Lee Rainie, "The Web at 25 in the U.S.", Pew Research Center (Feb. 27, 2014), *http://www.pewinternet.org/2014/02/27/the-web-at-25-in-the-U–S/.*
[140] See, *e.g.,* National Nurses Union (NNU); Professor Joel Cutcher-Gershenfeld; SEIU-United Healthcare Workers—West; Southwest Regional Joint Board, Workers United; Testimony of Brenda Crawford II; Testimony of Darrin Murray on behalf of SEIU II.

While * * * traditional means of communication remain in use, email, postings on internal and external websites, and other electronic communication tools are overtaking, if they have not already overtaken, bulletin boards as the primary means of communicating a uniform message to employees and union members. Electronic communications are now the norm in many workplaces, and it is reasonable to expect that the number of employers communicating with their employees through electronic methods will continue to increase. Indeed, the Board and most other government agencies routinely and sometimes exclusively rely on electronic posting or email to communicate information to their employees. In short, "[t]oday's workplace is becoming increasingly electronic."[141]

Moreover, our experience with campaigns preceding elections conducted under Section 9 of the Act indicates that employers are, with increasing frequency, using email to communicate with employees about the vote. See, *e.g., Arkema, Inc.,* 357 NLRB No. 103, slip op. at 14 (2011) (employer sent an email to employees broadly prohibiting "harassment" with respect to the upcoming election), enf. denied 710 F.3d 308 (5th Cir. 2013); *Humane Society for Seattle,* 356 NLRB No. 13, slip op. at 3 (2010) ("On September 27, the Employer's CEO, Brenda Barnette, sent an email to employees asking that they consider whether ACOG was the way to make changes at SHS. On September 29, HR Director Leader emailed employees a link to a third-party article regarding 'KCACC Guild's' petition and reasons the Guild would be bad for SHS."); *Research Foundation of the State University of New York at Buffalo,* 355 NLRB 950, 958 (2010) ("On January 12, Scuto sent the first in a series of email's [sic] to all Employer postdoctoral associates concerning the Petitioner's efforts to form a Union at the Employer[,]. . . . explaining the Employer's position on unionization . . . ."); *Black Entertainment Television,* 2009 WL 1574462, at *1 (NLRB Div. of Judges June 5, 2009) (employer notified several employees by email to attend a meeting in which senior vice-president spoke one-on-one with the employees regarding the election scheduled for the following day).[142]

---

[141] To be clear, the Board cites *J. Picini Flooring* and related examples simply to demonstrate its view of the changing realities of workplace communication, and not—as suggested in the comments of AHCA—to argue that simply because an employer might use a particular mode of communication that a union should therefore be entitled to use of that same mode as a quid pro quo.
[142] In addition, the rulemaking record reflects that employers sometimes use their employees' personal contact information to communicate about campaign issues. See United Nurses Associations of California/Union of Health Care Professionals

Continued

Box 7.8 _(continued)_

74338   **Federal Register** / Vol. 79, No. 240 / Monday, December 15, 2014 / Rules

Disclosure of the employees' personal email addresses, like the disclosure of personal phone numbers discussed below, will allow the nonemployer parties (including unions and decertification petitioners) to promptly convey their information concerning the question of representation to all the eligible voters. Disclosure of this contact information also makes it more likely that nonemployer parties can respond to employee questions, both individually and collectively, including questions that employees have, but may be uncomfortable raising on their own.[143] It also permits the nonemployer parties to engage with employees on campaign issues in a timely manner and specifically, prior to the election, as well as share those responses with other employees, thus making it more likely that employees can make an informed choice in the election. After all, it obviously takes less time for an employee to receive the nonemployer party's campaign communication when that message is sent via email than when it is sent via United States mail.[144] Nurse Brenda Crawford

explained the difficulty in organizing off-campus informational meetings when her colleagues work 12-hour shifts and have outside family responsibilities. In her view, modern communication tools, including email, would enhance the ability to provide information in a manner that is convenient to workers and their families. Testimony of Crawford II. The Board agrees, and has concluded that the required disclosure of available personal email addresses of eligible voters will permit the timely give-and-take of campaign information that will increase the likelihood that employees will be placed "in a better position to make a fully informed and reasonable choice." _Excelsior_, 156 NLRB at 1240.[145] And of course, the Board included employees' home and personal cell telephone numbers in the voter list proposals because the use of telephones to convey information orally and via texting is an integral part of the communications evolution that has taken place in our country since _Excelsior_ was decided.[146]

However, some comments question the inclusion of phone numbers in the final rule, implying that because the Board chose not to mandate disclosure of phone numbers in 1966, at a time

when at least basic telephone technology existed, then it should not do so today.[147] CDW attempts to lend force to this argument by asserting that in the late 1960s "the United States led the world in telephone usage . . . and . . . the average person had 701 telephone conversations", while simultaneously arguing that the home addresses disclosed under the current _Excelsior_ policy continue to be the "most reliable and near universal points of contact" for employees.

The Board believes that comments such as CDW's do not adequately appreciate the way phone communication has changed in the last 45 years. While it may be true that when the Board issued its _Excelsior_ decision, many households had at least one telephone, the telephone was not nearly as ubiquitous as it is presently, and those that existed bore little resemblance to the technology we have become accustomed to today. In particular, voicemail service had yet to be invented, and no commercially viable home answering machine had yet entered the marketplace. See "The History of . . . Answering Machines," _http://transition.fcc.gov/cgb/kidszone/history_ans_machine.html_ (last updated June 4, 2004). Because answering machine and voicemail technology was uncommon or nonexistent in 1966, a nonemployer party could not leave a message if the employee with whom it intended to speak about the upcoming election was not at home when the union called. By contrast, the employee would receive the nonemployer party's letter even if the employee was not at home when the post office delivered it. Today, however, even if the employee is not home when the call is placed, the caller is virtually always able to leave a voice message—to say nothing of the ability to send written messages via phone texting technology. And, of course, if an employee has a cell phone, the caller can reach the employee even if the employee is not at home when the call is received.

Contrary to CDW, the Board believes that the changes in phone ownership and use make personal phones a universal point of contact today in a way that was unimaginable in 1966. The share of U.S. households possessing a telephone has steadily increased since the 1960s, from 78% in 1960 to 95% in 1990. See Bureau of the Census, Census Questionnaire Content, 1990 CQC–26, "We asked . . . You told us: Telephone and Vehicle Availability" 1 (Jan. 1994), _http://www.census.gov/prod/cen1990/_

(UNAC/UHCP) II and testimony of Brenda Crawford II (describing an employer sending text message blasts to employees' personal cell phones as part of its election campaign).

[143] For example, Board caselaw provides examples of campaigns in which employees are presented with hypothetical "questions" to "ask" the organizing union. See, _e.g. Kellwood Co._, 178 NLRB 20, 23 (1969) (employer encouraged employees to ask organizing union what would happen when no contract was reached); _Smithtown Nursing Home_, 228 NLRB 23, 26 (1977) (employer encouraged employees to ask the organizing union for a "guarantee" of no strikes, and other strike related demands); _World Wide Press, Inc._, 242 NLRB 346, 357 (1979) (employer distributed leaflets encouraging employees to ask about discontinued pension negotiations at another plant); _Flamingo Hilton-Laughlin_, 324 NLRB 72, 80–83 (1997) (employer distributed leaflets encouraging employees to ask 18 questions of the organizing union including certain "guarantees"); _Eldorado Tool_, 325 NLRB 222, 224 (1997) (employer distributed leaflet encouraging employees to ask 15 rhetorical questions of the organizing union including whether the union could "guarantee" no job loss or facility closure).

[144] We recognize that nonemployer parties can reply by email to any voter who chooses to pose questions by email since the return email address is included in the email itself, but we would find unpersuasive any claim that voluntary disclosures of this sort establish that it is unnecessary to provide nonemployer parties with email addresses of all eligible voters. Looking at the matter so narrowly overlooks that an organizing campaign is not merely a series of discrete individual communications addressed to interested employees with particular questions. Union representatives may seek to answer questions that not all employees may have thought to ask and to provide information about representation issues that not all employees possess. The ability to communicate effectively with all employees is necessary for this purpose. Accordingly, the Board believes that requiring an employer to furnish the available personal email addresses of eligible voters to the nonemployer parties makes it more likely that

employees can make an informed choice in the election.

[145] To be sure, the Board believes that requiring the provision of employees' available personal email and phone numbers is a necessary improvement to the existing _Excelsior_ policy even in workplaces where employers do not choose to avail themselves of email and phones as a tool of their representation campaign, _i.e._, its importance and usefulness is not linked to, or dependent on, the employer's use of email or phone communication.

[146] SIGMA and others suggests that many employers do not keep records of employees' personal email addresses and so "the Board may overestimate the availability or utility" of personal email addresses as a means for petitioners to reach all employees with their message. Yet, the amendments merely require an employer to furnish its employees' "available personal email addresses" (and "available home and personal cellular ("cell") telephone numbers"). Accordingly, if the employer does not maintain those addresses and numbers, it does not need to ask its employees for them. As discussed below, the Board recognizes that delays in conducting elections would result if employers (or the Board) were required to collect personal information directly from employees after the parties entered into an election agreement or the regional director directed an election. However, the fact that some employers may not maintain records of their employees' personal email addresses and personal phone numbers does not demonstrate that it is not worthwhile to require those employers who do maintain such information to disclose it in the interests of fair elections and more efficient administrative proceedings. Similarly, the fact that an employer may not possess the personal email addresses and personal phone numbers for each and every one of its employees does not demonstrate that it is not worthwhile to require the employers to disclose those employees' personal email addresses and personal phone numbers that it does possess.

[147] See, _e.g._, SIGMA; Schnuck Markets, Inc.; INDA II.

DECISIONS AND ORDERS

Understanding Decisions and Orders

Many agencies also operate in ways that are quasi-judicial, meaning that they make decisions involving the application of law to specific facts and issue legally binding orders regarding the payment of damages or requiring or prohibiting certain conduct, for example. In fact, some agencies, including the NLRB, do most of their lawmaking by issuing decisions rather than promulgating regulations. Like judicial cases, agency decisions have a degree of precedential effect and can take on the flavor of a body of common law, with the names and holdings of certain administrative decisions having instantly recognizable meaning to practitioners in the field. Agency decisions fall into two main categories: formal adjudication and informal adjudication.

A *formal adjudication* resembles a judicial trial, with parties observing rules of procedure, presenting testimony and documentary evidence before an administrative law judge (ALJ), and making written and oral legal arguments about the final outcome. At the conclusion of a formal adjudication, the ALJ issues a written decision and recommendation about how he or she thinks that the case should be decided. If no one makes a timely request for further review by the agency, the ALJ's recommendation usually becomes the agency's binding order. If a party does make a timely request for further review, or if the agency itself disagrees with the ALJ's decision, then the agency's commissioners or other authorized high-level agency officials review the ALJ's decision and issue a final order. Just as an appellate court reviewing a trial court might affirm, reverse, or do something in between, agencies may adopt, reject, or take a mixed approach to the ALJ's opinion. The important point is that it is the agency's final decision — not the ALJ's recommended decision — that is the final agency word on the matter.

A formal agency decision more or less resembles the opinion of a judicial court. It includes a statement of facts as found by the agency, the agency's decision, and its reasoning behind the decision. That reasoning typically includes discussion of the statute, any pertinent regulations, and previous decisions of the agency.

Box 7.9 is a decision of the NLRB affirming an ALJ's decision and order discussing an employer's firing of employees who posted comments critical of coworkers on one of their personal Facebook pages. The ALJ ruled that the postings were concerted activity protected under the National Labor Relations Act, so that the firings were unlawful. Among other things, the ALJ ordered the employer to reinstate the employees and to compensate them for lost earnings, as well as to cease from engaging in similar conduct in the future.

Agencies are not always required to use these formal, courtlike procedures. In fact, most decisions and orders are the product of informal adjudication. Although the procedures are less formal, there are some procedural

| Box 7.9 | **BOARD DECISION AND ORDER (Social Media Policy)** |

NOTICE: This opinion is subject to formal revision before publication in the bound volumes of NLRB decisions. Readers are requested to notify the Executive Secretary, National Labor Relations Board, Washington, D.C. 20570, of any typographical or other formal errors so that corrections can be included in the bound volumes.

Hispanics United of Buffalo, Inc. *and* Carlos Ortiz.
Case 03–CA–027872

December 14, 2012

DECISION AND ORDER

BY CHAIRMAN PEARCE AND MEMBERS HAYES, GRIFFIN, AND BLOCK

On September 2, 2011, Administrative Law Judge Arthur J. Amchan issued the attached decision. The Respondent filed exceptions and a supporting brief, and the Acting General Counsel filed an answering brief. The Acting General Counsel filed cross-exceptions and a supporting brief, the Respondent filed an answering brief, and the Acting General Counsel filed a reply brief.[1]

The National Labor Relations Board has considered the decision and the record in light of the exceptions, cross-exceptions, and briefs and has decided to affirm the judge's rulings,[2] findings,[3] and conclusions[4] and to adopt the recommended Order.

---

[1] The Respondent has requested oral argument. The request is denied, as the record, exceptions, cross-exceptions, and briefs adequately present the issues and the positions of the parties.

[2] The Respondent excepts to several of the judge's evidentiary and procedural rulings, including (1) his revocation of its subpoena to Region 3 of the Board, seeking documents regarding "speakers, meetings, presentations, in-service, conferences and/or seminars presented by Board agents to the Respondent's employees at its main facility"; (2) his revocation of its subpoenas to the five discharged employees, seeking information such as communications among themselves, applications, if any, to the State for unemployment benefits and/or moneys received from the State, and any complaints or inquiries to State or Federal agencies seeking statutory relief; and (3) his denial of its request for the names and contact information of current and former employees that had been redacted from emails the Board agent investigating the underlying charge allegations had supplied the Respondent.

The Board accords judges' rulings substantial deference and sets them aside only where they constitute an abuse of discretion. *Santa Barbara News-Press*, 357 NLRB No. 51, slip op. 1 fn. 3 (2011). A "high burden" is imposed to make this showing. *Aladdin Gaming, LLC*, 345 NLRB 585, 588 (2005), petition for review denied sub. nom. *Local Joint Executive Board of Las Vegas v. NLRB*, 515 F.3d 942 (9th Cir. 2008). Having carefully reviewed the record, we find that the Respondent has failed to meet this burden.

First, the judge's revocation of the subpoena to Region 3 accords with longstanding precedent prohibiting Board agents from producing materials relating to the investigation of unfair labor practice charges. *G. W. Galloway Co.*, 281 NLRB 262 fn. 1 (1986), vacated on other grounds 856 F.2d 275 (D.C. Cir. 1988); see also *Earthgrains Co.*, 351 NLRB 733, 739 (2007). Second, as to the information subpoenaed from the discriminatees, the Respondent failed to show that it was relevant to any issue in dispute. Accordingly, the subpoena was properly revoked as an unwarranted "fishing expedition." *Santa Barbara News*, supra, slip op. fn. 3, citing *Parts Depot, Inc.*, 348 NLRB 152 fn. 6 (2006). Finally, with respect to its request for the redacted names and

At issue in this case is whether the Respondent violated Section 8(a)(1) of the Act by discharging five employees for Facebook comments they wrote in response to a coworker's criticisms of their job performance. Although the employees' mode of communicating their workplace concerns might be novel, we agree with the judge that the appropriate analytical framework for resolving their discharge allegations has long been settled under *Meyers Industries*[5] and its progeny. Applying *Meyers*, we agree with the judge that the Respondent violated 8(a)(1) by discharging the five employees.

The relevant facts are as follows. Marianna Cole-Rivera and Lydia Cruz-Moore were coworkers employed by the Respondent to assist victims of domestic violence. The two employees frequently communicated with each other by phone and text message during the workday and after hours. According to Cole-Rivera's credited testimony, Cruz-Moore often criticized other employees during these communications, particularly housing department employees who, Cruz-Moore asserted, did not provide timely and adequate assistance to clients. Other employees similarly testified that Cruz-Moore spoke critically to them about their work habits and those of other employees.

This "criticism" issue escalated on Saturday, October 9, 2010, a nonworkday, when Cole-Rivera received a text message from Cruz-Moore stating that the latter intended to discuss her concerns regarding employee performance with Executive Director Lourdes Iglesias. Cole-Rivera sent Cruz-Moore a responsive text questioning whether she really "wanted Lourdes to know . . . how u feel we don't do our job. . . ." From her home, and

---

contact information referenced in emails, we agree with the judge that there is no merit to the Respondent's argument that it was entitled to the information because these individuals were "potential witnesses" who might have relevant information about the case. The redacted information includes nondiscoverable information gathered by the Board agent during his investigation, and the request constituted further "fishing" for potentially relevant evidence.

[3] The Respondent has excepted to some of the judge's credibility findings. The Board's established policy is not to overrule an administrative law judge's credibility findings unless the clear preponderance of all the relevant evidence convinces us that they are incorrect. *Standard Dry Wall Products*, 91 NLRB 544 (1950), enfd. 188 F.3d 362 (3d Cir. 1951). We have carefully examined the record and find no basis for reversing the findings.

[4] For the reasons stated by the judge, we adopt his analysis and conclusion that the Board properly asserted jurisdiction over the Respondent.

[5] *Meyers Industries*, 268 NLRB 493 (1983)(*Meyers I*), remanded sub nom. *Prill v. NLRB*, 755 F.2d 941 (D.C. Cir. 1985), cert. denied 474 U.S. 948 (1985), supplemented 281 NLRB 882 (1986)(*Meyers II*), affd. sub nom. *Prill v. NLRB*, 835 F.2d 1481 (D.C. Cir. 1987), cert. denied 487 U.S. 1205 (1988).

359 NLRB No. 37

Box 7.9   *(continued)*

2   DECISIONS OF THE NATIONAL LABOR RELATIONS BOARD

using her own personal computer, Cole-Rivera then posted the following message on her Facebook page:

> Lydia Cruz, a coworker feels that we don't help our clients enough at [Respondent]. I about had it! My fellow coworkers how do u feel?

Four off-duty employees—Damicela Rodriguez, Ludimar Rodriguez, Yaritza Campos, and Carlos Ortiz—responded by posting messages, via their personal computers, on Cole-Rivera's Facebook page; the employees' responses generally objected to the assertion that their work performance was substandard.

Cruz-Moore also responded, demanding that Cole-Rivera "stop with ur lies about me." She then complained to Iglesias about the Facebook comments, stating that she had been slandered and defamed. At Iglesias' request, Cruz-Moore printed all the Facebook comments and had the printout delivered to Iglesias. On October 12, the first workday after the Facebook postings, Iglesias discharged Cole-Rivera and her four coworkers,[6] stating that their remarks constituted "bullying and harassment" of a coworker and violated the Respondent's "zero tolerance" policy prohibiting such conduct.[7]

In *Meyers I*, the Board held that the discipline or discharge of an employee violates Section 8(a)(1) if the following four elements are established: (1) the activity engaged in by the employee was "concerted" within the meaning of Section 7 of the Act; (2) the employer knew of the concerted nature of the employee's activity; (3) the concerted activity was protected by the Act; and (4) the discipline or discharge was motivated by the employee's protected, concerted activity. 268 NLRB at 497. See also *Correctional Medical Services*, 356 NLRB No. 48, slip op. at 2 (2010). Only the first and third elements are in dispute here: whether the employees' Facebook comments constituted concerted activity and, if so, whether that activity was protected by the Act.[8]

The Board first defined concerted activity in *Meyers I* as that which is "engaged in with or on the authority of other employees, and not solely by and on behalf of the employee himself." 268 NLRB at 497. In *Meyers II*, the Board expanded this definition to include those "circumstances where individual employees seek to initiate or to induce or to prepare for group action, as well as individual employees bringing truly group complaints to the attention of management." 281 NLRB at 887.

Applying these principles, as the judge did, there should be no question that the activity engaged in by the five employees was concerted for the "purpose of mutual aid or protection" as required by Section 7. As set forth in her initial Facebook post, Cole-Rivera alerted fellow employees of another employee's complaint that they "don't help our clients enough," stated that she "about had it" with the complaints, and solicited her coworkers' views about this criticism. By responding to this solicitation with comments of protest, Cole-Rivera's four coworkers made common cause with her, and, together, their actions were concerted within the definition of *Meyers I*, because they were undertaken "with . . . other employees." 268 NLRB at 497. The actions of the five employees were also concerted under the expanded definition of *Meyers II*, because, as the judge found, they "were taking a first step towards taking group action to defend themselves against the accusations they could reasonably believe Cruz-Moore was going to make to management."[9]

Our dissenting colleague contends that the employees' Facebook discussions about Cruz-Moore's criticisms were not undertaken for the purpose of their "mutual aid and protection." Specifically, he states that a group action defense to Cruz-Moore's criticisms could not have been intended because Cole-Rivera failed to tell her co-

---

[6] The judge noted that Jessica Rivera, Iglesias' secretary, was not discharged even though she also posted a responsive Facebook comment. The Respondent excepts, stating that it no longer employed Rivera at the time of the discharges. The record, however, shows otherwise.

[7] Although Cruz-Moore informed Iglesias on October 10 that she had suffered a heart attack as a result of the Facebook comments, the judge found that there was no record evidence of a heart attack, nor was there any evidence establishing a causal relationship between the comments and Cruz-Moore's health. In addition, although Iglesias informed the five employees when discharging them that they were responsible for Cruz-Moore's heart attack, we agree with the judge that Iglesias had no reasonable basis for making that statement.

[8] The Respondent does not, and could not, deny that it knew of the concerted nature of the employees' action, as Iglesias showed the five employees printouts of their October 10 Facebook comments during their discharge interviews. See, e.g., *Dresser-Rand Co.*, 358 NLRB

No. 34, slip op. at 26 (2012) (the "most obvious evidence" of employer knowledge was respondent's possession of a voice recording containing evidence of concerted activity). With respect to the fourth element, the judge found and the Respondent agrees that the Facebook postings were the sole reason for the discharges. Because this is a single-motive case where there is no dispute as to the activity for which discipline was imposed, the dual-motive analysis set forth in *Wright Line*, 251 NLRB 1083 (1980), enfd. 662 F.2d 899 (1st Cir. 1981), cert. denied 455 U.S. 989 (1982), is not applicable. See, e.g., *Dresser-Rand Co.*, 358 NLRB No. 97, slip op. at 25 (2012); *Nor-Cal Beverage Co.*, 330 NLRB 610, 611 (2000).

[9] The Acting General Counsel cross-excepts to the judge's failure to find—based on Cole-Rivera's testimony, corroborated by Damicela Rodriguez—that Cole-Rivera also intended to meet with Iglesias about Cruz-Moore's criticisms of employees. Because the group action objective of the Facebook postings was demonstrated, in part, by Cole-Rivera's knowledge that Cruz-Moore intended to meet with Iglesias about her workplace complaints, we find it unnecessary to address and resolve the Acting General Counsel's argument that Cole-Rivera also intended to meet with Iglesias about the issue.

Box 7.9   (continued)

HISPANICS UNITED OF BUFFALO, INC.   3

workers that Cruz-Moore was going to voice her criticisms to Iglesias. We disagree.

In *Relco Locomotives, Inc.*, 358 NLRB No. 37, slip op. at 17 (2012), the Board reiterated established precedent that the "object or goal of initiating, inducing or preparing for group action does not have to be stated explicitly when employees communicate," citing *Whittaker Corp.*, 289 NLRB 933, 933 (1988). Even absent an express announcement about the object of an employee's activity, "a concerted objective may be inferred from a variety of circumstances in which employees might discuss or seek to address concerns about working conditions . . . ." Id. Relying on this authority, the Board in *Relco* found unlawful the discharge of two employees for discussing among themselves and other employees their "concern" about the rumored discharge of a fellow employee. Notwithstanding that the two never "talk[ed] specifically about working together to address their concerns about [the employee's] termination," the Board adopted the judge's finding that they "engaged in concerted activities when they communicated with other employees about their concern . . .[and i]t matter[ed] not that [they] had not yet taken their concerns to management—their discussions with coworkers were indispensable initial steps along the way to possible group action" Id., slip op. at 17.

Here, too, Cole-Rivera's Facebook communication with her fellow employees, immediately after learning that Cruz-Moore planned to complain about her coworkers to Iglesias, had the clear "mutual aid" objective of preparing her coworkers for a group defense to those complaints. Contrary to our colleague, Cole-Rivera was not required under *Relco* to discuss this object with coworkers or tell them it was made necessary by Cruz-Moore's impending visit with Iglesias. Her "mutual aid" object of preparing her coworkers for group action was implicitly manifest from the surrounding circumstances. *Timekeeping Systems, Inc.*, 323 NLRB 244, 248 (1997).[10]

As to the third element of the violation, whether the employees' concerted activity was protected, we find that the Facebook comments here fall well within the Act's protection. The Board has long held that Section 7 protects employee discussions about their job performance,[11] and the Facebook comments plainly centered on that subject. As discussed, the employees were directly re-

sponding to allegations they were providing substandard service to the Respondent's clients. Given the negative impact such criticisms could have on their employment, the five employees were clearly engaged in protected activity in mutual aid of each other's defense to those criticisms.[12]

The Respondent does not argue that the employees' comments were unprotected because they were made via Facebook. To the contrary, the Respondent asserts that, "regardless of where the comments and actions of the five terminated at-will employees took place, the result herein would have been the same." According to Respondent, it was privileged to discharge the five employees because their comments constituted unprotected harassment and bullying of Cruz-Moore, in violation of its "zero tolerance" policy. The judge rejected this argument, and so do we.

First, as the judge found, the Facebook comments cannot reasonably be construed as a form of harassment or bullying within the meaning of the Respondent's policy.[13] Second, even assuming that the policy covered the comments, the Respondent could not lawfully apply its policy "without reference to Board law." *Consolidated Diesel Co.*, 332 NLRB 1019, 1020 (2000), enfd. 263 F.3d 345 (4th Cir. 2001). As the Board explained in *Consolidated Diesel*, "legitimate managerial concerns to prevent harassment do not justify policies that discourage the free exercise of Section 7 rights by subjecting employees to . . . discipline on the basis of the subjective reactions of others to their protected activity." Id. Here, as in *Consolidated Diesel*, the Respondent applied its harassment policy to the discharged employees based solely on Cruz-Moore's subjective claim (in a text message) that she felt offended by the Facebook comments. As the United States Court of Appeals for the Fourth Circuit noted in enforcing the Board's decision, "[s]uch a wholly subjective notion of harassment is unknown to the Act," 263 F.3d 354, and discipline imposed on this basis violates Section 8(a)(1).

---

[10] *Daly Park Nursing Home*, 287 NLRB 710 (1987), relied on by our colleague, bears no resemblance to this case. Rather than preparing for group action in that case, employee Heard and her coworkers essentially agreed that group action in aid of a terminated fellow employee would be futile.

[11] *Praxair Distribution, Inc.*, 357 NLRB No. 91, slip op. at 11 (2011); *Jhirmack Enterprises*, 283 NLRB 609 fn. 2 (1987).

---

[12] In affirming the judge's finding that the employees' activity was protected, we find it unnecessary to rely on his analysis under *Atlantic Steel Co.*, 245 NLRB 814 (1979). That analysis typically applies when determining whether activity that is initially protected has been rendered unprotected by subsequent misconduct. See, e.g., *Crowne Plaza LaGuardia*, 357 NLRB No. 95 (2011). Here, however, where the Respondent contends that the Facebook postings were unprotected from the outset, an *Atlantic Steel* analysis is unnecessary.

[13] As found by the judge, there was no evidence that any of the five employees harassed Cruz-Moore by their comments, or that any purported harassment was covered by the zero tolerance policy, which refers to "race, color, sex, religion, national origin, age, disability, veteran status, or other prohibited basis."

Box 7.9   *(continued)*

In sum, because we have found that the Facebook postings were concerted and protected, and because it is undisputed that the Respondent discharged the five employees based solely on their postings, we conclude that the discharges violated Section 8(a)(1).

ORDER

The National Labor Relations Board adopts the recommended Order of the administrative law judge and orders that the Respondent, Hispanics United of Buffalo, Inc., Buffalo, New York, its officers, agents, successors, and assigns, shall take the action set forth in the Order.

Dated, Washington, D.C. December 14, 2012

Mark Gaston Pearce,	Chairman

Richard F. Griffin, Jr.,	Member

Sharon Block,	Member

(SEAL)   NATIONAL LABOR RELATIONS BOARD

MEMBER HAYES, dissenting.

I agree with my colleagues and the judge that *Meyers Industries*[1] and its progeny control in determining whether the Respondent violated Section 8(a)(1) of the Act by discharging five employees for their Facebook postings about a coworker's criticisms of their work. Correctly applied, however, the *Meyers* test mandates dismissal of the complaint. This is so because "[i]n order for employee conduct to fall within the ambit of Section 7, it must be both concerted and engaged in for the purpose of 'mutual aid or protection.' These are related but separate elements that the General Counsel must establish in order to show a violation of Section 8(a)(1)."[2] In this case, the colloquy around the Facebook "virtual water cooler" may have been concerted, in the sense that it was actual group activity, but the Acting General Counsel has failed utterly to prove that it was activity undertaken for "mutual aid and protection." As a result, I

would find that the Respondent lawfully discharged the employees for their unprotected Facebook comments.[3]

Not all shop talk among employees—whether in-person, telephonic, or on the internet—is concerted within the meaning of Section 7, even if it focuses on a condition of employment.[4] With respect to the second element of the Acting General Counsel's burden, the *Meyers* test expressly incorporates the requirement of *Mushroom Transportation Co. v. NLRB*, 330 F.2d 683 (3d Cir. 1964), that for conversations among employees to fall within the definition of concerted activity protected by Section 7 "it must appear at the very least that it was engaged in with the object of initiating or inducing or preparing for group action or that it had some relation to group action in the interest of the employees."[5] Absent evidence of a nexus to group action, such conversations are mere griping, which the Act does not protect.

Here, the group griping on Facebook was not protected concerted activity because there is insufficient evidence that either the original posting or the views expressed in response to it were for mutual aid or protection. Specifically, in her initial Facebook post, Marianna Cole-Rivera informed her coworkers that Lydia Cruz-Moore had complained that "we don't help our clients enough," and solicited her coworkers' views about this criticism. Four coworkers posted responses on Cole-Rivera's Facebook page, generally objecting to Cruz-Moore's claims that their work performance was deficient. Cole-Rivera posted another comment, essentially agreeing with her coworkers' posts. Subsequent posts diverged to discussion of a party planned for that evening.

My colleagues find that the employees' conduct was concerted because, in responding to Cole-Rivera's initial Facebook post, her four coworkers made "common cause" with her. They did not. As previously stated, the mere fact that the subject of discussion involved an aspect of employment—i.e., job performance—is not enough to find concerted activity for mutual aid and protection. There is a meaningful distinction between sharing a common viewpoint and joining in a common cause. Only the latter involves group action for mutual aid and protection. While the Facebook posts evidenced the employees' mutual disagreement with Cruz-Moore's criticism of their job performance, the employees did not

---

[1] *Meyers Industries*, 268 NLRB 493 (1983)(*Meyers I*), remanded sub nom. *Prill v. NLRB*, 755 F.2d 941 (D.C. Cir. 1985), cert. denied 474 U.S. 948 (1985), supplemented 281 NLRB 882 (1986)(*Meyers II*), affd. sub nom. *Prill v. NLRB*, 835 F.2d 1481 (D.C. Cir. 1987), cert. denied 487 U.S. 1205 (1988).

[2] *Hollings Press, Inc.*, 343 NLRB 301, 302 (2004).

[3] For purposes of this opinion, I assume, arguendo, that the judge correctly found the Board has jurisdiction over the Respondent.

[4] See, e.g. *Adelphi Institute, Inc.*, 287 NLRB 1073, 1074 (1988).

[5] 330 F.2d at 685.

requirements to ensure that all parties receive due process of law. For example, an agency may have the authority to decide a dispute based only on written submissions from the parties, without providing the opportunity for a live hearing before an ALJ. Even though these kinds of decisions do not use court-like procedures, they still result in decisions that have the force of law.

Formal and informal agency decisions, like agency regulations, are subject to judicial review. The organic statute creating the agency typically specifies whether the review begins in a district or appellate court. In some situations, it may be possible to introduce new facts before the court that were not introduced before the agency; usually this is not permitted. In the typical situation, the court's review of agency action looks more like an appellate proceeding, with the facts fixed during the agency proceedings. The issues before a reviewing court often are limited to whether there is substantial evidence in the record to support the agency's decision, whether the agency has exceeded its statutory authority or failed to follow required procedures, and whether the agency has abused its discretion.

Researching Decisions and Orders

Agency decisions involve legal issues governed by statutes and possibly regulations. Thus, these sources of law should be included in your research in agency decisions. As you read the organic statute for the agency, you should look for a description of the agency's authority to adjudicate and the process that the agency must follow, including any substantive standards governing the issue. Also, research regulations that may apply to the issue.

Some agencies publish their decisions in print reporters, others in databases made available through public websites, and others in a combination of the two. A standard pattern is that recent decisions are available on the websites and older ones are available in print. Furthermore, agency decisions appear in the commercial resources Bloomberg Law, HeinOnline, Lexis, and Westlaw. As with regulations, however, it is often best to start with the free online materials that are already provided to you by the government.

You should read administrative orders as carefully as you would a judicial case. As with judicial cases, you should look for the outcome of the decision, discern the rule used by the agency to decide the case, understand the facts of the case and the agency's reasoning about those facts, identify the leading authorities cited in the reasoning, and examine any dissenting and concurring opinions.

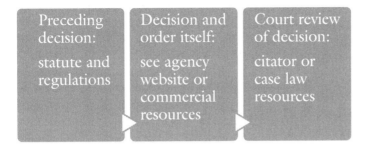

| Preceding decision: statute and regulations | Decision and order itself: see agency website or commercial resources | Court review of decision: citator or case law resources |

As with judicial cases, the law made through agency decisions evolves over time. Later agency decisions may affect the validity of an earlier agency decision in various ways (e.g., overruling, modifying, distinguishing, and citing with approval). As noted previously, agency decisions are appealable to courts, so a necessary step is to cite the decision in question to ascertain whether it has been reviewed on appeal and, if so, to what effect. The standard tools for citing agency decisions are the same as for citing cases: KeyCite on Westlaw and Shepard's on Lexis.

For example, the NLRB has published its decisions for many years in a print reporter system, *Decisions and Orders of the National Labor Relations Board*, accompanied by a finely detailed classification outline and digest. Now, the NLRB website provides the Board's decisions, including ALJ recommendations, online, along with various ways to find them.

When researching the Exact Electronics request for information on social media policy, we went to the NLRB website. We went to the online version of the classification outline (CiteNet) and selected *employer interference with employee section 7 rights*, which we already knew to be a legal principle that protects employees' ability to communicate with each other (even in a non-union setting). We then entered the search term *social media* and obtained the pertinent subtopic, *use of social media*. Clicking on that link and *Board* (for decisions of the NLRB rather than ALJs) brought us to digests of NLRB decisions regarding employee use of social media. See Box 7.10. Through this method, we located the *Hispanics United* case featured in Box 7.9.

Box 7.10   **AGENCY WEBSITE DIGESTS OF DECISIONS (Social Media Policy)**

Classified Index - The Electronic Network

Skip Navigation   Comments   Using CiteNet (video)

NLRB.GOV   Banner   Search Heading   Search Digest   Search Case Name   User Guide

Classification Digest Search Results
Criteria: 512501267300000: Decision Type B
Total Found: 75

Do Search Within Search	View CiteNet Abbreviations

List All Results in new window (this will allow you to view and/or print the entire list)

FIRST   BACK   NEXT   LAST

512-5012-6730-0000 Use of social media

Digest: [E's discharge of 5 Ees for Facebook comments they wrote in response to a coworker's criticisms of their job performance, unlawful; applying "Meyers Industries," 268 NLRB 493 (1983), Bd analyzes the 2 "Meyers" factors at issue here: whether the Ees' Facebook comments constituted concerted activity, and, if so, whether that activity was protected by Act; Bd finds Ees' conduct was concerted for purpose of "mutual aid or protection" as required by Act; first Ee's initial post to Facebook alerted her fellow Ees to a coworker's complaints about their work, and by responding to this post with comments of protest, her fellow Ees made common cause with her, and, together, their actions were concerted because they were undertaken with other Ees; Ees' actions were also concerted under "Meyers II," 281 NLRB 882 (1986), because they were taking a first step towards taking group action to defend themselves against accusations they could reasonably believe the coworker was going to make to E]

Case Name: Hispanics United of Buffalo, Inc.

Case Number: 03-CA-027872 **Decision Date:**December 14, 2012

Type: Board   **Citation Number:** 359 NLRB No. 037

Members: PGB   **Tracking ID:** 2013-3

FIRST   BACK   NEXT   LAST

NLRB.GOV   BANNER   SEARCH HEADING   SEARCH DIGEST   SEARCH CASE   USER GUIDE   ABBREVIATIONS

INTERPRETIVE RULES AND OTHER GUIDANCE MATERIALS

Legislative regulations and decisions and orders issued by agencies are primary authority, just as statutes and case law are. Agencies also create additional types of quasi-authoritative materials that, although not binding in a legal sense, are vital to understanding how an agency interprets the law. They may carry significant weight with courts interpreting the law.

One type of quasi-authoritative material is a rule known in administrative law parlance as an *interpretive* or *nonlegislative rule*; unlike legislative regulations, it does not make law but rather expresses the agency's interpretation of the statute it administers. Other quasi-authoritative materials do not take the form of rules or cases at all. A classic example is a *guidance memo,* in which an authoritative agency official explains how he or she interprets regulations or statutes without actually applying them to specific situations. Another example is the agency *advice letter,* in which the agency responds to questions about a specific factual situation without actually adjudicating the outcome in a binding way. Yet another example is an agency's *internal procedures manual,* used by agency staff in conducting official inspections.

Because these materials are not themselves law, guidance materials are not as readily or consistently available as regulations and decisions. Your best resource is usually the agency's website, perhaps followed up with a call to an agency official.

When we researched the Exact Electronics issue about social media policy, we found on the NLRB website a report from the NLRB's general counsel. In it, the general counsel summarized recent decisions analyzing various employers' social media policies, including one that it found lawful. The document was addressed to his staff, but it also proved very helpful to employers seeking to avoid charges under the NLRA. See Box 7.11.

Box 7.11   **GUIDANCE DOCUMENT (Social Media Policy)**

REPORT OF THE GENERAL COUNSEL

In August 2011 and in January 2012, I issued reports
presenting case developments arising in the context of
today's social media. Employee use of social media as it
relates to the workplace continues to increase, raising
various concerns by employers, and in turn, resulting in
employers' drafting new and/or revising existing policies
and rules to address these concerns. These policies and
rules cover such topics as the use of social media and
electronic technologies, confidentiality, privacy,
protection of employer information, intellectual property,
and contact with the media and government agencies.

My previous reports touched on some of these policies
and rules, and they are the sole focus of this report, which
discusses seven recent cases. In the first six cases, I
have concluded that at least some of the provisions in the
employers' policies and rules are overbroad and thus
unlawful under the National Labor Relations Act. In the
last case, I have concluded that the entire social media
policy, as revised, is lawful under the Act, and I have
attached this complete policy. I hope that this report,
with its specific examples of various employer policies and
rules, will provide additional guidance in this area.

_____/s/_____
Lafe E. Solomon
Acting General Counsel

2

Box 7.11 *(continued)*

As explained above, rules that are ambiguous as to their application to Section 7 activity and that contain no limiting language or context to clarify that the rules do not restrict Section 7 rights are unlawful. In contrast, rules that clarify and restrict their scope by including examples of clearly illegal or unprotected conduct, such that they could not reasonably be construed to cover protected activity, are not unlawful.

Applying these principles, we concluded that the Employer's revised social media policy is not ambiguous because it provides sufficient examples of prohibited conduct so that, in context, employees would not reasonably read the rules to prohibit Section 7 activity. For instance, the Employer's rule prohibits "inappropriate postings that may include discriminatory remarks, harassment and threats of violence or similar inappropriate or unlawful conduct." We found this rule lawful since it prohibits plainly egregious conduct, such as discrimination and threats of violence, and there is no evidence that the Employer has used the rule to discipline Section 7 activity.

Similarly, we found lawful the portion of the Employer's social media policy entitled "Be Respectful." In certain contexts, the rule's exhortation to be respectful and "fair and courteous" in the posting of comments, complaints, photographs, or videos, could be overly broad. The rule, however, provides sufficient examples of plainly egregious conduct so that employees would not reasonably construe the rule to prohibit Section 7 conduct. For instance, the rule counsels employees to avoid posts that "could be viewed as malicious, obscene, threatening or intimidating." It further explains that prohibited "harassment or bullying" would include "offensive posts meant to intentionally harm someone's reputation" or "posts that could contribute to a hostile work environment on the basis of race, sex, disability, religion or any other status protected by law or company policy." The Employer has a legitimate basis to prohibit such workplace communications, and has done so without burdening protected communications about terms and conditions of employment.

We also found that the Employer's rule requiring employees to maintain the confidentiality of the Employer's trade secrets and private and confidential information is not unlawful. Employees have no protected right to disclose trade secrets. Moreover, the Employer's rule provides sufficient examples of prohibited disclosures (i.e., information regarding the development of systems, processes, products, know-how, technology, internal reports, procedures, or other internal business-related communications) for employees to understand that it does not reach protected communications about working conditions. [Walmart, Case 11-CA-067171]

20

Box 7.11   *(continued)*

Social Media Policy

Updated: May 4, 2012

At [Employer], we understand that social media can be a fun and rewarding way to share your life and opinions with family, friends and co-workers around the world. However, use of social media also presents certain risks and carries with it certain responsibilities. To assist you in making responsible decisions about your use of social media, we have established these guidelines for appropriate use of social media.

This policy applies to all associates who work for [Employer], or one of its subsidiary companies in the United States ([Employer]).

Managers and supervisors should use the supplemental Social Media Management Guidelines for additional guidance in administering the policy.

GUIDELINES

In the rapidly expanding world of electronic communication, *social media* can mean many things. *Social media* includes all means of communicating or posting information or content of any sort on the Internet, including to your own or someone else's web log or blog, journal or diary, personal web site, social networking or affinity web site, web bulletin board or a chat room, whether or not associated or affiliated with [Employer], as well as any other form of electronic communication.

The same principles and guidelines found in [Employer] policies and three basic beliefs apply to your activities online. Ultimately, you are solely responsible for what you post online. Before creating online content, consider some of the risks and rewards that are involved. Keep in mind that any of your conduct that adversely affects your job performance, the performance of fellow associates or otherwise adversely affects members, customers, suppliers, people who work on behalf of [Employer] or [Employer's] legitimate business interests may result in disciplinary action up to and including termination.

Know and follow the rules

Carefully read these guidelines, the [Employer] Statement of Ethics Policy, the [Employer] Information Policy and the Discrimination & Harassment Prevention Policy, and ensure your postings are consistent with these policies. Inappropriate postings that may include discriminatory remarks, harassment, and threats of violence or similar inappropriate or unlawful conduct will not be tolerated and may subject you to disciplinary action up to and including termination.

Be respectful

Always be fair and courteous to fellow associates, customers, members, suppliers or people who work on behalf of [Employer]. Also, keep in mind that you are more likely to resolved work-related complaints by speaking directly with your co-workers or by utilizing our Open Door Policy than by posting complaints to a social media outlet. Nevertheless, if you decide to post complaints or criticism, avoid using statements, photographs, video or audio that reasonably

Box 7.11   *(continued)*

could be viewed as malicious, obscene, threatening or intimidating, that disparage customers, members, associates or suppliers, or that might constitute harassment or bullying. Examples of such conduct might include offensive posts meant to intentionally harm someone's reputation or posts that could contribute to a hostile work environment on the basis of race, sex, disability, religion or any other status protected by law or company policy.

Be honest and accurate

Make sure you are always honest and accurate when posting information or news, and if you make a mistake, correct it quickly. Be open about any previous posts you have altered. Remember that the Internet archives almost everything; therefore, even deleted postings can be searched. Never post any information or rumors that you know to be false about [Employer], fellow associates, members, customers, suppliers, people working on behalf of [Employer] or competitors.

Post only appropriate and respectful content

- Maintain the confidentiality of [Employer] trade secrets and private or confidential information. Trades secrets may include information regarding the development of systems, processes, products, know-how and technology. Do not post internal reports, policies, procedures or other internal business-related confidential communications.
- Respect financial disclosure laws. It is illegal to communicate or give a "tip" on inside information to others so that they may buy or sell stocks or securities. Such online conduct may also violate the Insider Trading Policy.
- Do not create a link from your blog, website or other social networking site to a [Employer] website without identifying yourself as a [Employer] associate.
- Express only your personal opinions. Never represent yourself as a spokesperson for [Employer]. If [Employer] is a subject of the content you are creating, be clear and open about the fact that you are an associate and make it clear that your views do not represent those of [Employer], fellow associates, members, customers, suppliers or people working on behalf of [Employer]. If you do publish a blog or post online related to the work you do or subjects associated with [Employer], make it clear that you are not speaking on behalf of [Employer]. It is best to include a disclaimer such as "The postings on this site are my own and do not necessarily reflect the views of [Employer]."

Using social media at work

Refrain from using social media while on work time or on equipment we provide, unless it is work-related as authorized by your manager or consistent with the Company Equipment Policy. Do not use [Employer] email addresses to register on social networks, blogs or other online tools utilized for personal use.

Retaliation is prohibited

[Employer] prohibits taking negative action against any associate for reporting a possible deviation from this policy or for cooperating in an investigation. Any associate who retaliates against another associate for reporting a possible deviation from this policy or for cooperating in an investigation will be subject to disciplinary action, up to and including termination.

23

BUILD YOUR UNDERSTANDING

Test Your Knowledge

1. What is an agency's organic statute? Why would you research it?

2. Explain how regulations resemble statutes.

3. How do the *Federal Register* and the C.F.R. relate to each other?

4. You are researching a regulation pertinent to a client's case. Order the sources listed here in chronological order, and for each, indicate whether it is a primary authority or not. Also, identify the major publication in which it is published.
   - Codified version
   - Congressional grant of authority to the agency to promulgate the regulation
   - Explanation by the agency
   - Final adoption by the agency
   - Judicial review of the regulation
   - Public comments
   - Notice of Proposed Rulemaking

5. How does formal adjudication resemble court litigation?

6. If you have found a pertinent agency decision and order, what other sources of law are likely to also be involved in forming the complete rule of law controlling your client's situation?

7. List at least three types of quasi-authoritative materials created by administrative agencies. If these are not actually law, why are they useful to research?

Put It into Practice

Recall your client's situation (detailed in Chapter 1 at pages 20-21): Your client, Emmet Wilson, is a veteran who has developed post-traumatic stress disorder (PTSD). Among other treatments, he has been assigned a therapy dog. Mr. Wilson's landlord has raised concerns because the building is a no-pets building. Indeed, the lease (which is for a year) so specifies, and the landlord says that other tenants have raised the issue. So she has given Mr. Wilson notice that if he does not give up the dog, he will be evicted in a month.

For the following questions, focus on the federal Fair Housing Act, which is administered by the Department of Housing and Urban Development (HUD).

1. Find the section or sections in the Fair Housing Act that indicate (1) whether HUD may (or must) promulgate regulations to implement the Fair Housing Act and (2) how it is to handle individual instances of

housing discrimination. Explain what you found, and cite the pertinent section or sections.

2. In e-CFR, find the current regulation identifying what *mental impairment* means for the purposes of the nondiscrimination provision of the Fair Housing Act.
   a. Explain how you located that section.
   b. Provide the precise citation.
   c. Quote the language that pertains to Mr. Wilson's situation.
   d. Note the *Federal Register* citations pertaining to that section.

3. To learn the backstory of the regulation, find and read the materials in the *Federal Register* that accompanied the pertinent language when it was finally adopted. Do the comments add anything to your understanding of the regulation? Explain.

4. To enrich your understanding of HUD's approach to the issue of service animals, proceed to the HUD website and to the Fair Housing and Equal Opportunity program page. Search for documents addressing disability discrimination and service animals. Provide the title of any pertinent document that you find, and summarize the information that it provides.

Make Connections

Try to identify at least five federal or state agencies that have an impact on your daily life. Is it desirable to have agencies make law in those areas through the processes described here, in addition to the lawmaking of legislatures through enacting statutes and courts through deciding cases? Explain.

Answers to Test Your Knowledge Questions

1. An organic statute is the law that creates the agency. Regulations as well as decisions and orders must conform to it. Also, you should find useful references when you read an organic statute in an annotated code.

2. Like statutes, regulations are generally applicable laws that are adopted after a public, deliberative process. They may be amended. They are codified in a topical arrangement (in the C.F.R.).

3. The *Federal Register* is a chronological record of the activity of federal agencies, containing not only adopted regulations but also proposed regulations and explanations of adopted regulations. The C.F.R. is a topically organized code of federal regulations currently in effect.

4. The documents, listed in sequence with their categories and publications where appropriate, are:
   - Congressional grant of authority to the agency to promulgate the regulations — primary; statutory code
   - Notice of Proposed Rulemaking — not primary; *Federal Register*
   - Public comments — not primary; agency record and summarized in *Federal Register*
   - Explanation by the agency — not primary; *Federal Register*
   - Final adoption by the agency — primary; *Federal Register*
   - Codified version–primary; C.F.R.
   - Judicial review of the regulation — primary; case reporters

5. As with court litigation, formal adjudication involves rules of procedure, testimony and documents, and written and oral arguments in a sort of trial before an administrative law judge, who renders a written decision and recommended outcome. Furthermore, agency decisions and orders are sometimes reviewed by appellate courts.

6. If you have found a pertinent agency decision and order, it is most likely the case that the organic statute, probably a regulation, other decisions from the agency, and possibly judicial case law as well will combine to form the complete rule of law.

7. Quasi-authoritative materials created by administrative agencies include interpretive rules, advisory letters, guidance memos, and internal procedures manuals. All of these reflect how the agency thinks about the law that it administers and may be given credence by the courts.

BEYOND U.S. LAW

TRIBAL LAW AND INTERNATIONAL LAW

The law that controls activities in the United States is, in some situations, broader than that covered in the preceding chapters. In some situations, the law of American Indian tribes — separate sovereignties located in various areas around the United States — comes into play. In other situations, international law controls.

American Indian Tribal Law
by Prof. Sarah Deer[1]

One complex dimension of American legal research is how to research laws for the various tribes existing in the United States. Over 560 indigenous tribal nations are recognized by the U.S. government. These tribal nations have existed on the North American continent for thousands of years and therefore predate the United States. Tribal governments retain limited forms of legal independence under the U.S. legal system; each tribal nation retains its own capacity as a self-governing entity.

Tribal nations have a wide range of demographics and circumstances. In terms of population, the smallest tribe has less than fifty citizens. The largest tribes have over 200,000 citizens. There are dozens of distinct cultural groups, languages, and legal traditions represented among the many tribes. Some tribal governments still operate under ancient traditional governance structures. Other tribal governments have a contemporary structure identical to most state governments. Most tribal governments, however, are hybrid systems that include components from both tribal and Western (Anglo-American) legal traditions. Each tribal nation has an independent government, and most operate a tribal court.

Many people in the United States (including lawyers) are not familiar with tribal governments or tribal courts. This is likely because indigenous people

---

1. For more detail, consult Justin B. Richland & Sarah Deer, *Introduction to Tribal Legal Studies* (3d ed. 2015).

make up a very small portion of the overall population. However, tribal courts have become more prominent in recent years and are growing in strength and visibility. For this reason, a comprehensive approach to legal research in the United States should include basic information on tribal law.

There are two major categories of Indian law: *federal Indian law* (the law governing the relationship between tribal governments and the U.S. government) and *tribal law* (the internal laws of individual tribal governments).

Federal Indian Law

Federal Indian law has an extraordinarily complicated set of statutes and case law that govern the extent of tribal legal authority. This brief summary cannot cover all of the complex rules. An example of an issue of federal Indian law is this increasingly common situation: A tribal government is planning to form a contract with a privately owned business to develop a new business on tribal land. Because the title to the tribal land is legally held in trust by the federal government, the privately owned business needs to negotiate a contract that will be approved by the federal government.

Federal Indian law is reasonably accessible to the legal researcher but complex due to the many different agencies that may be involved with Indian issues. The U.S. Code has a specific title governing federal Indian law, Title 25, but Indian law issues arise in a variety of other contexts. There are also specific administrative agencies that implement much of the statutory law pertaining to tribal governments. For example, the Department of the Interior includes the Bureau of Indian Affairs, a subagency of which administers much of the relationship between the United States and tribal governments. All of these federal agencies have publicly accessible websites, including all of the applicable statutes and regulations.

The U.S. Supreme Court is the final arbiter on federal Indian law, and there are a number of crucial decisions that form the foundation for the relationship between the United States and tribal governments. Decisions dating back to the early 1800s still have significant relevance today. For this reason, legal research in Indian law usually requires historical research.

The most well-known legal treatise on Indian law is *Cohen's Handbook of Federal Indian Law*, which was most recently updated in 2012; it is published by LexisNexis and available in a Lexis online database. Another very helpful book is *American Indian Law in a Nutshell*, written by Judge William C. Canby, Jr. of the Ninth Circuit (published by West Academic); the sixth edition was released in 2015. These two resources can serve as starting points for the newcomer to federal Indian law. HeinOnline has an American Indian Law Collection, which contains over 1,000 titles spanning from the eighteenth century to the twenty-first century.

TRIBAL LAW

An example of an issue arising in tribal law is the following: Two tribal citizens are seeking a divorce in tribal court. They are having a dispute about custody of their children. The tribal judge has determined that the custody matter should be referred to a respected tribal elder who has traditional spiritual authority in times of conflict.

Tribal courts are difficult to generalize about due to the number and variety of legal structures. However, there are some common philosophical differences between indigenous legal theory and Anglo-American legal theory. Tribal laws tend to be more community-based than individual-based. Tribal criminal law is usually based on reparations rather than on punishment. Tribal legal procedure is more likely to be collaborative than adversarial. These qualities are not universal, however. Many tribal courts operate under typical Anglo-American structures and legal principles.

Another common difference is the appellate process. Most tribal governments have only one appellate court rather than two. In addition, some tribal courts rely on an inter-tribal court of appeals, which is a collaborative appellate court established by agreement by the tribal governments. The inter-tribal courts are particularly useful for very small tribes. Since tribal caseloads are typically much smaller than those of state and federal courts, the appellate infrastructure is not as complicated.

A case that arises in tribal court will be controlled first and foremost by the tribal government's own laws. Tribal courts may consider and consult laws from other tribes, the states, and the federal government in deciding cases, but usually they are not bound by decisions other than those issued by the highest court of the tribal government. Tribal judges must also be aware of important federal Indian law cases that delineate the scope and reach of tribal government power. In certain circumstances, a party that is not satisfied with the decision at the highest court of a tribal government may be able to bring an action in federal court, where the tribal court decisions may be scrutinized using federal Indian law cases.

Researching tribal law requires more time and preparation than researching other areas of U.S. law. The main reason is that there is no centralized comprehensive electronic database of tribal laws. Each tribe publishes laws, regulations, and cases differently.

The oldest Indian law case reporter is the *Indian Law Reporter*, which contains tribal court opinions dating back to the 1970s. It is available in print only in most academic law libraries. In 2009, West introduced *West's American Tribal Law Reporter* in print and a tribal law database, both containing laws and cases from a few tribes. Another resource is the National Indian Law Library (NILL), which is part of the Native American Rights Fund, based in Boulder, Colorado. NILL collects and catalogs tribal constitutions, laws, regulations, and cases and makes them available free of charge. Some of its catalog is available online, but some of the materials remain offline due to requests of the tribes. NILL has a very useful website at www.narf.org/nill/, which is constantly updated with new material.

Most tribal courts have a court clerk or a court judge who can usually provide an overview of where to find tribal law specific to that tribe. It may or may not be digital and searchable. Impoverished tribes may not have the infrastructure to digitize and post their laws and cases online. Fortunately, the federal government has been providing funding to some tribes to help them with the process of making tribal law more accessible to everyone.[2]

More traditional tribal courts sometimes incorporate tribal customary law or oral tradition, which may or may not be codified in written form. In these unusual cases, performing tribal legal research might be especially difficult. Some tribal law may be accessed only through ceremony, song, or prayer by the people of that community. An example of this kind of court is the Navajo Peacemaking Court system, which relies on traditional spiritual leaders to resolve a dispute and heal relationships that have been damaged through conflict. Lawyers are typically not allowed in these sessions.

Public International Law
by Prof. Anthony S. Winer

The first thing to realize is that there is a distinction between foreign law, public international law, and private international law. This part focuses on researching in the second of these areas, public international law. Nonetheless, the chapter opens with a discussion of foreign law and closes with private international law.

FOREIGN LAW

The phrase *foreign law* refers to a country's law or legal system — *domestic law* — other than that of the person using the phrase. So, to a legal researcher located in the United States who is practicing law in the United States, the domestic law of France, China, or Peru (or any other non-U.S. country) would be foreign law. However, to a legal researcher in France, China, or Peru, the domestic law of the United States would be foreign law.

Often lawyers in the United States are confronted with a situation involving the domestic law of a country other than the United States. When that happens, the U.S. lawyer is presented with an issue of foreign law, not of international law. In those circumstances, there are several websites and

---

2. For additional resources, see David Selden, *Researching American Indian Tribal Law*, Colo. Law., Feb. 2014, at 51; David Selden & Monica Martens, *Basic Indian Law Research Tips* (2012) at www.narf.org/nill/resources/tribal_law_research_2012.pdf; Bonnie Shucha, *"Whatever Tribal Precedent There May Be": The (Un)availability of Tribal Law*, 106 Law Libr. J. 199 (2014).

other authorities that provide a basic overview of the legal systems of various countries around the world. Among these are:

- The Yale Law School Lillian Goldman Law Library's *Country-by-Country Guide to Foreign Law Research*
- The Harvard Law School Library *Foreign and International Law Gateways*
- The World Law Guide
- The World Legal Information Institute
- The Law Library of Congress

If they wish, lawyers in the United States can consult these websites and other similar authorities to get basic background regarding the law or legal systems in a foreign country with which their clients may be involved. However, the utmost caution is warranted. Most lawyers practicing law in the United States are not educated, trained, or licensed regarding the domestic legal systems of other countries. Unless a lawyer is also educated, trained, and licensed under the domestic law of a foreign country, that lawyer should generally not give advice to U.S. clients regarding any foreign country's law if that advice purports to be thorough, comprehensive, and of the type that the client can rely on.[3] If the client of a U.S. lawyer needs reliable advice on the domestic law of a foreign country, the usual approach is for the U.S. lawyer to obtain for the client competent co-counsel in that country. This, of course, usually involves added time and expense for the client and can be undertaken only with the client's informed consent.

PUBLIC INTERNATIONAL LAW

The phrase *public international law* generally refers to the legal rules affecting the relations of different countries, in this context called "sovereign states" or "states," while acting vis-à-vis one another. So, legal rules involving the creation and enforcement of international treaties, the external use of armed force by states, the law of armed conflict (formerly the law of war), and other similar subjects are all aspects of public international law. Unlike foreign law, public international law does not necessarily concern the domestic law of any particular state. It is instead a legal system that generally operates largely externally to the domestic legal systems of states.

---

3. *See, e.g.,* American Bar Association Model Rule of Professional Conduct 5.5 (stating, *inter alia*, that a lawyer "shall not practice law in a jurisdiction in violation of the regulation of the legal profession in that jurisdiction, or assist another in doing so"). *See also* Comment 1 to Rule 5.5 ("A lawyer may practice law only in a jurisdiction in which the lawyer is authorized to practice."). These provisions do not explicitly address the situation of a U.S. lawyer in the United States practicing the law of a foreign state in violation of the law of that foreign state, but it is clear that such behavior can raise serious ethical issues.

Unlike the situation with foreign law, there is no formal restriction against a U.S. lawyer (educated, trained, and licensed only under the law of a U.S. jurisdiction) from providing advice on public international law.

The sources of public international law are listed in a United Nations (UN) document, the Statute of the International Court of Justice. The International Court of Justice (ICJ), or World Court, is the chief judicial body of the UN. It sits in The Hague, a city that is the seat of government of the Netherlands. The ICJ Statute is the document through which the ICJ was established, along with the UN itself, in 1945. Article 38(1) of the ICJ Statute establishes five types of sources for public international law.[4] These are:

1. International treaties and conventions
2. Customary international law
3. General principles of law
4. Judicial decisions in courts and tribunals
5. Scholastic works of prominent commentators on public international law

The last two types of authority are stated to be a "subsidiary means" for determining rules of public international law. They are, therefore, not primary sources for rules of public international law but rather secondary sources that serve as indirect indications. The extent to which there is a hierarchical relationship among the other three types of sources is itself a subject of interpretation and discussion.

Treaties and Conventions

Treaties are international agreements among states, usually in written form, that the parties intend to be binding.[5] Many international agreements that states enter into have significance only for building mutual foreign relations and are not formal documents with binding effect. It is only when states enter into agreements that they intend to be internationally binding that a treaty is created.

Treaties can be viewed as falling into distinct categories. For example, bilateral treaties (treaties between only two states) can be distinguished from multilateral treaties (treaties among three or more states). Each state that has become party to a multilateral treaty is often called a "state party" to that treaty, while each party to a bilateral treaty is often called a "counterparty." A *convention* is usually a special kind of treaty, generally multilateral, that enunciates new rules of legal conduct for the parties to it. Conventions

---

4. The language of Article 38(1) of the ICJ Statute varies somewhat from the five points stated here, but the presentation of the points here reflects a more conversational vocabulary and more pragmatic arrangement.

5. Vienna Convention on the Law of Treaties art. 2, ¶ (1)(a), May 23, 1969, 1155 U.N.T.S. 331 (entered into force Jan. 27, 1980) [hereinafter "VCLT"]. The VCLT "constitutes the basic framework for any discussion of the nature and characteristics of treaties." Malcolm N. Shaw, *International Law* 655 (7th ed. 2014).

Box 8.1	**MAJOR TREATY RESOURCES**
Organization	**Resources**
United Nations	*United Nations Treaty Series* (UNTS)* United Nations Treaty Collection *League of Nations Treaty Series* (LNTS)*
U.S. Government	*Treaties in Force* (index)* *United States Statutes at Large** *United States Treaties and Other International Agreements** (UST) The Treaty Affairs page of the U.S. State Department website
Unofficial Resources	Bevans and Kavass series* *International Legal Materials* * *American Journal of International Law* *
*Available through HeinOnline, Lexis, or Westlaw.	

are thus sometimes called "law-making" treaties, as opposed to "treaty-contracts," which would be treaties that only resolve certain more particular issues between their parties.[6]

Researching treaties can involve a range of resources, summarized in Box 8.1.

The UN Charter requires that all treaties entered into by any UN members be registered with the UN secretary-general.[7] The secretary-general then publishes them in a print serial set called the *United Nations Treaty Series* (UNTS). The UNTS also appears as an online electronic database, maintained by the UN, as part of the United Nations Treaty Collection at http://treaties .un.org/pages/UNTSOnline.aspx?id=1. This online database allows for searching by title, party names, full-text search, and certain other parameters. The UN Treaty Collection also contains an online database for the now-discontinued *League of Nations Treaty Series* (LNTS). The online LNTS is also searchable by a variety of parameters.

For access to treaties dating from before 1945 (or to very recent treaties not yet published under UN auspices), one often refers to treaty collections maintained by individual states. Over the generations, the United States has done a reasonably complete job of recording, cataloguing, and publishing the treaties to which it has become a party. The Treaty Affairs Office of the U.S. State Department's Legal Advisor has general authority in this regard.

---

6. *Starke's International Law* 37–41 (I.A. Shearer ed., 11th ed. 1994).
7. UN Charter Article 102(1).

Retrieving a treaty to which the United States is a party, other than through UN sources, involves two steps.

The first step is using an index. The indexing tool most commonly used is *Treaties in Force*, published annually by the Treaty Affairs Office. It is now available in print at most comprehensive law libraries, online at the Treaty Affairs page of the State Department website, and online through Lexis and Westlaw (for recent years). *Treaties in Force* broadly consists of two major lists. One list covers all bilateral treaties to which the United States is a party as of the relevant year, arranged alphabetically by counterparty. The second covers all multilateral treaties to which the United States is a party that year, arranged alphabetically according to subject matter. Because *Treaties in Force* serves only as an index, its entries for each treaty merely give bibliographic data. These include the dates of signature and effectiveness, the names of other parties (for multilateral treaties), and the dates of any amendments. Also, most of the index entries (but not all) provide a citation to a treaty source publication or a serial number.

Second, several publications contain treaty texts. From 1776 to 1949, treaties were published chronologically in *Statutes at Large*. So when an entry in *Treaties in Force* lists a "Stat." citation, the text for that treaty can be found in *Statutes at Large*. From 1950 to 1984, treaties were published in a multivolume print series called *United States Treaties and Other International Agreements* (UST). This is available in print in most comprehensive law libraries and online through HeinOnline, Lexis, and Westlaw.

Entries in *Treaties in Force* also often refer to a serial number, called a "TIAS" number; the acronym refers to "Treaties and Other International Acts Series." The TIAS serial number, assigned to all U.S. treaties chronologically since 1945, can be used to find treaty texts not available through *Statutes at Large* or UST. Historically under the TIAS system, treaties to which the United States became a party were initially published in the form of slip pamphlets before appearing in a UST volume. There was one slip pamphlet per treaty, and each slip pamphlet was given a chronologically consecutive TIAS serial number. Comprehensive law libraries shelved these TIAS slip pamphlets until they were included in the next published volume of UST. With the discontinuance of UST volumes in 1984, libraries continued to shelve later TIAS slip pamphlets until the slip pamphlets also seemed to be discontinued in 2006. (Some releases from 2007 may be available at some locations.) Many more recent treaty texts can be retrieved electronically by TIAS number at the Treaty Affairs page of the State Department website.

These official resources have been complemented by unofficial compilers of U.S. treaties during various time periods. Of these, perhaps the most frequently cited is the Bevans series, which was compiled by Charles I. Bevans for U.S. treaties from 1776 to 1949. Another private treaty compilation (1987–2013) is by Igor Kavass, who has also maintained a separate Kavass finding index. The Bevans and Kavass series are both available through HeinOnline.

When a treaty cannot easily be located in an official resource or a major unofficial resource, it may have been published in periodical form by the American Society of International Law in either of its two flagship publications: *International Legal Materials* and the *American Journal of International Law*. These can be retrieved and searched in the same manner that one would retrieve and search any other legal periodical, including on Westlaw, Lexis, and HeinOnline.

Also, treaties sometimes can be located in other unofficial resources (such as additional academic periodicals or the websites of related professional organizations) or other official resources (such as the websites of sovereign states that serve as depositaries for multilateral treaties).

Customary International Law

Rules of *customary international law* develop over time through the real-world practice of states. There is no written or published source or catalog of all these rules. Rather, they are determined to exist on a case-by-case basis by courts, arbitration tribunals, academic treatise authors, and other authorities.

For a pattern of state behavior to develop into a rule of customary international law, two things must be true. First, the behavior pattern must be engaged in by a sufficient number of states as to be considered a general practice, and it must be sufficiently uniform and of sufficient duration over time to be considered a consistent practice.[8] This is sometimes referred to as the "material" requirement. Second, the states engaging in this behavior pattern must do so out of a conviction that the behavior is required under international law. This is sometimes referred to as the "psychological" requirement and is frequently described by the Latin phrase *opinio juris.*[9]

Using formal research methods, one would accumulate evidence of state practice to establish compliance with the material requirement. This evidence could come from news reports, historical works, legal treatises, government press releases and policy statements, and other similar materials.[10] Similarly, one would retrieve evidence of official opinion regarding the psychological requirement. This evidence could come from diplomatic correspondence, official government manuals, executive decisions, military orders, and other similar materials.[11] These kinds of materials used in formal research can be difficult to obtain and use, however. See Box 8.2.

As a practical matter, for most nonspecialists, research into customary international law can begin with academic articles in law journals, legal treatises, and other academic publications (especially those specializing in

---

8. *See, e.g., Brownlie's Principles of Public International Law* 24-25 (James Crawford ed., 8th ed., 2012).

9. *E.g.*, Rebecca Wallace & Olga Martin-Ortega, *International Law* 17 (rev. 7th ed. 2013).

10. *See, e.g., Brownlie's Principles of Public International Law, supra* note 8, at 24. (This most recent edition of the Brownlie treatise does not refer to the first three items indicated in the text (beginning with news reports), but these are still acceptable sources for a general-interest researcher.)

11. *E.g.*, Shaw, *supra* note 5, at 63. (In his most recent edition, Shaw emphasizes the conduct of international organizations, patterns of UN General Assembly resolutions, and the work of the UN General Assembly's International Law Commission. The sources indicated in text are also acceptable for the general-interest researcher.)

Box 8.2   COMPONENTS OF CUSTOMARY INTERNATIONAL LAW

The Material Component: State Practice

- The observed practice of states should demonstrate *general* and *consistent* state behavior.
  General state behavior is engaged in by a sufficient quantity of states around the world.
  Consistent state behavior is sufficiently uniform and of sufficient duration over time.
- Among the sources from which one could discern state practice would be:
  - News reports
  - Historical works
  - Legal treatises
  - Domestic state legislation
  - International and national judicial decisions
  - Government press releases
  - Government policy statements
  - Treaties and conventions
  - UNGA resolutions addressing legal issues

The Psychological Component: *Opinio Juris*

- States must engage in the general and consistent state behavior out of a conviction that the behavior is *required* under international law.
- Among the sources from which one could discern *opinio juris* would be:
  - Diplomatic correspondence
  - Official government manuals
  - Opinions of legal advisors to governments and international organizations
  - Executive decisions
  - Manuals of military law
  - Military orders
  - International and national judicial decisions
  - Treaties and conventions, in draft and completed form
  - UNGA resolutions addressing legal issues

international subjects). These authorities frequently simply declare and discuss their views as to the existence of various rules of customary international law. Depending on the extent of influence of each authority and the degree of unanimity among them, these declarations and discussions can for many purposes be a substantial indication of the rules' existence.

Determinations derived from academic sources can (and usually should) be fortified by research in other sources. Prominent among these would be treaties and conventions. If a particular treaty or convention has a very large number of states as parties to it, and there is general compliance with its terms over an appreciable period, it arguably satisfies the requirements for a rule of customary international law. To the extent that the treaty or convention has these characteristics, the customary international law rules that it embodies will apply to all states, whether or not they are parties to the treaty or convention. Sometimes advocates even assert that draft treaties or treaties not yet in force state rules of customary international law, if they believe that states generally and consistently comply with their terms out of a sense of legal obligation.

The decisions of courts and arbitration tribunals also frequently declare the existence of rules of customary international law and discuss their application. This is especially true of courts and arbitration tribunals charged with international duties. (Examples are the ICJ and the arbitration tribunals established by the Permanent Court of Arbitration.[12])

Additionally, resolutions passed by the UN General Assembly (UNGA) and other international deliberative bodies can be helpful in identifying rules of customary international law. Indeed, it is not unusual for the resolutions themselves to purportedly declare rules of customary international law. Such declarations can be useful in building the case for a rule of customary international law, but they are usually not dispositive, absent other evidence of general and consistent practice that is engaged in out of a sense of legal obligation.

Decisions by Courts and Arbitration Panels

Decisions by courts and arbitration panels are a tool for building arguments about customary international law. Furthermore, Article 38(1) of the ICJ Statute also refers to "judicial decisions" directly, as a subsidiary means for the determination of rules of law.

The ICJ is perhaps the most authoritative international court currently operating in the world. However, it hears and decides only cases between sovereign states.[13] No private persons, individual or corporate, can be parties to contested actions before it. In fact, not even international organizations can be parties before the ICJ. The ICJ is authorized, however, to give advisory opinions at the request of the UNGA and certain other bodies.[14] The decisions of the ICJ, both for contentious cases and for advisory opinions, are published in a print, annual, multivolume set called the *International Court of Justice Reports of Judgments, Advisory Opinions and Orders (ICJ*

---

12. The Permanent Court of Arbitration was established through the Hague Peace Conventions of 1899 and 1907.

13. I.C.J. Statute art. 34, ¶ (1).

14. *Id.* arts. 65–68.

Reports). These decisions are available online at the ICJ website (www.icj-cij.org/), Lexis, HeinOnline, and Westlaw.

The Permanent Court of Arbitration (PCA) has been for generations the administrator of some of the most influential international arbitration proceedings. The disputes addressed in these arbitrations all involve at least one state, although sometimes private persons (individuals or corporate) have also been parties. States, therefore, have chosen arbitration under PCA auspices when jurisdiction would not exist in the ICJ or when, for other reasons, the parties have chosen arbitration over the established framework of the ICJ. Since the establishment of the UN, the UN has published the PCA's most significant arbitration decisions (even including those issued before 1945) in a multivolume print set called the *Reports of International Arbitration Awards*. The RIAA is available at many law libraries, online in conjunction with the UN website (www.un.org/law/riaa/), and in HeinOnline.

Some international commercial arbitration awards are from arbitrations between or among states; others are from arbitrations among or with private parties, either corporations or individuals or both. While these private international arbitrations might involve issues of public international law, their decisions would not normally have the same influence on later arbitrations between states as would decisions from arbitrations among states. Many international commercial arbitration awards are available through Lexis (which includes materials from, among other sources, *International Arbitration: Mealey's Litigation Report*) and Westlaw.

There are also several important regional and special-purpose courts and tribunals. Some of the most significant websites including the decisions issued by the relevant courts and tribunals, are:

- International Criminal Court (www.icc-cpi.int)
- European Court of Human Rights (www.echr.coe.int)
- Inter-American Court on Human Rights (corteidh.or.cr)
- African Court on Human and Peoples' Rights (www.african-court.org)
- International Criminal Tribunal for the Former Yugoslavia (ICTY) (www.icty.org)
- International Criminal Tribunal for Rwanda (ICTR) (www.unictr.org)

Westlaw also provides access to documents of the ICTY and ICTR, the Iran-U.S. Claims Tribunal, and panels of the World Trade Organization.

UN Materials

Certain official documents issued by some bodies of the UN can also have a significant effect on the development of public international law. This is especially true of resolutions passed by the UN Security Council (UNSC) and the UNGA.

UNSC resolutions are generally binding in accordance with their terms. Article 25 of the UN Charter requires UN members to "accept and carry out the decisions" of the UNSC.

UNGA resolutions can be influential in the development of customary international law, although they are not in themselves customary international law or any kind of binding international law. Indeed, they do not come within any of the classifications set out in Article 38(1) of the ICJ Statute. However, UNGA resolutions often make statements about rules of customary international law. These can be especially useful when the statements asserting a particular point appear in a large number of UNGA resolutions, these resolutions are frequent enough to be consistent, and the resolutions are carried by sufficiently large majorities to indicate very broad consensus. Then the resolutions are good evidence that the point of law asserted has attained the required *opinio juris* to become a rule of customary international law.[15]

Similarly, some authorities have also used UNGA resolutions, if they are sufficiently unanimous and consistent over time, to fulfill the material requirement for a rule of customary international law as well. That is, the resolutions can be used to show a general and consistent state practice. This is more controversial because resolutions may reflect simply what states say, rather than their actions.

For many purposes, the easiest way to retrieve and work with UN resolutions is to use the UN website. The UNGA and the UNSC maintain separate catalogs of resolutions, dating back to the founding of the UN. The resolutions can be easily retrieved, by resolution number and by date, at the UNGA and UNSC pages of the UN website.

If you are researching a subject but do not know the resolution number or date of a resolution, you can use several search features at the UN website. First, the UN Bibliographic Information System Network (UNBISNet) uses a sophisticated advanced search protocol to access all the titles indexed in the official library of the UN in New York (called the Dag Hammarskjöld Library) and the official UN library in Geneva. The system involves searching bibliographic records for UNGA and UNSC resolutions and linking to the resolutions. If you know the title of a resolution, it can be easily retrieved in the title field of the advanced search. Subject and key-word searching are also available. However, at the present time, UNBISNet only goes back to 1979, although documents (including some UN resolutions) dating from earlier years can sometimes be found due to ongoing retrospective conversions by UN staff.[16]

---

15. UNGA resolutions can also serve as a basis for later adoption in the form of conventions, as occurred with the International Covenant on Civil and Political Rights and the International Covenant on Economic, Social, and Cultural Rights. This does not mean that any particular UNGA resolution, when passed unanimously or by a large majority, automatically becomes a rule of international law. Rather, resolutions passed unanimously or by very large majorities, when they are part of a set of similar resolutions passed with the same degree of consensus over an appreciable period of time, can become rules of customary international law if they are so recognized by courts and other authorities.

16. UNBISNet also allows searching for voting records for UN resolutions (back to 1946) and maintains an index to speeches made before the principal bodies of the UN, generally from 1983.

The second major UN tool is the UN Official Document System (ODS). Its scope is narrower than UNBISNet: it covers only official UN documents. In addition to resolutions, verbatim records of meetings (called by their French name, "procès-verbaux"), letters to and from the UN principal bodies that are admitted into their records, and reports delivered to or issued by the UN principal bodies or their subsidiary bodies, other official items are included. In general, ODS goes back only to 1993 (although older documents are added on a regular basis), but its database of UN resolutions goes back to 1946.

Some of the documents retrievable through UNBISNet and ODS other than resolutions (such as procès-verbaux, letters, and reports) can also be used to build cases for both the material and psychological requirements for the existence of a rule of customary international law.[17]

Commentary and General Principles

Commentary, particularly treatises and articles in legal periodicals, can be used to build arguments regarding customary international law. In addition, Article 38(1) of the ICJ Statute directly refers to "the teachings of the most highly qualified publicists of the various nations" as a "subsidiary means for the determination of rules of law."

The discovery, retrieval, and use of treatises and articles in legal periodicals to research issues of public international law are not much different from the methods used to research issues of U.S. domestic law. Most of the significant legal periodicals focused on public international law issues are available through Westlaw, Lexis, and HeinOnline. The leading treatises on public international law are available in print at most comprehensive law libraries. Among the leading treatises on public international law in the English language are:

- Anthony Aust, *Handbook of International Law* (2d ed. 2010)
- *Brierly's Law of Nations* (Andrew Clapham ed., 7th ed. 2012)
- *Brownlie's Principles of Public International Law* (James Crawford ed., 8th ed. 2012)
- Antonio Cassese, *International Law* (2d ed. 2005)
- Malcolm N. Shaw, *International Law* (7th ed. 2014)
- *Starke's International Law* (I.A. Shearer ed., 11th ed. 1994)
- Rebecca Wallace & Olga Martin-Ortega, *International Law* (rev. 7th ed. 2013)

---

17. A third UN bibliographic tool, UN Info Quest (UN-I-QUE), is mostly useful for advanced researchers who are using the UN's complex system of document numbering as a basis for their searching.

The third category of sources for public international law, listed here, is *general principles of law*. There are varying interpretations of this phrase, and it has been reasonably interpreted as covering a variety of principles of various types. One category is principles "intrinsic to the idea of law and basic to all legal systems."[18] Examples are the idea that no one can transfer more rights than he or she possesses and the canon that the later of two rules supersedes the earlier, if both address the same subject and have the same source. Basic concepts of equity, proportionality, and fairness could also be cited in this connection.

The language of the ICJ Statute on this point is somewhat vague and general. The availability of this potential source of public international law can be viewed by some advocates as an opportunity to mold arguments based on considerations most conducive to their cause. For most purposes, it is best to base the arguments on court or tribunal decisions or on the works of commentators.

PRIVATE INTERNATIONAL LAW

Private international law is distinct from public international law. There are distinctions among conceptions of private international law. The first, the traditional conception, views private international law as identical to international conflict of laws.[19] The phrase "conflict of laws" refers to the body of rules used to determine which state's law applies to a litigated fact pattern that has plausible connections to more than one state. When two or more private parties are involved in a contested matter that involves more than one national jurisdiction, an international conflict of laws problem can arise.

Classically, each state develops and maintains its own conflict of laws rules. The institutions of the European Union (EU) have promulgated certain conflict of laws rules for contractual disputes adjudicated within the EU.[20] However, in general, there are no universally applicable treaties or conventions setting forth conflict of laws rules. General treatises exist in the area, and the case law of a common law state in many instances will contain that state's conflict of laws regime.

Under the more modern and expansive interpretation, private international law is comprised of treaties and other legal rules that pertain to the activities of private persons acting across national boundaries. For example, to a much greater extent now than before, treaties and conventions as

---

18. Oscar Schachter, *International Law in Theory and Practice* 53 (1991).

19. James R. Fox, *Dictionary of International and Comparative Law* 66, 264 (3d ed. 2003).

20. Commission Regulation 593/2008 of 17 June 2008, 2008 O.J. (L 177) 6.

instruments of public international law apply to and restrict the actions of private persons. When a treaty or convention does so, it can be thought of as also being an instrument of private international law. An example would be the Convention on Contracts for the International Sale of Goods,[21] which directly applies to many private buyers and sellers of goods in international trade.

Similarly, when individual states issue laws that affect the international operations of their citizens or residents, those domestic laws can also be viewed as rules of private international law. An example would be the immensely influential U.S. Foreign Corrupt Practices Act, which applies to U.S. persons engaging in corrupt activities with officials of foreign states. Furthermore, international organizations such as the Hague Conference on Private International Law and the International Institute for the Unification of Private Law (UNIDROIT) have a role in creating international agreements directly affecting private persons acting internationally. Finally, some private organizations, such as the International Chamber of Commerce (ICC) and the International Law Institute (known by the acronym for its French title, IDI), also promulgate or help develop rules that can be applied to private persons acting internationally.

The methods used when researching these instruments of private international law depend on the source involved. Treaties and conventions involving private international law are researched in much the same manner as any other treaty and convention, as discussed previously. Domestic statutes in any state setting forth rules of private international law are researched in whatever manner is normal for statutory research in that state. And materials issued by the Hague Conference, UNIDROIT, the ICC, and the IDI are researched as one would research the activities of any other modern association or organization, especially including their online databases.

---

21. United Nations Convention on Contracts for the International Sale of Goods, Apr. 11, 1980, 1489 U.N.T.S. 3.

Unlike the situation with foreign law, there is no formal restriction against a U.S. lawyer (educated, trained, and licensed only under the law of a U.S. jurisdiction) from providing advice on public international law.

The sources of public international law are listed in a United Nations (UN) document, the Statute of the International Court of Justice. The International Court of Justice (ICJ), or World Court, is the chief judicial body of the UN. It sits in The Hague, a city that is the seat of government of the Netherlands. The ICJ Statute is the document through which the ICJ was established, along with the UN itself, in 1945. Article 38(1) of the ICJ Statute establishes five types of sources for public international law.[4] These are:

1. International treaties and conventions
2. Customary international law
3. General principles of law
4. Judicial decisions in courts and tribunals
5. Scholastic works of prominent commentators on public international law

The last two types of authority are stated to be a "subsidiary means" for determining rules of public international law. They are, therefore, not primary sources for rules of public international law but rather secondary sources that serve as indirect indications. The extent to which there is a hierarchical relationship among the other three types of sources is itself a subject of interpretation and discussion.

Treaties and Conventions

Treaties are international agreements among states, usually in written form, that the parties intend to be binding.[5] Many international agreements that states enter into have significance only for building mutual foreign relations and are not formal documents with binding effect. It is only when states enter into agreements that they intend to be internationally binding that a treaty is created.

Treaties can be viewed as falling into distinct categories. For example, bilateral treaties (treaties between only two states) can be distinguished from multilateral treaties (treaties among three or more states). Each state that has become party to a multilateral treaty is often called a "state party" to that treaty, while each party to a bilateral treaty is often called a "counterparty." A *convention* is usually a special kind of treaty, generally multilateral, that enunciates new rules of legal conduct for the parties to it. Conventions

---

4. The language of Article 38(1) of the ICJ Statute varies somewhat from the five points stated here, but the presentation of the points here reflects a more conversational vocabulary and more pragmatic arrangement.

5. Vienna Convention on the Law of Treaties art. 2, ¶ (1)(a), May 23, 1969, 1155 U.N.T.S. 331 (entered into force Jan. 27, 1980) [hereinafter "VCLT"]. The VCLT "constitutes the basic framework for any discussion of the nature and characteristics of treaties." Malcolm N. Shaw, *International Law* 655 (7th ed. 2014).

nal Conduct, 264
    n8
    nsibility, 258n8

    94

    Rights, 318

    , 294

    making, 275, 276

CFR Index and Finding Aids, 277
Code of Federal Regulations, 275
e-CFR, 276–277, 280–282
effective date, 286
FDsys, 276–277, 280, 282
Federal Register, 275, 276, 278, 283–284, 286
HeinOnline, 277
KeyCite, 282, 285
LexisNexis, 277
regulatory history, 286–288
Shepard's, 282
statutory annotation, 277, 279
updating, 280–282
Westlaw, 277
ALWD Citation Manual, 50, 124
American Bar Association, Model Rules of Professional Conduct. *See* Model Rules of Professional Conduct
American Indian Law Collection, HeinOnline, 308
American Indian Law in a Nutshell, 308
American Journal of International Law, 314
American Jurisprudence 2d, 69
American Law Institute, 77, 171
American Law Reports (A.L.R.) Annotations, 59, 61, 85–88, 191
American Society of International Law, 314
Analysis
    agency decisions, 294
    agency regulations, 282
    cases, 123–124
    rules of procedure, 243
    statutes, 170–171
Annotated code
    commentary references, 181
    finding tools, 277
    main volume and updates, 181
    notes of decision, 181
    online, 191
    print, 179–181
    session law references, 181
Appellate courts
    agency actions, review of, 282
    appeal as of right, 122
    discretionary review, 122
    process, 109
    standard of review, 109
Arbitration decisions, international law, 317–318
Authority, defined, 6n5. *See also* Primary authority; Secondary sources

Bar, defined, 13n10
BCite, 147
Bevans, Charles I., 314
Bill, 165

Conference committees, 208
Conflict of laws, defined, 321
Congress.gov, 224, 231–232
Congressional Information Service, 223
Congressional Record, 208, 221
Congress, U.S.
    administrative law, authorization by, 272
    Congress.gov, 224, 231–232
    Congressional Information Service, 223
    Congressional Record, 208, 221
    House or Senate documents, 208, 210
    U.S.C.C.A.N., 221
Consequences of poor research, 4
Constitutions
    defined, 165–166
    distinguished from charters, 165
    federal, 204–205
    interpretation, 204–205
    process of enactment, 204
    state constitutions, 204–205
    statutes, constitutionality of, 7n8
Continuing legal education, 93
Convention on Contracts for the International Sale of
        Goods, 322
Conventions, international law, 312–315, 317
Corpus Juris Secundum, 69
Costs of resources, 18, 33–34
Courts. *See also specific courts*
    federal court sanctions, 4, 258
    federal system, 6
    rules of procedure, 243
    specialized courts, 240n3
    state courts, 103–110
    structures
        federal, 111–122
        hierarchy, 104
        state, 104, 109
    websites, 128, 129, 245, 255
Credibility of resources, 33–34
Customary international law, 315–317, 320–321

Database alerts, 93n14
Decision, defined, 103
Defamation, 10–13, 16, 62–68, 83–84, 86–88,
        104–108, 129
Deskbooks, 244–245
Dictionaries, 29, 171
Discipline, 4
Diversity jurisdiction, 122

E-CFR, 276–277, 280–282
Electronic filing, 255–256
Enacted law, 165–238. *See also* Statutes
    bill, 165
    charter, 165, 205–206
    constitutions, 165–166, 204–205
    ordinances, 165, 205–206
    session laws, 165
    statutes, 165
Encyclopedias, 69–72
    American Jurisprudence 2d, 69
    Corpus Juris Secundum, 69
    LexisNexis, 69

    as secondary source, 60
    state encyclopedias, 69, 83
    Westlaw, 69, 191
Ethics. *See* Professional responsibility law
European Court of Human Rights, 318
European Union, 321

Family leave, 177, 187–190, 195–204, 210–218, 223,
        227–231
FAQs, 297
FastCase
    case research, 148–153
    online resource, 17
    statutes, 202–204
    terms-and-connectors searches, 148, 202
FDsys (Federal Digital System), 129, 276–277, 280, 282
Federal law
    family leave. *See* Family leave
    federal court sanctions, 4, 258
    protected concerted activity, 289
Federal Practice and Procedure, 245
Federal Register, 275, 276, 278, 283–284, 286
Federal Rules Decisions, 246n7
Federal Rules Enabling Act of 1934, 240n2
Federal system
    administrative law, 271
    constitutions, 204–205
    courts, 6
    described, 6
    legislation, 177
    procedural rules, 240, 243
Finding tools
    abstracts, 224
    annotated code, 277
    categories of sources, 12–17
    CFR Index and Finding Aids, 277
    indexes, 35–40, 50, 62
    library catalogs, 61, 223
    organization, 35–40, 50, 62
    periodical indexes, 73
    tables of contents, 35–40, 50, 62
Findlaw, 18
Floor debates, 207–208
Foreign Corrupt Practices Act (U.S.), 322
Foreign law, 310–311. *See also* International law
Formal rulemaking, 275n4
Framing research, 27–28

General Assembly of UN, 317, 318–320
Google Scholar, 18, 128, 154–158
Government Publishing Office, 186
Graphical Statutes, 226, 231

Hague Conference on Private International Law, 322
HeinOnline
    administrative materials, 277, 294
    American Indian Law Collection, 308
    international law, 315, 318, 320
    law reviews, 73–76
    legislative history, 220, 223, 226
    legislative history — research, 223
    Restatements, 77, 79

HeinOnline (*continued*)
  searching, 73
  tribal law, 308
  UST, 314
Holdings, 289

IDI (International Law Institute), 322
Indexes
  CFR Index and Finding Aids, 277
  finding tools, 35–40, 50, 62
  Index to Legal Periodicals and Books (ILPB), 73
  Index to Legal Periodicals Retrospective, 73
  Legal Resource Index, 73
  periodical indexes, 73
Index to Legal Periodicals and Books (ILPB), 73
Index to Legal Periodicals Retrospective, 73
Indian Law Reporter, 309
Informal/notice-and-comment rulemaking, 275, 276
Information management, 49–51
Interaction of authorities, 104, 111, 171, 177, 243,
    271, 282
Inter-American Court on Human Rights, 318
*International Arbitration: Mealey's Litigation
    Report*, 318
International Chamber of Commerce, 322
International Court of Justice, 312, 317
*International Court of Justice Reports of Judgments,
    Advisory Opinions and Orders*, 317
International Criminal Court, 318
International Criminal Tribunal for Rwanda, 318
International Criminal Tribunal for the Former Yugoslavia,
    318
International Institute for the Unification of Private Law, 322
International law. *See also* Foreign law
  African Court on Human and Peoples' Rights, 318
  American Journal of International Law, 314
  American Society of International Law, 314
  arbitration decisions, 317–318
  commentary, 320–321
  conflict of laws, defined, 321
  Convention on Contracts for the International Sale of
      Goods, 322
  conventions, 312–315, 317
  court decisions, 317–318
  customary international law, 315–317, 320–321
  European Court of Human Rights, 318
  European Union, 321
  Foreign Corrupt Practices Act (U.S.), 322
  foreign law, 310–311
  General Assembly of UN, 317, 318–320
  general principles, 321
  Hague Conference on Private International Law, 322
  HeinOnline, 315, 318, 320
  Inter-American Court on Human Rights, 318
  International Arbitration: Mealey's Litigation Report,
      318
  International Chamber of Commerce, 322
  International Court of Justice, 312, 317
  *International Court of Justice Reports of Judgments,
      Advisory Opinions and Orders*, 317
  International Criminal Court, 318
  International Criminal Tribunal for Rwanda, 318
  International Criminal Tribunal for the Former
      Yugoslavia, 318

International Institute for the Unification of Private Law,
    322
International Law Institute, 322
International Legal Materials, 314
Iran-U.S. Claims Tribunal, 318
LexisNexis, 315, 318, 320
LNTS, 313
opinio juris, 315, 316, 319
organizations creating private international actions, 322
Permanent Court of Arbitration, 318
private international law, 321–322
public international law, 311–321
Report of International Arbitration Awards, 318
Security Council of UN, 318–319
TIAS numbers, 314
treaties, 312–315, 317
Treaties in Force, 314
treatises, 315, 320
UN Bibliographic Information System Network, 319
UN Info Quest, 320n17
United Nations, 312, 313, 317, 318–320
UN Official Document System, 320
UNTS, 313
U.S. State Department, 313
UST, 314
Westlaw, 315, 318, 320
International Law Institute, 322
International Legal Materials, 314
Interpretive regulations, 272n1
Iran-U.S. Claims Tribunal, 318

Judicial review of agency actions, 282. *See also* Appellate
    courts
Jurisdiction
  concurrent, 122
  contract clause, 122
  defined, 6
  diversity, 122
  geography, 123
  mandatory/binding versus persuasive, 109
  resources, 33
  statutory research, 179
Jury instruction guides, 60, 83–84
Justia, 18

Kansas law on defamation, 62, 83, 86, 104–110, 125,
    129–134
Kavass, Igor, 314
KeyCite. *See also* Westlaw
  agency decisions, 295
  agency regulations, 282, 285
  cases, 134–138
  cited and citing authorities, 134–138
  pending legislation, 194, 231
  statutes, 194

Law.com, 18
Law reviews, 72–73
League of Nations Treaty Series (LNTS), 313
Legal ethics. *See* Professional responsibility law
Legal publishing, 17–19
Legal Resource Index, 73

Legal rules, 109, 123, 239. *See also* Rules of procedure
LegalTrac, 73
Legislative history
  materials
    bills, 207
    committee hearing transcripts, 208
    committee prints, 209, 224, 226
    committee reports, 208
    floor debates, 208
    House or Senate documents, 208, 210
    legislative intent, 171, 207, 208
    presidential messages, 210
  research
    generally, 210, 219–220
    annotated code, 221
    Bloomberg Law, 220, 231
    compiled legislative histories, 221, 223
    Congress.gov, 224, 231–232
    Federal Digital System. *See* FDsys
    Graphical Statutes, 231
    HeinOnline, 220, 223, 226
    LexisNexis, 220, 223, 226, 231
    ProQuest Congressional, 223, 224, 226, 231
    purpose provision, 221
    session laws, 210, 221
    statutory codes, 220–221
    THOMAS, 224
    U.S.C.C.A.N., 221
    Westlaw, 220, 223, 226, 231
Legislative intent, 171, 207, 208
Legislative process
  committee action, 207
  conference committees, 208
  Congressional Record, 208, 221
  floor debates, 207–208
  introduction of bill, 207
  lobbying, 208
  overview, 165–166
  pocket veto, 208
  presidential action (signature, veto, pocket veto), 208
  public law numbers, 221
  veto, 208
Legislative websites, 186–204
LexisNexis
  administrative materials, 277, 294
  A.L.R. Annotations, 85
  cases, 139–147
    databases, 139
    editorial matter, 140
    filters, 147
    Get a Document, 139
    natural language, 139
  Cohen's Handbook of Federal Indian Law, 308
  encyclopedias, 69
  headnotes, 139
  International Arbitration: Mealey's Litigation Report, 318
  international law, 315, 318, 320
  jury instruction guides, 83
  legislative history, 220, 223, 226, 231
  Moore's Federal Practice, 245
  online resource, 17
  professional responsibility law, 264
  Restatement case citations, 77
  statutes, 191, 195–202

terms-and-connectors, 139
topic searches, 139
treatises, 62
United States Code Service, 186
UST, 314
Library catalogs, 61, 223
Litigation process, 109
LNTS (League of Nations Treaty Series), 313
Lobbying, 208
Local laws
  charter, 165, 205–206
  ordinances, 165, 205–206
  rules of procedure, 243
Loose-leaf services, 49, 89, 181

Magazines, 93
Malpractice, 4
Manuals, 297
Marital status discrimination, 7, 36, 40, 42, 181
Mining sources, 68–69, 123–124
Minnesota law, 40, 181–186
Model laws, 171
Model Rules of Professional Conduct. *See also* Professional
      responsibility law
  preamble, 5
  as primary authority, 258
  Rule 1.1, 4
  Rule 1.6, 259–262, 265
  Rule 5.5, 311n3
  Rule 6.1, 21n18
  Monitoring research, 128, 179
Moore's Federal Practice, 245
Municipal charters, 165

National Conference of Commissioners on Uniform State
      Laws, 171
National Indian Law Library, 308
National Labor Relations Board, 289, 295
Native American Rights Fund, 309
Newsletters, 93
Newspapers, 93

Office of the Law Revision Counsel (OLRC), 186, 187
Official case reporters, 124, 126
Official codes
  legislative websites, 186–204
  print, 179–186
Online searches
  generally, 35
  annotated codes, 191
  database alerts, 93n14
  database selection, 40, 130, 139, 147
  field searching, 35, 319
  keyword search drafting, 41–42, 62, 73
  legislative websites, 186–204
  natural language, 41
  sample searches, 41–42, 130–133, 135–138, 141–146,
        187–190, 225
  statutory research, 186–204
  terms-and-connectors searches, 41
    Bloomberg Law, 147
    FastCase, 148, 202

Online searches (*continued*)
   LexisNexis, 139
   proximity connectors, 41
   samples, 130–131, 139–140
   Westlaw, 130–131
   wildcards, 41
   treatises, 61–62
Opinio juris, 315, 316, 319
Opinion, defined, 103
Ordinances, 165, 205–206
Organic statutes, 272, 294

Parties, 7n7
Pending legislation
   KeyCite, 194, 231
   ProQuest Congressional, 231
   Shepard's, 200–201, 231
Periodicals, 72–76
Permanent Court of Arbitration, 318
Piggyback on others' work, 34–35, 59
Pocket parts, 49, 181
Pocket veto, 208
Popular name tables, 182, 188
Practice guides, 61, 85, 89–95
Practices, 25–35. *See also* Searching steps
   access angles, 35–42
   client's situation, mastering, 26–27
   currency of sources, 45–49
   information management, 49–51
   looking back, 42–45
   piggyback on others' work, 34–35, 59
   research libraries, 50–51
   research logs, 50–51
   research plan creation, 31–32
   research term development, 28–31
   resource choice, 32–34
   stopping research, 52
   synthesizing and summarizing, 26–27
Precedent (stare decisis), 104, 109
Precision vs. recall, 28
Presidential actions, legislative, 208, 210
Primary authority, 101–164. *See also specific types*
   case law, 103–164
   categories of sources, 5–12, 26
   defined, 6n5
   Model Rules of Professional Conduct, 258
   rules of procedure, 240
Print
   agency decisions and orders reporters, 294
   annotated code, 179–181
   committee prints, legislative history, 209, 224, 226
   official codes, 179–186
   statutory codes, 179–186
   updating publications (pocket parts, supplemental
      pamphlets, loose-leaf pages), 49, 181
Private international law, 321–322
Pro bono publico, defined, 21n18
Procedural law
   generally, 239–244
   cases, 243
   consequences of violations, 240
   statutes, 239
Professional responsibility law, 258–265
   ABA/BNA Lawyers' Manual on Professional Conduct, 264

ABA Canons of Professional Ethics, 258n8
ABA Model Code of Professional Responsibility,
   258n8
ABA Model Rules of Professional Conduct. *See* Model
   Rules of Professional Conduct
   advisory opinions as quasi-authority, 258
   annotated statutes, 264
   Bloomberg Law, 264
   cases, 264
   commentary as quasi-authority, 258
   deskbooks, 264
   discipline, 4
   enforcement systems, 258
   LexisNexis, 264
   malpractice, 4
   research, 264–265
   Restatement (Third) of Law Governing Lawyers, 258,
      263
   Rule 11, 240n5
   sanctions, 4, 258
   as secondary source, 258, 264
   state rules, 258
   Westlaw, 264
ProQuest Congressional
   Advanced Search, 226
   comprehensiveness, 224
   Congressional Information Service, 223
   coverage, 223
   Get a Document, 223
   Legislative Insight, 223
   pending legislation, 231
Publication of cases, 121
Public international law, 311–321
Public law numbers, 221
Public policy, 79

Quasi-authority
   advisory committee notes, 243
   advisory opinions, 258
   agency decisions and orders, 289
   agency regulations, 272
   categories of sources, 6, 7, 12
   commentary as, 258

Recall vs. precision, 28
Regulations. *See* Agency regulations
Reporters
   agency decisions and orders, 294
   cases, 124, 126
   Indian Law Reporter, 309
   *International Court of Justice Reports of Judgments,
      Advisory Opinions and Orders*, 317
   official reporters, 124, 126
   print reporters, 294
   United States Reports, 127
   West Reporter System, 126–127
   West's American Tribal Law Reporter, 309
Report of International Arbitration Awards, 318
Researcher-driven searching. *See* Online searches
Research issues, 27
Research libraries, 50–51
Research logs, 50–51
Research plan creation, 31–32

Research term development, 28–31
Research vocabulary, 28–31
Resources generally, 3
  breadth and depth, 33
  choosing, 32–34
  commercial, 18
  cost, 18, 33–34
  credibility, 33–34
  ease of use, 33–34
  government, 6–7
  jurisdiction, 33
  legal publishing, 17–19
  resource, defined, 26
  social media, 13–15
  time range, 33
Restatements of the Law, 77–82
  adoption by courts, 77
  citation, 77
  components, 77
  derivation, 77
  HeinOnline, 77, 79
  jury instruction guides compared, 83
  Law Governing Lawyers, 258, 263
  LexisNexis, 77
  Shepard's, 79, 82
  topics, 78
  Westlaw, 77
Rule 11, 240n5
Rulemaking
  formal rulemaking, 275n4
  informal/notice-and-comment rulemaking, 275, 276
Rules. See specific types
Rules of procedure
  process
    advisory committee notes as quasi-authority, 243
    appellate procedure, 240
    application by courts, 243
    civil procedure, 240
    creation, 240
    criminal procedure, 240
    evidence, 240
    Federal Rules Enabling Act of 1934, 240n2
    federal system, 240, 243
    local rules, 243
    organization, 240
    as primary authority, 240
    specialized courts, 240n3
  researching
    analysis, 243
    annotated rules, 246
    cases, 246
    court websites, 245, 255
    deskbooks, 244–245
    electronic filing, 255–256
    Federal Practice and Procedure, 245
    forms, 243
    Moore's Federal Practice, 245
    organization, 240
    overview of resources, 244
    treatises, 245–246

Sanctions, 4, 258
Searching steps, 25–35. See also Practices
  generally, 25–35

author-driven tools, 35–40
mining references, 68–69
recall versus precision, 28
researcher-driven tools, 40–42
updating, 45–49
Secondary sources, 59–99. See also specific sources
  generally, 12–17
  commentary as, 59
  continuing legal education, 93
  database alerts, 93n14
  defined, 26
  magazines, 93
  mining, 68–69
  newsletters, 93
  newspapers, 93
  piggyback on others' work, 34–35, 59
  professional responsibility law, 258, 264
  statutory interpretation, 171
  treatises, 61–67
  updating, 49
Security Council, UN, 318–319
Seminal cases, 123
Session laws
  code vs., 165, 181
  historical research, 210, 221
  new laws, 210
  official session laws, 210
  Statutes at Large, 210, 221, 276, 314
Shepard's
  agency decisions, 295
  agency regulations, 282
  cases, 139
  pending legislation, 200–201, 231
  Restatements, 79, 82
  statutes, 200–201
  table of authorities, 147n26
Social media, 13–15, 89–92, 271, 290–293, 297–301
Split decisions (concurrence, dissent, majority, plurality),
        120–121
Stare decisis, 104, 109
States
  administrative law, 271
  case law, 103–110
  constitutions, 204–205
  encyclopedias, 69, 83
  National Conference of Commissioners on Uniform
        State Laws, 171
  professional responsibility law, 258
  state courts, 103–110
  statutes, 177
Statutes. See also Enacted law
  amendment, 167, 171
  analysis, 170–171
  briefing, 177–178
  citators, 191
  components: opening, operative, implementation,
        technical sections, 166–167
  constitutionality, 7n8, 170
  effective date, 166
  FastCase, 202–204
  hierarchy, 177
  interpretation. See Statutory interpretation
  "law" defined, 165
  prospective application, 272
  reading, 177–178

Statutes (*continued*)
  repeal, 167
  session laws, 165, 181
  Shepard's, 200–201
  states, 177
  "statute" defined, 165
  structure, 166–167
  sunset provision, 167
Statutes at Large, 210, 221, 276, 314
Statutory codes
  annotated in print, 179–181
  annotated online, 191
  contents, 40
  federal, 186
  legislative history research, 220–221
  official, 179
  official versus unofficial, 179
  organization, 179–180
  print codes, 179–186
  selection factors, 180
  versus session laws, 165, 181
Statutory interpretation
  canons of construction, 172
  cases, 171
  dictionaries, 171
  legislative intent, 171, 207, 208
  model laws, 171
  related statutes, 171
  secondary sources, 171
  uniform laws, 171
Statutory research. *See also* Session laws; Statutory codes;
    specific resources
  commercial resources, 191–204
  jurisdiction, 179
  key words, 188
  legislative websites, 186–204
  online, 186–204
  pocket parts, 181
  popular name tables, 182, 188
  recommended approaches, 178–204
  time frame, 178–179
Stopping research, 52
Substantive legal rule, 239
Supplemental pamphlets, 49, 181
Supreme Court, U.S., 6, 111, 121–122, 205, 243, 308
Synthesizing and summarizing, 26–27

Tables of authorities, 134n20, 147n26, 277
Tables of contents, 35–40, 50, 62
Temporary injunction, defined, 28n3
Terms-and-connectors searches
  generally, 41
  Bloomberg Law, 147
  FastCase, 148, 202
  LexisNexis, 139
  proximity connectors, 41
  samples, 130–131, 139–140
  Westlaw, 130–131
  wildcards, 41
Thesauri, 29
TIAS numbers, 314
Treaties
  citation, 314
  international law, 312–315, 317
  LNTS, 313

Treaties in Force, 314
*United States Treaties and Other International
    Agreements* (UST), 314
  UNTS, 313
Treaties in Force, 314
Treatises, 61–67
  Bloomberg Law, 62
  citation, 61, 69
  defined, 61
  example, 62–67
  international law, 315, 320
  LexisNexis, 62
  note-taking, 68–69
  online searches, 61–62
  rules of procedure, 245–246
  Westlaw, 62
Trial courts
  motion practice, 109
  trial, 109
Tribal law
  administrative law and, 308
  appellate process, 309
  federal Indian law, 308
  HeinOnline, 308
  Indian Law Reporter, 309
  laws of tribes, 309–310
  National Indian Law Library, 308
  Native American Rights Fund, 309
  oral tradition, 310
  tribes generally, 307
  West's American Tribal Law Reporter, 309

UN Bibliographic Information System Network, 319
Uniform laws, 171
UN Info Quest, 320n17
United Nations
  Bibliographic Information System Network, 319
  General Assembly, 317, 318–320
  Info Quest, 320n17
  international law, 312, 313, 317, 318–320
  Official Document System, 320
  Security Council, 318–319
  UNTS, 313
United Nations Treaty Series (UNTS), 313
United States Code, 186
United States Code Congressional and Administrative News
    (U.S.C.C.A.N.), 221
United States Reports, 127
*United States Treaties and Other International
    Agreements* (UST), 314
Updating
  agency regulations, 280–282
  annotated code, 181
  publications (pocket parts, supplemental pamphlets,
    loose-leaf pages), 49, 181
  searching steps, 45–49
  secondary sources, 49

Veto, 208

Websites
  agency regulations, 278, 280
  courts, 128, 129, 245, 255

legislative websites, 186–204
Westlaw. *See also* KeyCite
    administrative materials, 277, 294
    A.L.R. Annotations, 85
    case law research, 130–139
        databases, 130
        filters, 139
        KeyCite, 134–138
        key number as search term, 132–134
        Key Search, 132–134
        terms-and-connectors, 130–131
    compiled legislative histories, 220
    encyclopedias, 69, 191
    Federal Practice and Procedure, 245
    international law, 315, 318, 320
    jury instruction guides, 83
    legislative history, 220, 223, 226, 231
    online resource, 17
    professional responsibility law, 264
    Restatements, 77

    statutes, 191–195
    treatises, 62
    United States Code Annotated, 186
    UST, 314
West Reporter System
    digests, 126
    Federal Appendix, 127
    Federal Reporter, 127
    Federal Rules Decisions, 246n7
    Federal Supplement, 127
    headnotes, 126
    key number, 126
    regional reporters, 127
    Supreme Court Reporter, 127
    West's American Tribal Law Reporter, 309
Work-flow
    planning, 31–32
    searching, 25–35
    steps described, 25–35
    stopping, 52